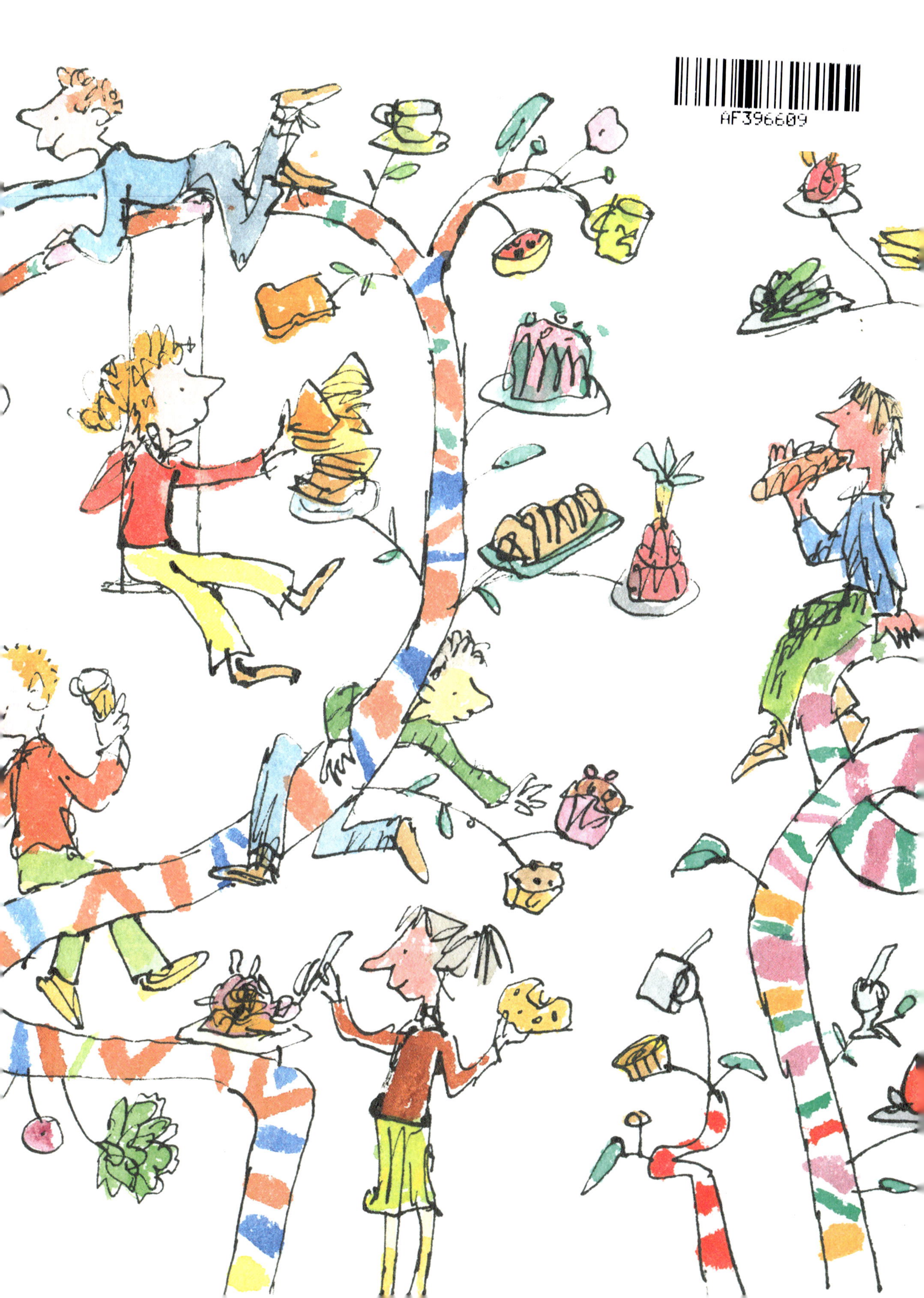
AF396609

*Quentin Blake* is one of Britain's most distinguished illustrators. He has illustrated both his own books for children and those of many celebrated collaborators as well as classic books for adults. He has been knighted for his services to illustration and was appointed Commander of Honour in 2022. He is also a Chevalier of the Légion d'Honneur in France.

*Claudia Zeff* is an art director who has worked on book jackets and magazines. Since 2011 she has worked as Creative Consultant to Quentin Blake and has helped set up The Quentin Blake Centre of Illustration with Quentin where she is now Deputy Chair.

Quentin Blake and Claudia Zeff are, respectively, Series Consultant and Series Editor of Thames & Hudson's series 'The Illustrators'.

*Quentin Blake*

# Not for Art's Sake

*To my fellow artists*
**QB**

*For John*
**CZ**

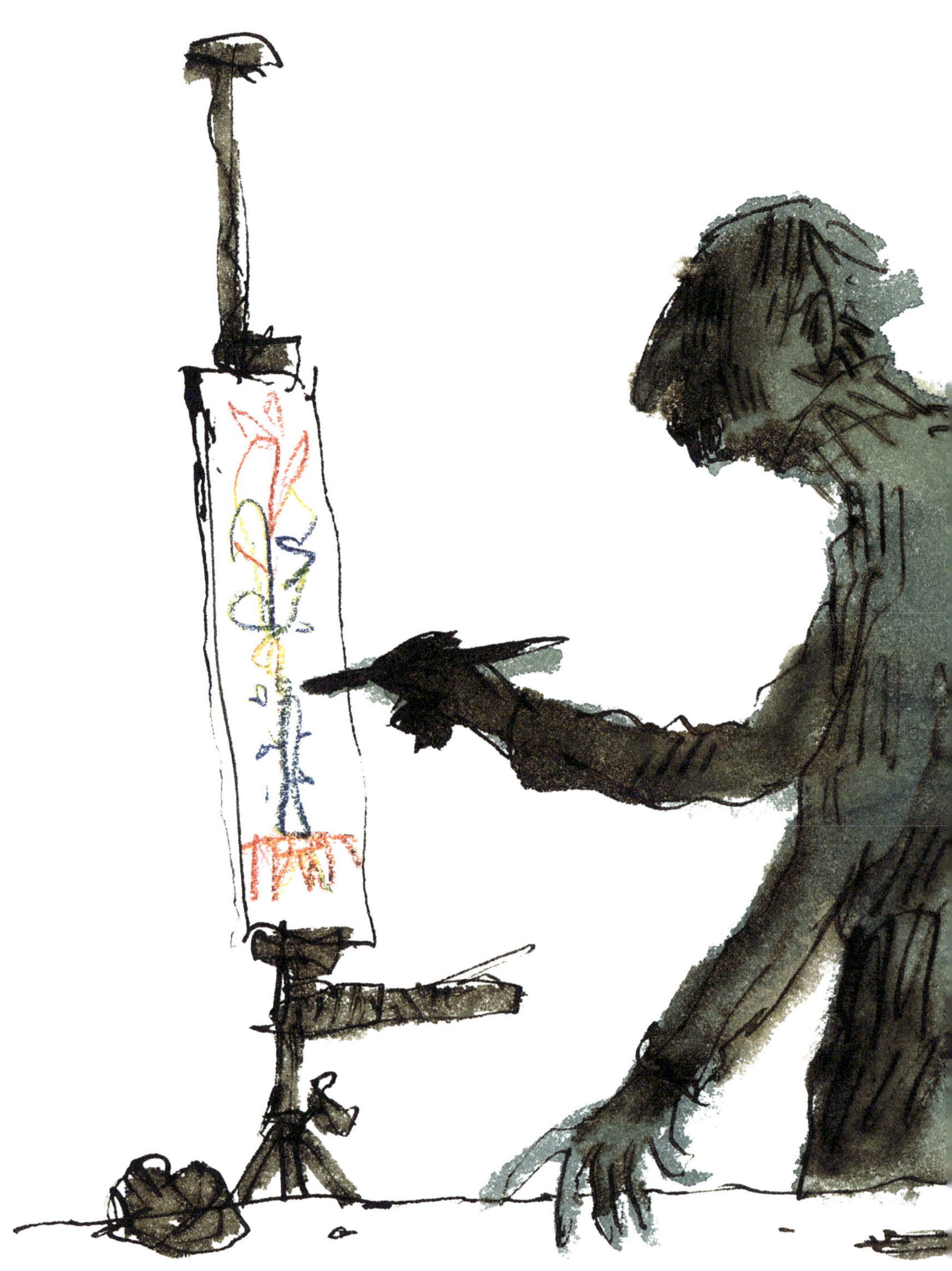

# Quentin Blake

# Not for Art's Sake

*Edited by*
Claudia Zeff

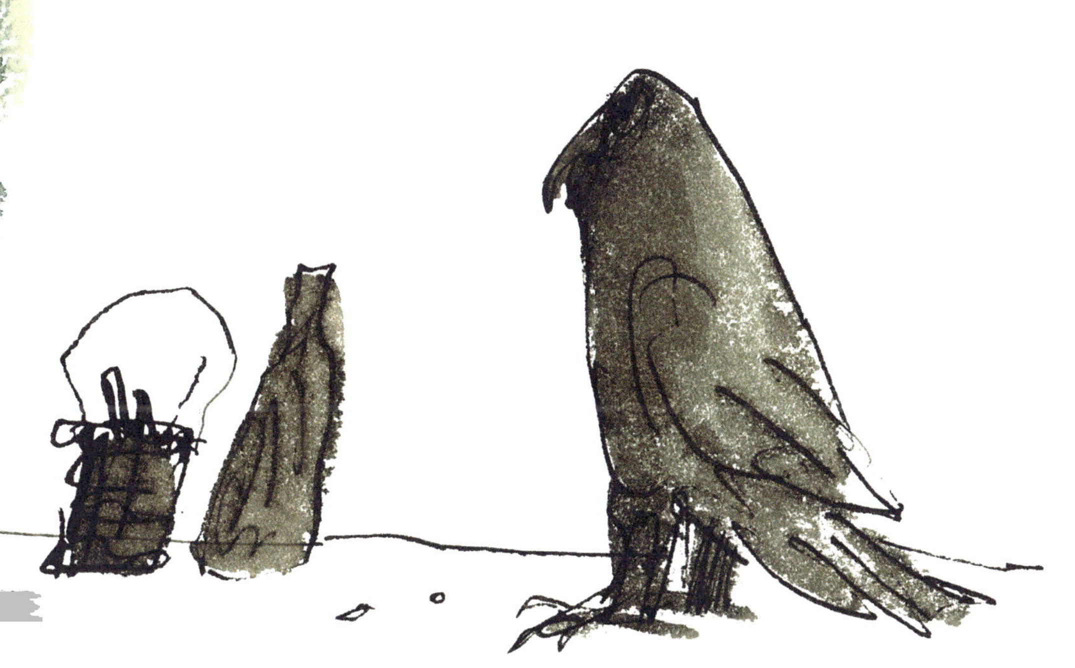

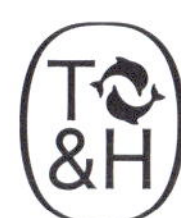

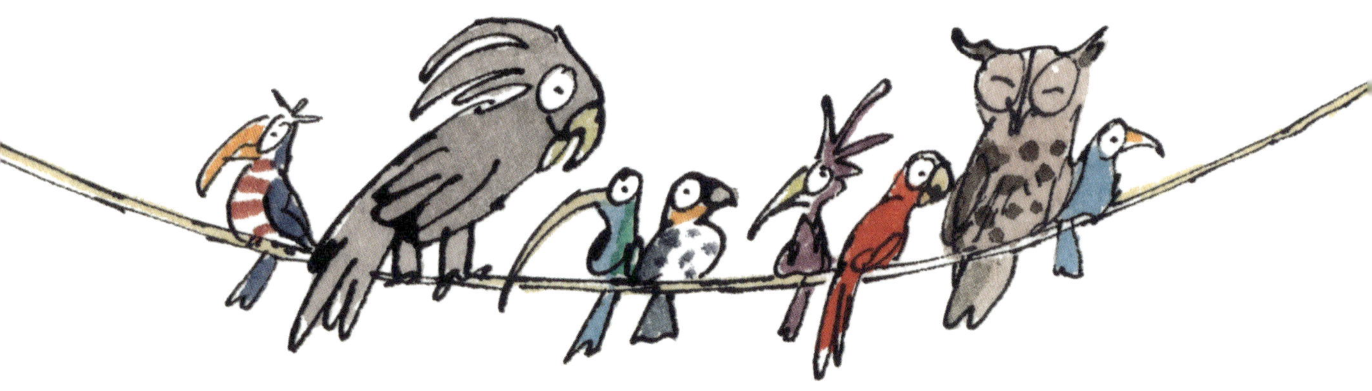

# Contents

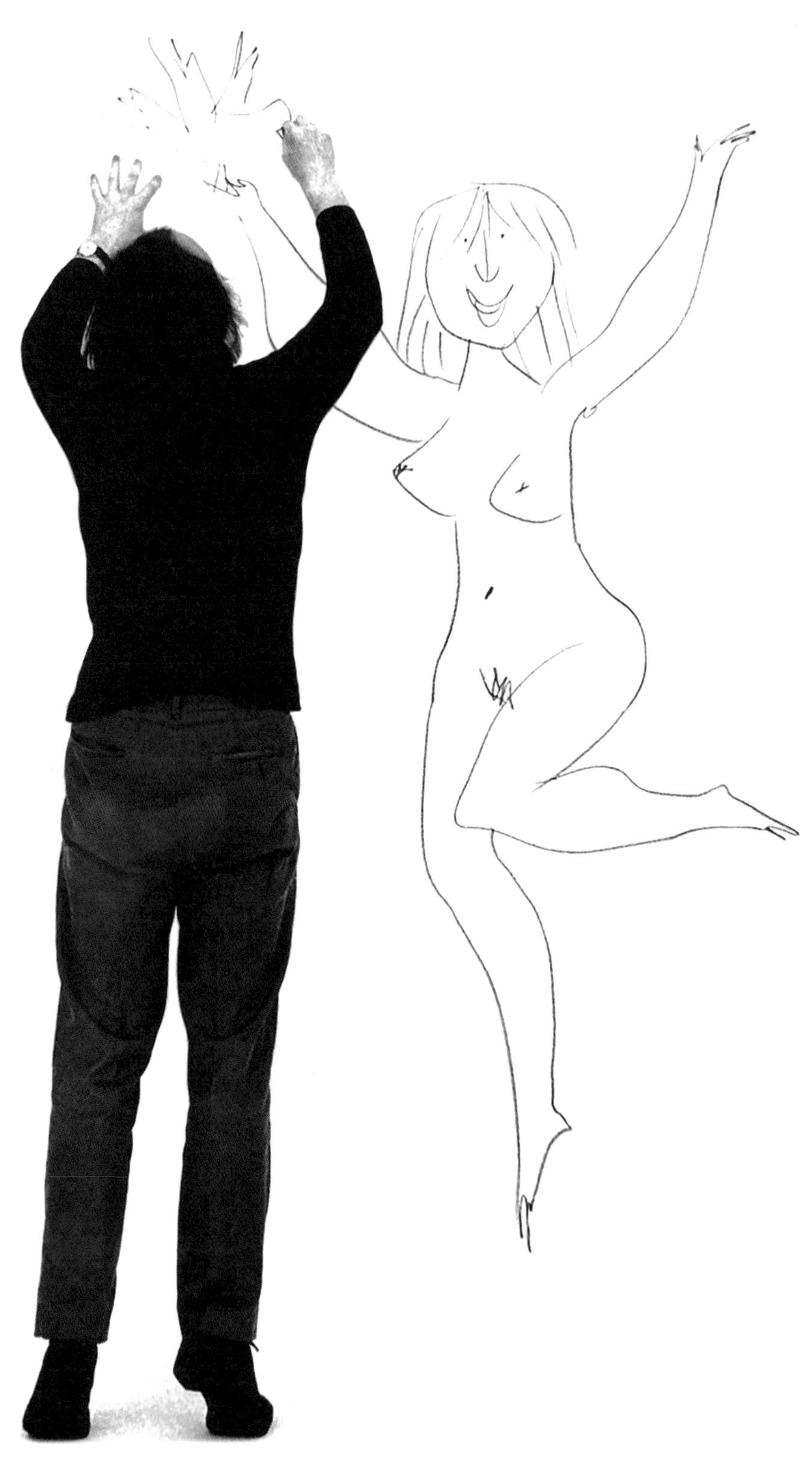

*Foreword*

# Not for Art's Sake

For most of his life, Quentin has illustrated books, either written by himself or someone else, but in the last 20 years or so he has also been commissioned to draw for other purposes.

The pieces in this book were created for specific audiences, sites or occasions and have not been seen by the general public unless they happened to be, for example, at the Royal opening of St Pancras International or visiting a maternity hospital in France.

Some years ago, Quentin asked me if I would act as his Creative Consultant, so my role became that of an intermediary, taking care of the relationship between him and his clients. He explained that an essential part of my role would be to say 'no' to requests that he didn't have the time to do, or which didn't interest him. But I soon found that any drawing which was for a purpose 'beyond the page' was irresistible to Quentin and that he'd always want to say 'yes'. He never seemed daunted by the most sensitive subject matter and felt keenly the privilege of being asked. The appeal of his work being seen in unexpected places and contexts was an adventure for him and the arrival of sophisticated digital printing made changes in size and scale possible.

This book is a celebration of these works and where they have taken Quentin.

*Claudia Zeff,* 2024

'All the works shown in this book use art in their making. However, what I want to record are the places that circumstantial requirements have taken me to. To mention only three I'm sure that I would not spontaneously have found myself making family drawings for people in prison, drawings to encourage young people recovering from anorexia, or to do a drawing suitable to wrap two sides of a five-storey building. How fortunate can a working artist get?'

*Quentin Blake,* 2024

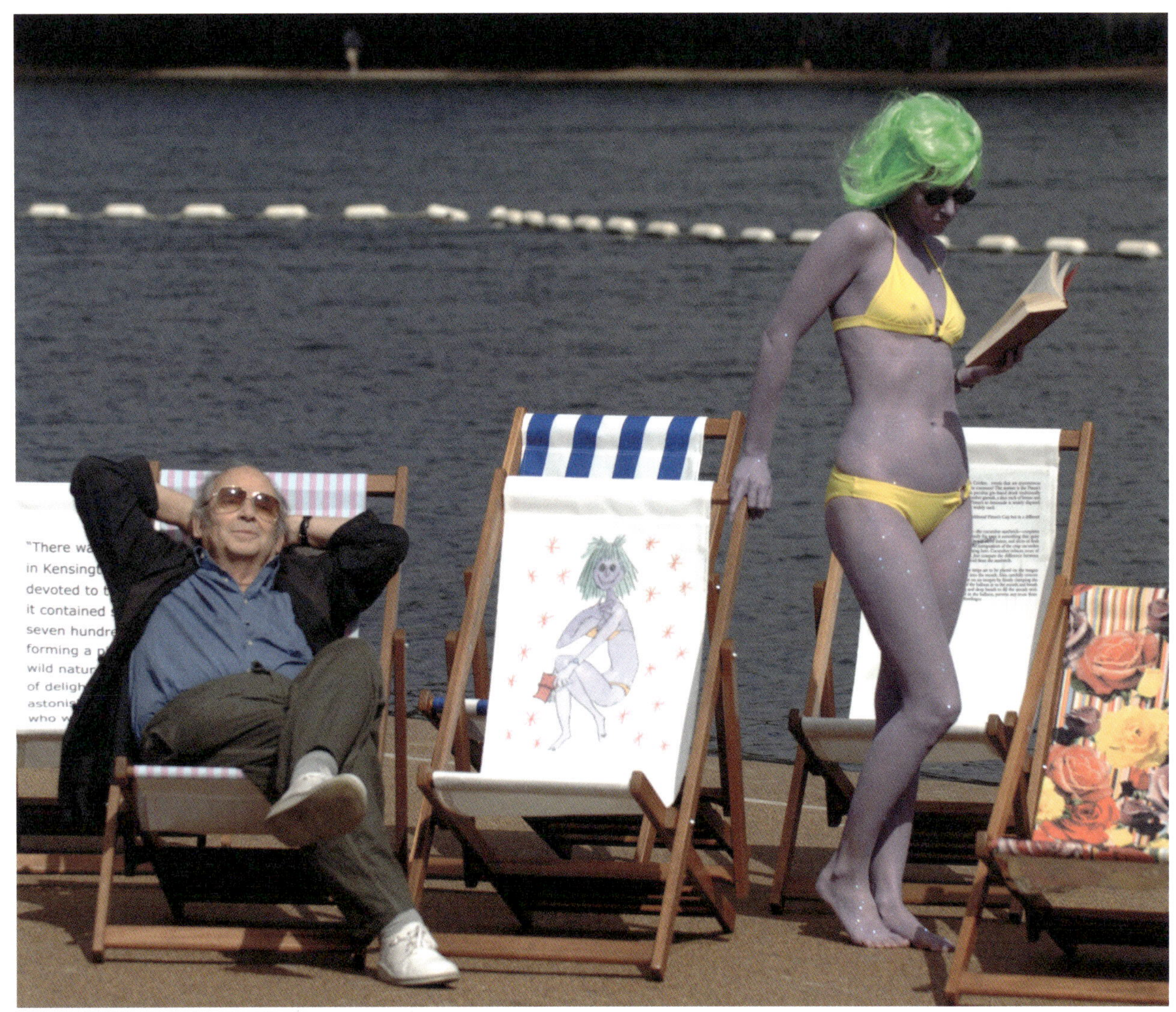



*Royal Parks Foundation Deckchair, 2006*

*Chapter One*

# Public Places

In 1999, Quentin was made the first Children's Laureate, a prize given to a 'children's writer or illustrator to celebrate outstanding achievement in their field'. There was no road map as to what he should do in his two-year tenure. For Quentin it meant many more public appearances.

When he went to a London police station to help launch a reading scheme, he had a realisation: 'Sometimes I have felt that the label Children's Laureate sounds antiquated or quaint, but it certainly does the business – the television people are on the scene and we make it onto the evening news.'

Quentin was becoming famous beyond the world of children's books and people started asking him to draw off the page…

# Deckchair for Royal Parks

In 2006, The Royal Parks invited artists and designers to donate a deckchair design. Among them were Tracey Emin, Peter Blake, Alexander McQueen and Quentin.

'My version of what you might like to find on a deckchair was a sunbathing woman, but she was purple with green hair to remind you that she was fictional. At a photo opportunity to announce the appearance of the chairs, beside the Serpentine in Hyde Park, the organisers had the idea of producing a brave young woman in the same colours, which also gave me the chance, in the half an hour after the photo-shoot, and no doubt before hypothermia set in, to draw her from life, in a moment of art imitating life imitating art.'

Quentin has often been asked how new technology has affected the way he works:

'The answer is hardly at all except in one very significant respect. I want to go on drawing with those old-fashioned implements: brushes, reed pens, quills. But today these drawings can be reproduced at any size. It's a change of technical possibility which offers a change of outlook.'

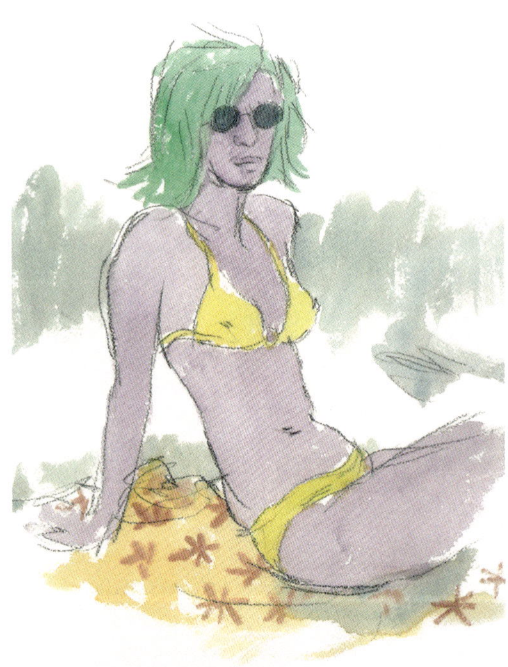

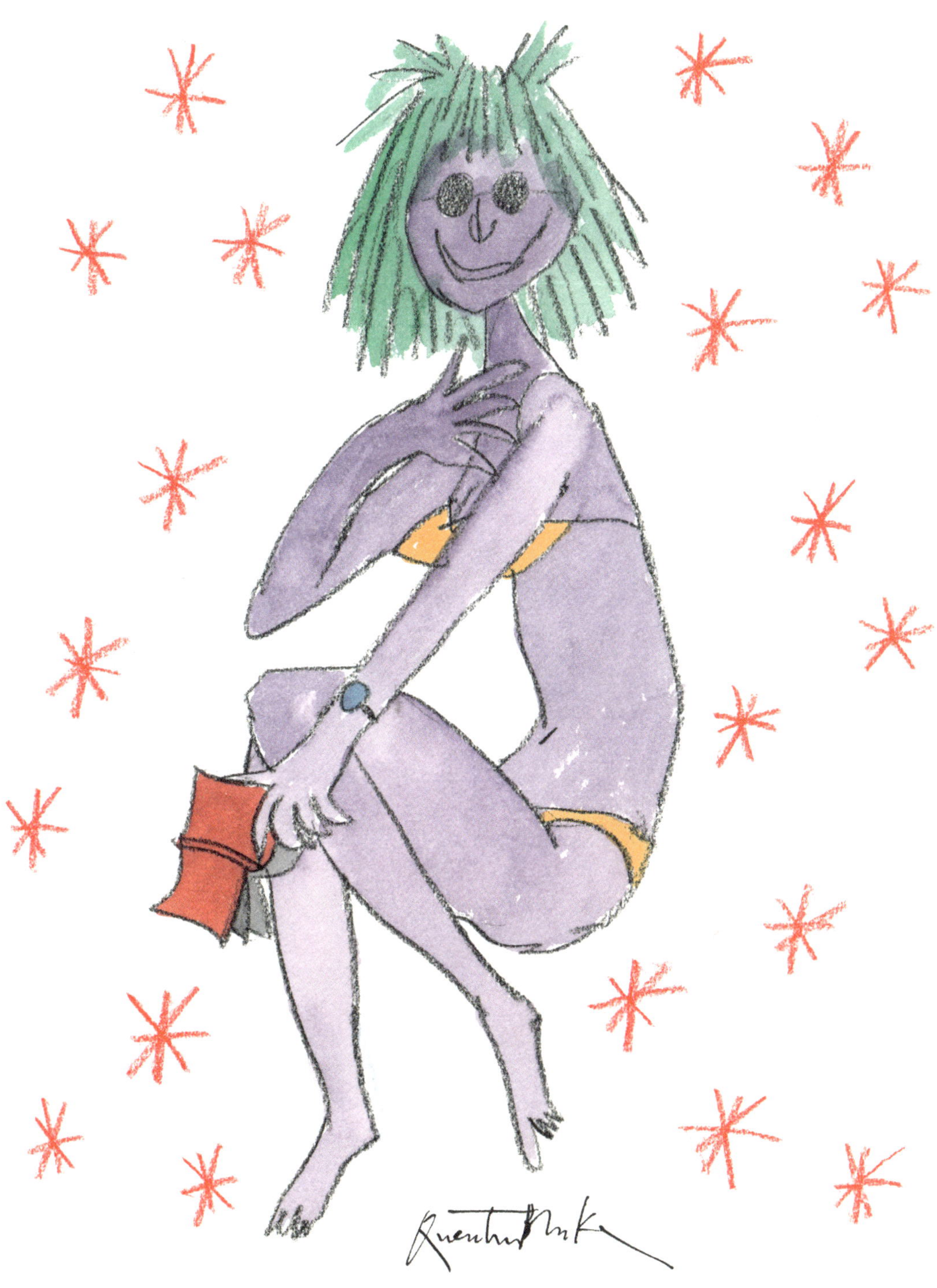

# The Big Wrap at St Pancras

The House of Illustration was in discussion with Argent, the developers of the huge King's Cross regeneration site, about a building in the corner of Granary Square. The Royal opening of St Pancras International Station opposite the site was scheduled in the summer of 2007 but there was a problem: the Stanley Building, a derelict Victorian tenement block, was directly in Queen Elizabeth's line of sight and would be a blot on the landscape. So Argent asked Quentin if he could do something to improve its appearance.

'I talked to the designer Lexi Burgess and he came back with the answer, "We can only wrap it"; and so we did – at least on the two St Pancras-facing sides.… I was keen to keep the sense that this was a drawing, so it was scratchy, in black and only one other colour. It was produced on the drawing board but printed five storeys high. The cast of characters were such that you might meet now that you had arrived in London…'

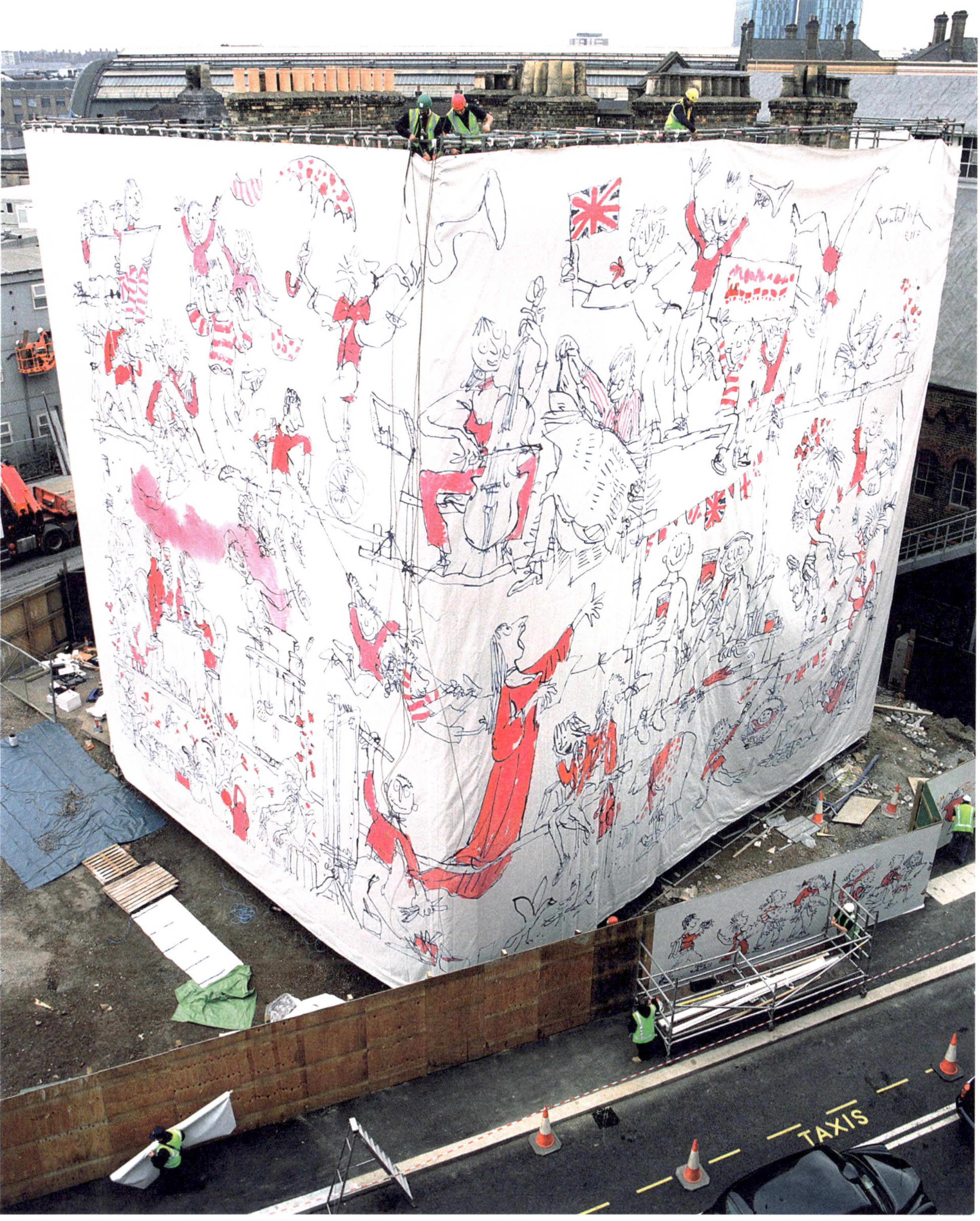

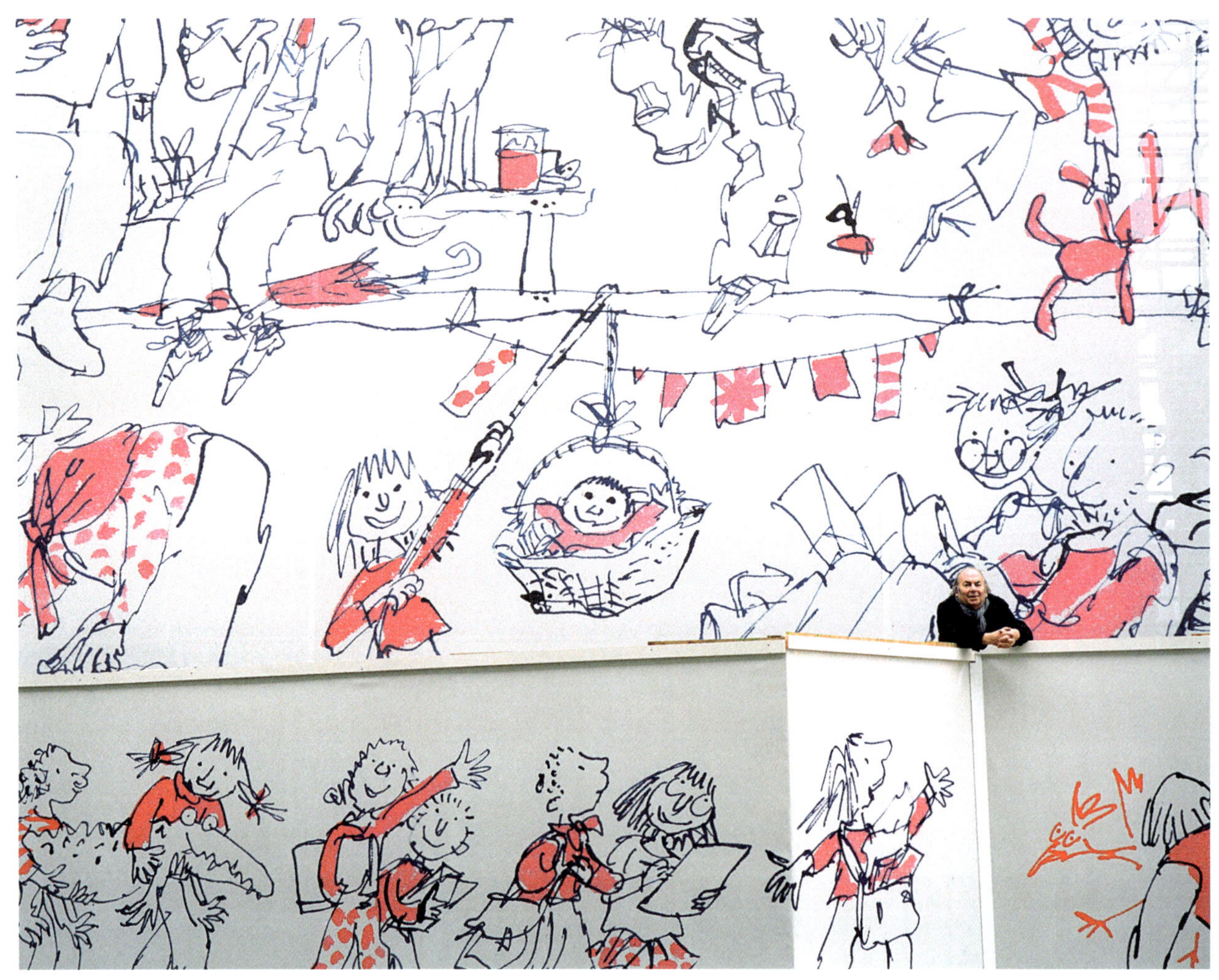

ABOVE & OPPOSITE – *Stanley Building Wrap*, 2007

'I was keen to keep the sense that this was a drawing
so it was scratchy, in black and only one other colour.'

QB

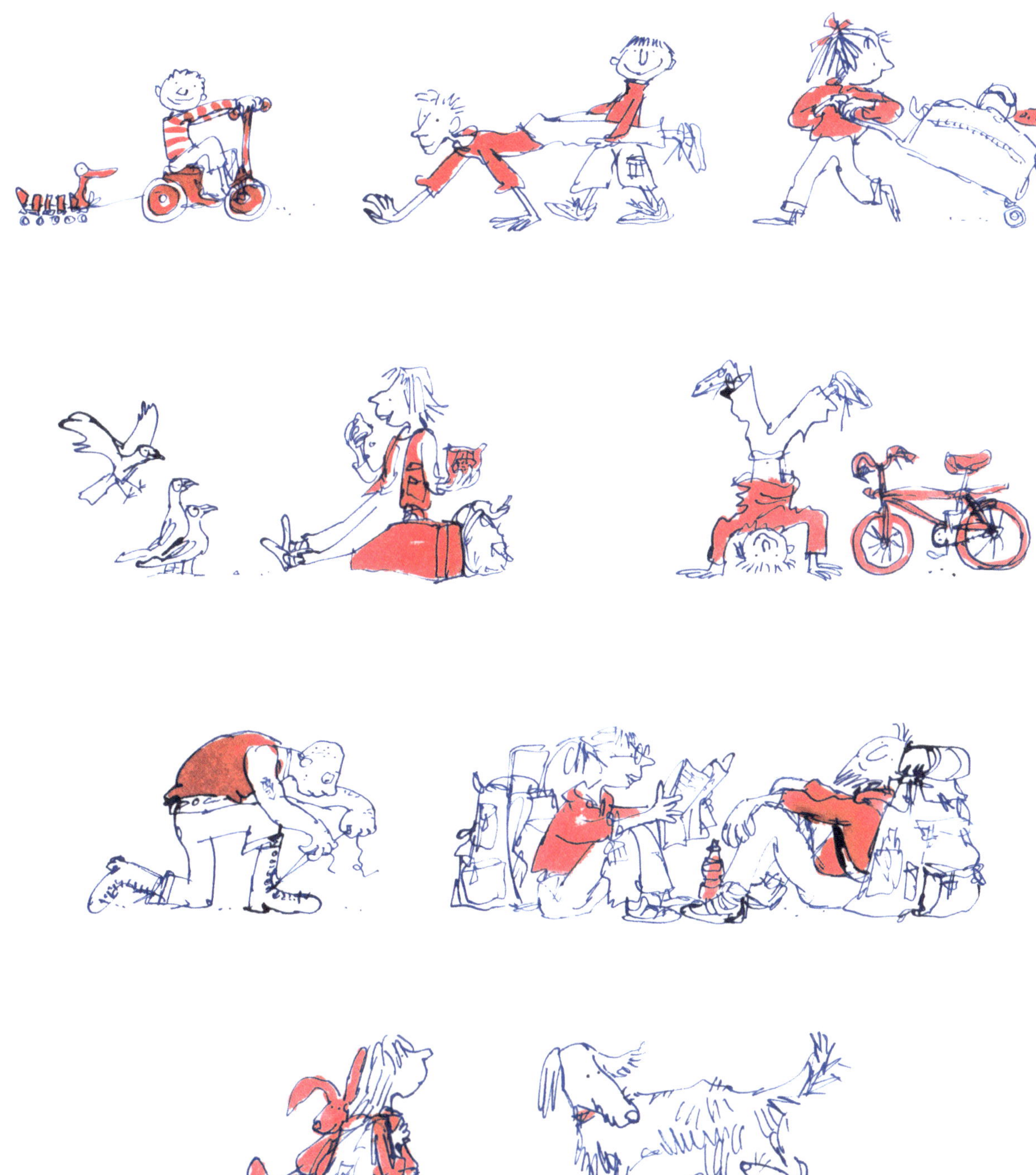

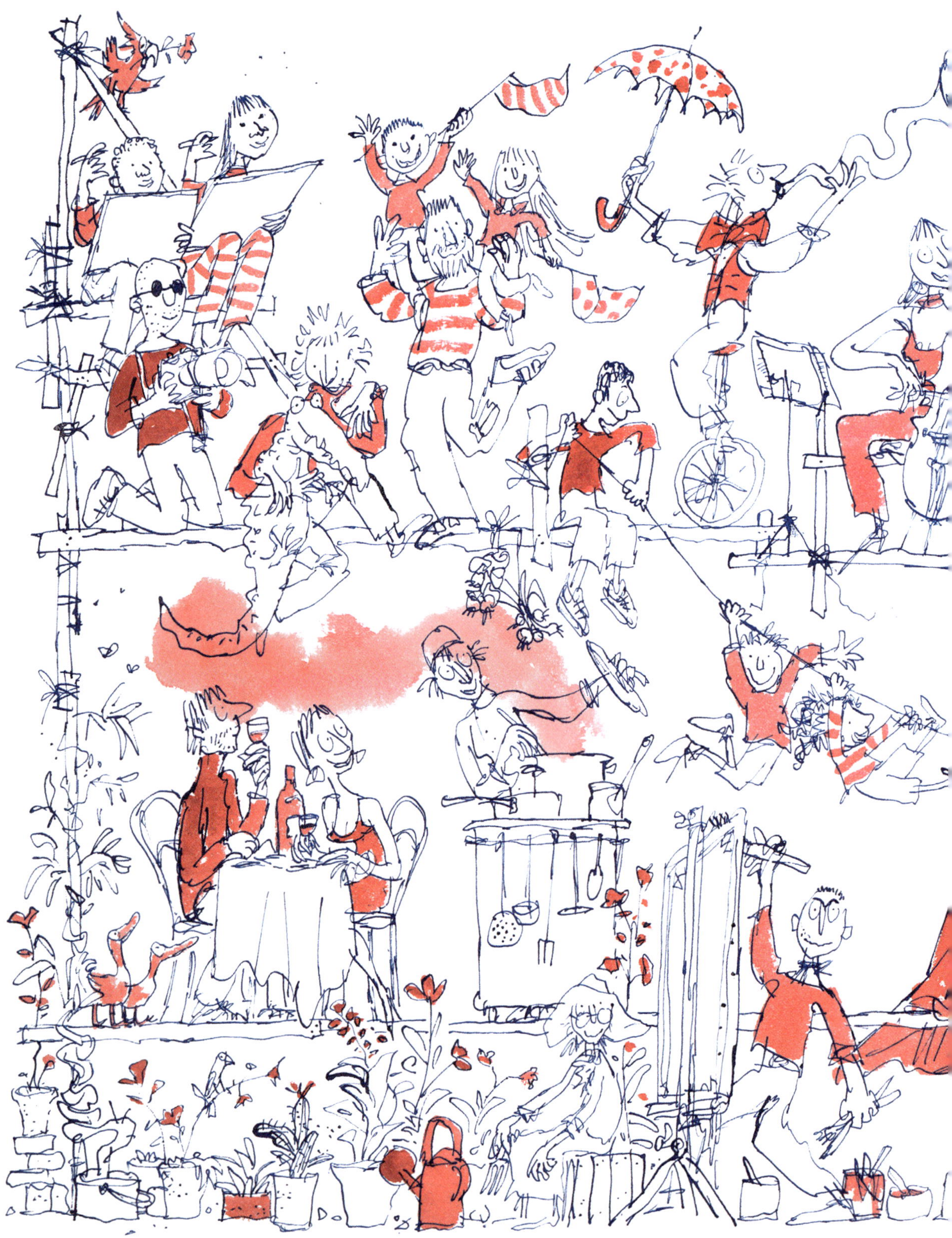

*Stanley Building Wrap*, 2007

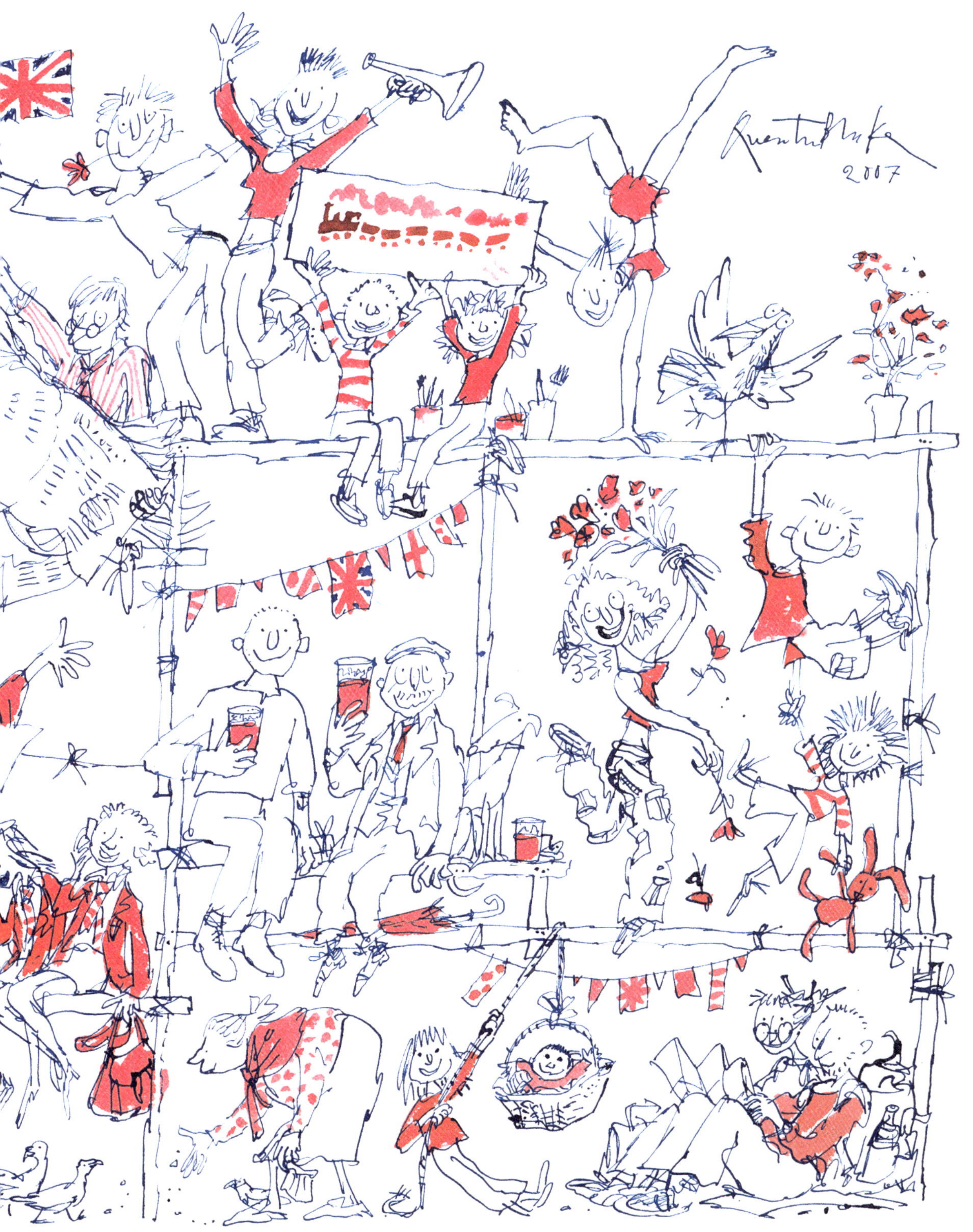

# Famous Alumni for the Cambridge 800 Light Show

As a student Quentin had gone to Cambridge where he read English:

'I wish I had more to say about my time as an undergraduate apart from reading books, visiting plays or films, going to life classes at Cambridge Art School and doing some drawings for the student magazine *Granta*.... An interview on *Desert Island Discs* revealed a pathetic lack of outrage or dissipation, to the contempt of one or two reviewers in the popular press. At any rate, at some point Cambridge discovered that they owned me, with various happy results for me.'

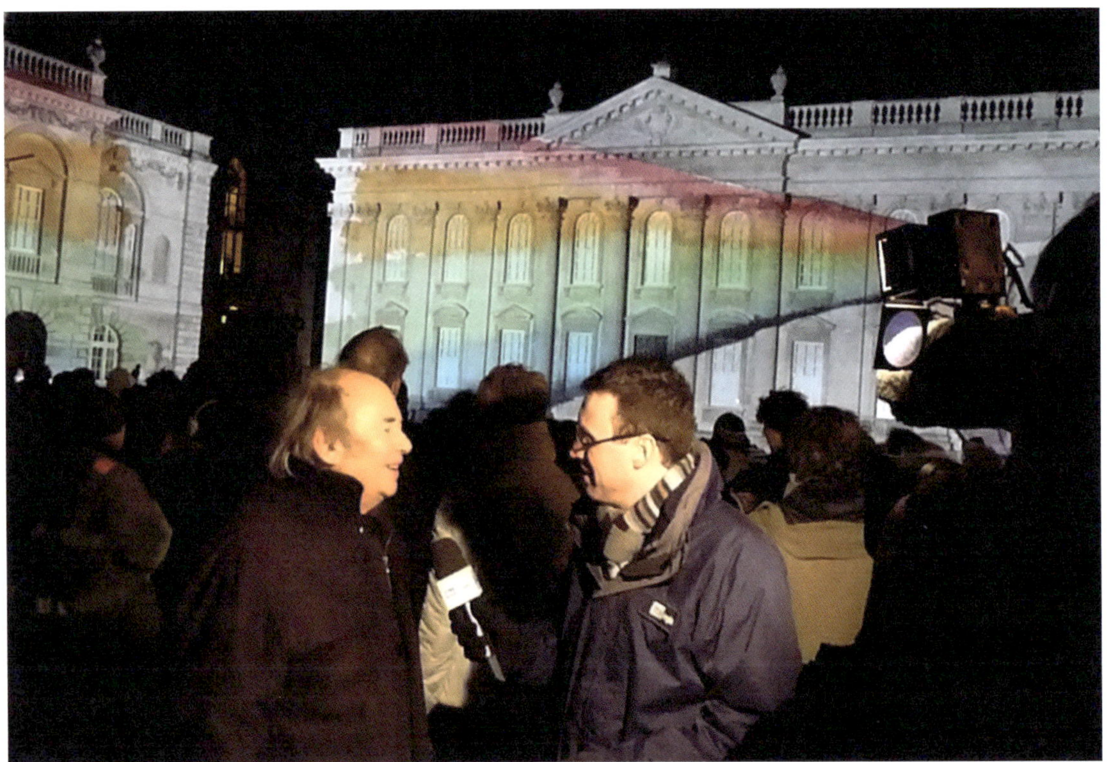

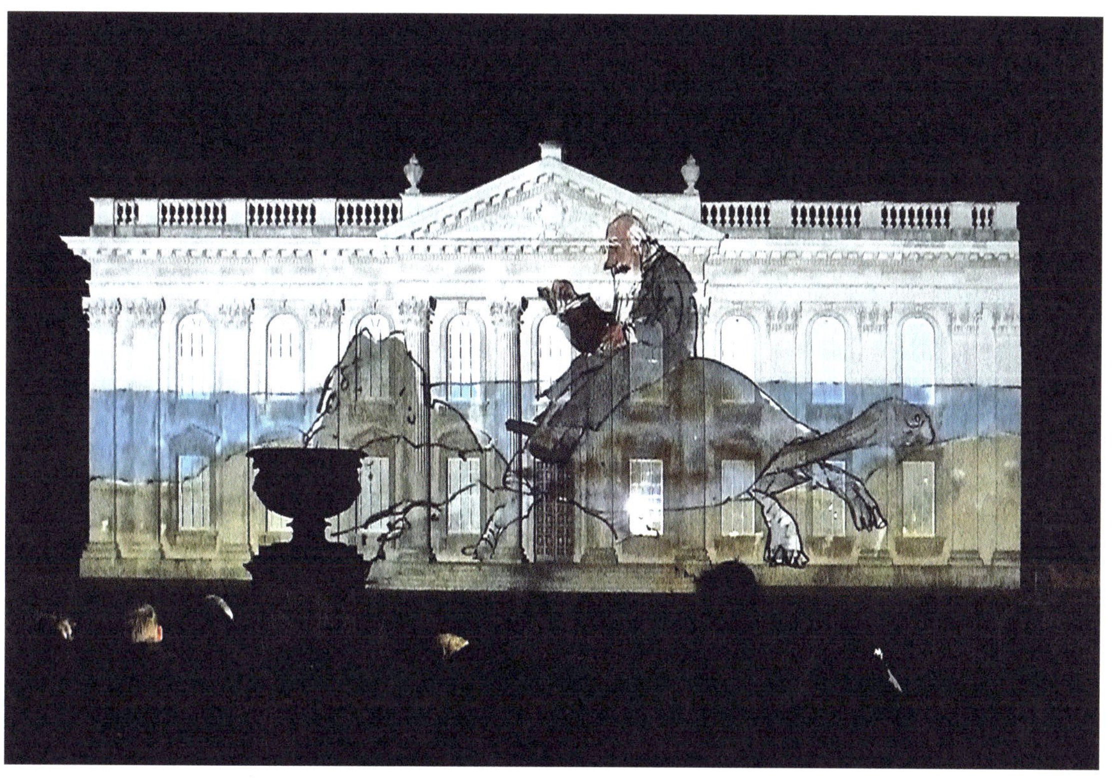

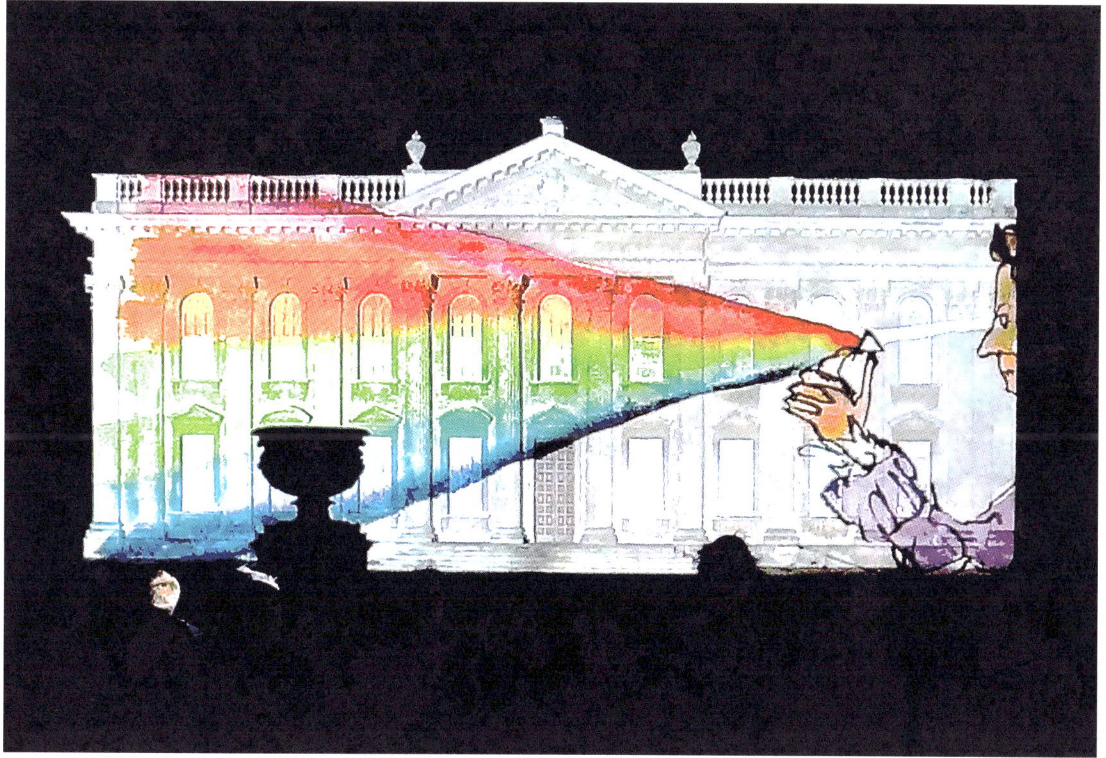

*Cambridge 800*, 2009

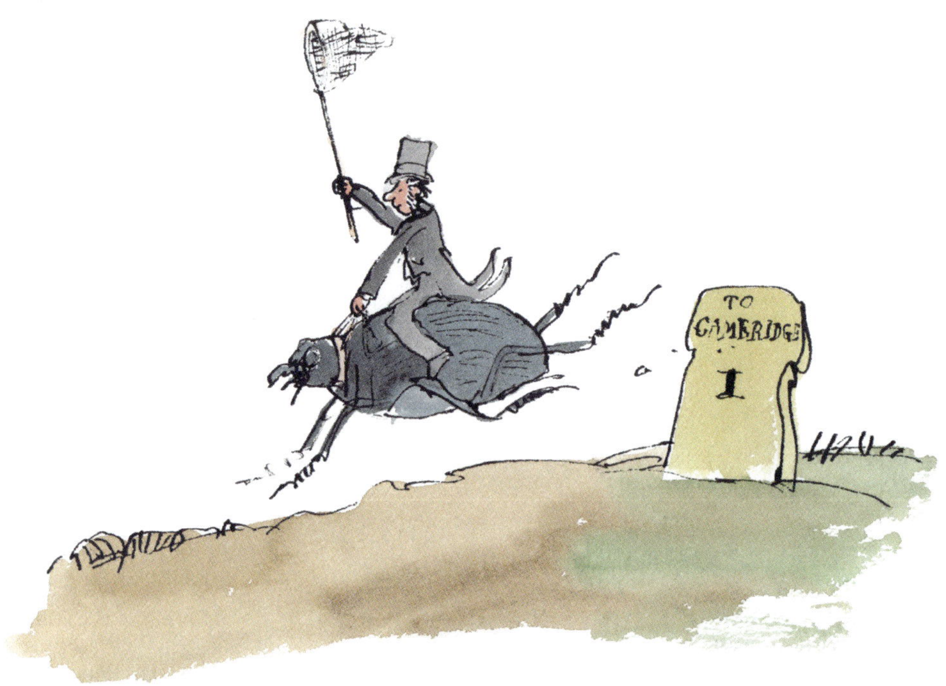


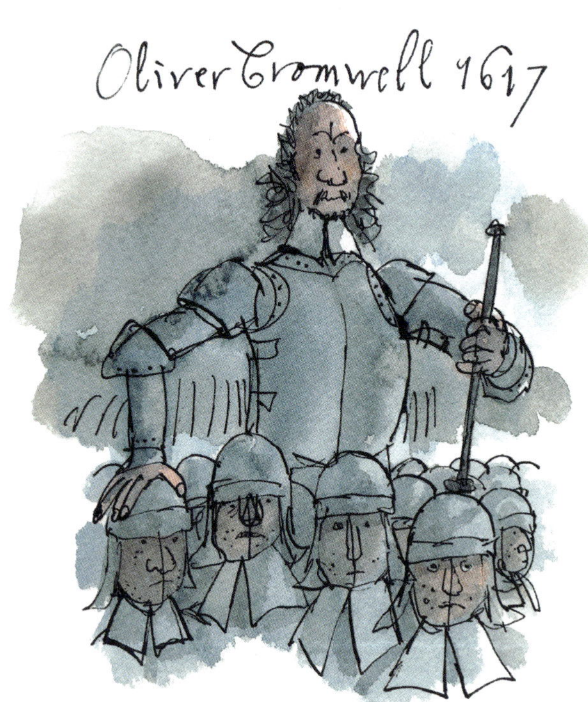

Oliver Cromwell 1617

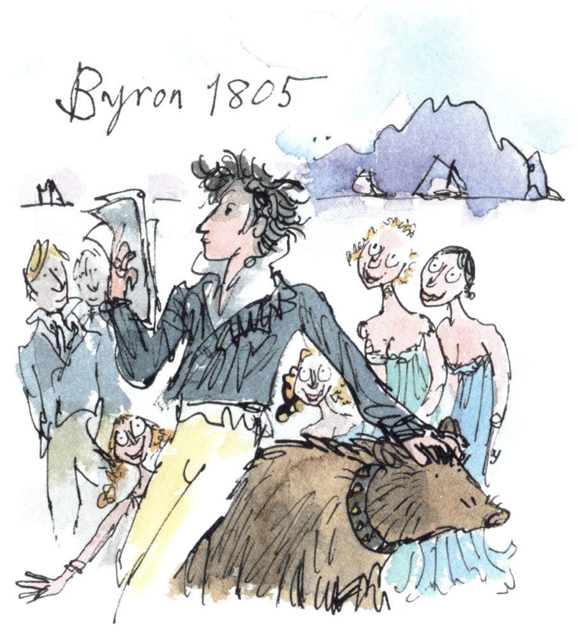


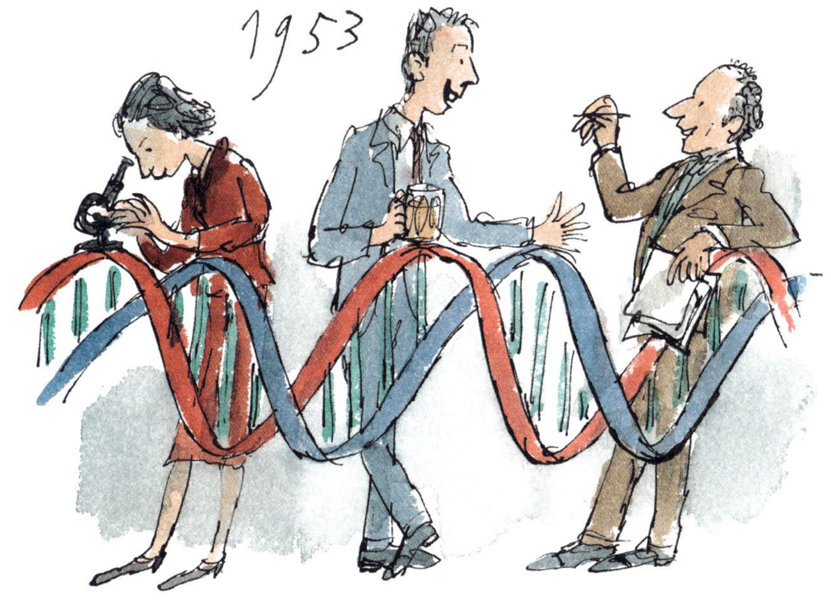


*Cambridge 800*, 2009

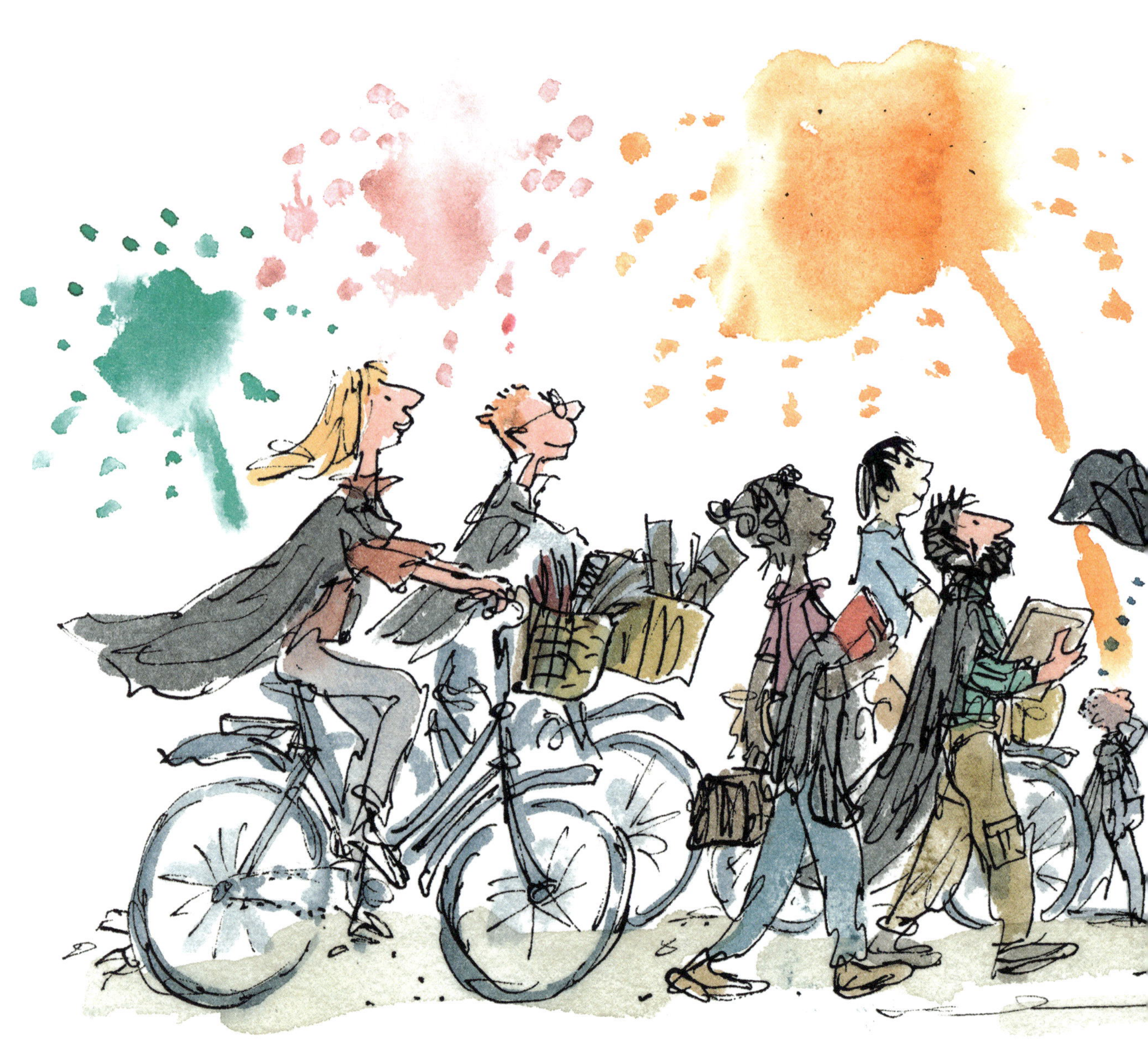

*Cambridge 800*, 2009

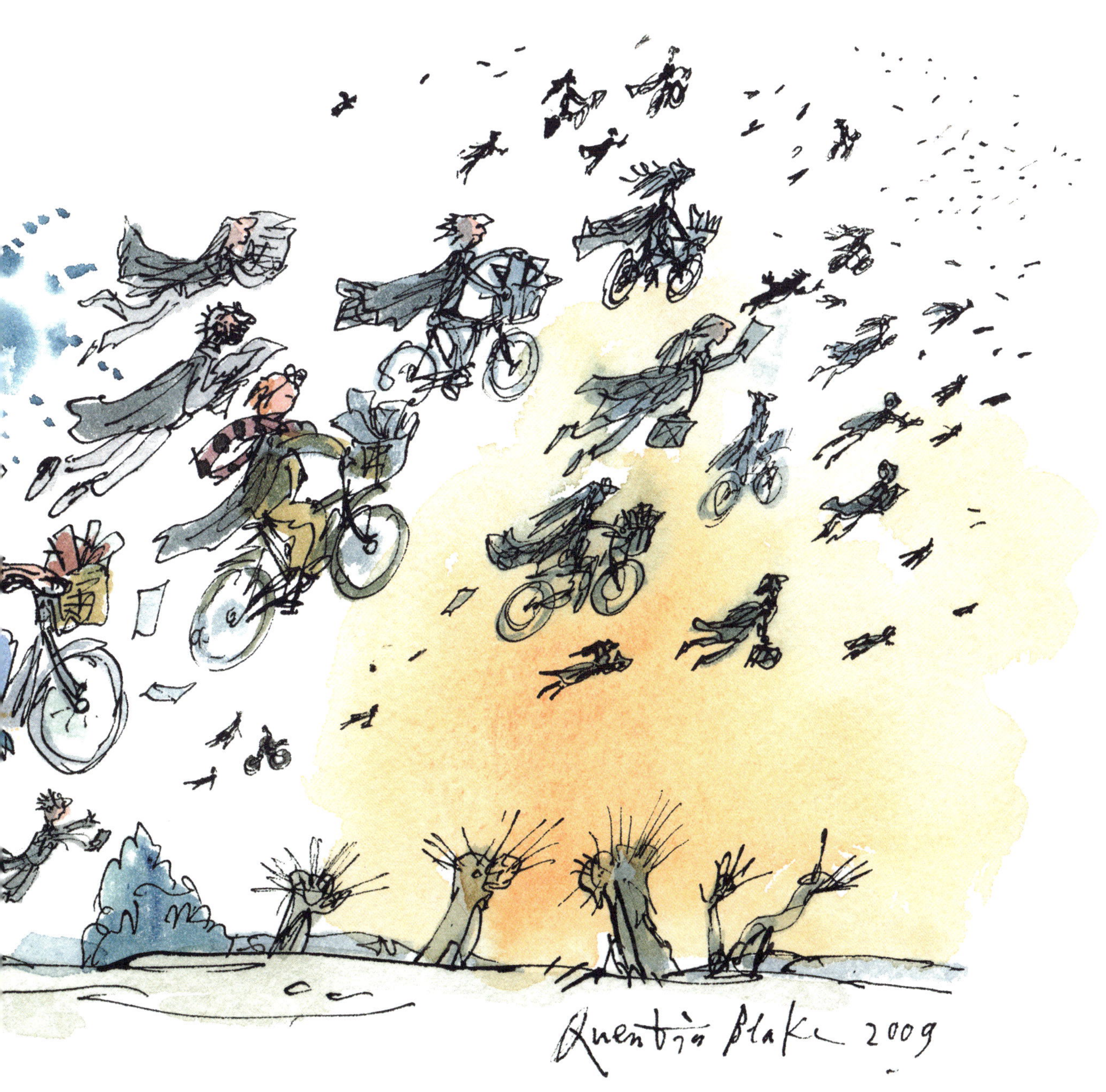

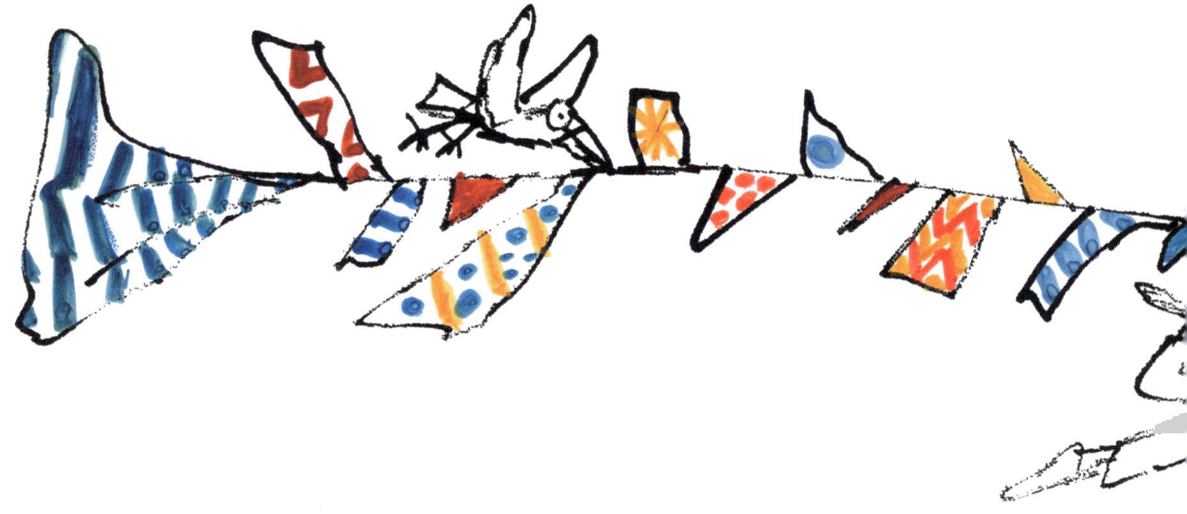

# Murals for the Unicorn Theatre

### *London South Bank*

For Quentin there is an element of performance in drawing; he has said that he 'acts the part' when he's drawing a character and that he sees the double pages of a book like a stage. When the Unicorn Theatre for children and young adults asked him to decorate the white walls of their new building in London's South Bank he remembered a performance he'd seen over forty years ago.

'The play began with the cast uniformly dressed in white jump-suits, to which they added elements of costumes as they went into character. I've always remembered it as expressive of what theatre performance is about, and I adopted it for the Unicorn drawings. My characters are entirely black and white except when they blossom out into coats, trousers, hats, all of extravagant colour.'

Quentin's drawings were enlarged and then copied by a sign painter on to the walls. Because the drawings would be seen up close, he wanted the texture of the murals to be as similar as possible to his illustrations.

'The pressures and variations of the reed pen they were drawn with are preserved, but evenly black and flat. One has the interesting sensation that they are somehow printed on the wall so that the visitor could be cheerfully welcomed and accompanied up the stairs to the auditorium with a suggestion of the theatricality to come.'

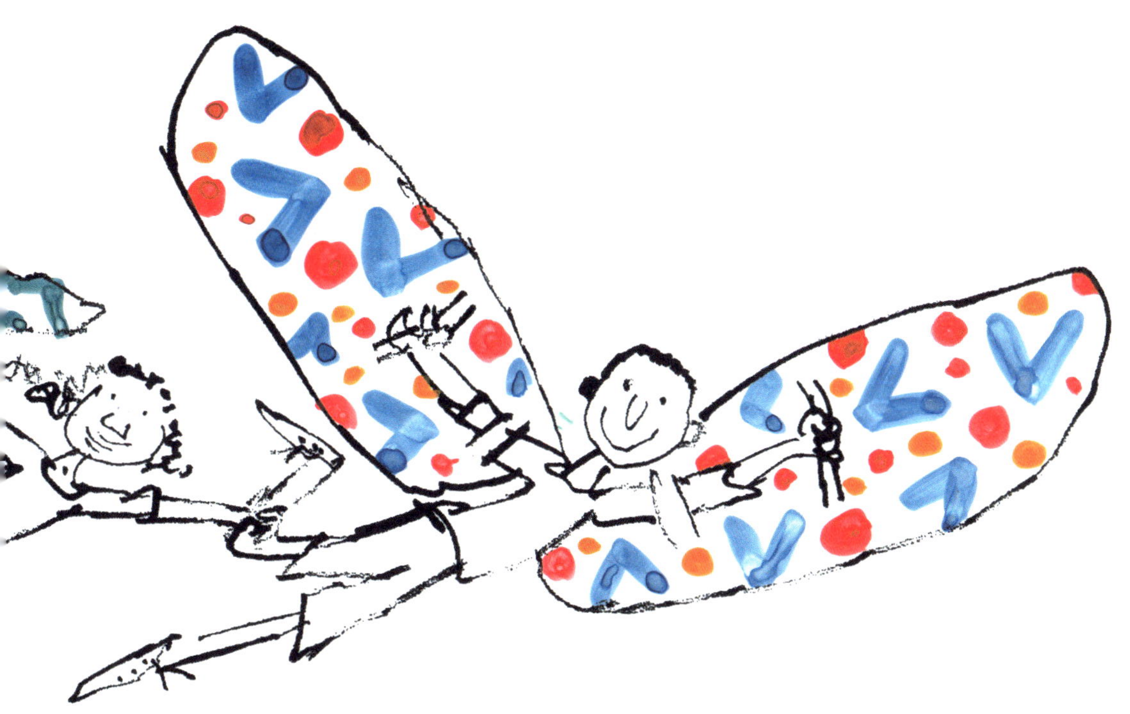

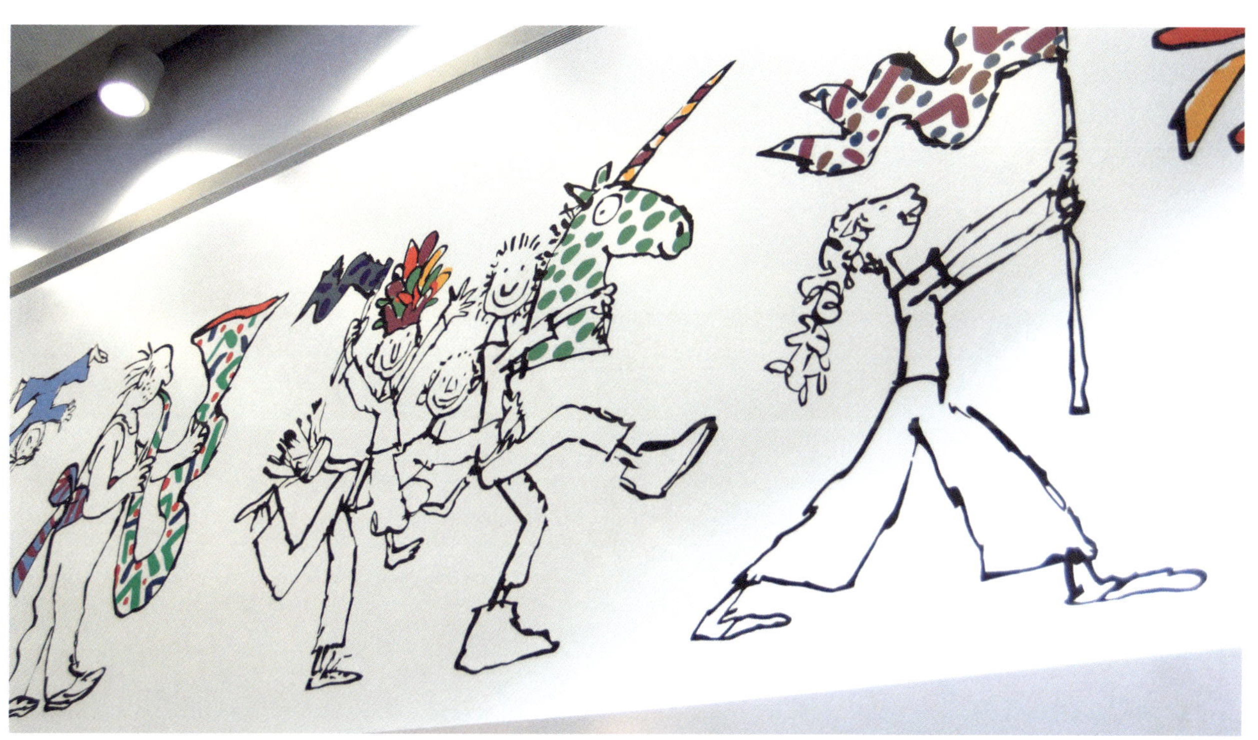

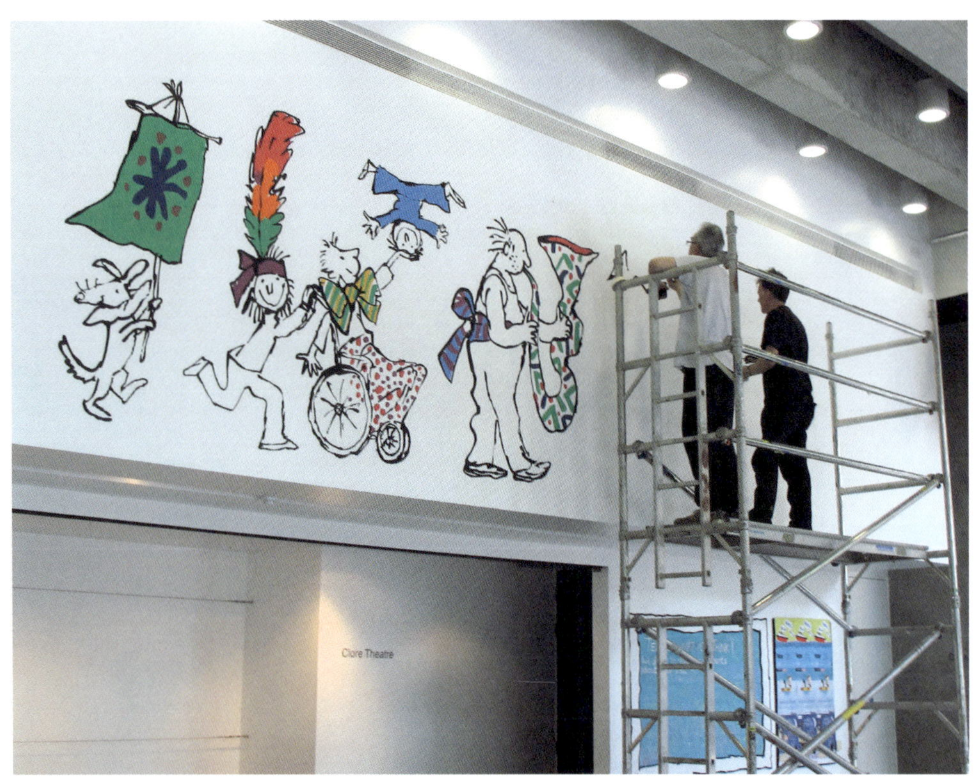
Clore Theatre

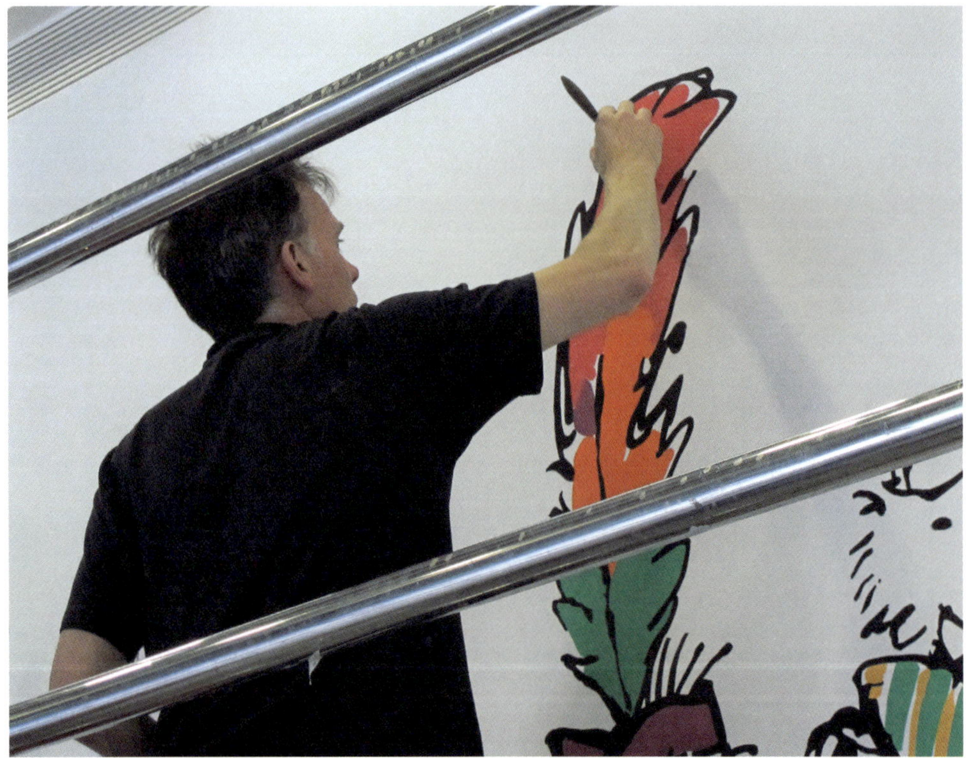

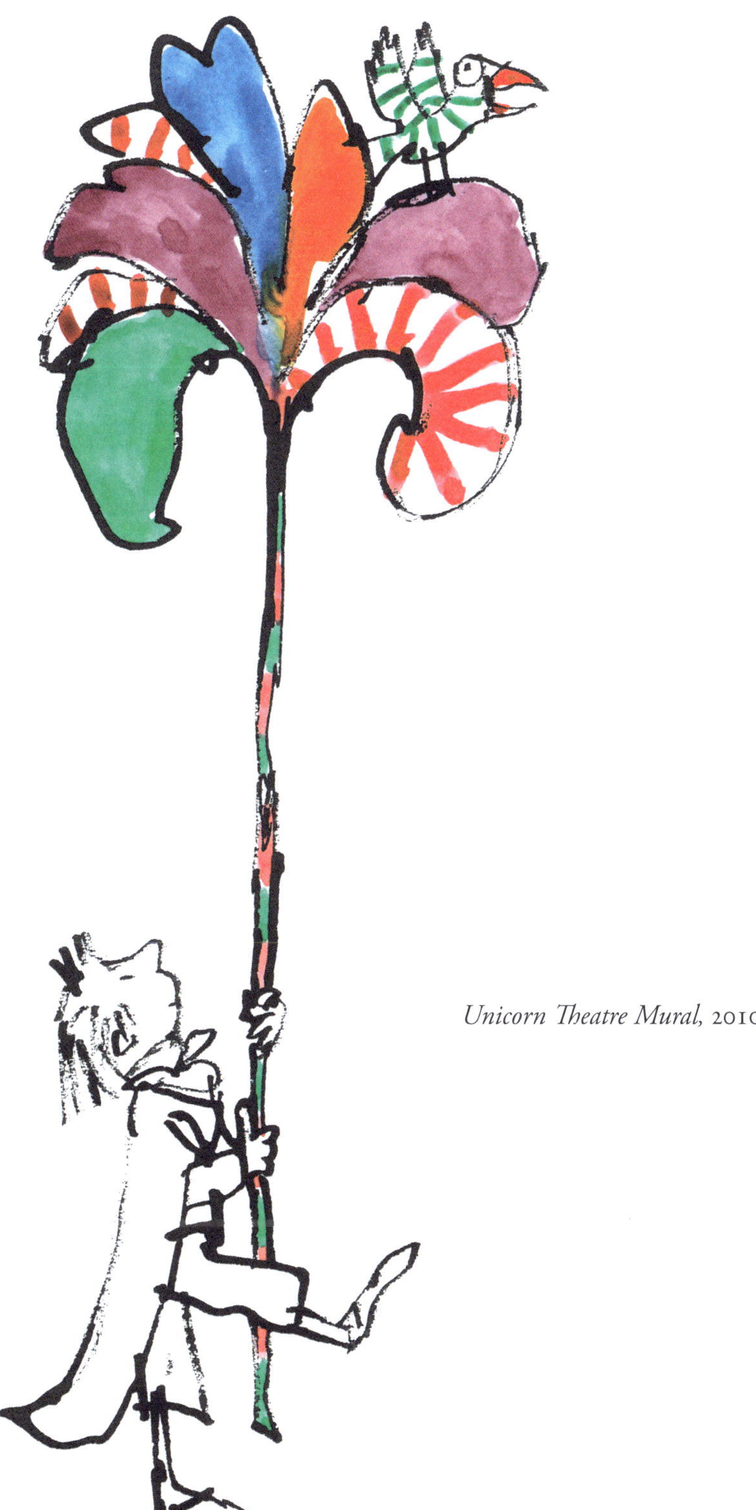

*Unicorn Theatre Mural,* 2010

*Unicorn Theatre Mural*, 2010

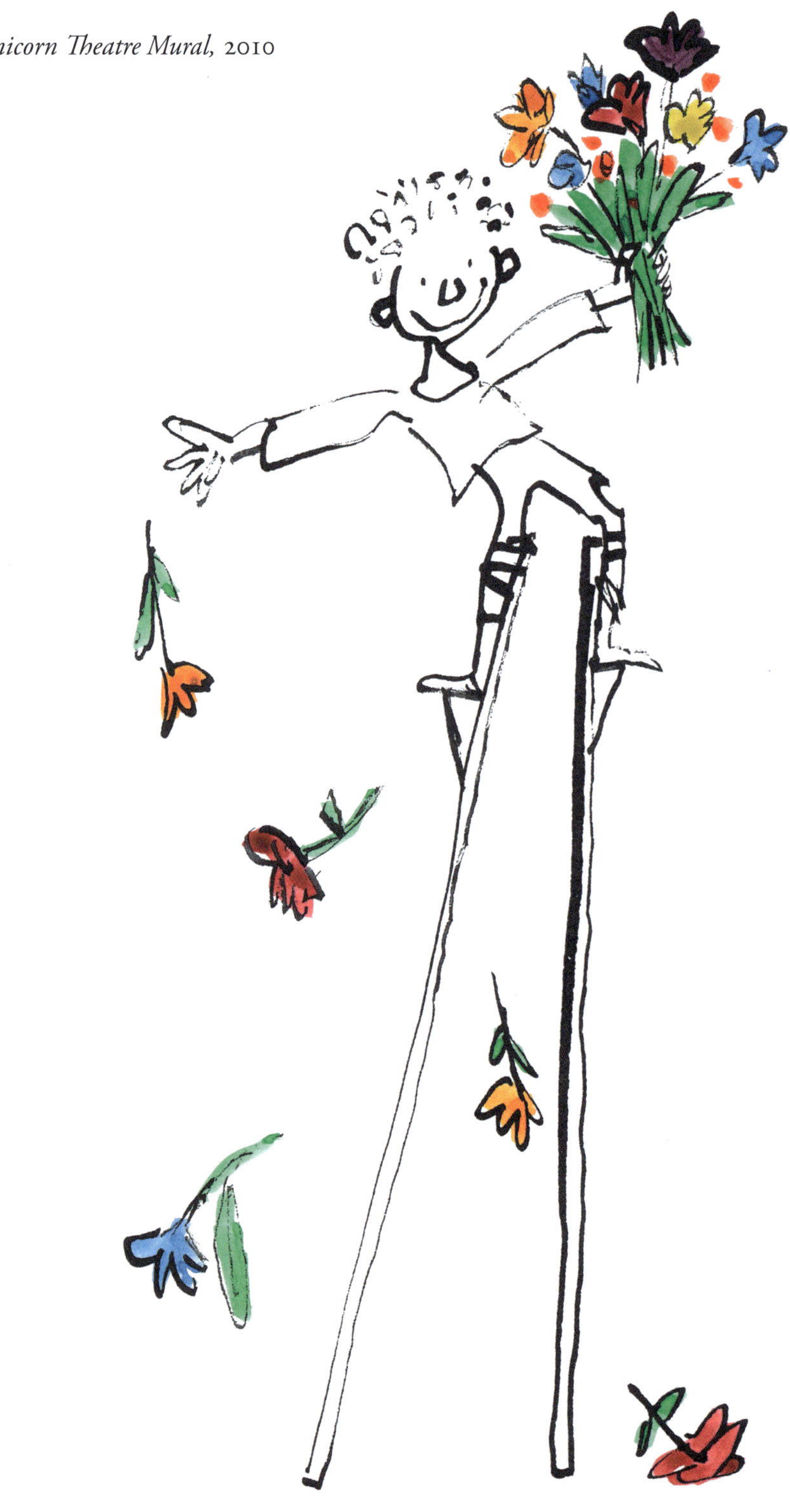

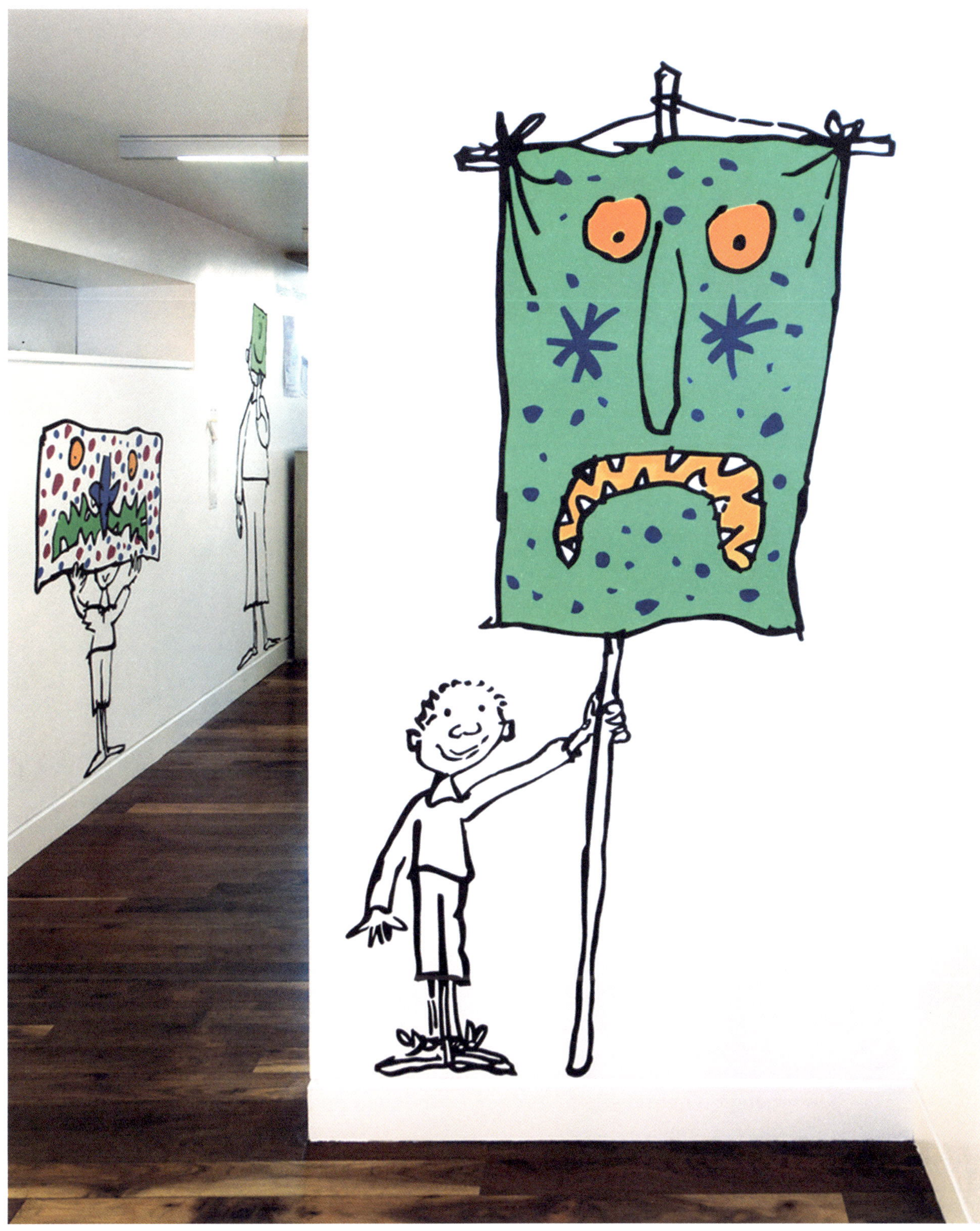

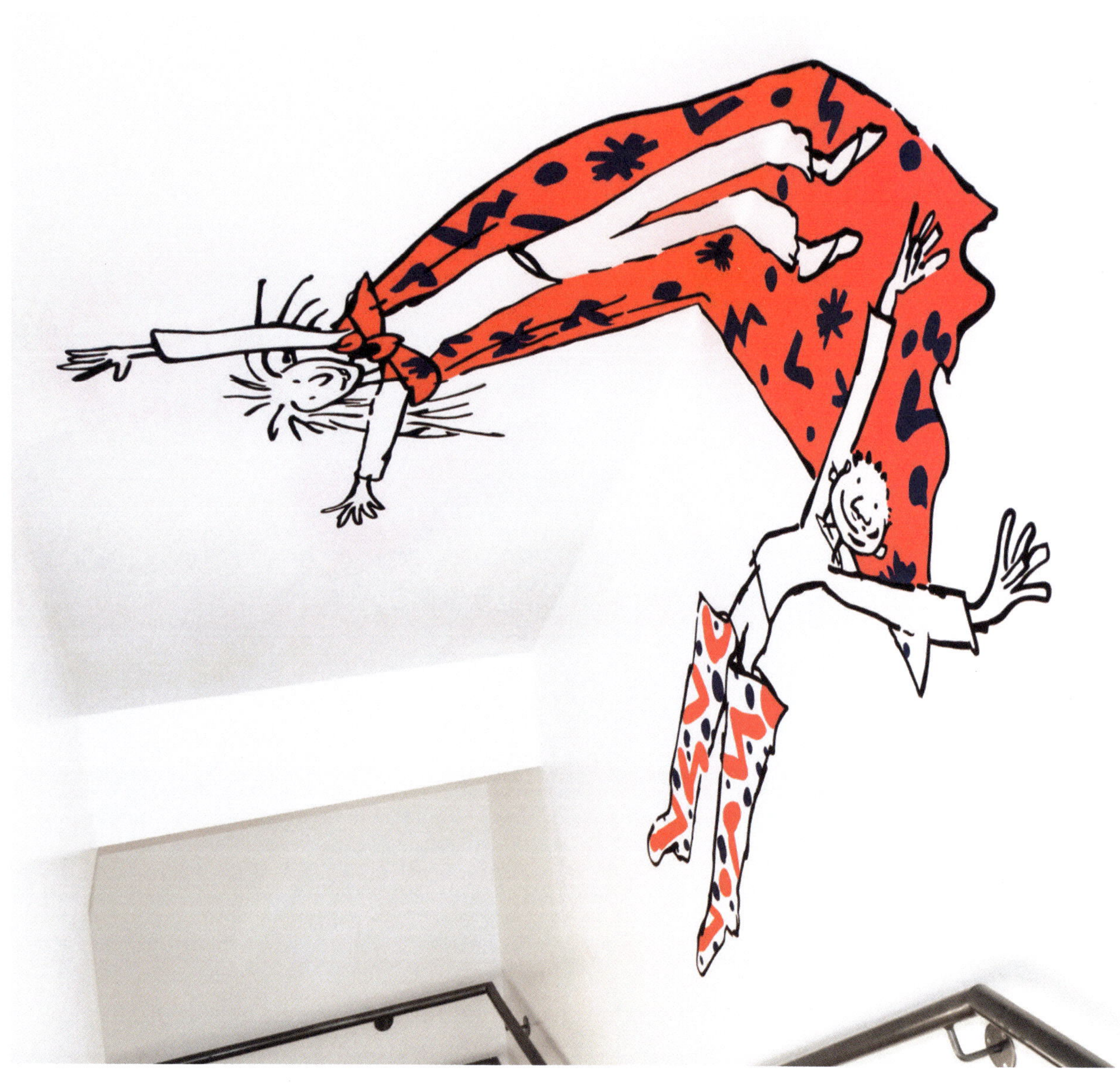

*Unicorn Theatre Mural,* 2010

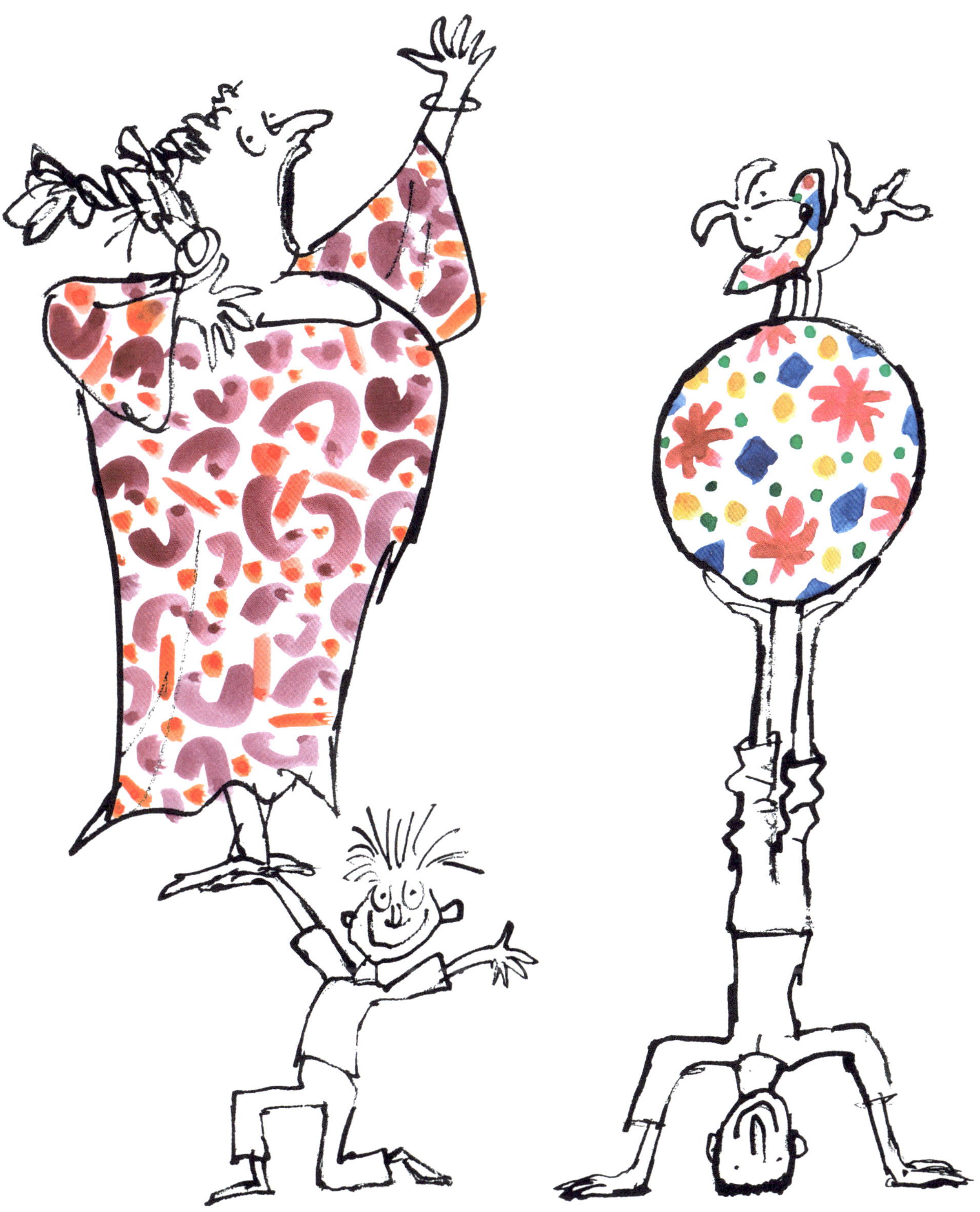

# A Pillar at the Barbican Centre

When Sir Nicholas Kenyon was put in charge of the Barbican Arts Centre, he asked Quentin if he could decorate a large pillar in his office. The idea that the drawings should have a performance element to them seemed an obvious one, but the *type* of performers was more surprising. Quentin loves birds, both real and fantastic. And, because they stand on two legs, he can give them human attributes to represent people; it is his way of using satire without ridiculing or causing offence.

'The advantage of this approach was that I could draw a variety of artistic activities without specifying the individual performers, and indeed the fact that they were all birds gave the thing a certain unity. I soon had a sequence of them pursuing a gamut of artistic activities, and they became *A Barbican Ornithology*.'

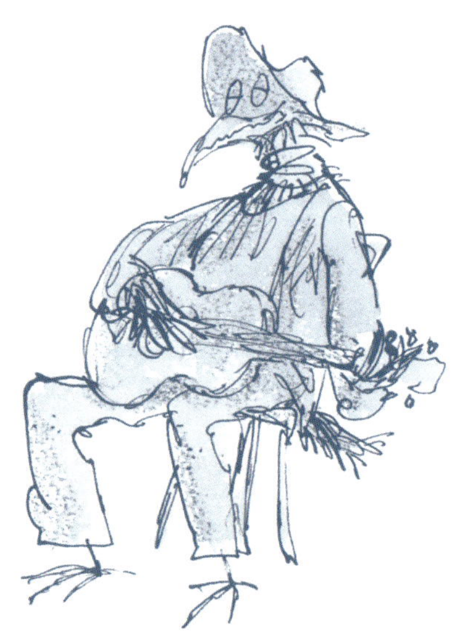

OPPOSITE –
*A Barbican Ornithology*

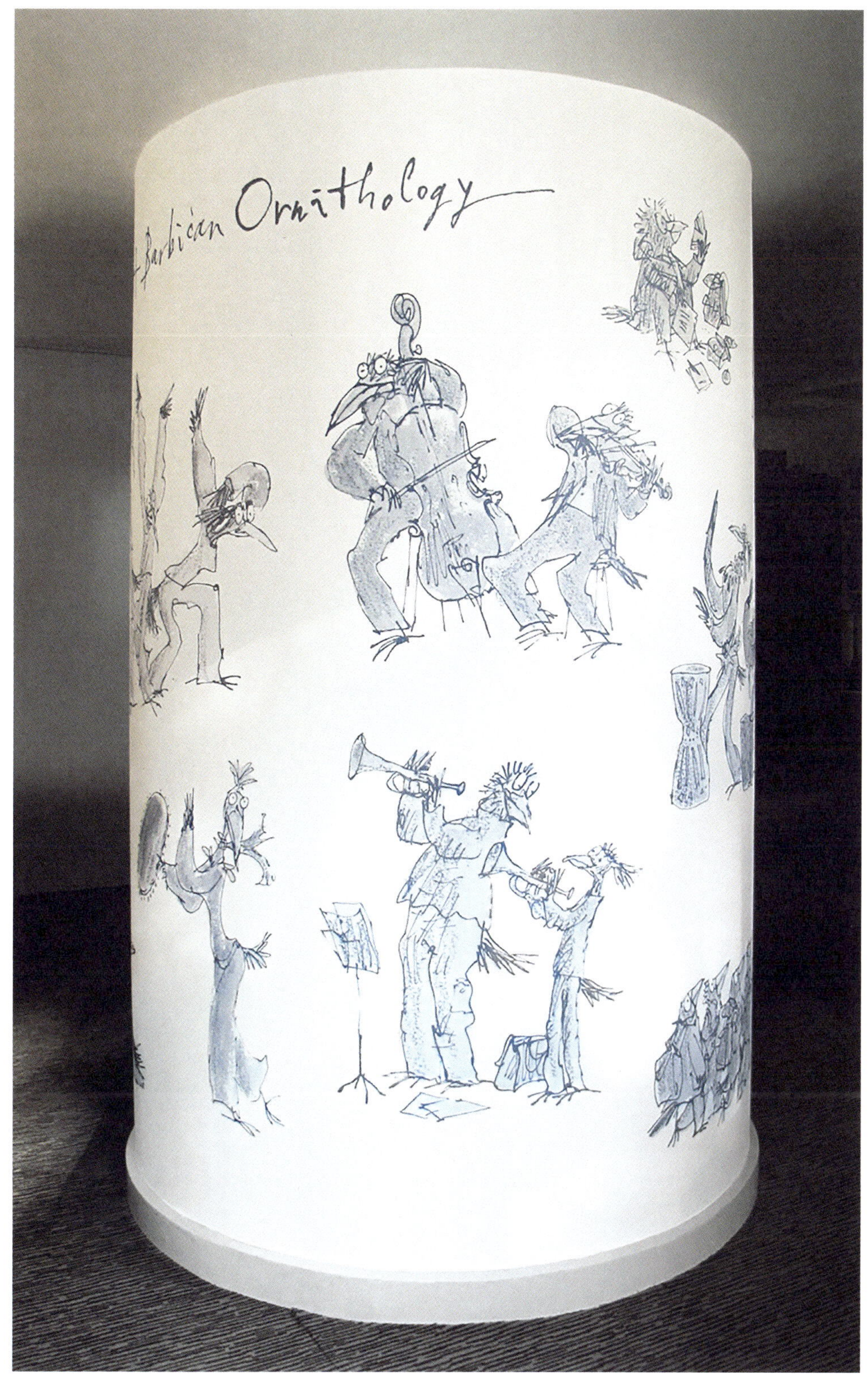
Barbican Ornithology

# A Barbican Ornithology

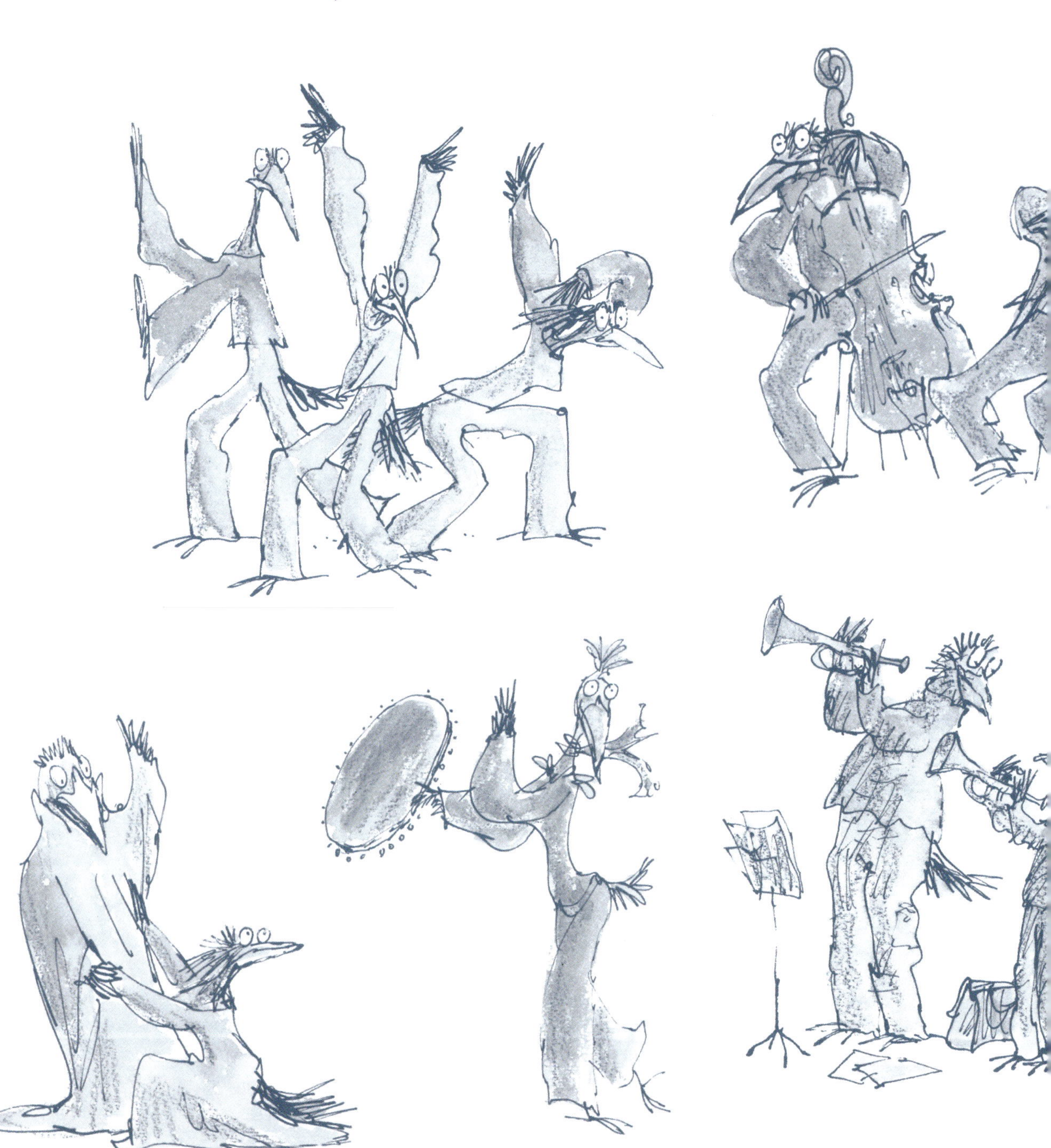

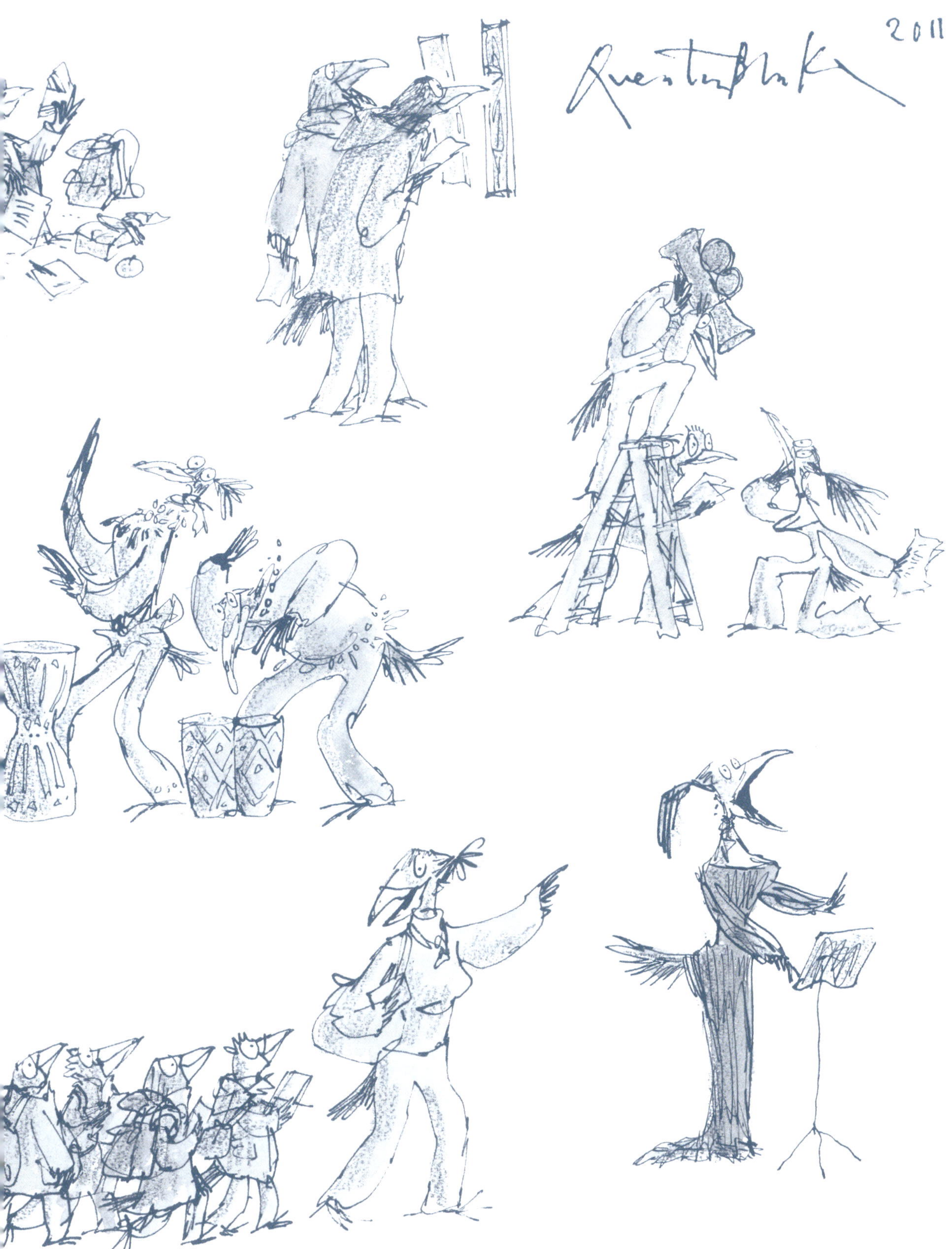

# The Downing College Tapestry

Quentin's old college at Cambridge, Downing, has a griffin for its insignia. Having already produced drawings of it for college merchandise, he was invited to do a large-scale tapestry to be hung in a new building.

'My response was two scratchy drawings of griffins rampant, with subdued colour that was evidently watercolour… my griffins became wall hangings, with the use of a mechanical process that produces the effect of tapestry. I confess that there was something that appealed to me in the idea of two small informal drawings translated into the traditional formality of tapestry.'

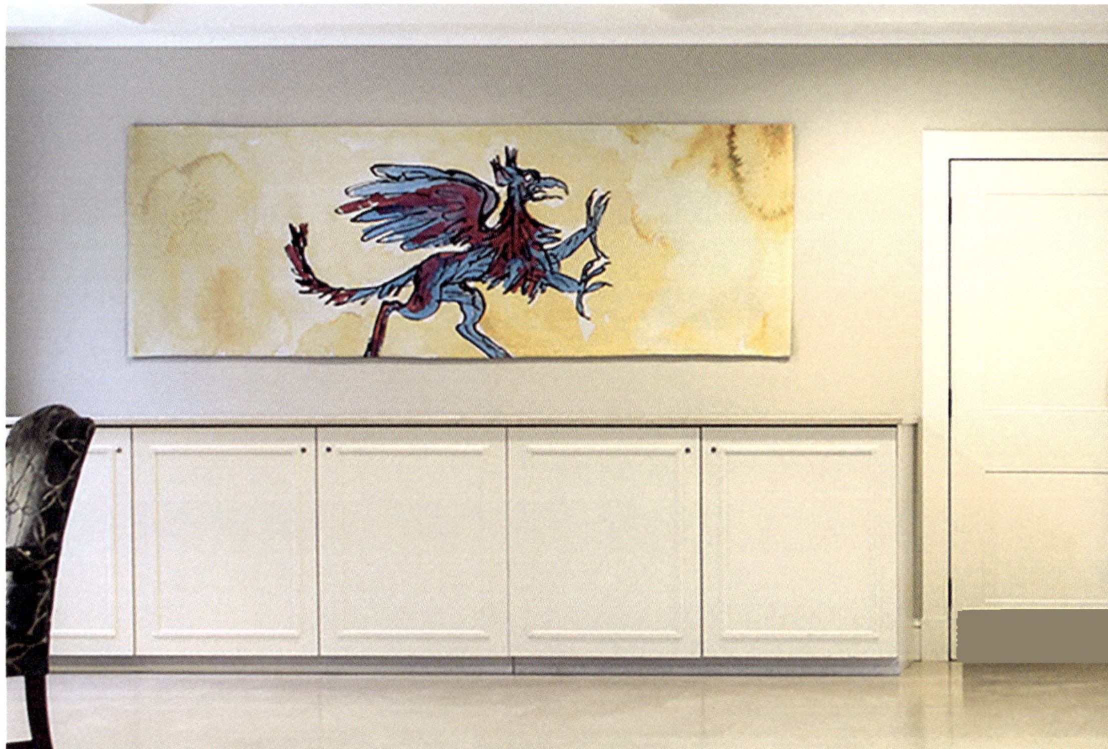

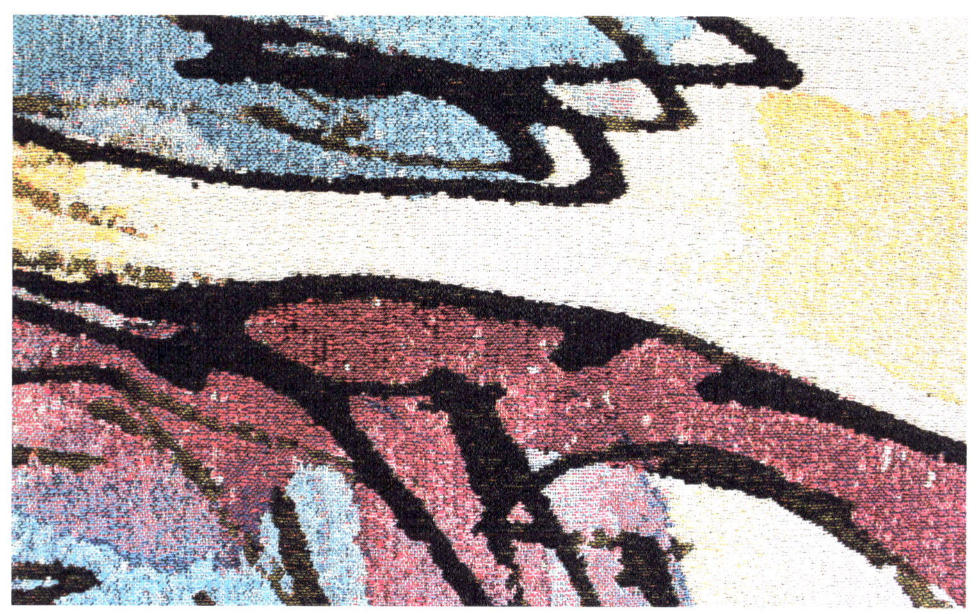

*Downing College Griffin Tapestry (detail above)*, 2015

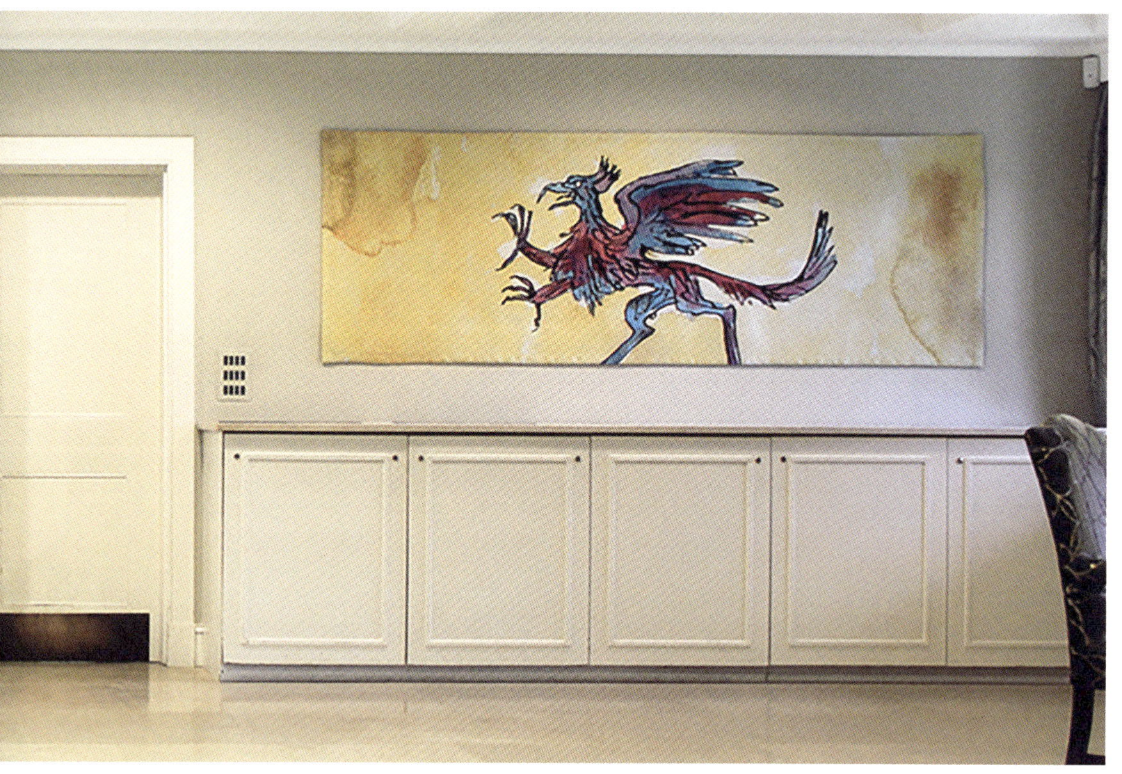

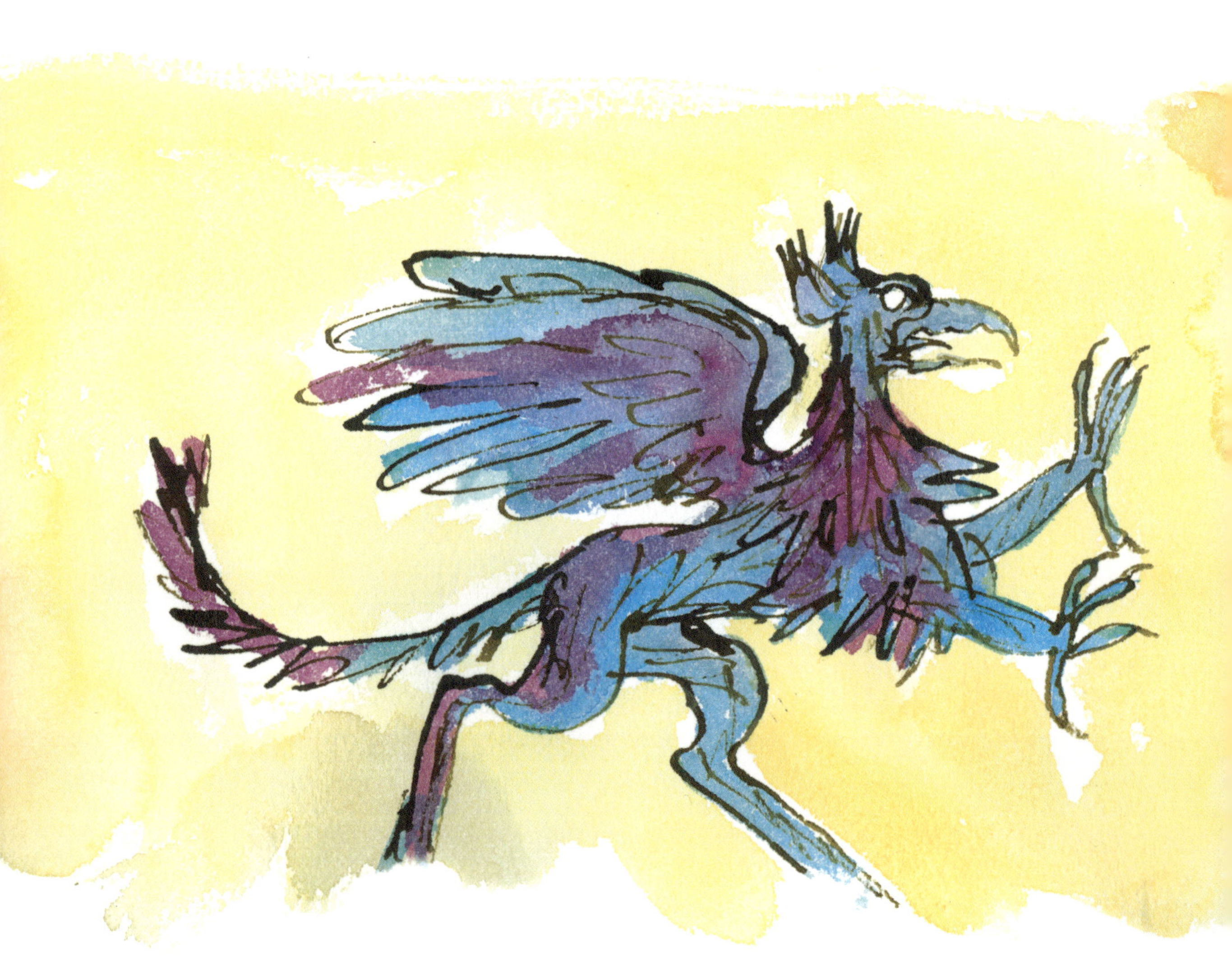

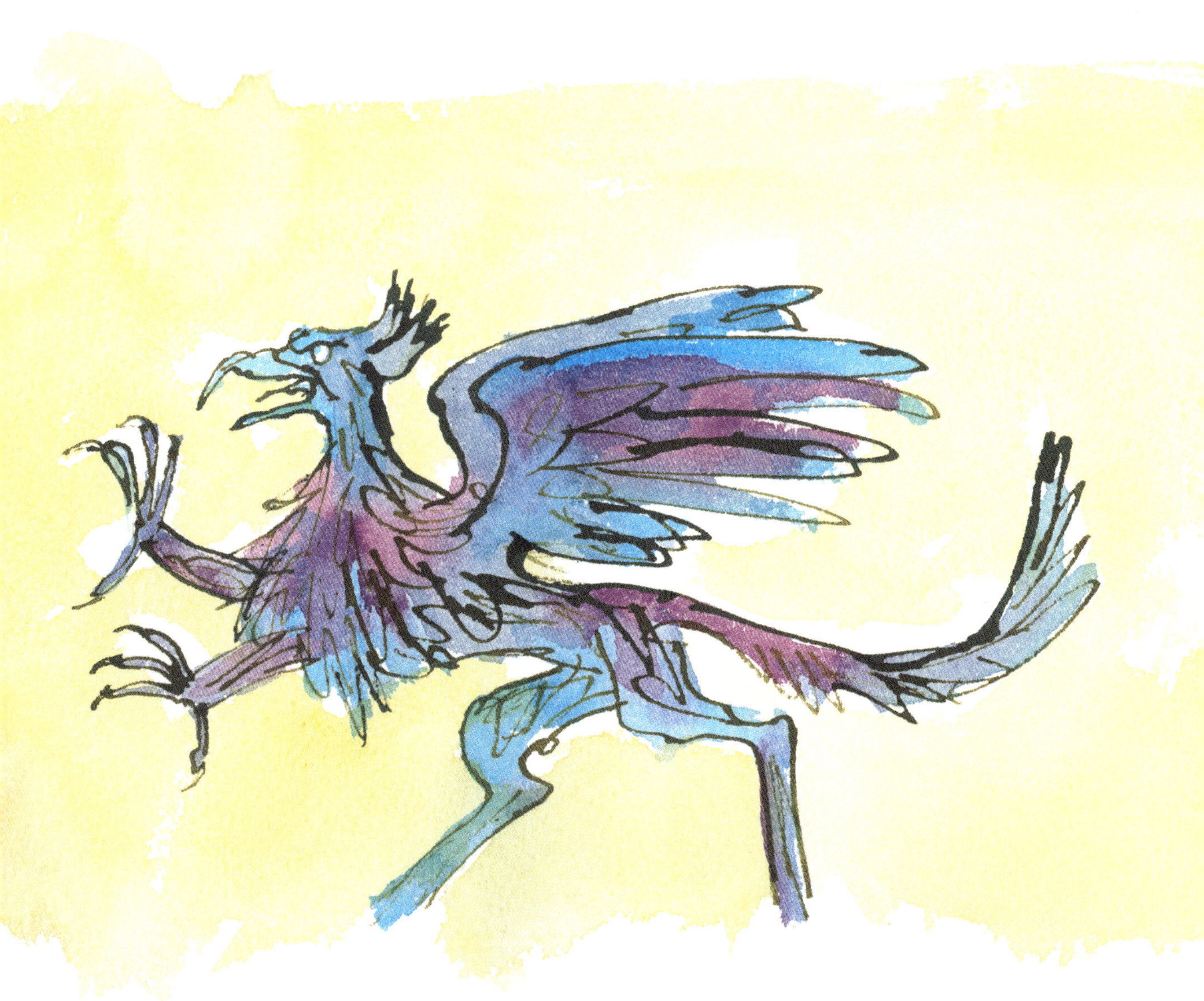

# A Mural for Buckingham Palace

Every summer, when Queen Elizabeth went to Balmoral, Buckingham Palace was opened to public tours. Quentin was asked to do a drawing of the BFG for a tented pavilion, which appealed to him because of the scene in the book when the BFG and Sophie visit the Queen.

But there was a problem of how to fit him in. 'I pointed out, however, that as the pavilion was only to be fourteen or fifteen feet in height it would have to be rather a small version of our hero. That led me to think of another solution: if he were sitting down he could comfortably fill the wall and perhaps for the first time actually be depicted at life size. I also thought that it might be nice if he were to hold out his hand at a level where a child could sit on it. Needless to say, I would not have been able to bring any of this about without the collaboration of Lexi Burgess. He was the person who knew how to get my drawing enlarged to the size of the wall, and to construct a secure and unobtrusive seat. In striking contrast with much work for publishing, where your drawings go off to reappear in proof several months later and in book form even later than that, this had to be completed within days...'

*BFG Mural at Buckingham Palace,* 2016

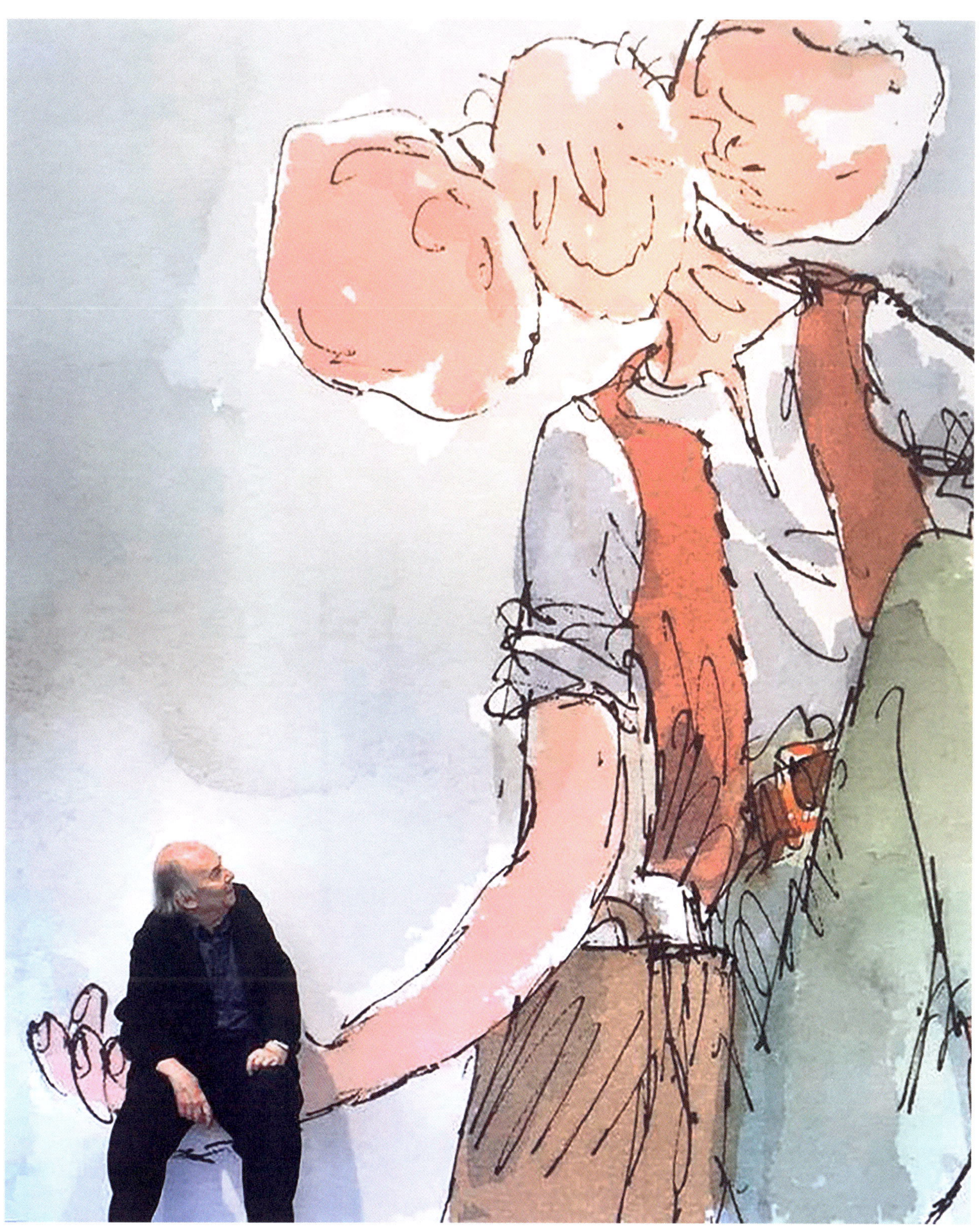

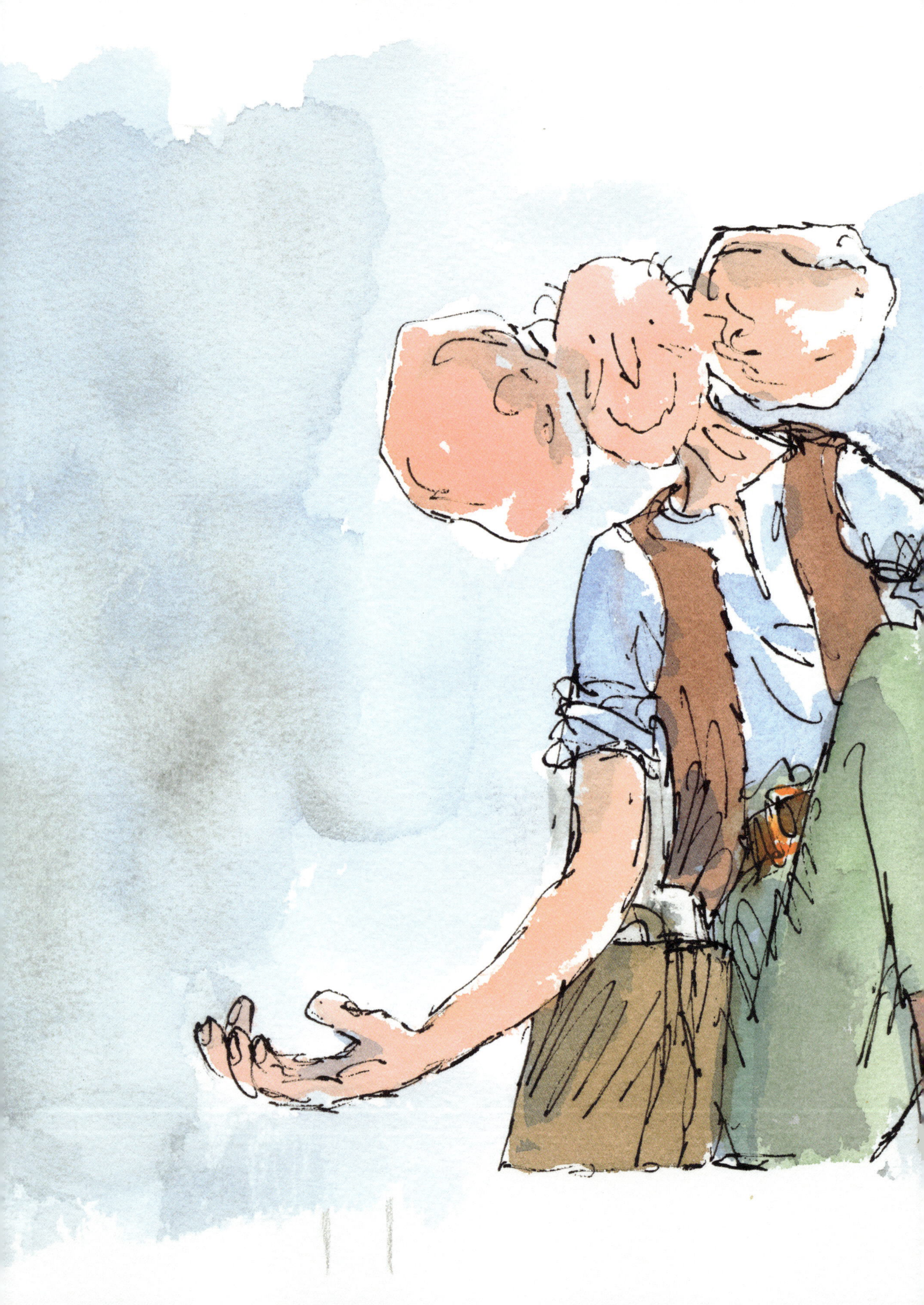

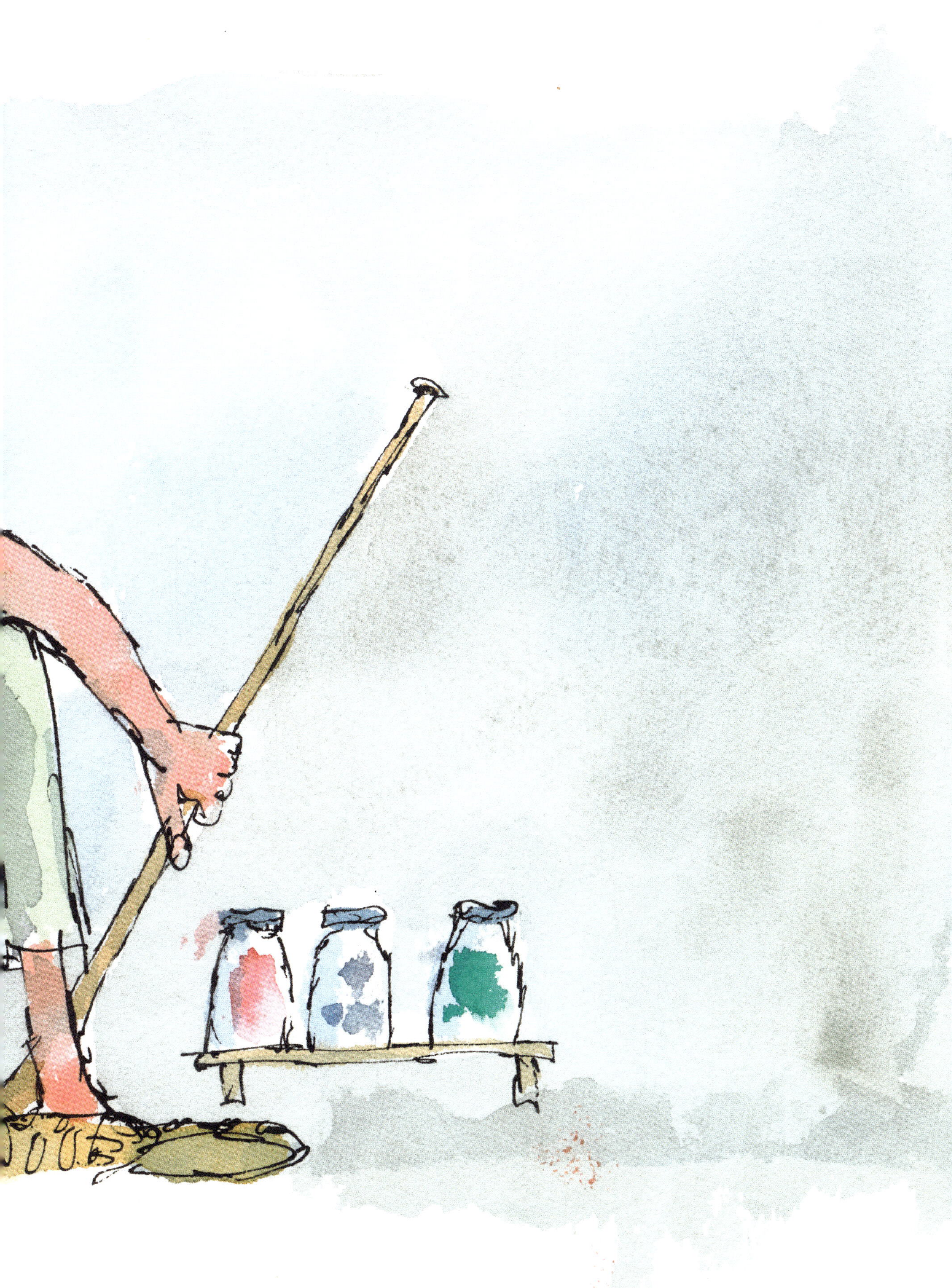

# The Zoology Museum

'I had worked with Shelley Bolderson on the Cambridge 800 project, and on her arrival at the Zoology Museum she had the idea that there may be something appropriate for me to do there too. I set to work on a set of drawings for the blinds; they are permanently lowered to keep the light off the specimens on display on the ground floor. My drawings show visitors to the museum encountering them, as though in real life. An advantage of this was that we could show creatures such as the dodo and the giant sloth as they would once have looked, although they only exist in the collections as skeletons.'

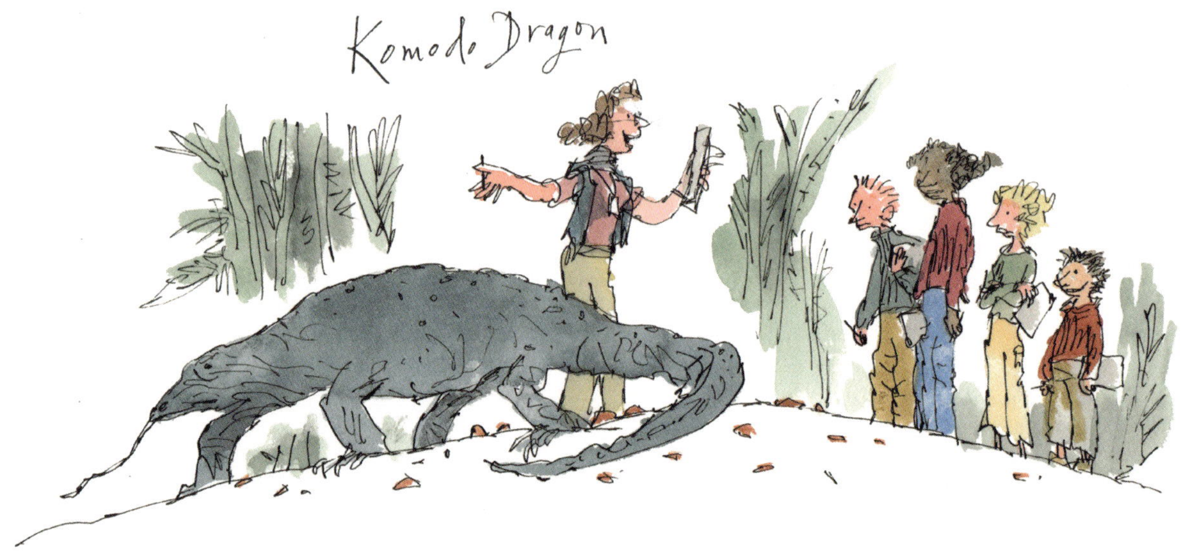

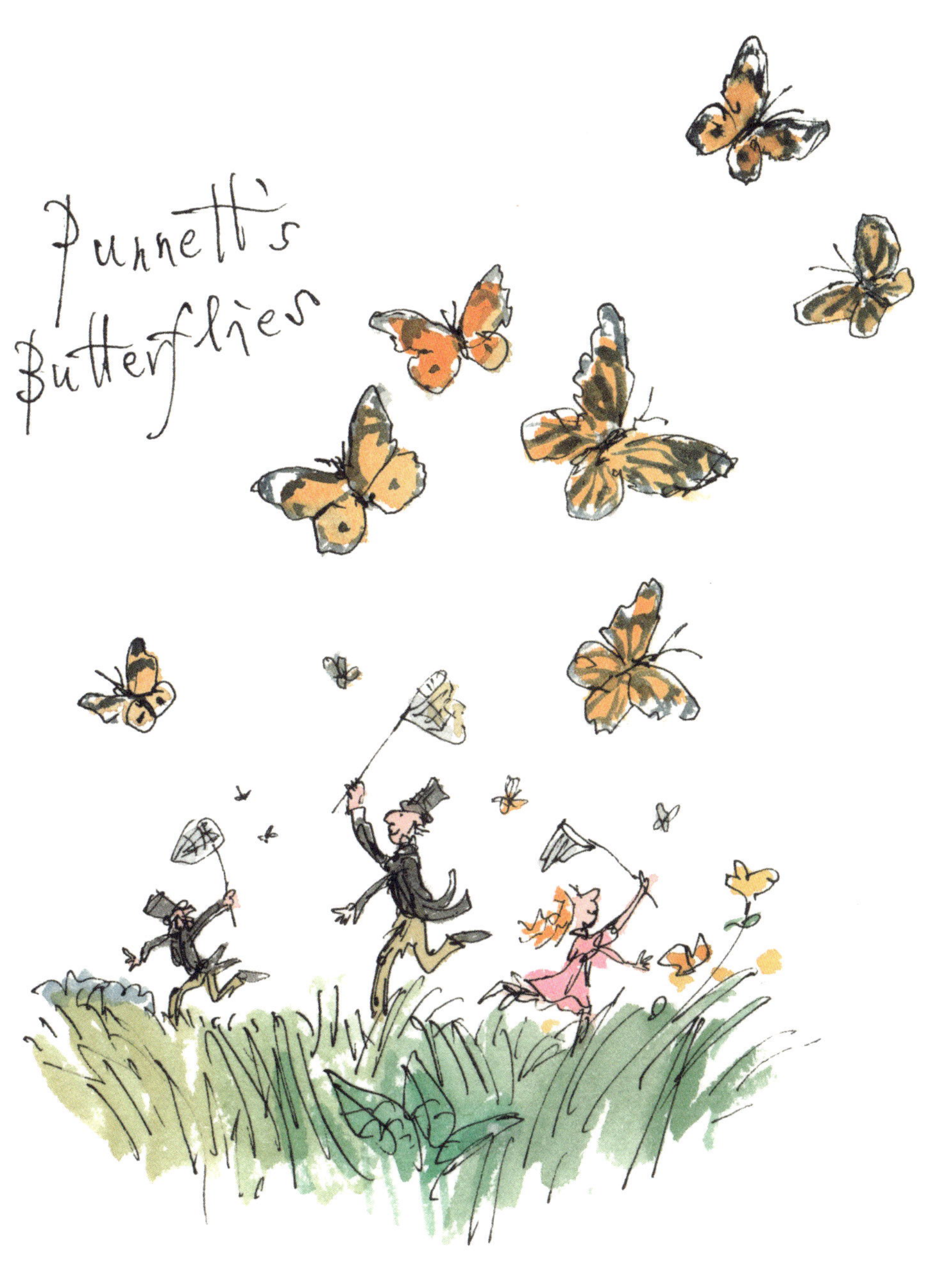


OPPOSITE & ABOVE – *Cambridge Museum of Zoology*, 2017

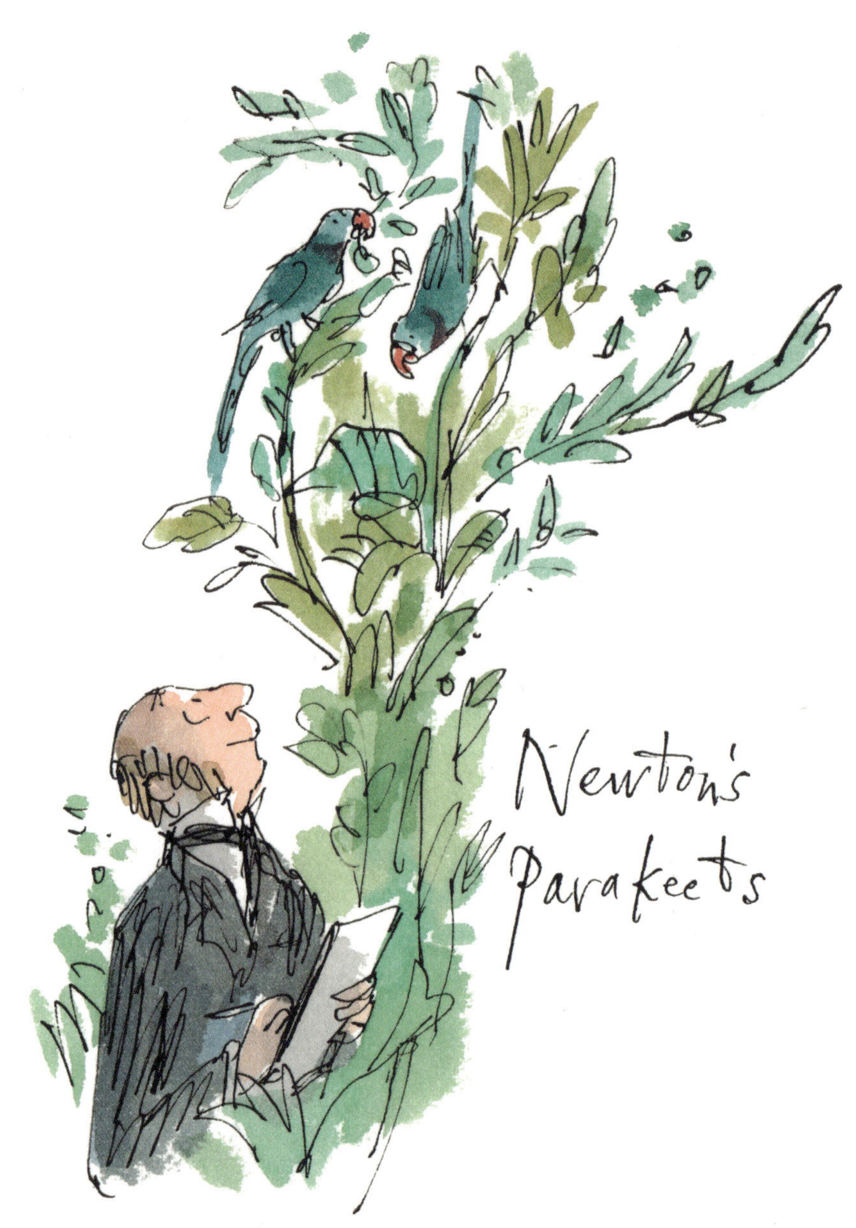
Newton's
Parakeets

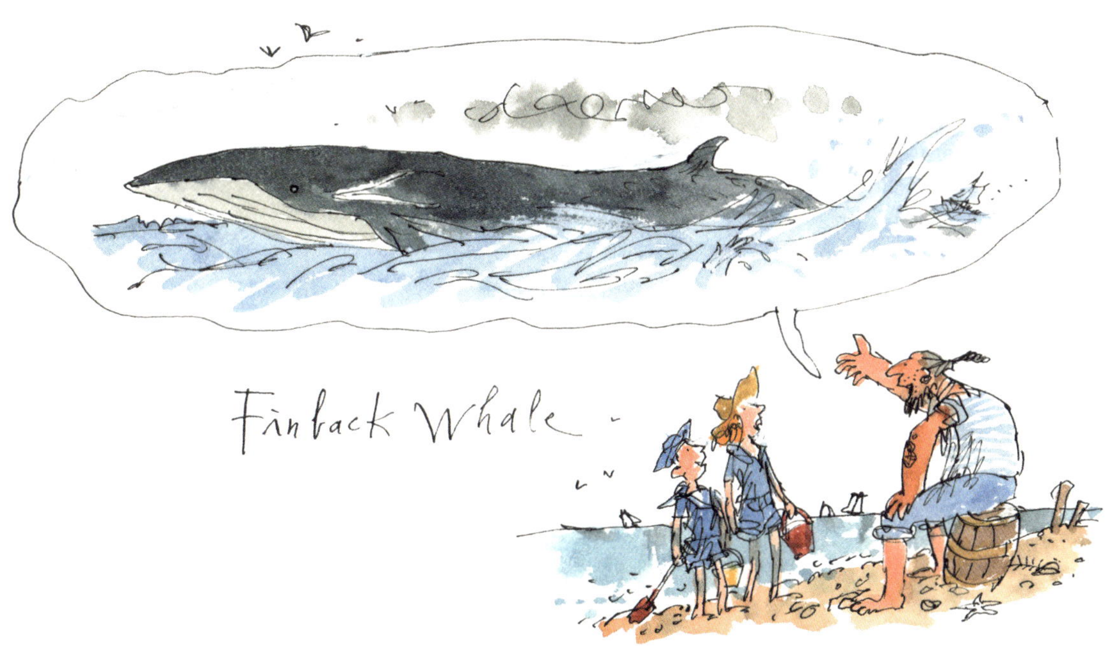


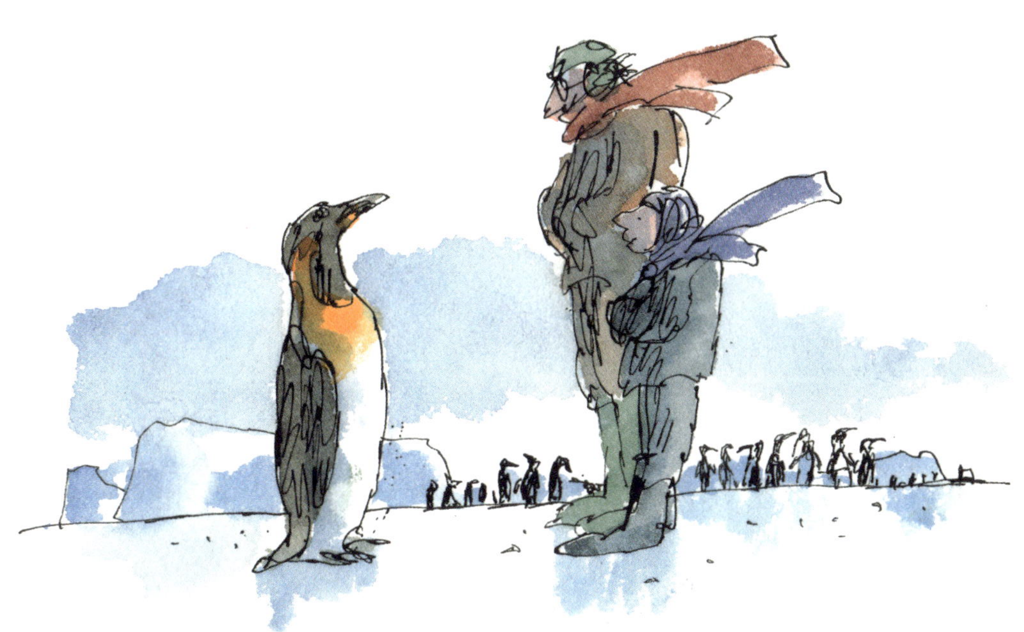

OPPOSITE & ABOVE – *Cambridge Museum of Zoology*, 2017

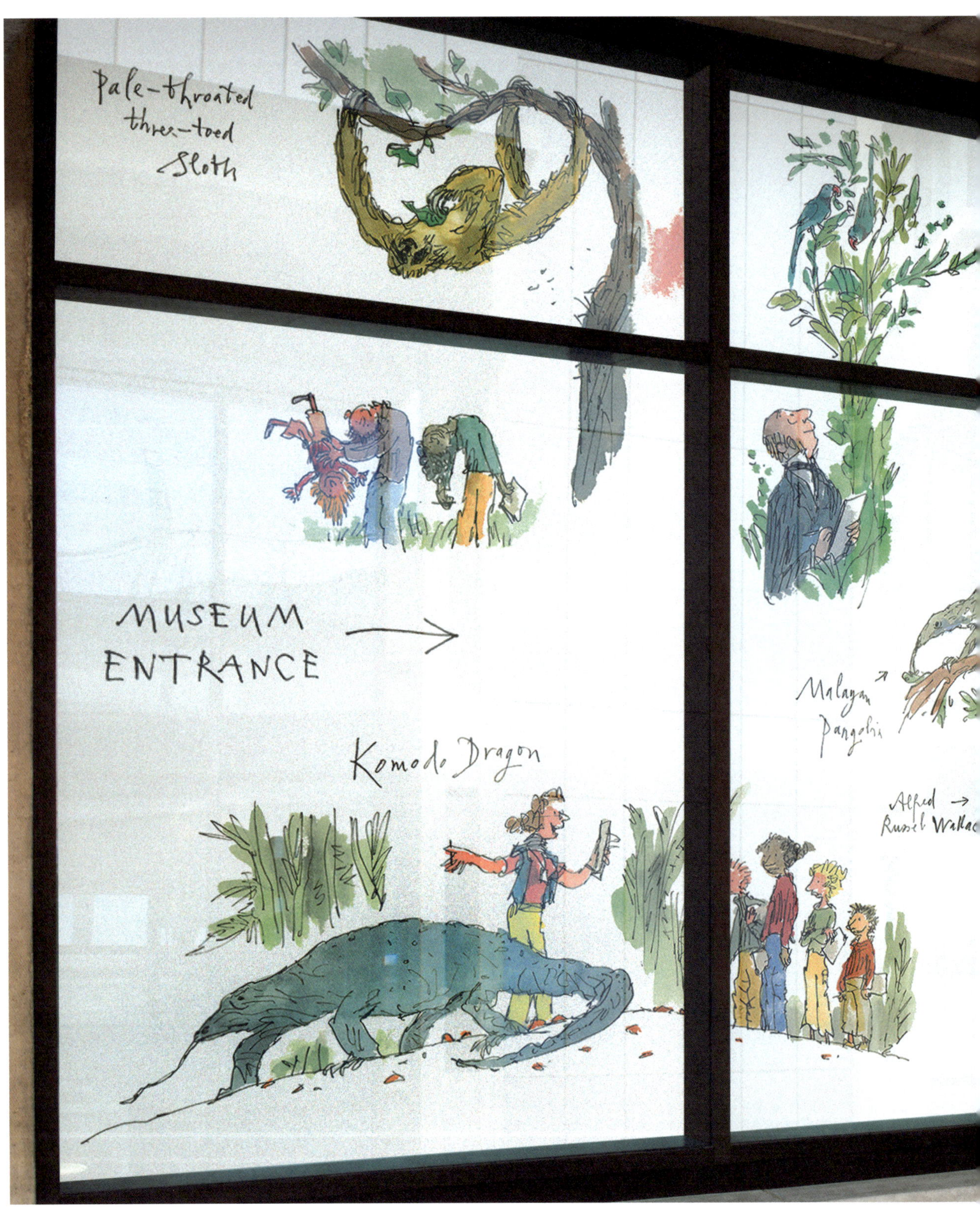


*Cambridge Museum of Zoology, 2017*

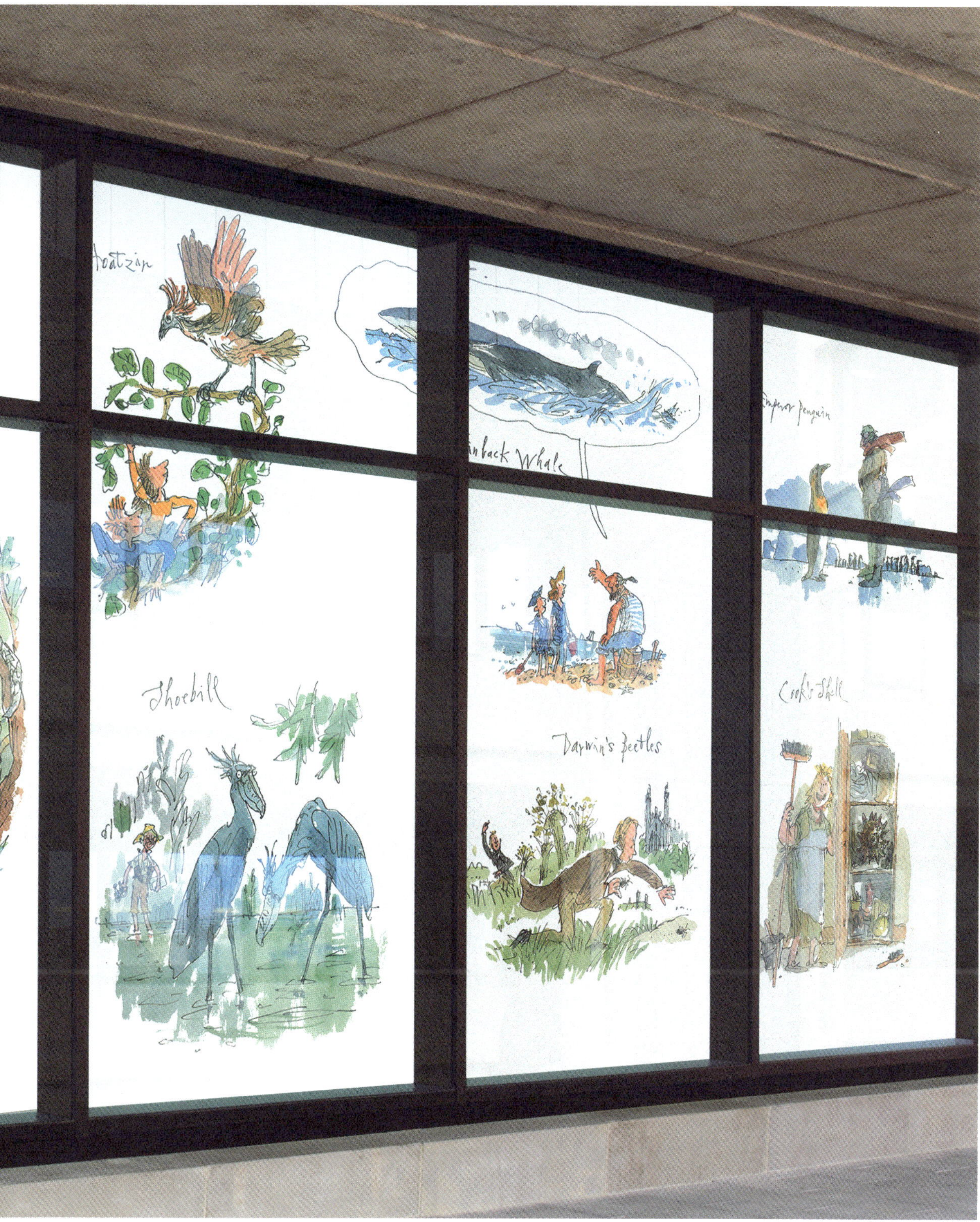
Hoatzin
...nback Whale
Emperor Penguin
Shoebill
Darwin's Beetles
Cook's Shell

# A Mural for the Science Museum

Quentin was approached by the Science Museum to do a sequence of drawings for the Wonderlab Gallery, depicting the scientists and inventors whose creations were owned by the museum.

'Stephenson and his Rocket, Arkwright and the spinning machine. Amy Johnson was an exception to the rule, but her aeroplane is one of the most dramatic exhibits in the museum and she and it demanded to be drawn.

All that was left for me to do was to get reasonably convincing portraits of the protagonists (plenty of useful whiskers) and reasonably convincing (though relaxed) drawings of their inventions. What I also had to take into consideration was that the drawings would have another, in some respects even more important, function when they appeared on items of merchandise in the museum's flourishing shop. It was another of those interesting situations in which drawings produced in the studio find themselves both much smaller and much larger than life.'

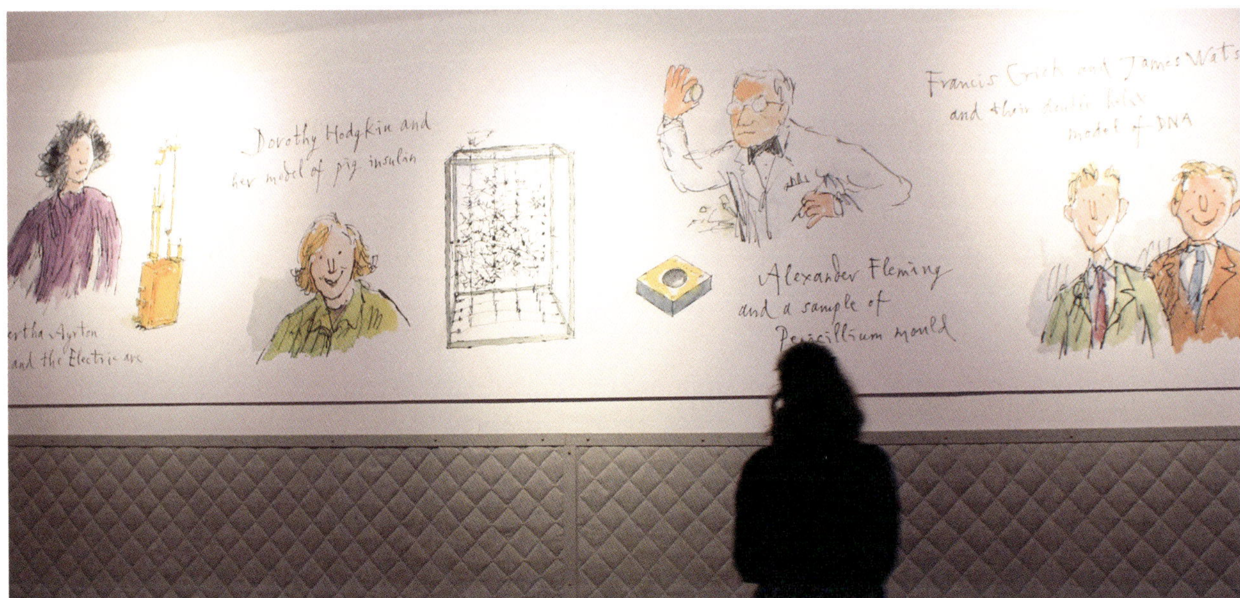


above & opposite – Science Museum Mural, 2018

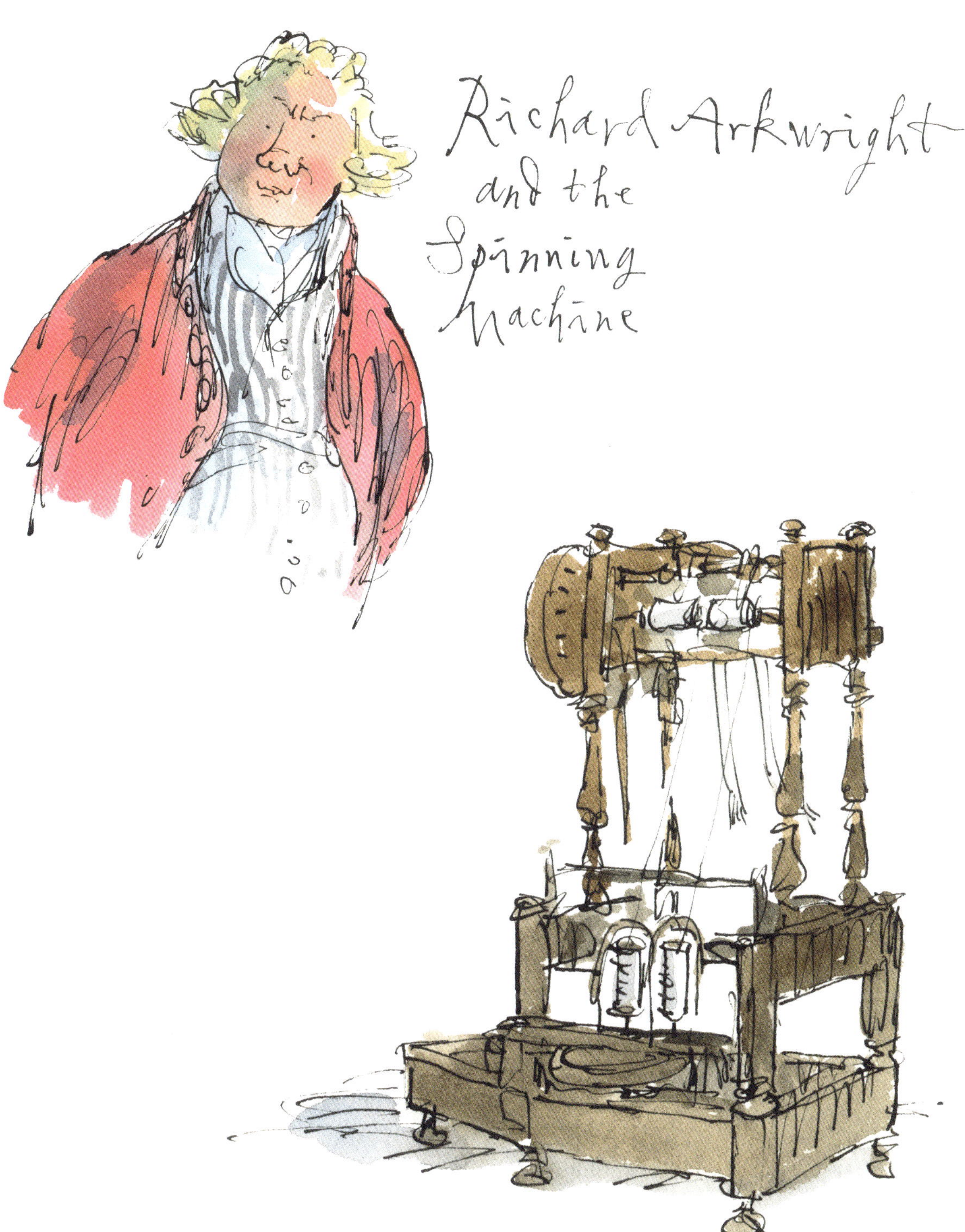

Richard Arkwright
and the
Spinning
Machine

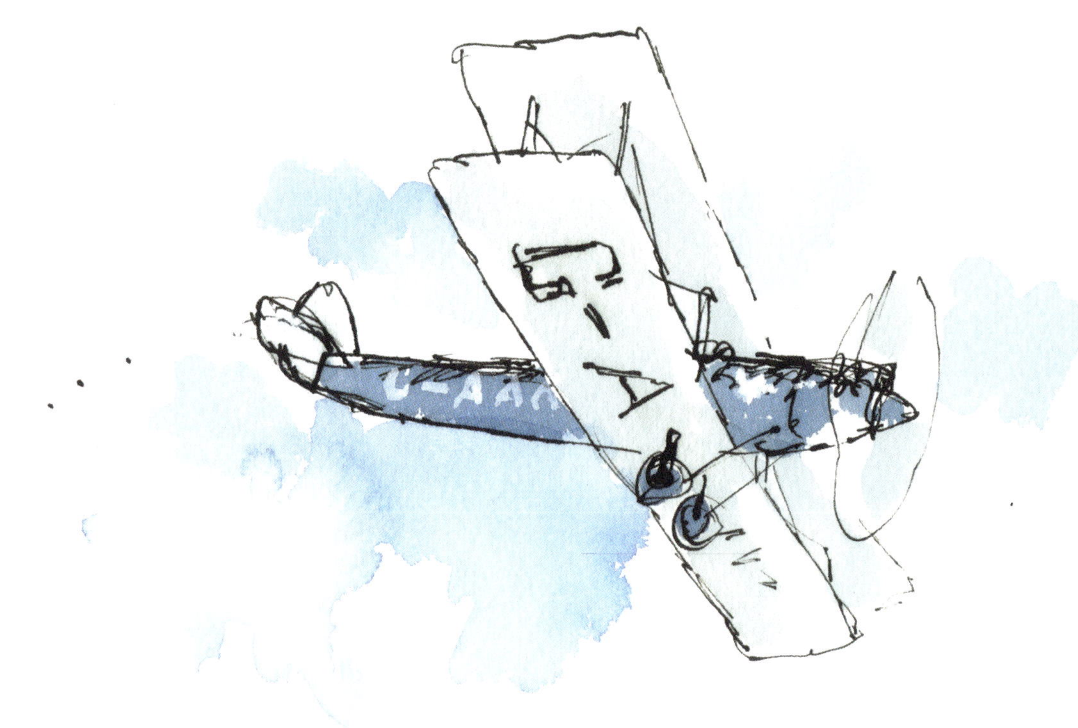

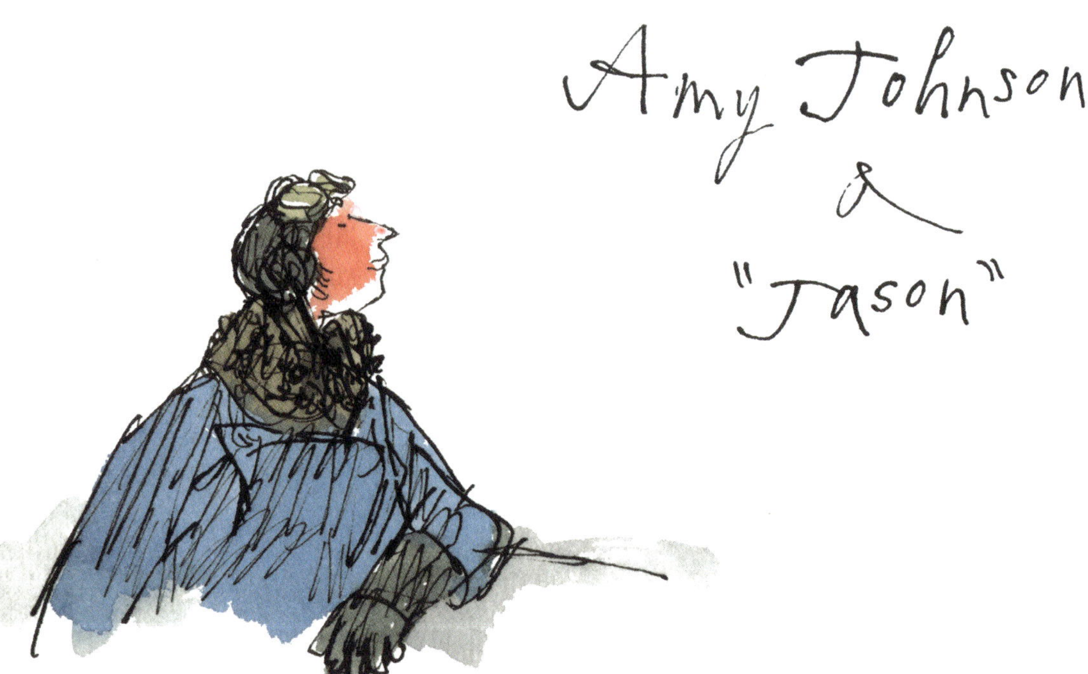

Amy Johnson & "Jason"

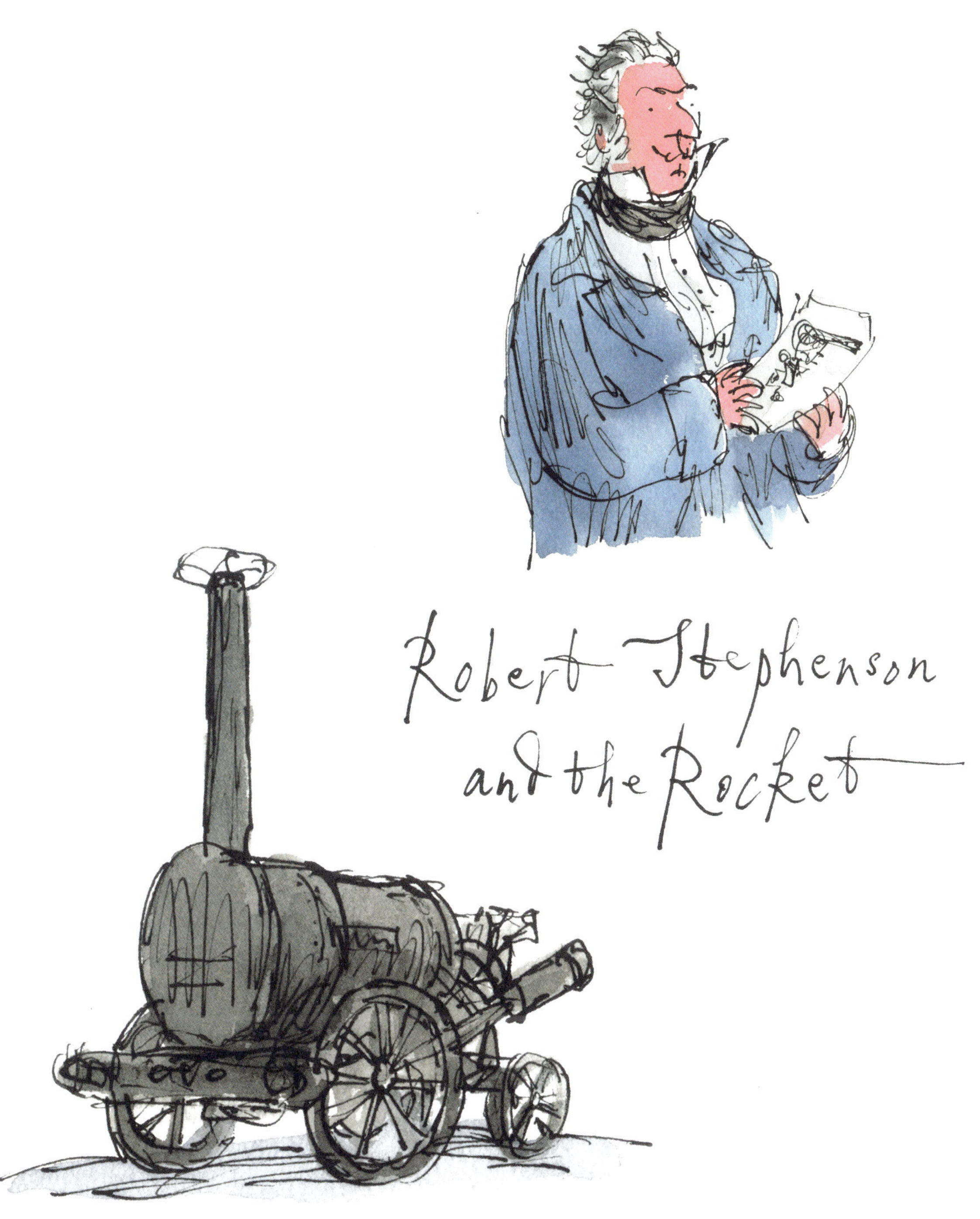


OPPOSITE & ABOVE – *Science Museum Mural*, 2018

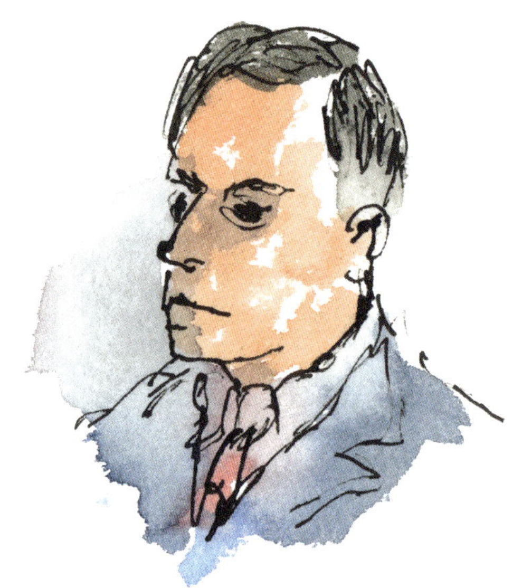

# Alan Turing and the Automatic Computing Engine

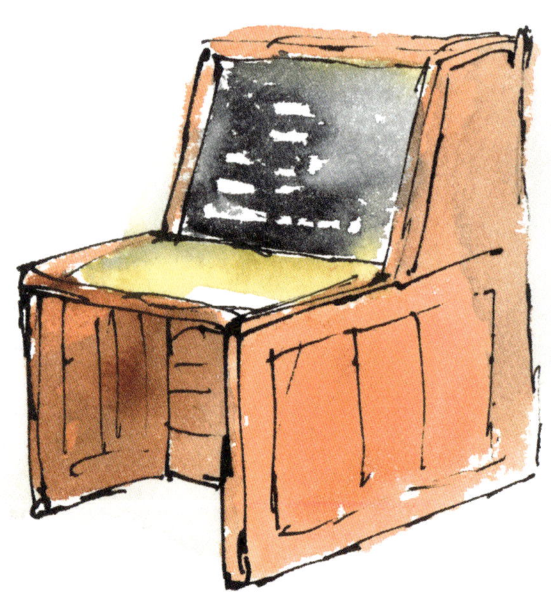

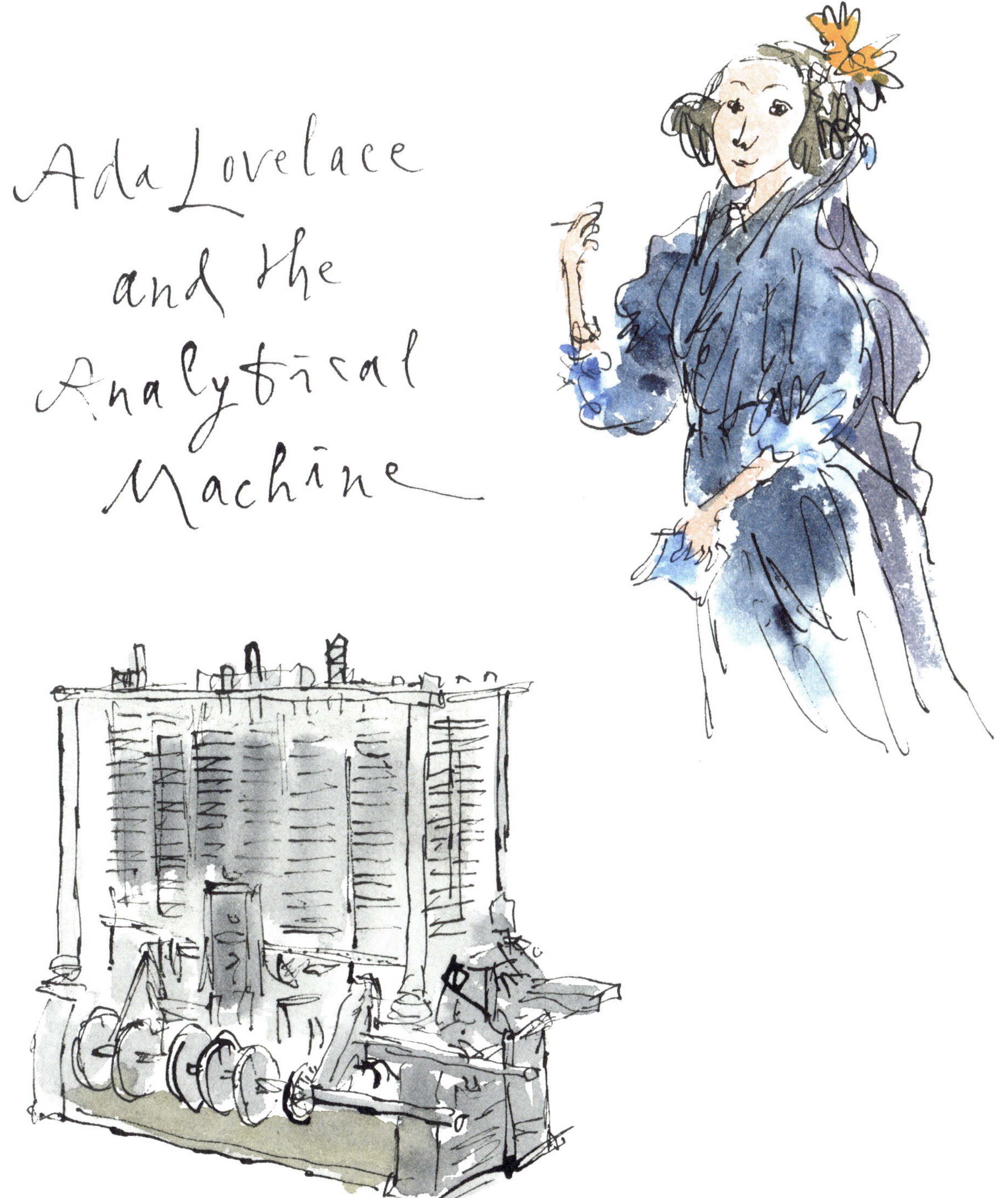



OPPOSITE & ABOVE – *Science Museum Mural*, 2018

# The Foundling Portraits

The Foundling Hospital was set up in 1739 by Thomas Coram to care for and educate some of the many vulnerable children in London. William Hogarth donated his work to help realise Coram's vision and to encourage other artists to do the same and the UK's first public gallery was established. The Foundling Museum still involves artists today; Yinka Shonibare, Grayson Perry and Lauren Child as well as Quentin have all given their work and time to the museum.

'I had known about the Foundling Hospital and the involvement of William Hogarth in its setting up. Years ago I visited Coram's Fields and saw Hogarth's portrait of Captain Coram…

This explains at least how my head came to be quite full of a sense of the foundlings; what I can't explain is why, one day, I started to make drawings of the foundlings themselves. They were done in china marker, this is a pencil really intended for drawing on ceramics but which gives a wonderfully sensitive mark on paper.'

The sequence of forty young people – aged ten or twelve – are drawn from Quentin's imagination.

'They are to some extent like illustration pulled inside out. If you are providing drawings for a book you take the description of the character in question and try to create what that person looks like. Here I simply imagined their slightly troubled faces with a silent invitation to the spectator to speculate about their situation.'

*The Foundling Portraits*, 2021

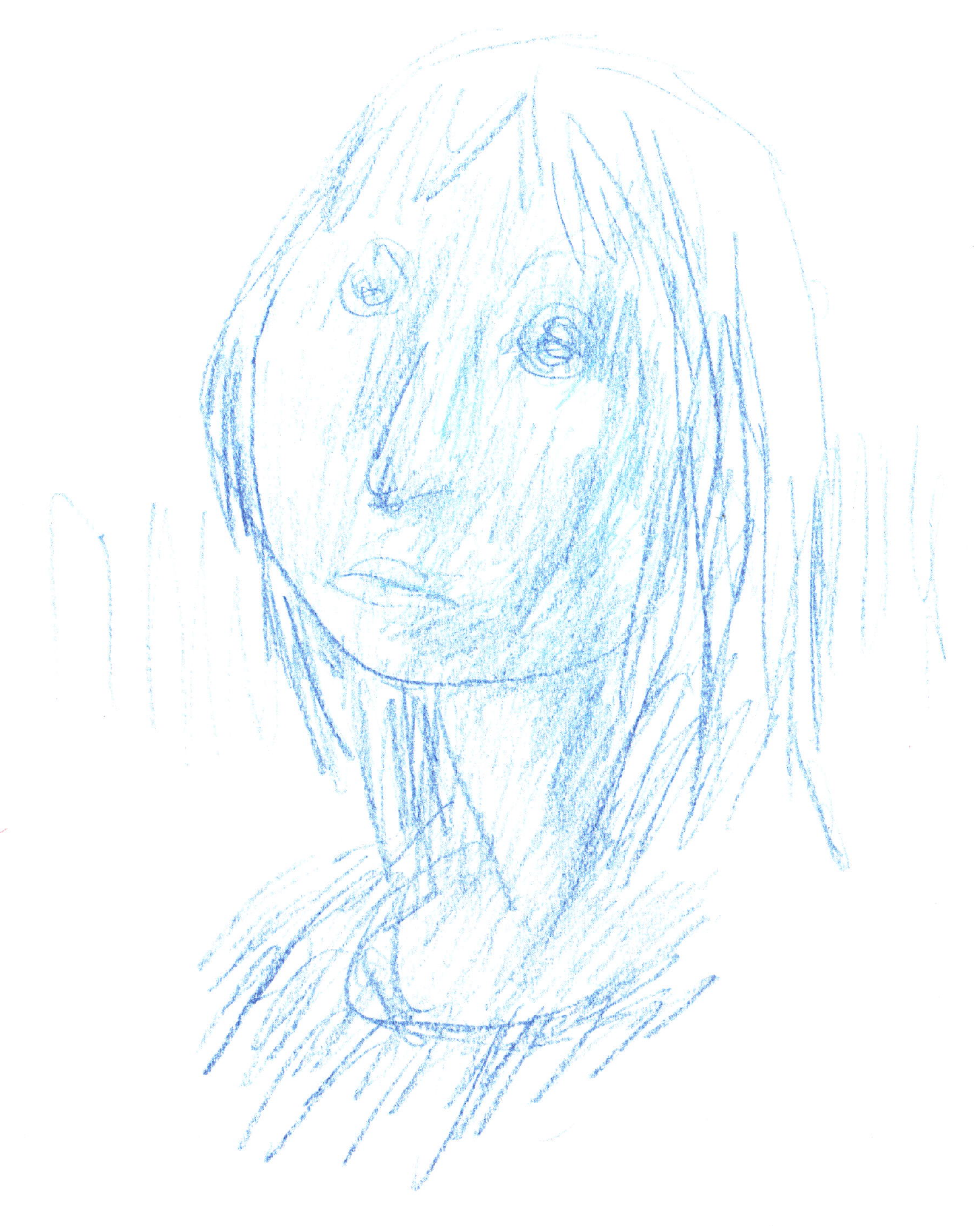

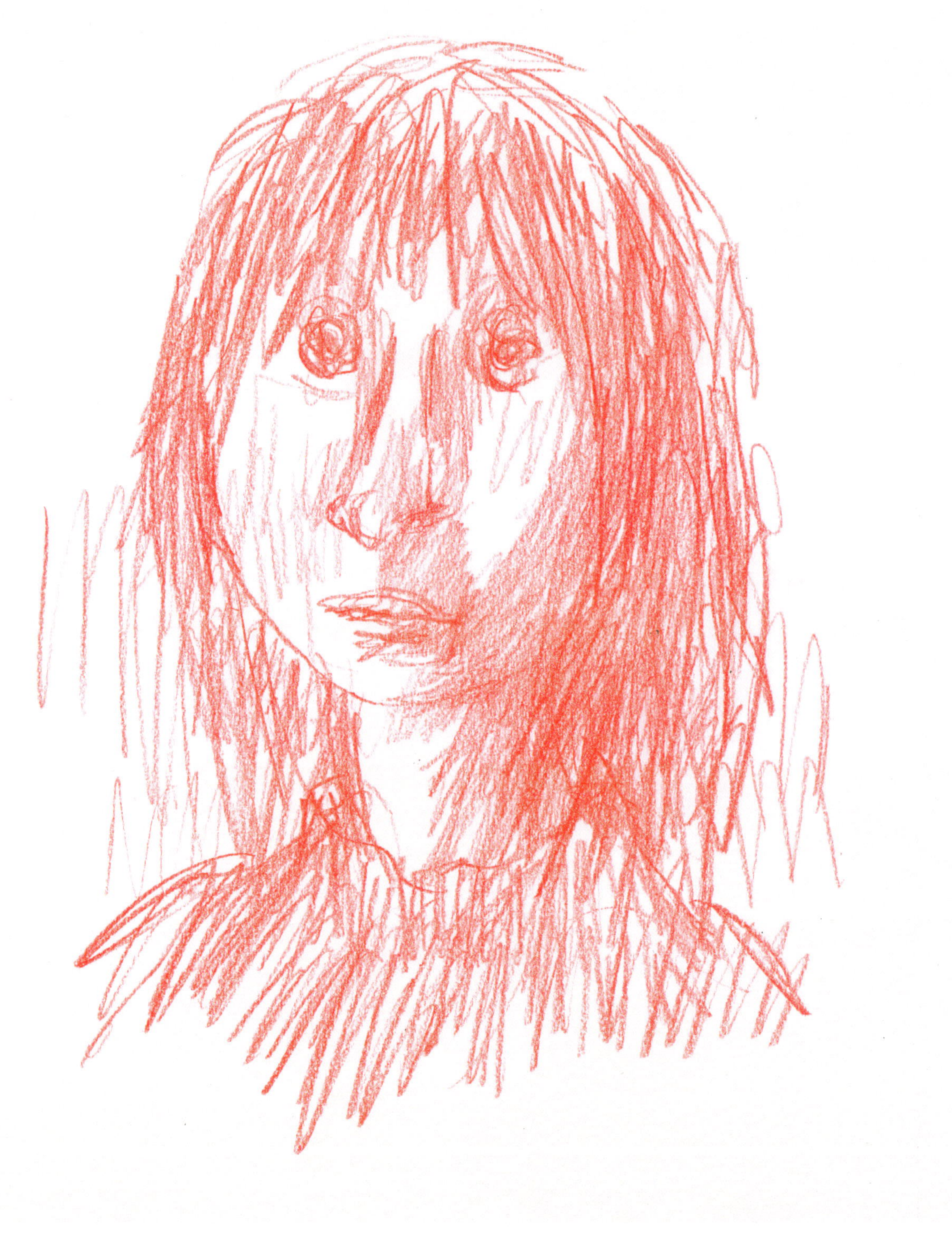

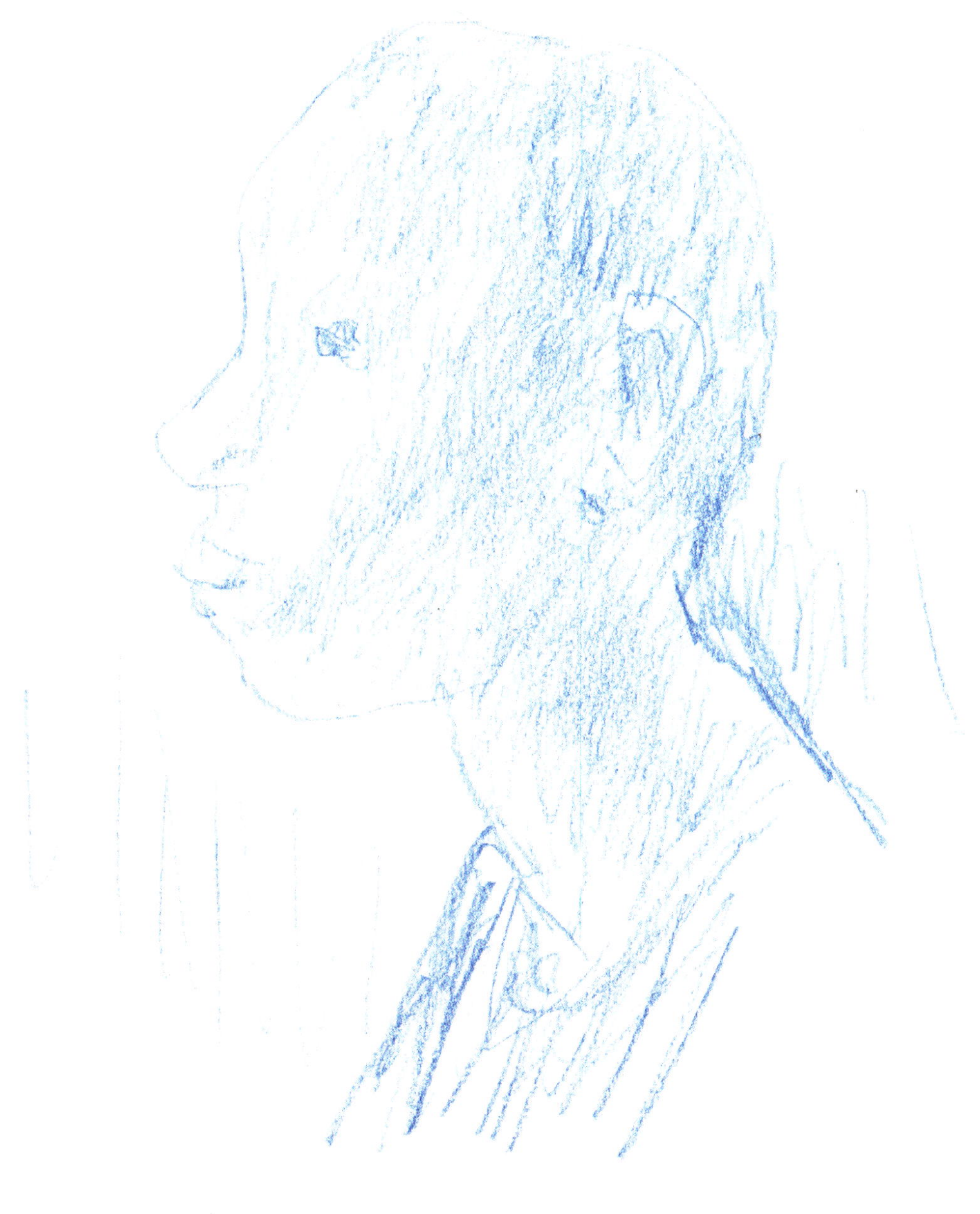

OPPOSITE & ABOVE – *The Foundling Portraits,* 2021

# 'The Taxi Driver'
# at Hastings Contemporary

Some years ago, a taxi came to pick Quentin up from his flat. He told Jenny Uglow about it for her book:

'Rather to my surprise the taxi driver got in as well, and sat opposite me and said, "we live in worrying times."'

He told Quentin that he'd seen Picasso's *Guernica* in Spain: 'what we need is something like that for our own times. And you're the person to do it.'

'So I said, "Well, it's not quite my kind of thing, is it?"

And he said, "Yes, you're the man… Cometh the hour, cometh the man."

So I said, "Well, I'll see what I can do…".'

Quentin asked for the driver's name, but he said there was no need, as he keeps 'an eye on everything.'

Quentin thought if he was going to take up the taxi driver's challenge to create a new *Guernica* it would need to be big. So when Liz Gilmore, the director of Hastings Contemporary, offered him a gallery with a 10-metre-long wall he seized the opportunity. He painted on a roll of paper 5FT by 30FT attached to the wall using a thick brush and watered-down acrylic paint. The mural shows displaced people struggling to carry their children and possessions in a desolate, war-torn landscape. In the far distance there is a London taxi, 'with nowhere to go.' Quentin completed the mural in a day. It is raw and striking; he wanted to capture the human suffering in the world and, like Picasso, he did it by painting.

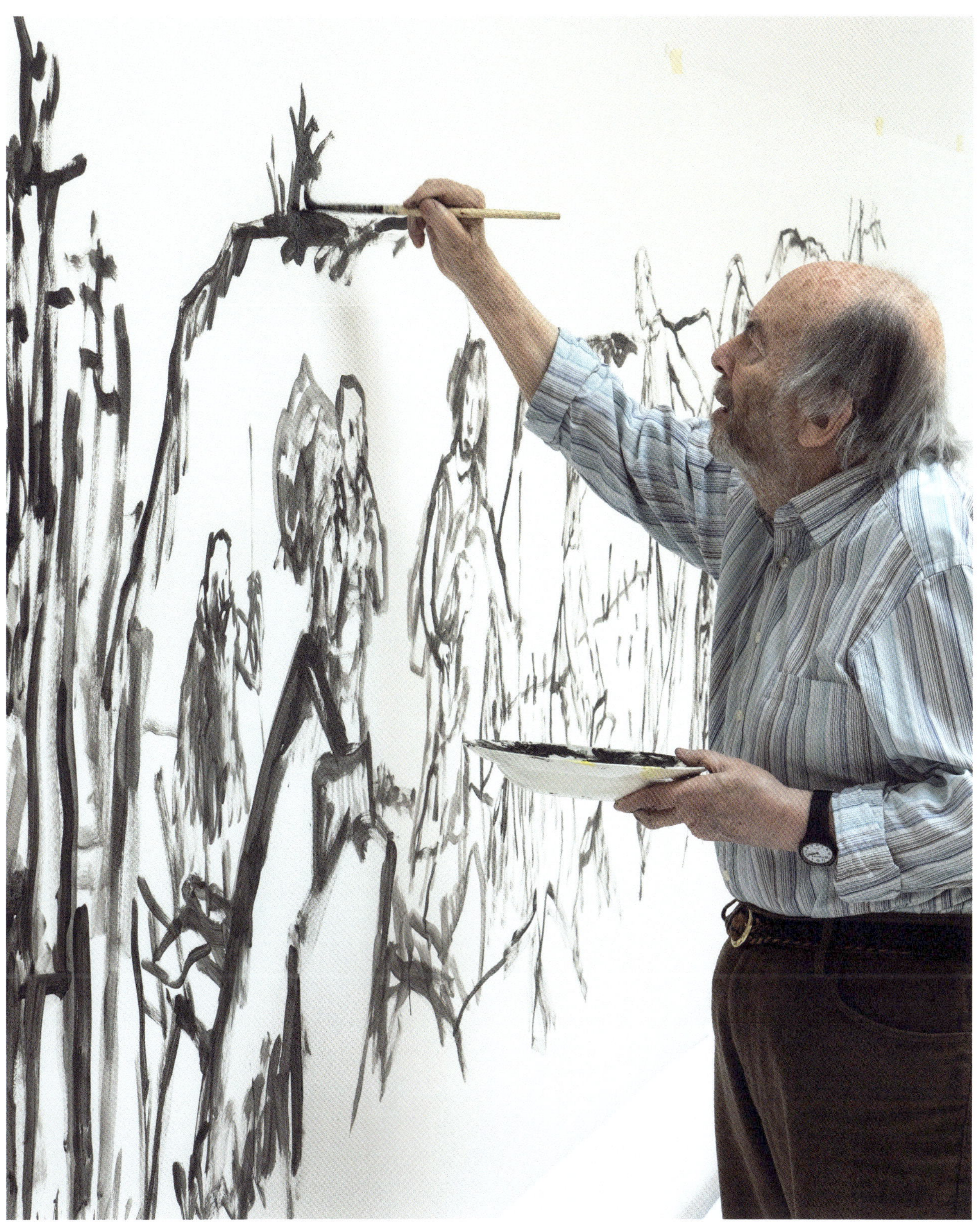

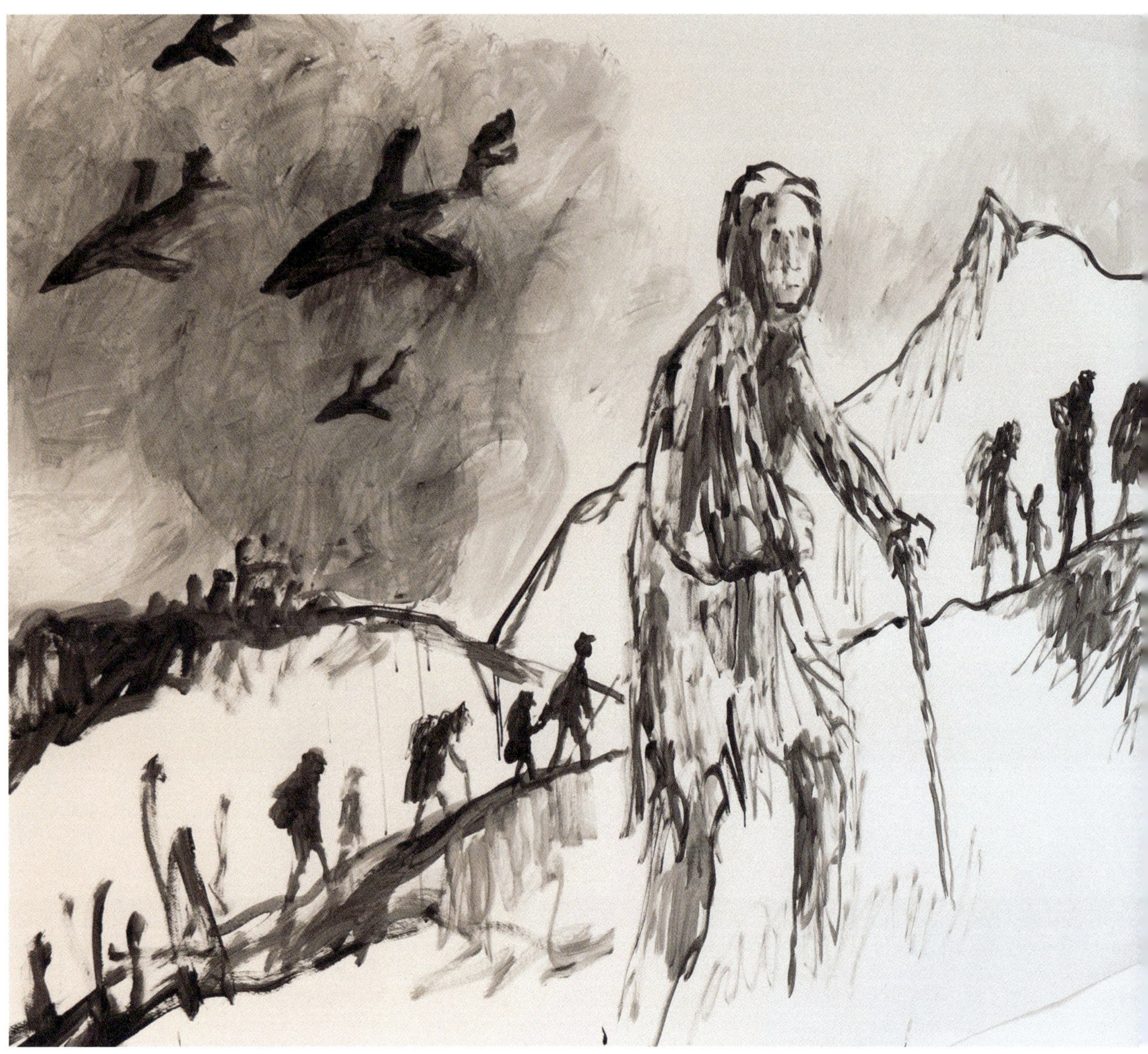

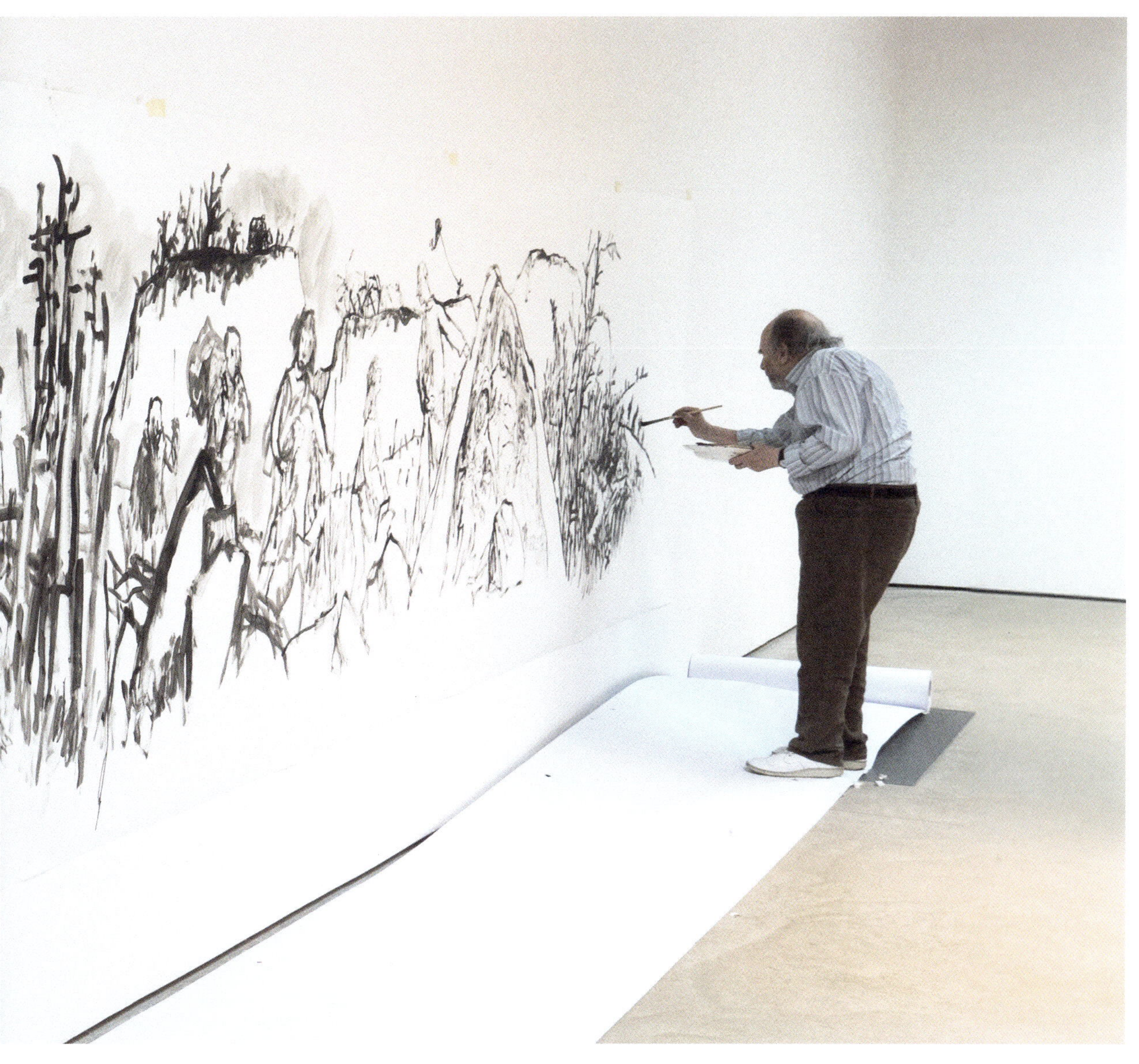

'We need art because it's got life in it... you may be drawing a
very distressing thing... but what I hope is that it's not entirely
distressing, because the way you present it, the way it's drawn,
has got something enhancing in it. So that no matter how
grisly it is, the fact that there is drawing in it means you are
embracing it, you're moving forward, you're doing something
with it, and that something is very fascinating...'

*THE QUENTIN BLAKE BOOK, 2022*

# Signs for the Royal Parks

The Royal Parks commissioned Quentin to illustrate twenty-seven posters to be attached to the railings of London parks.

'I didn't realise what a good opportunity it was till they asked me. The inclusion of my drawings with park rules and admonitions might create a better relationship with the visitor – you're entertaining them rather than castigating them. It's enjoyable for instance, to invent a drawing that says "Keep off the Grass".'

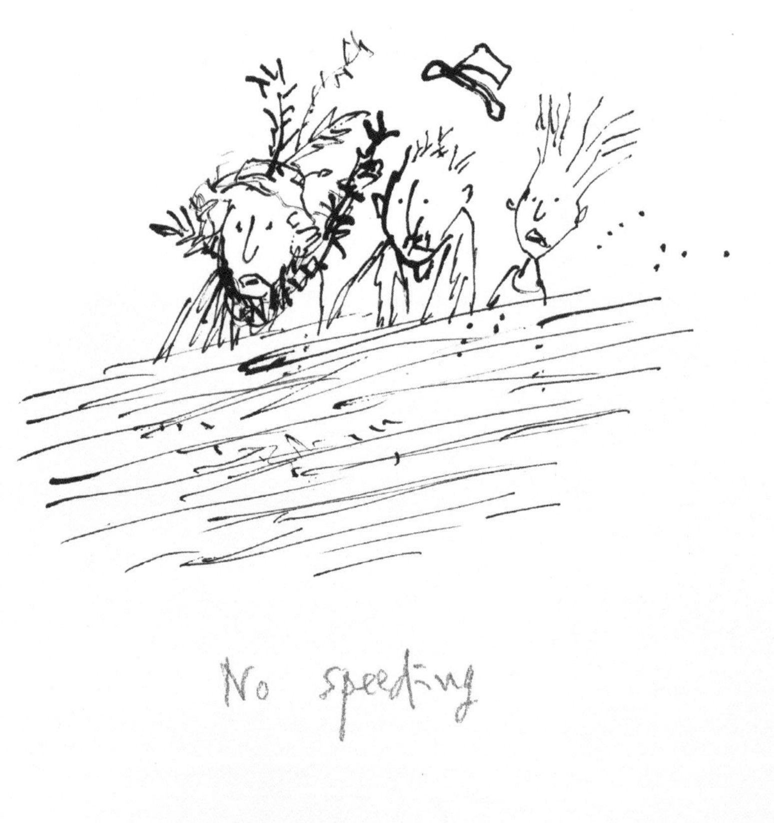

No speeding

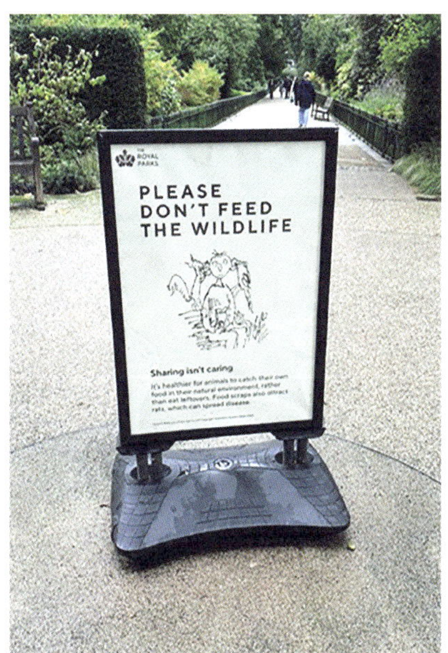
THE ROYAL PARKS

PLEASE
DON'T FEED
THE WILDLIFE

Sharing isn't caring
It's healthier for animals to catch their own
food in their natural environment, rather
than eat leftovers. Food scraps also attract
rats, which can spread disease.

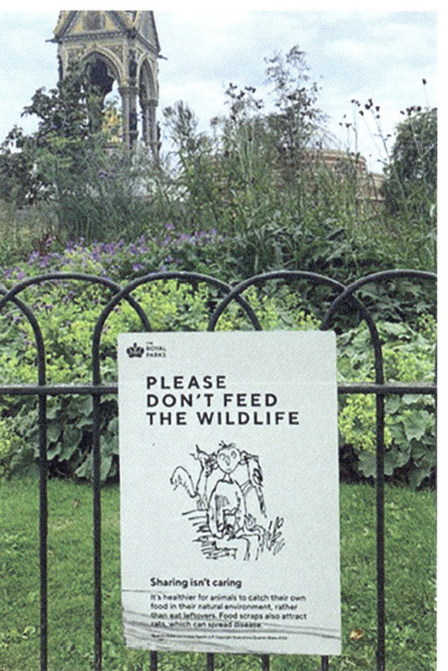
THE ROYAL PARKS

PLEASE
DON'T FEED
THE WILDLIFE

Sharing isn't caring
It's healthier for animals to catch their own
food in their natural environment, rather
than eat leftovers. Food scraps also attract
rats, which can spread disease.

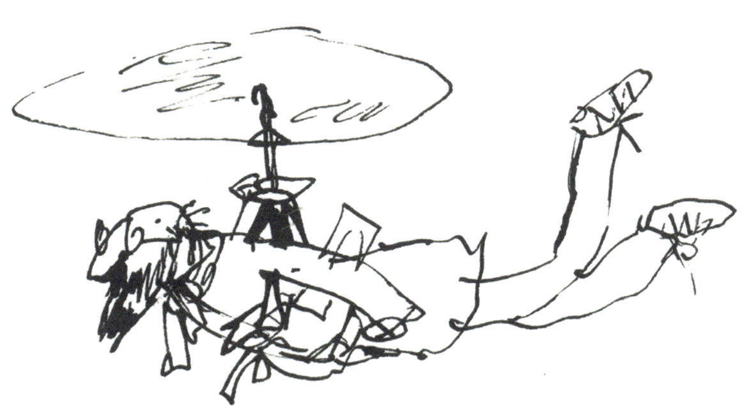

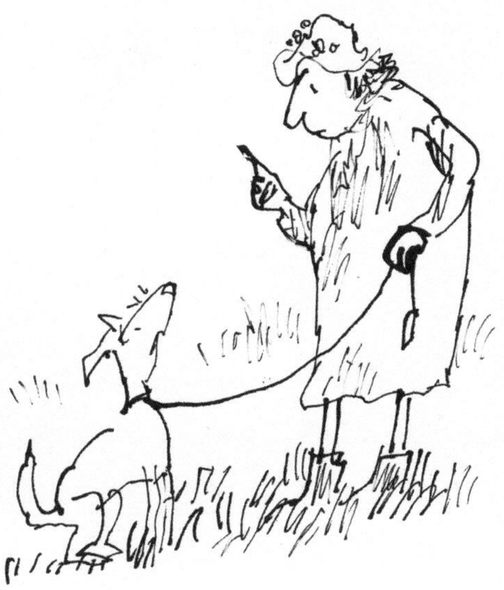

No dog fouling

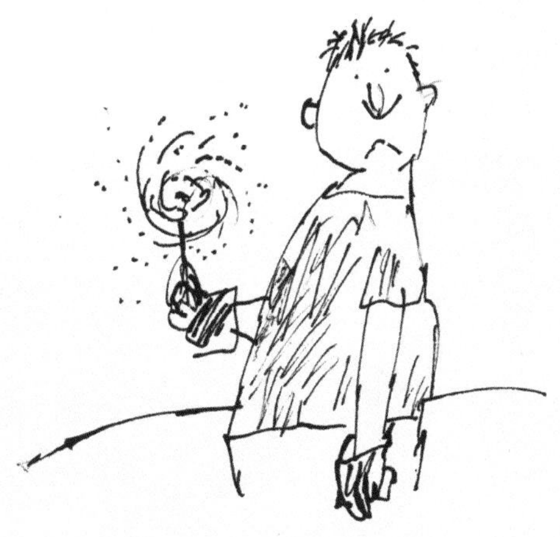

No fireworks

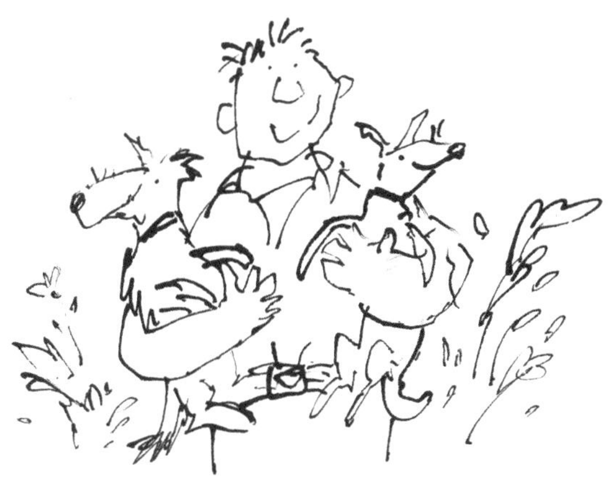



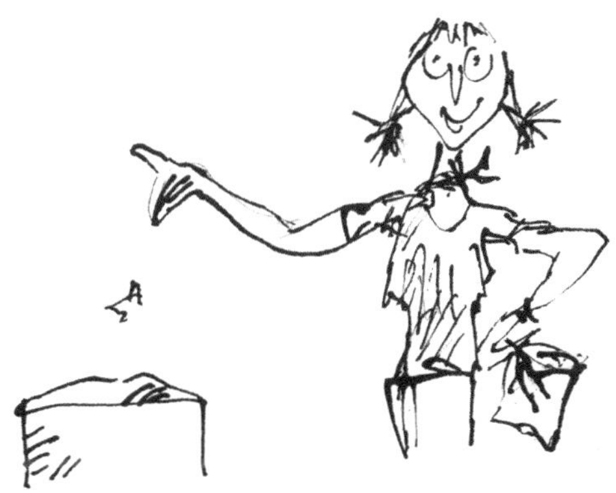



OPPOSITE & ABOVE – *Royal Parks Signage*, 2024

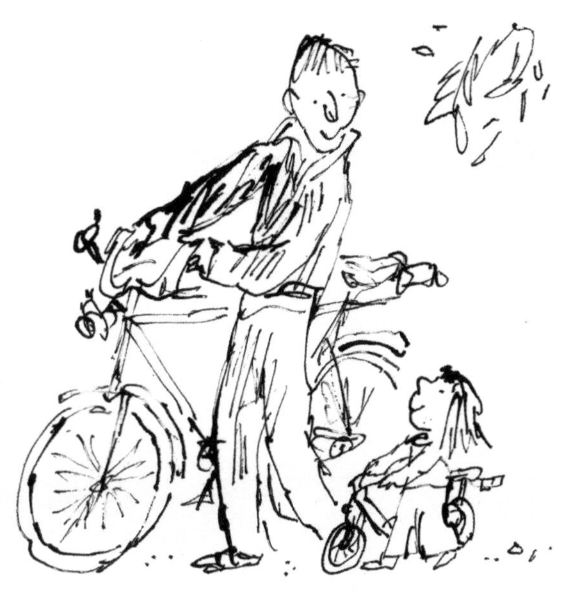

No cycling

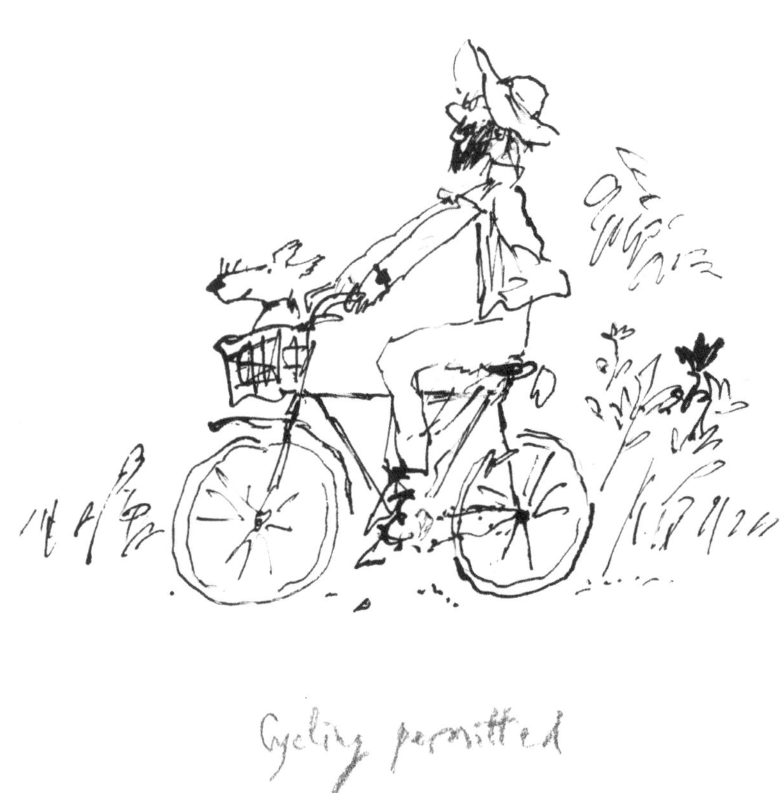



OPPOSITE & ABOVE – *Royal Parks Signage,* 2024

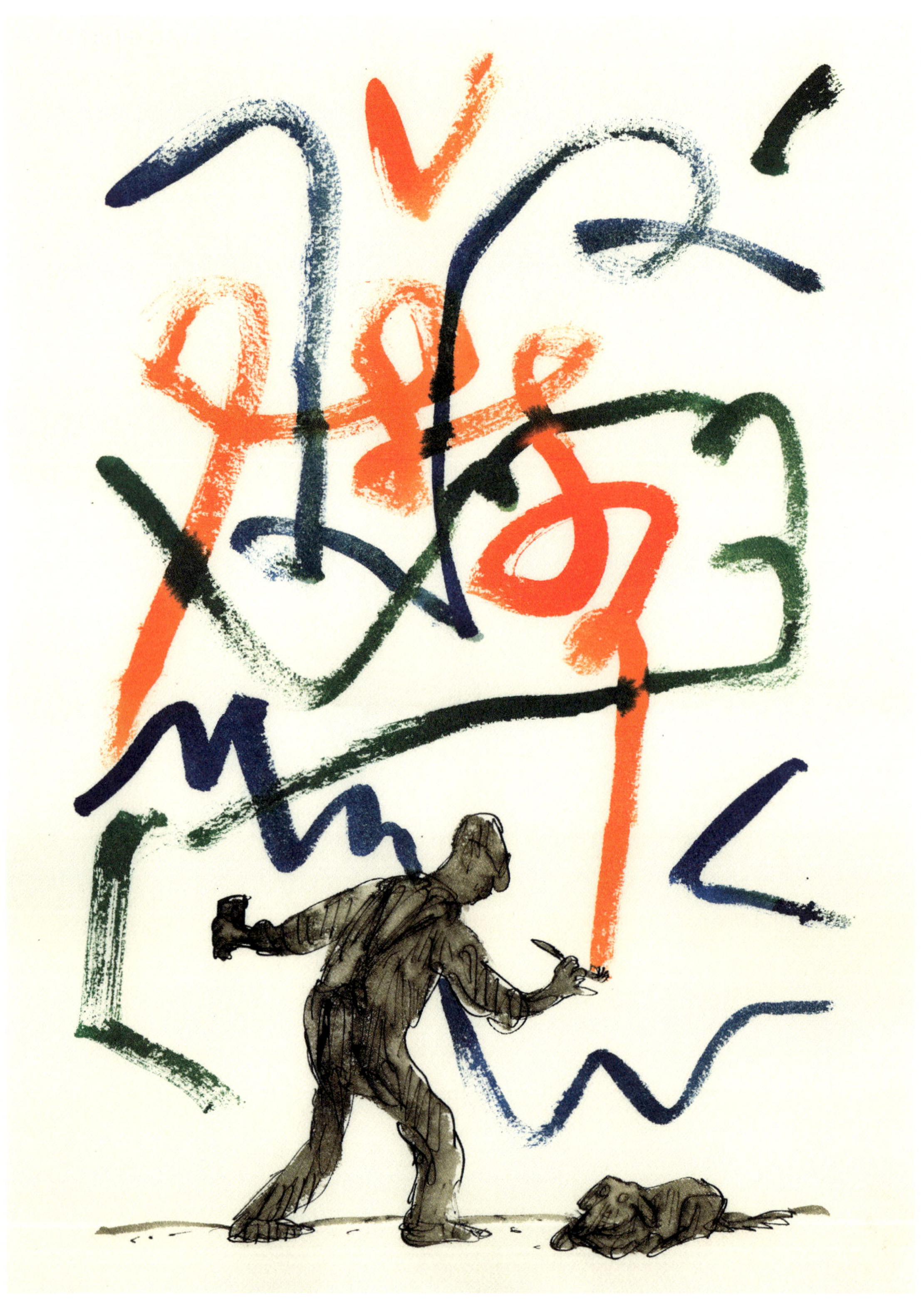

Kershaw Ward, 2006

*Chapter Two*

# Hospitals

The Nightingale Project was set up by Dr Nick Rhodes and Stephen Barnham to put art into hospitals and mental health units run by the Central and North West London NHS Foundation Trust.

Nick and Stephen asked Quentin to do a set of drawings for the Kershaw Ward, an adult Mental Health Centre at the South Kensington and Chelsea Hospital in West London: 'The meeting… took place in Carluccio's café on Fulham Road in December 2005. It happened to be on my birthday. The question of age wasn't entirely inappropriate, either, since being approximately the age of my prospective audience I felt it gave me if not a qualification at least a sort of licence.'

These drawings, and all the others Quentin has done for hospitals, are reproduced digitally as giclée prints. They are enlarged and printed by a printmaker on the same paper as the original, so that it is almost impossible to tell the printed version from the original. The hospital has the right to reproduce the image and, if necessary, the print can be replaced. Mounted in shallow Perspex boxes with no frame so that impression is of a mural, 'What you see are, in a sense, illustrated walls.'

The drawings are humorous, 'the style a form of caricature that I used in children's books.… If there is any levity it isn't because I want to make fun of the characters I am depicting.' Quentin had read a description by Sickert of Japanese artists, explaining the way they present 'simple daily works… before us in a whimsical light. This quaint, gently grotesque touch brings the Japanese artist into closer relationship with his subject than we are able to get: poking fun at his models, he rallies them into friendship': 'I hope that something like this might happen with my Kershaw residents.'

He was pleased when one delighted patient observed that the drawings showed them doing things they weren't allowed to or weren't able to do anymore. The Nightingale Project originally asked for nineteen drawings, but Quentin enjoyed doing them so much he did sixty-five, varying the theme and the medium from one sequence of drawings to the next. In one, he used only grey and gold to represent old and young people together, and there's a series of cats and birds, 'some of which came out looking as though they might have psychological problems of their own.'

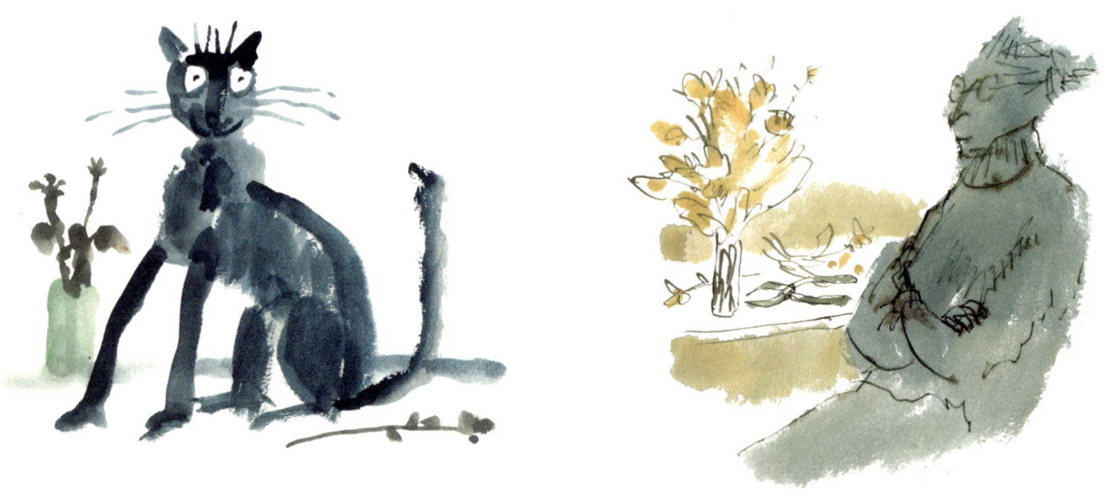

ABOVE & OPPOSITE – Kershaw Ward, 2006

Quentin used trees as the structure for many of the images in the Kershaw Ward: 'they free you from the background' and 'every incident is well in view at the same distance. It's a *mise-en-scène* that allows both comforting situations, on platforms and in hammocks, as well as nervous wobbly ones. The fundamental idea, of course, is that if you jump (or fall) out of the trees there is always someone there to catch you.'

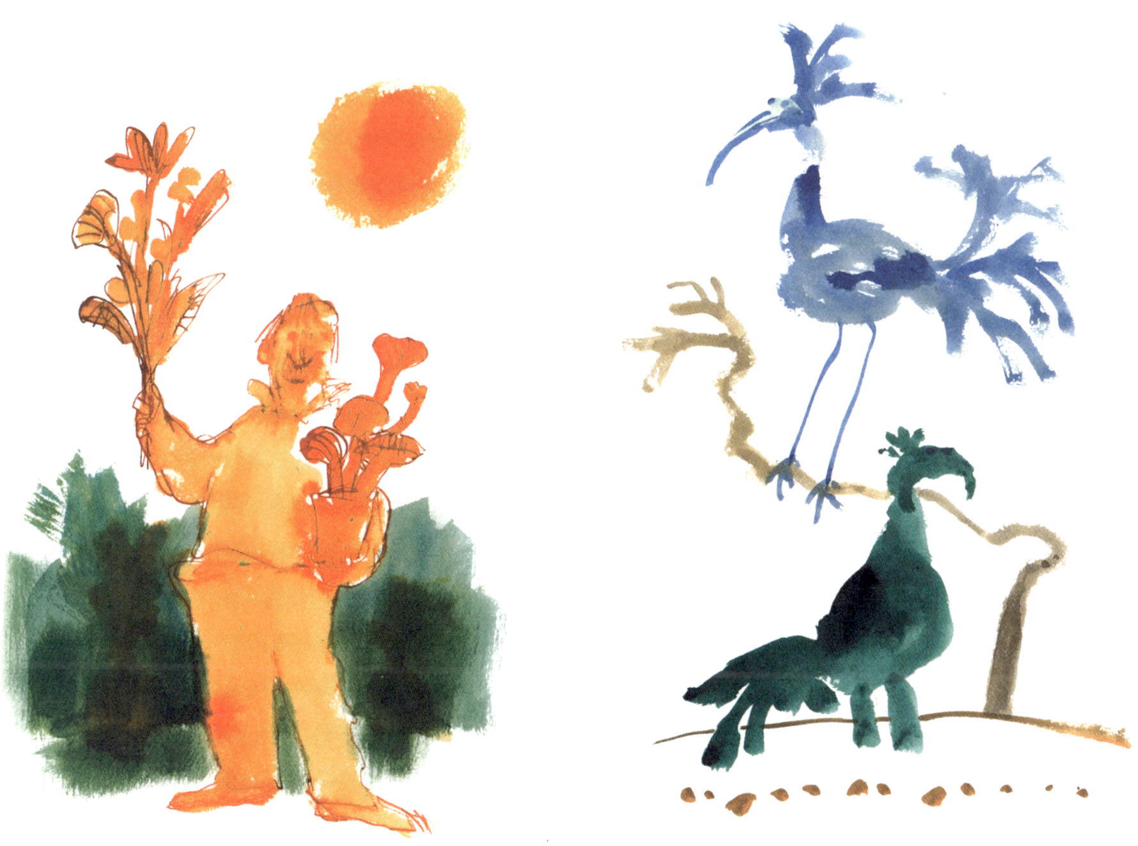

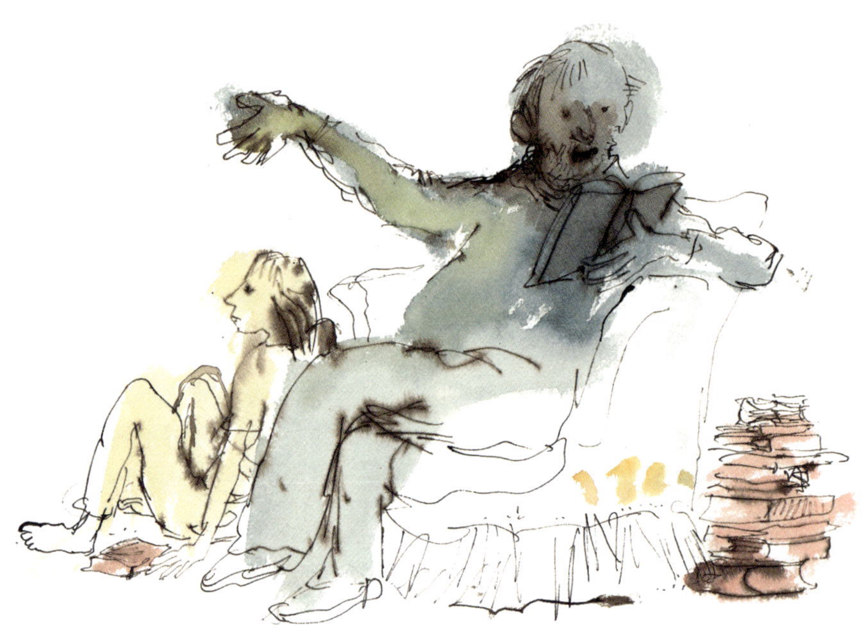

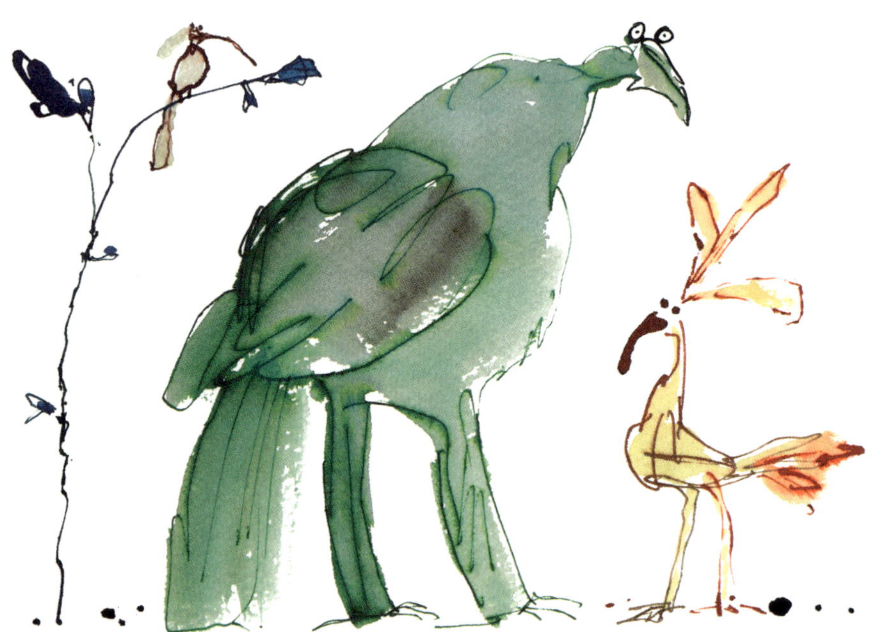

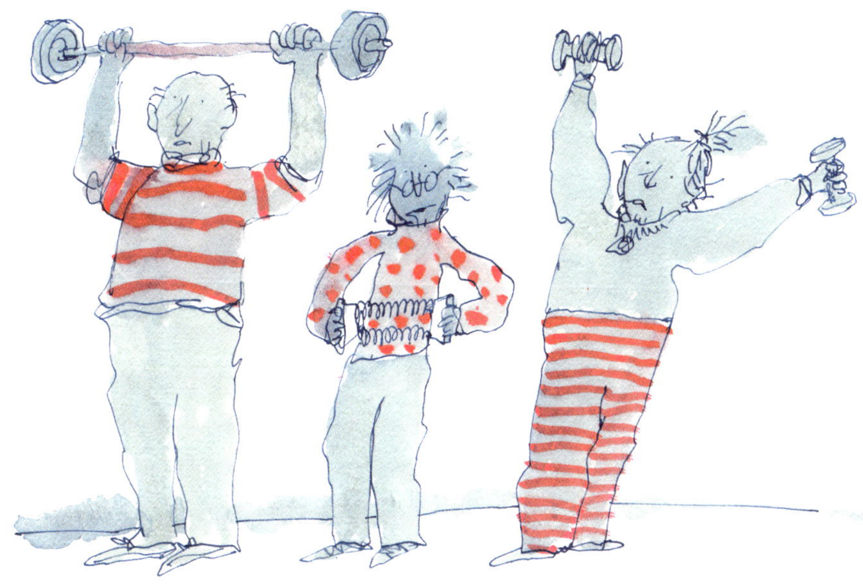

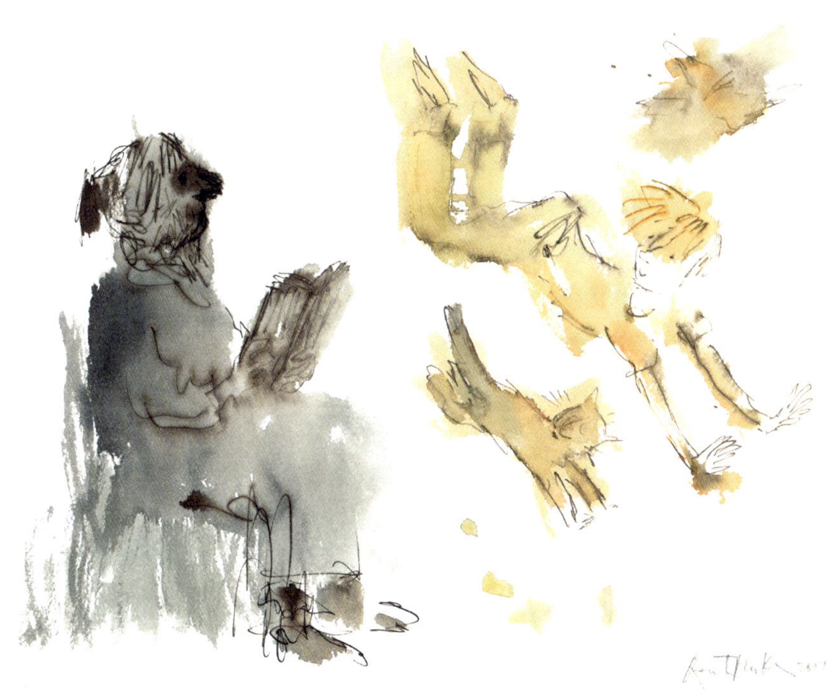

OPPOSITE & ABOVE – Kershaw Ward, 2006

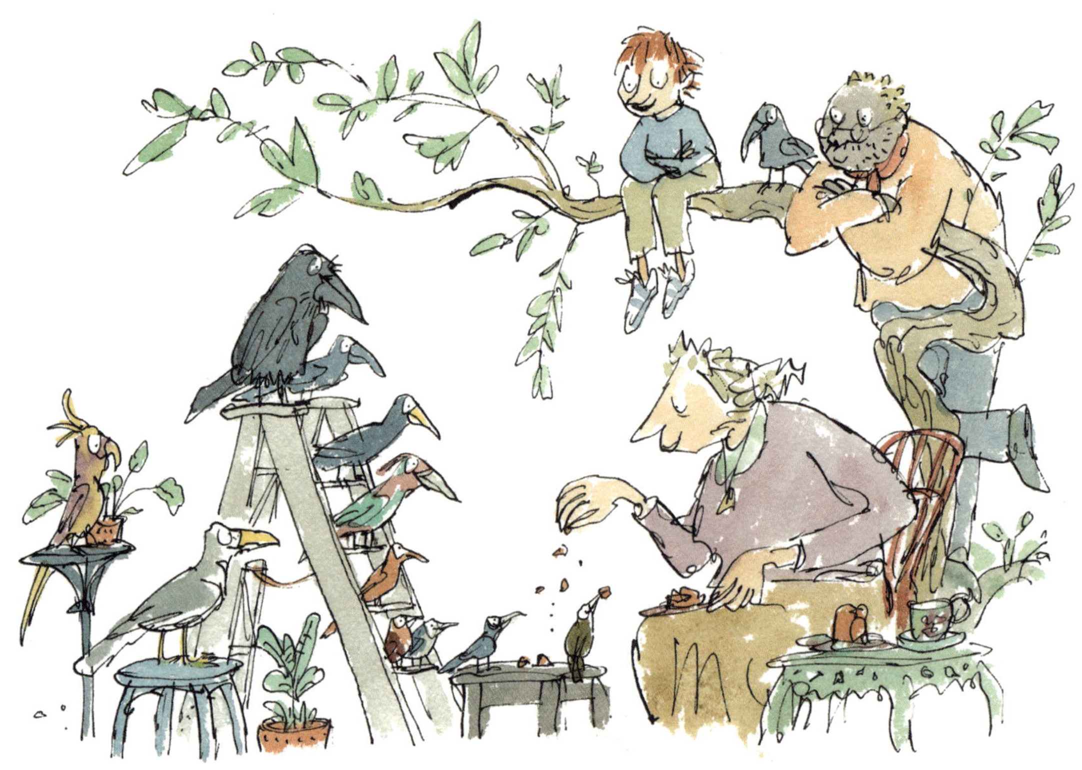



ABOVE & OPPOSITE – Kershaw Ward, 2006

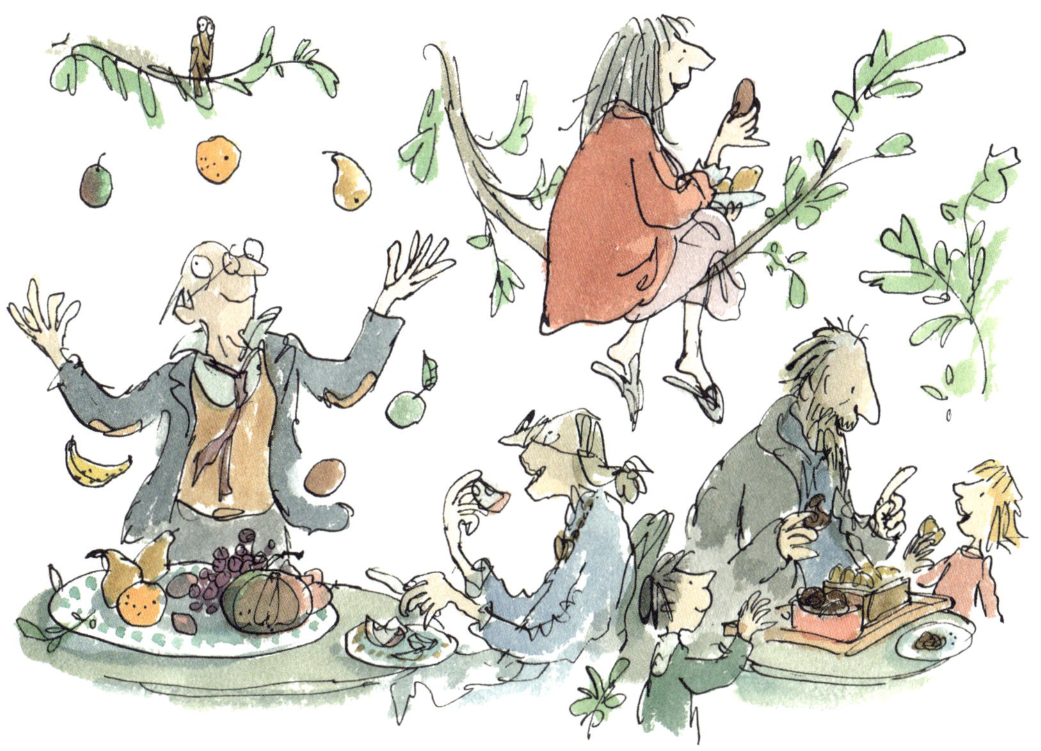

'The fundamental idea, of course, is that if you jump (or fall)
out of the trees there is always someone there to catch you.'

**QB**

# Alexandra Avenue Health
# & Social Care Centre

## *Harrow*

'Trees again, but this time very strange, patterned ones, because the fiction is that
we are on Planet Zog. The parallel, of course, is between our experience on an
alien planet and that in an almost equally alien hospital.... I don't think I have
ever made any claims that pictures like these have a therapeutic effect, at least
beyond helping to put people at ease. However, it's impossible not to hope that
sometimes they might have…'

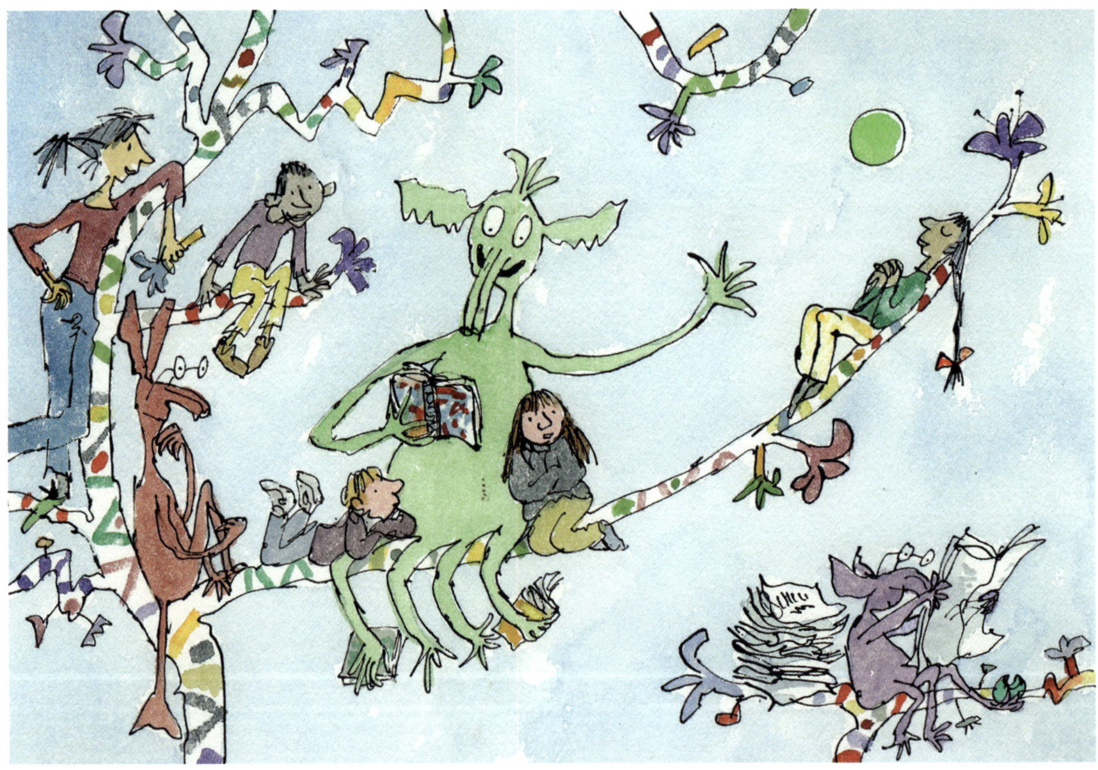

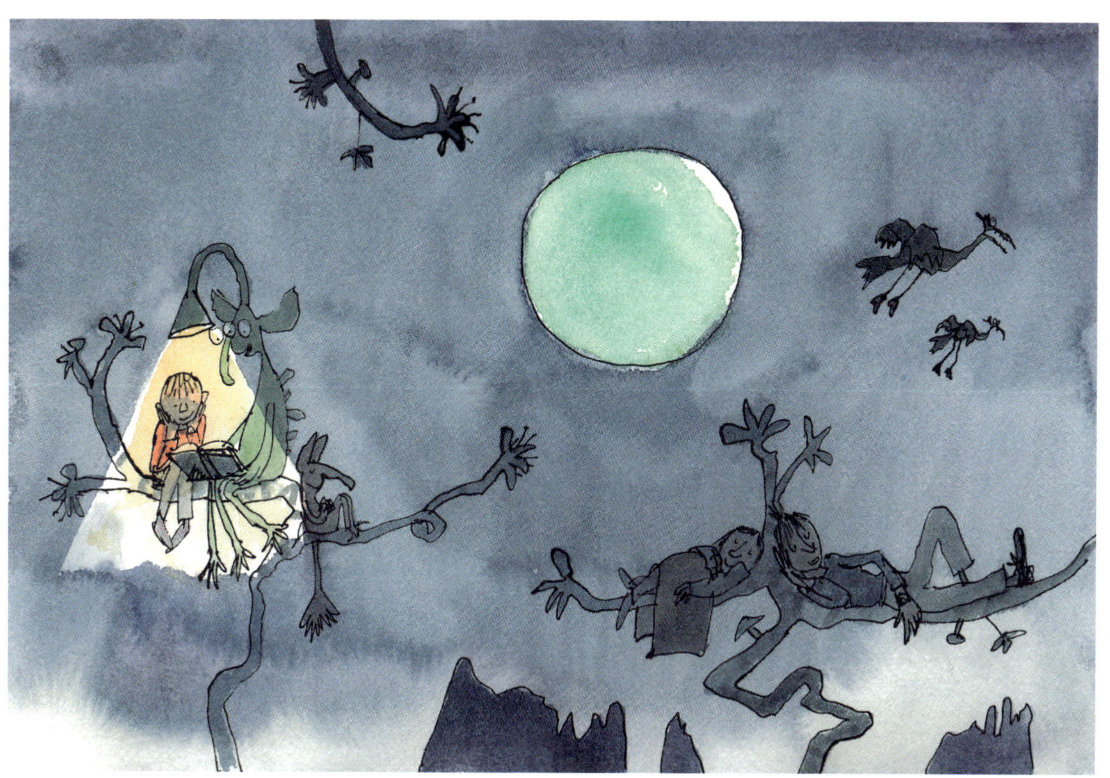

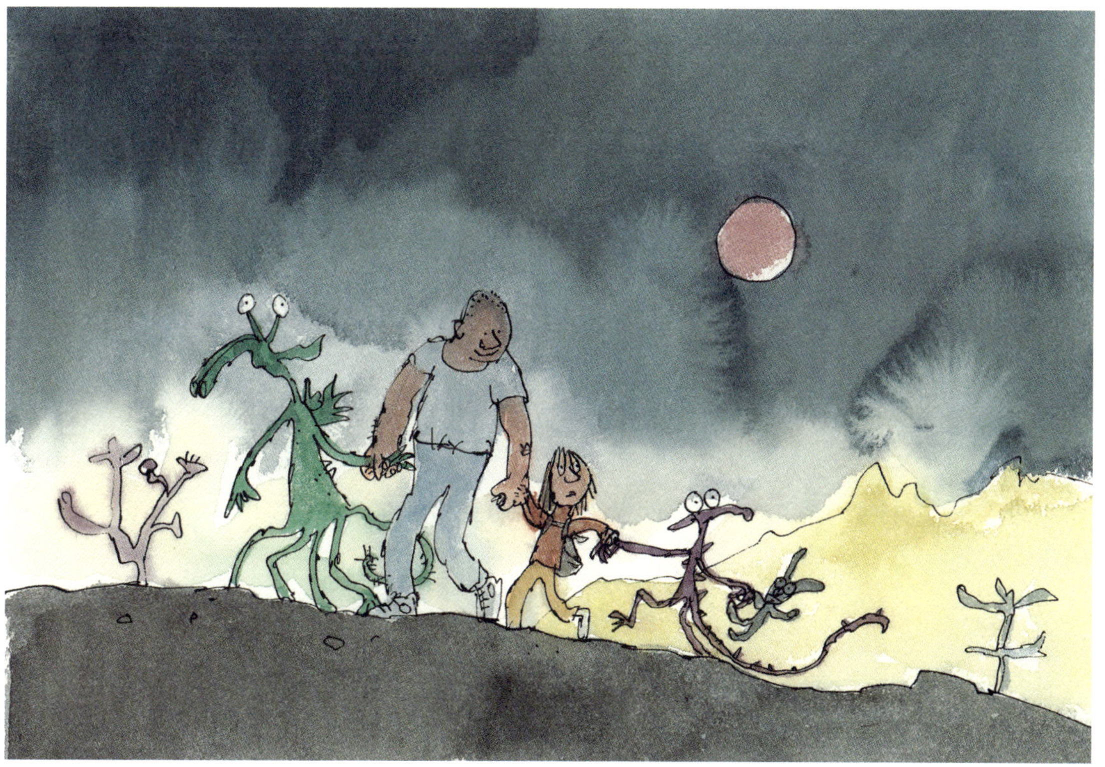

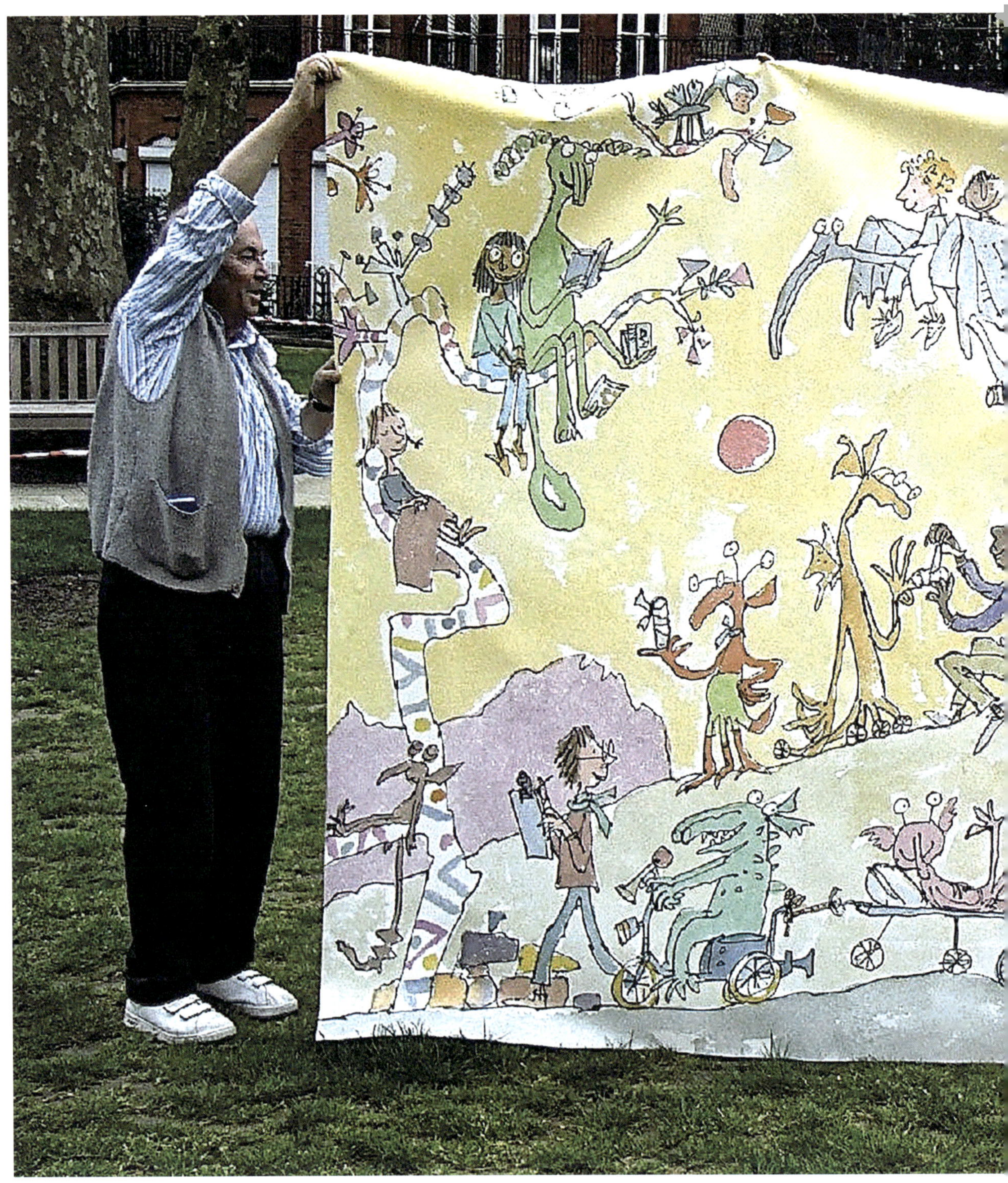

*Welcome to Planet Zog,* Banner, 2007

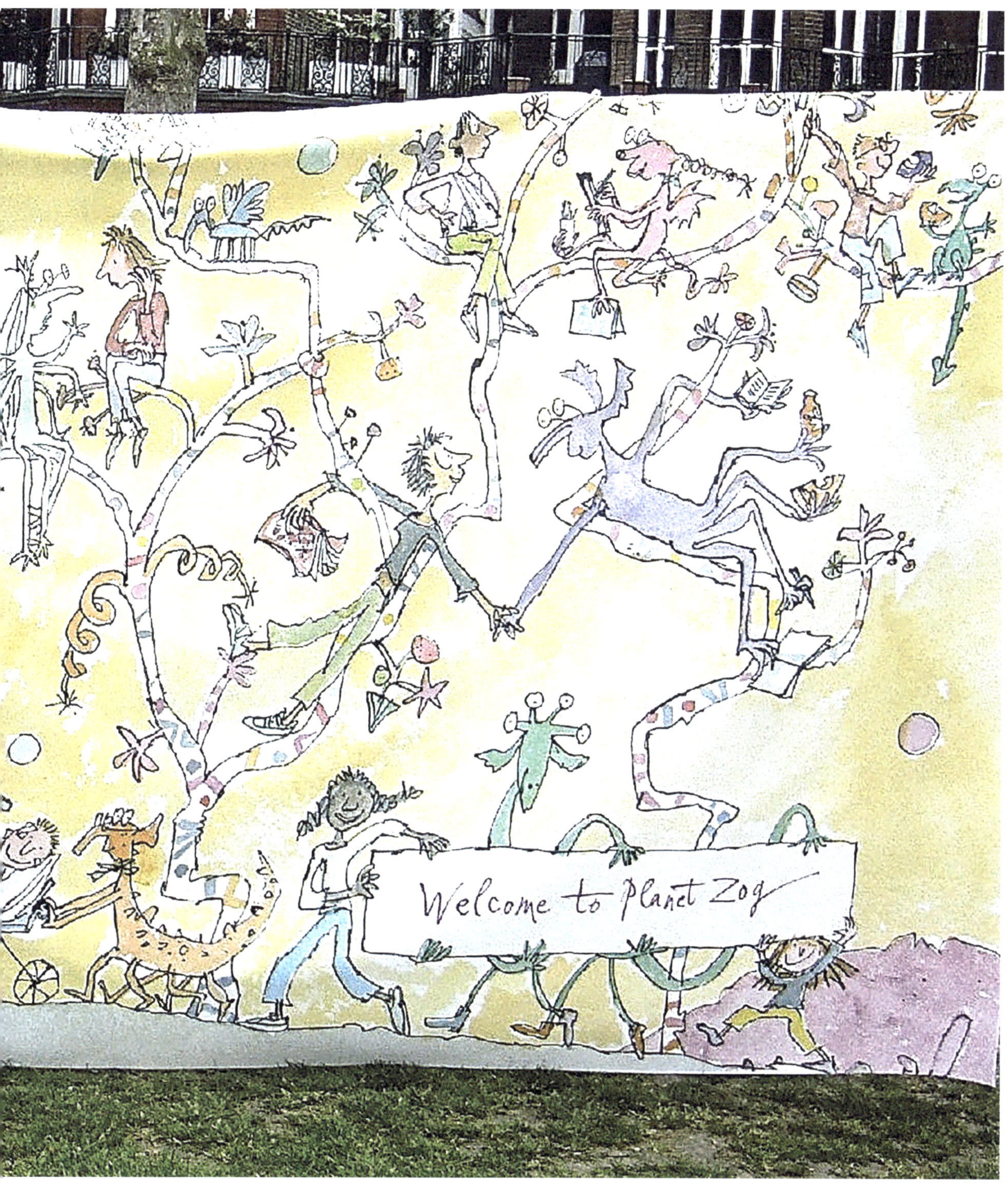
Welcome to planet Zog

# Ellington Ward,
# Northwick Park Hospital

*Harrow*

In this mental health unit for older patients, the elderly are often helped by young people. Quentin depicts these young assistants here, helping the patients while they 'set about circus acts with a certain aplomb, and in a comfortably less extreme form than is usual, except perhaps for the fire-eating. Perhaps because of its open defiance of any possible health and safety regulations this has proved to be one of the most popular in the series.'

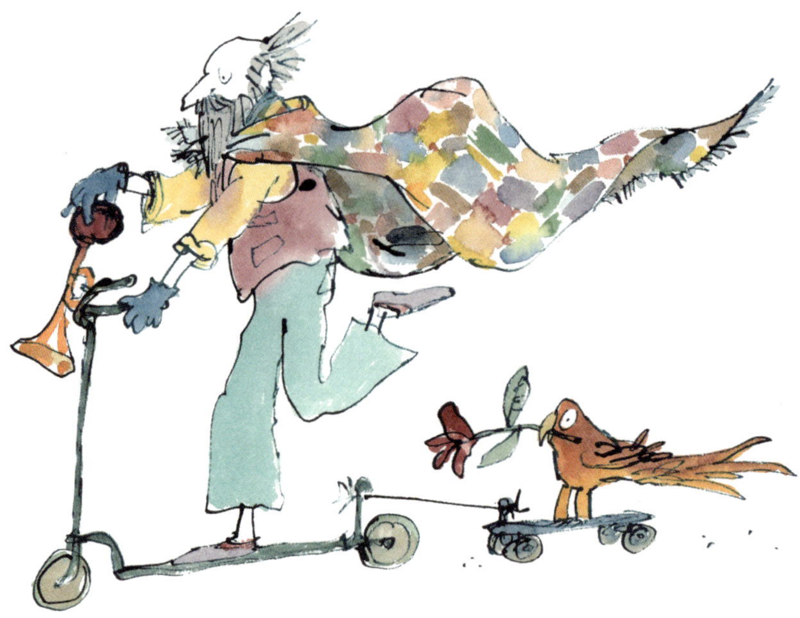

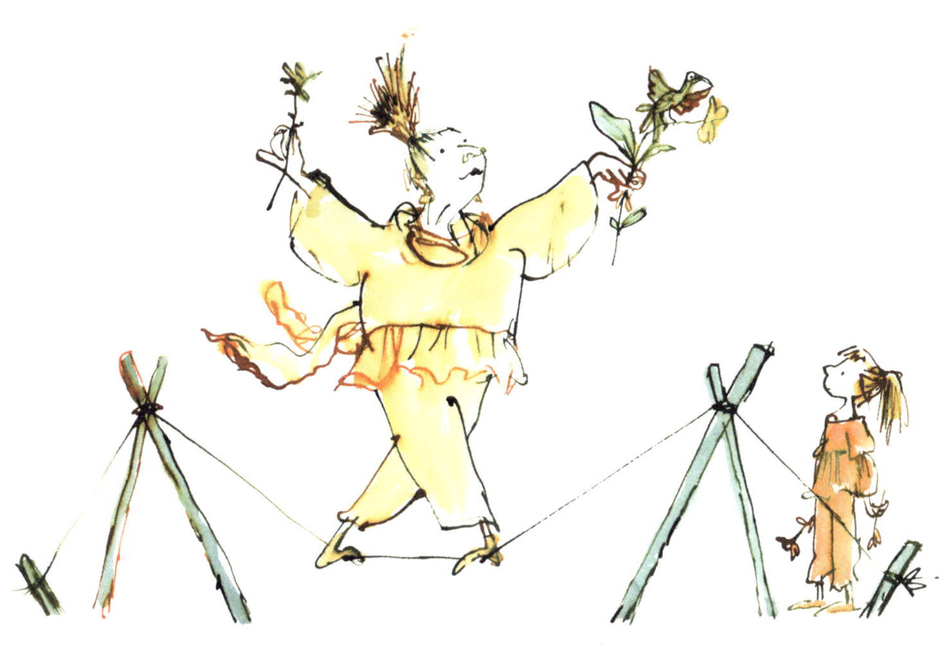

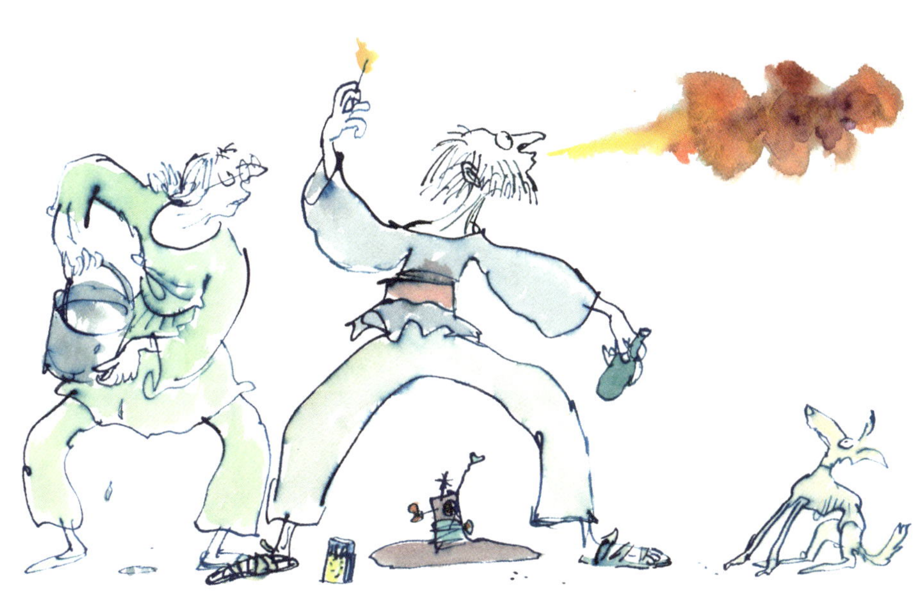

# Hôpital Armand Trousseau

### *Paris*

As a result of his work with the Nightingale Project, hospitals outside London approached him to do drawings, including the Hôpital Armand Trousseau, which contacted him in 2008. This hospital in Paris is for children and young people with medical and psychological problems, many of whom are from immigrant African families. There was no brief, and for an artist who has spent most of his working life illustrating a narrative this was real freedom:

'…having to create a brief for yourself is part of the fascination of the exercise. Hanging about in the reception area to draw the young patients, and talking to the medical staff, aided my sense of what ought to happen. In the final pictures all the different clients managed to appear, in varying states of optimism or despair, together with a number of helpers and specialists.'

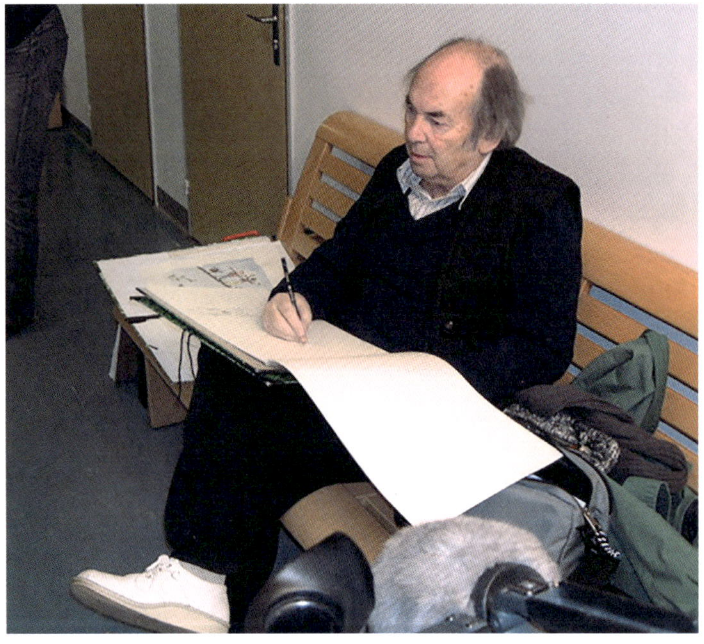

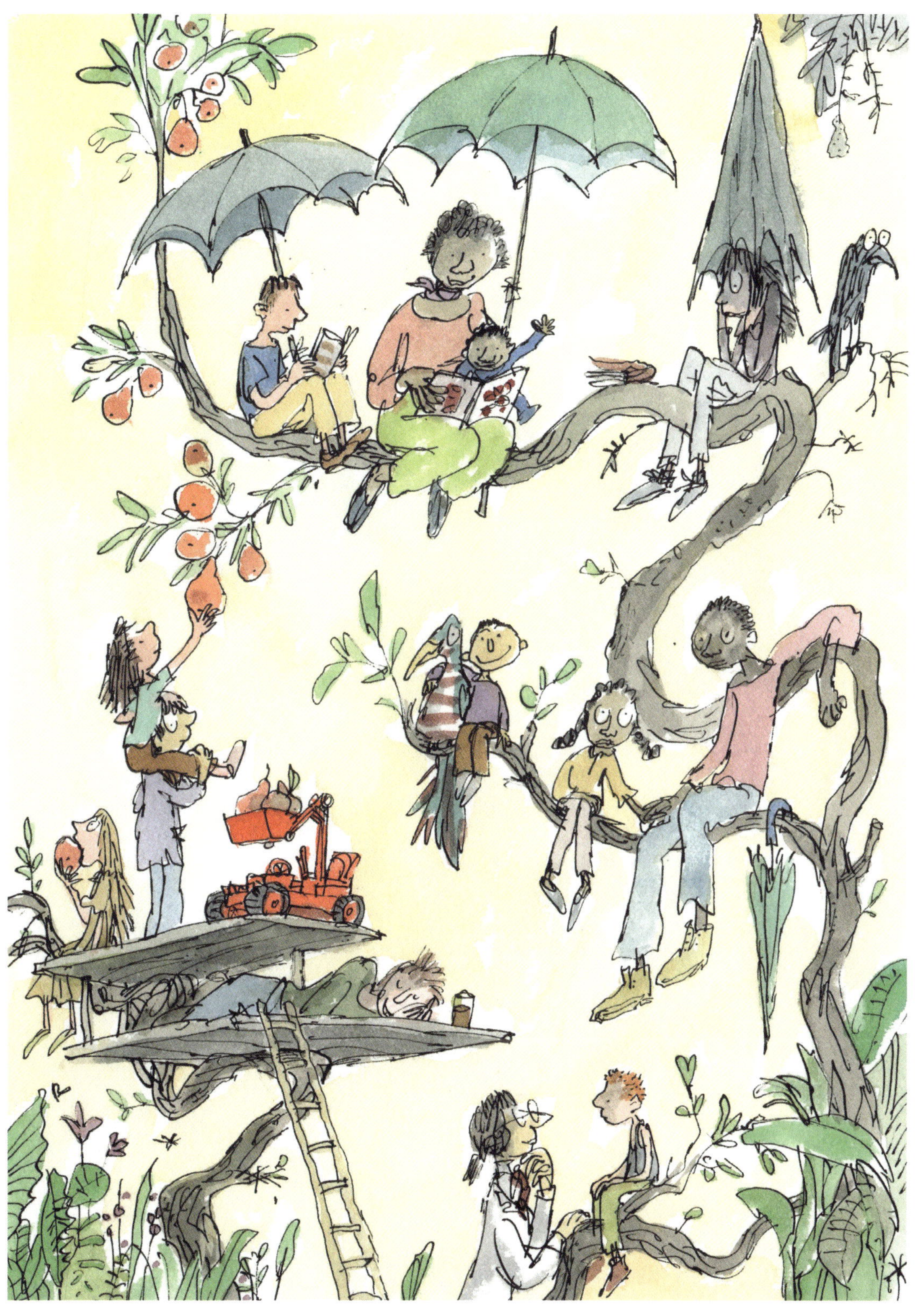

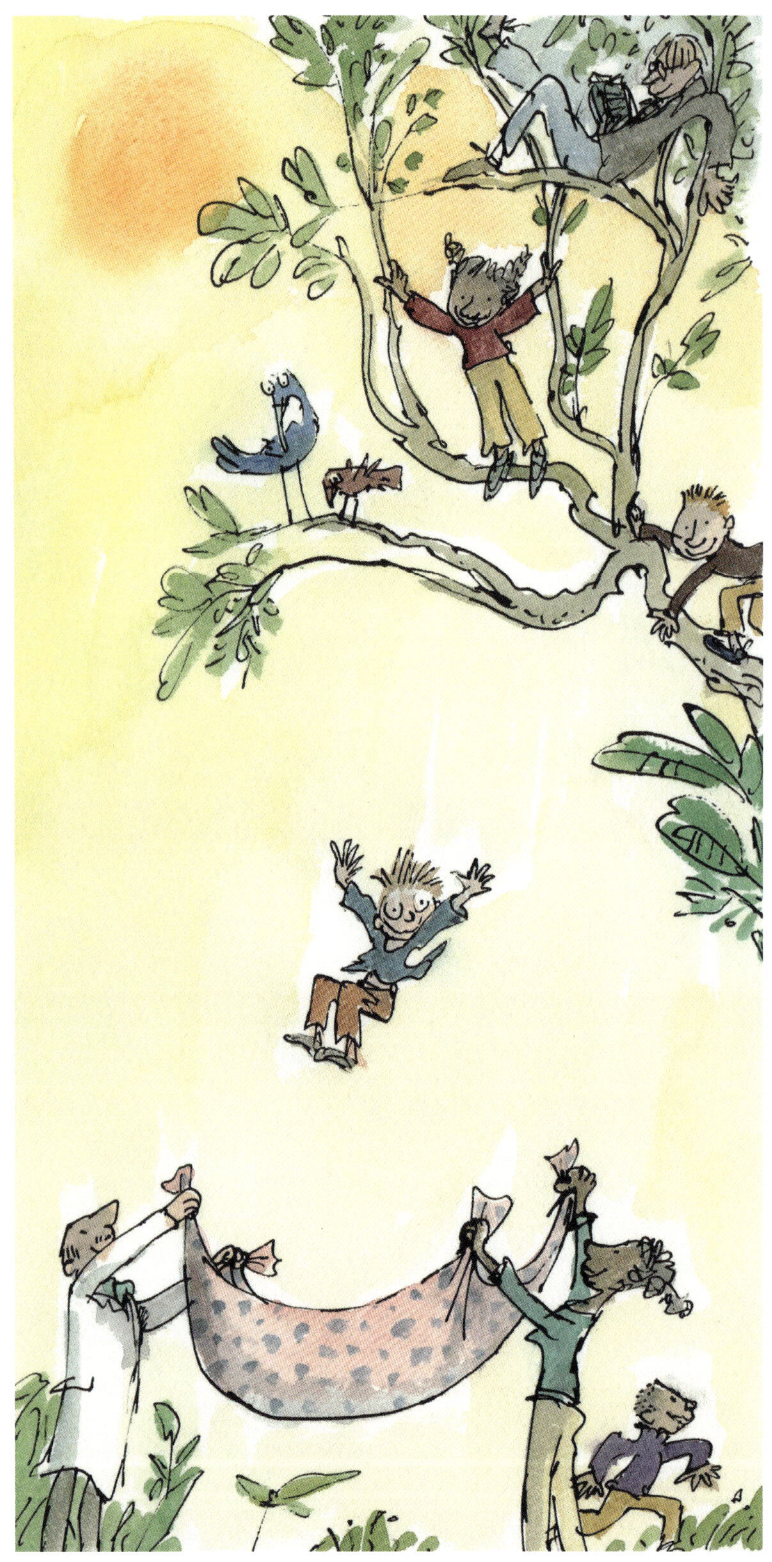

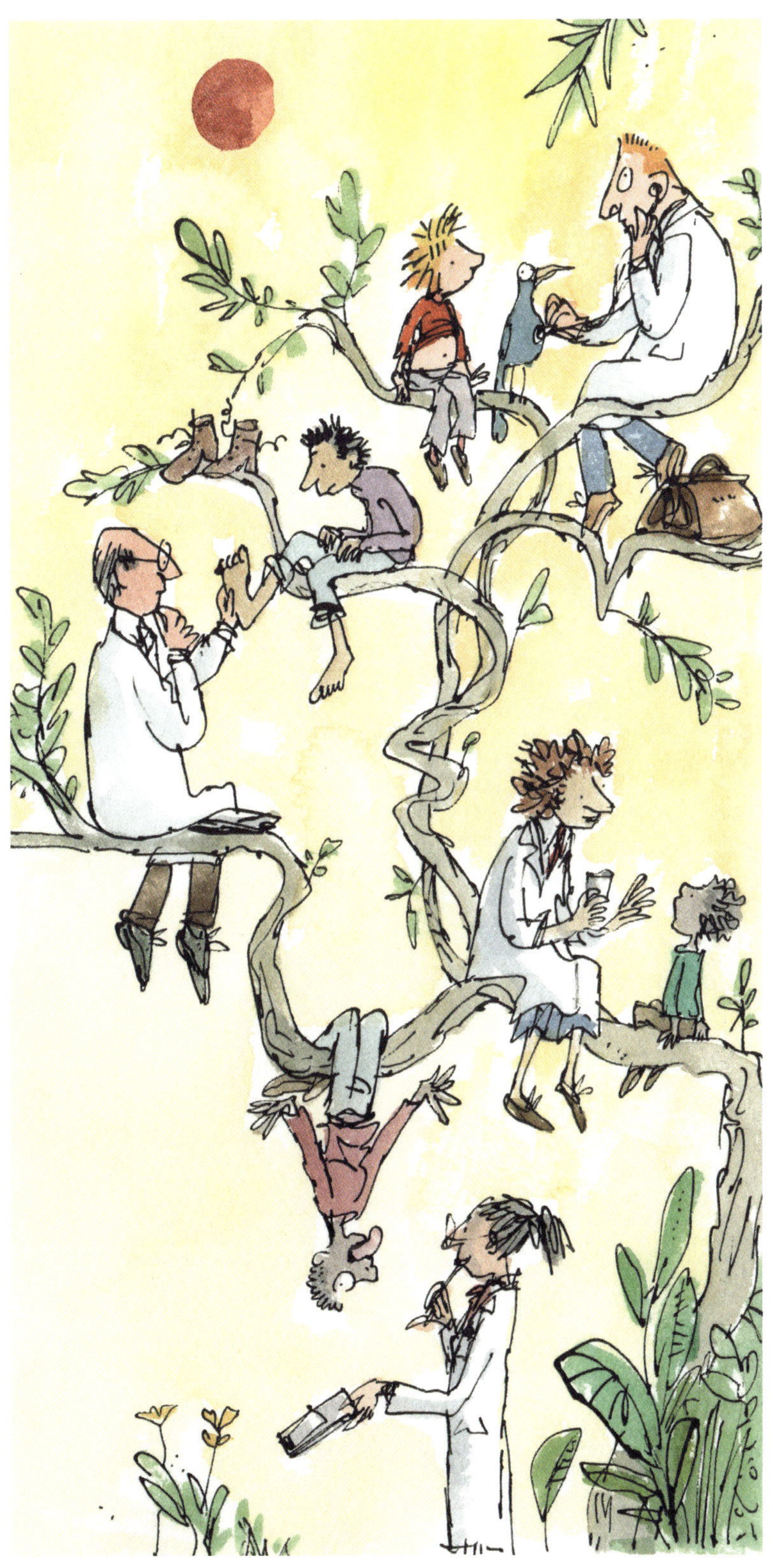

opposite & above — *Hôpital Armand Trousseau,* 2008

# Eating Disorder Unit

## *Westminster*

Quentin and I visited the EDU in Vincent Square and, in order for him to get a sense of what was needed, we met some of the patients and staff. The patients were mostly young, open and intelligent. As ever Quentin listened respectfully and quickly understood that these patients needed something very different from what he had done before:

'In some of the hospital drawings I made use of fantasy, to help people imagine they can do things which they actually can't at the moment. The situation here is the opposite. These patients have enough fantasy about their own selves so that I thought it was appropriate to be realistic and offer pictures of ordinary life in what I hope would be a reassuring way.'

The staff and the patients encouraged him to draw whatever he liked, 'though it's acknowledged that food is a sensitive issue. The rooms to have drawings include the dining-room, where, as one young woman puts it, "I've got enough on my plate as it is."… It seemed to me that what was in order were pictures which did not avoid reference to some of the issues that concerned them, but which are, I hope helpfully relaxed and at ease – so that food may appear just as part of everyday life and self-image becomes a self-portrait or a snapshot. The pictures are drawn with quills, which give a slightly untidy sort of line, and coloured with watercolour, which soften away at the edges.'

With his characteristic empathy, it's as if Quentin were holding a mirror up to the patients in which 'they saw themselves not criticized or judged, but accepted with an easy goodwill.'

(Jenny Uglow, *The Quentin Blake Book,* 2022)

*Ordinary Life,* 2010 – 2011

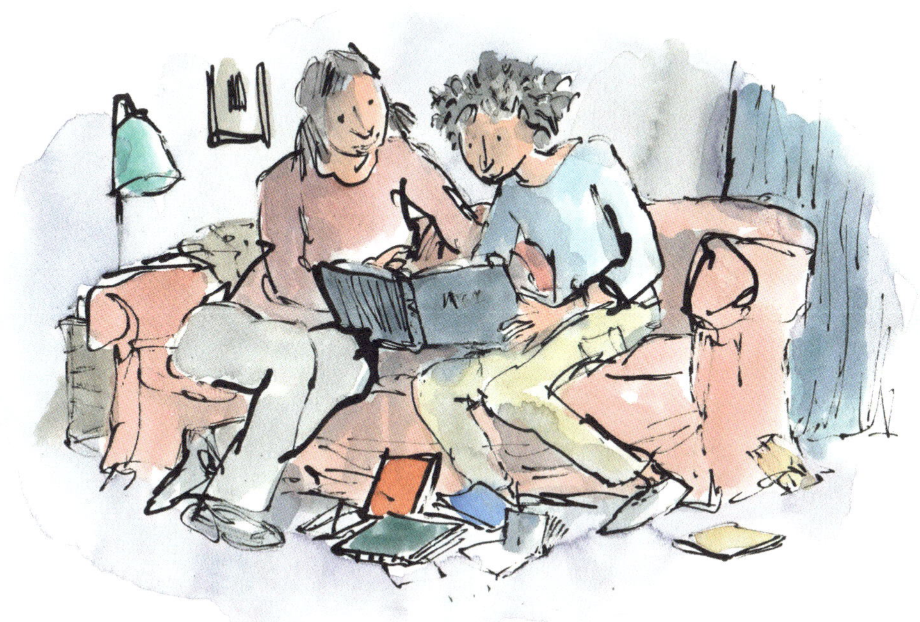

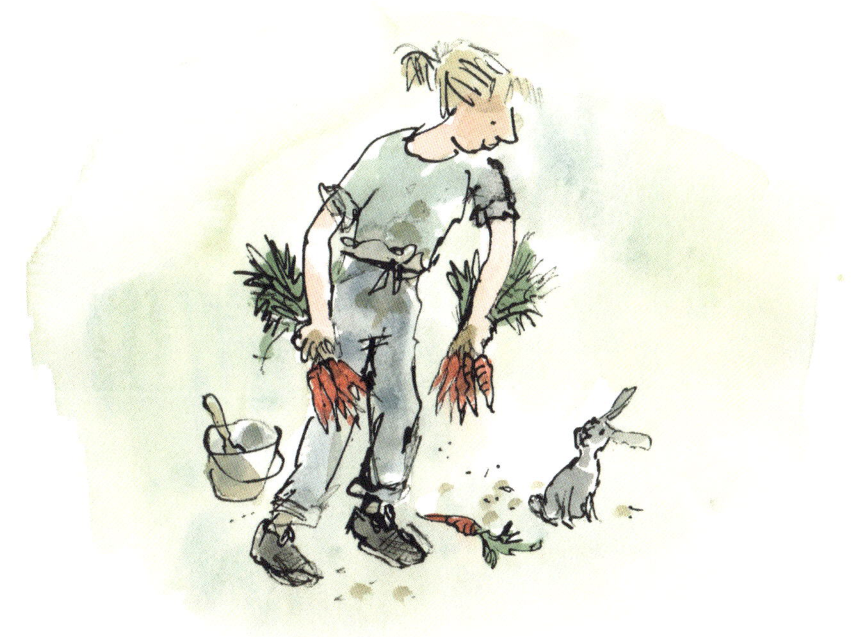

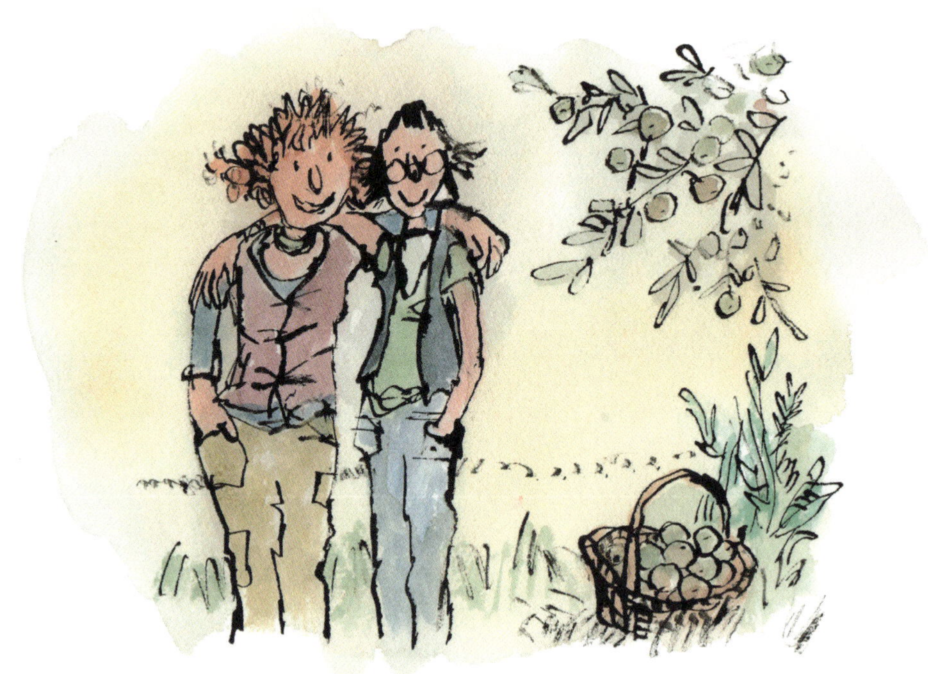

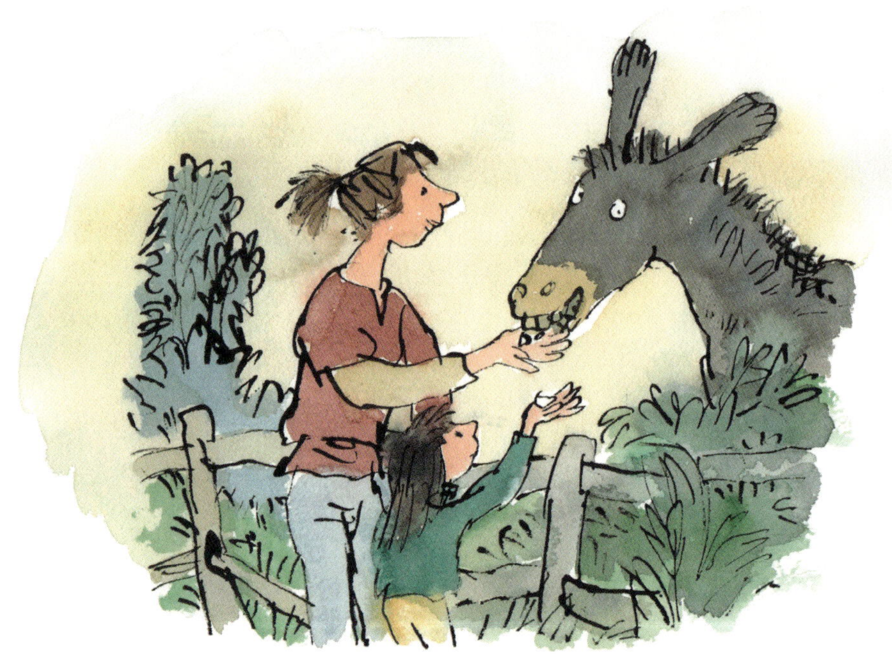

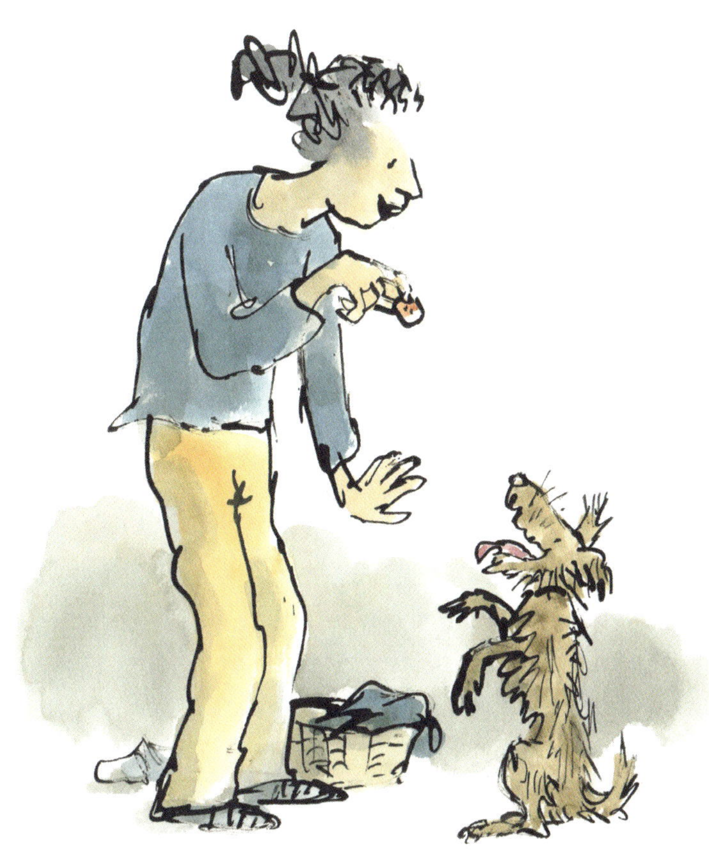

OPPOSITE & ABOVE –
*Ordinary Life*, 2010 – 2011

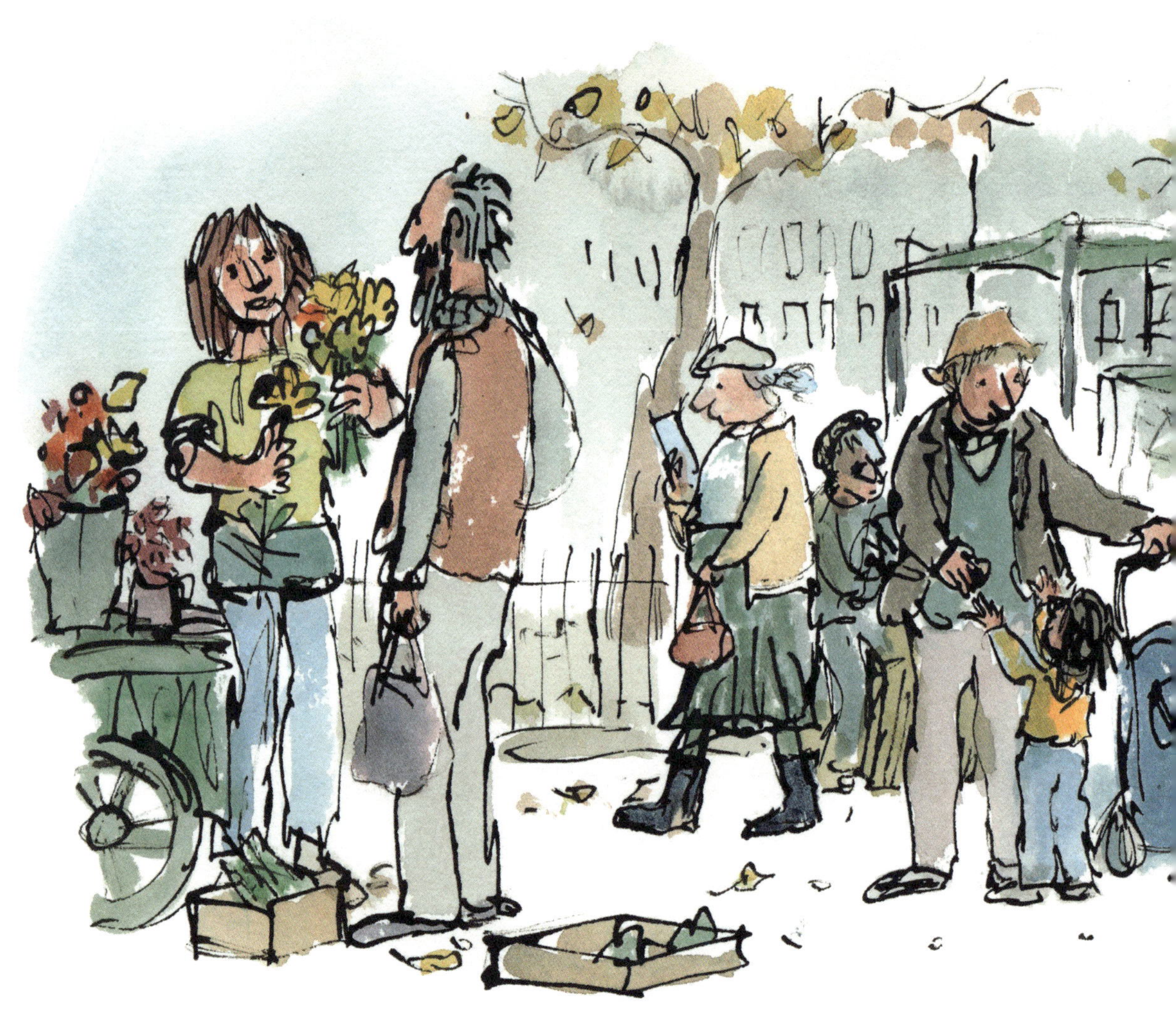

*Ordinary Life*, 2010 – 2011

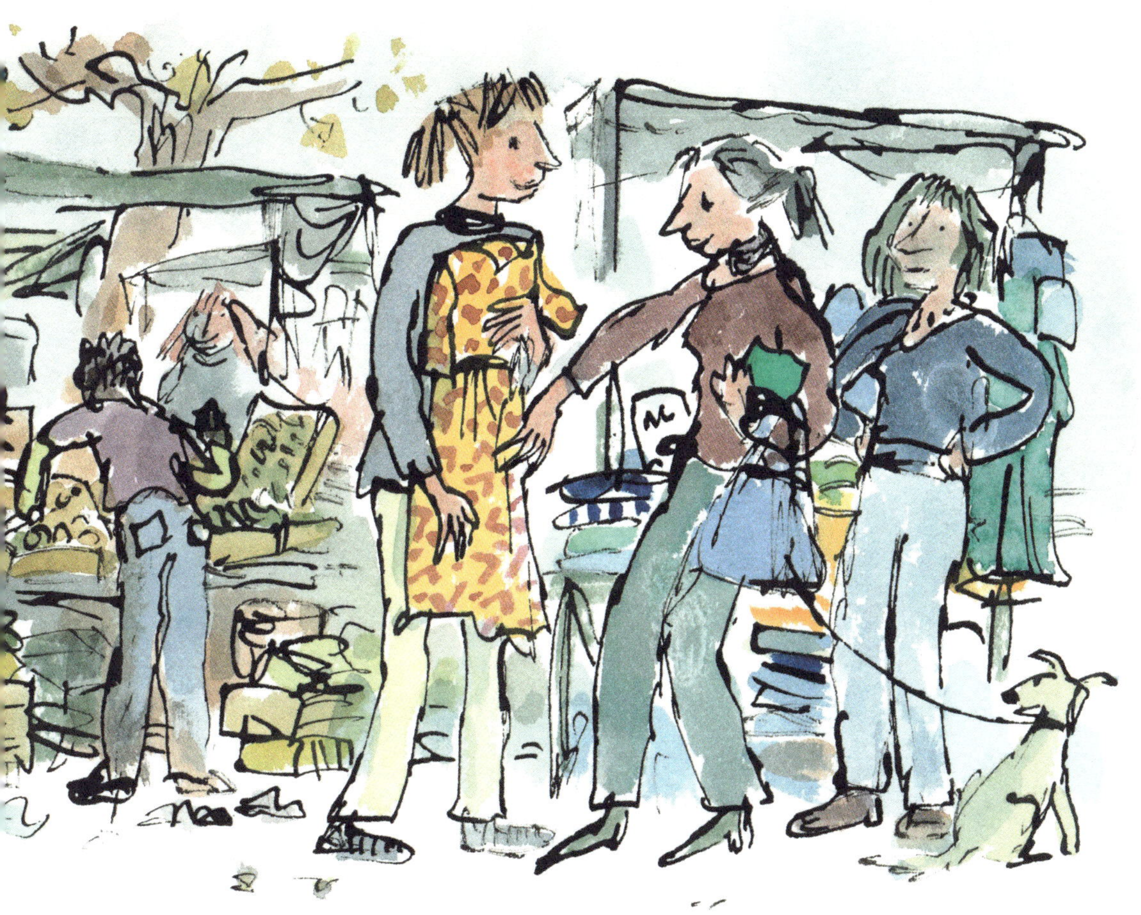

# The Gordon Hospital

## *Westminster*

The experience of visiting hospitals and thinking about what he could put on hospital walls was a new source of inspiration for Quentin; it fed his imagination and allowed him to freewheel:

'…and so it was I found myself in the room that serves as my studio in France drawing people swimming about under water. I have no idea where they came from. They are accompanied by an assortment of fish, and occasionally one or two small crocodiles, but their distinctive feature is that they are dressed in ordinary everyday clothes. They are drawn with a brush in a more naturalistic style than any of the other hospital pictures so far, which makes it even more possible for them to behave as though nothing untoward was happening.'

When he brought the drawings back to London and showed them to the Nightingale Project, they immediately knew that they belonged in the Gordon Mental Health Centre for Adults in Vincent Square.

*Life Under Water,* 2008

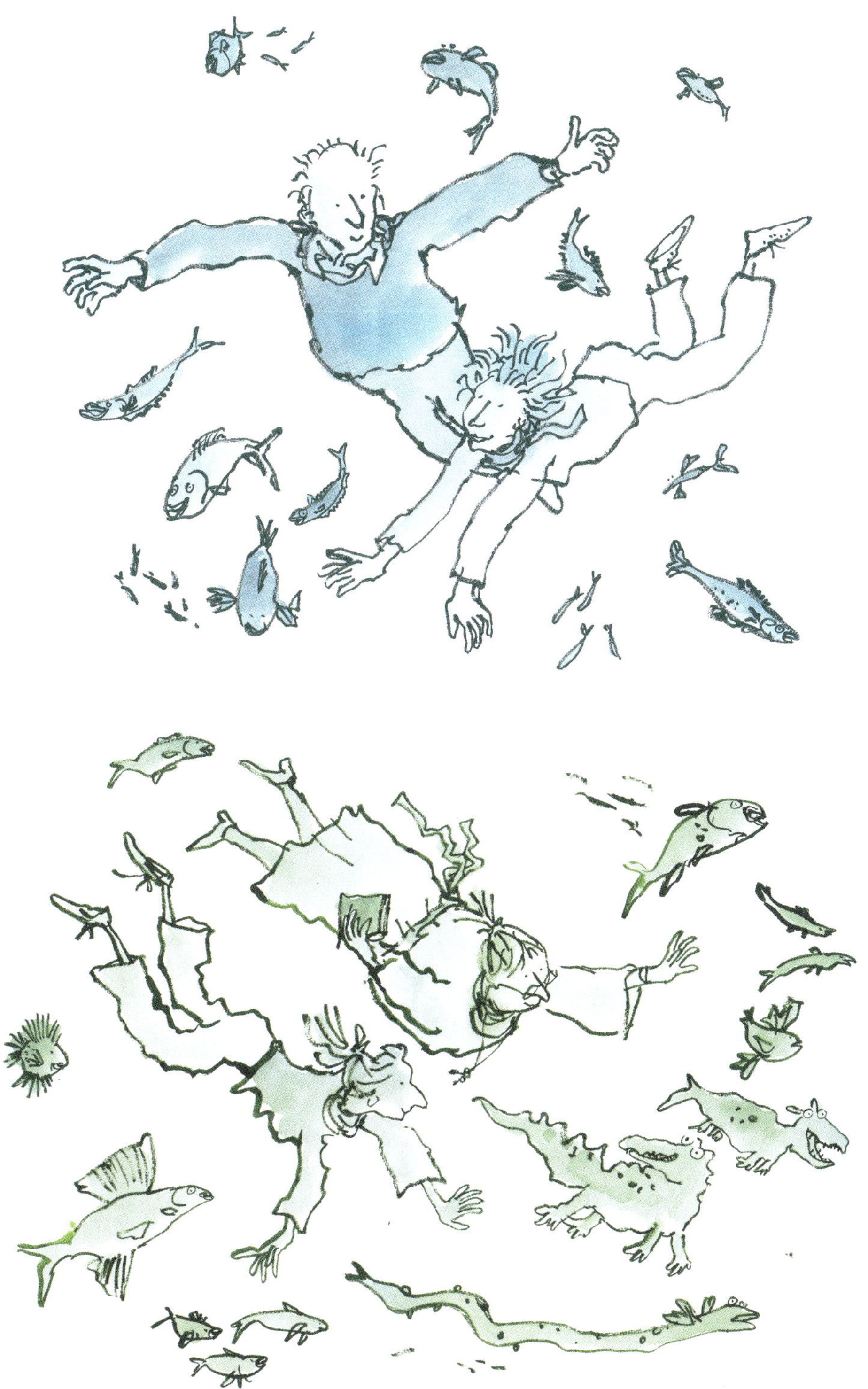

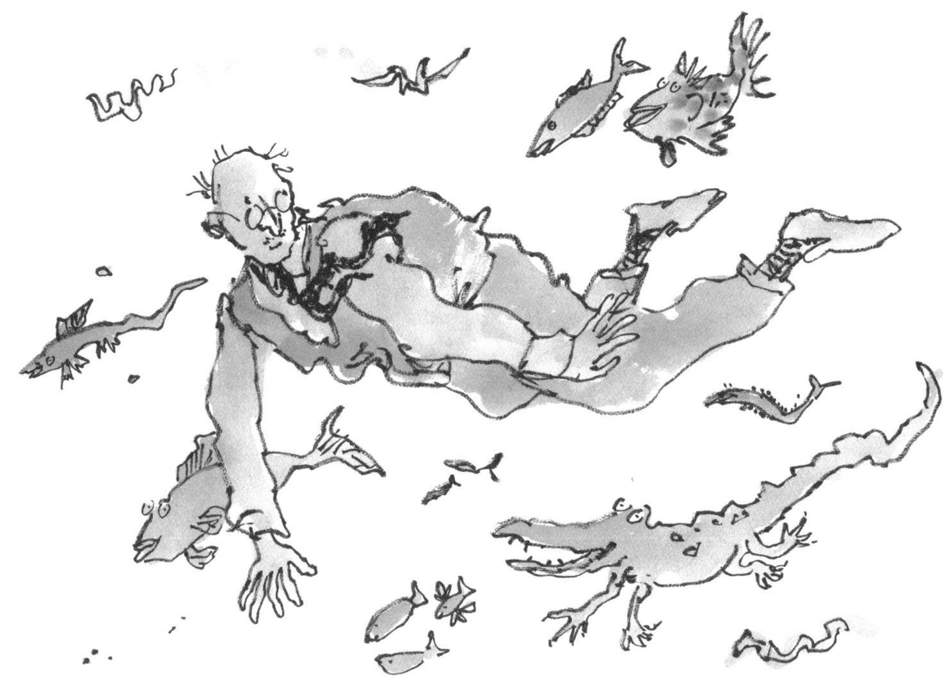

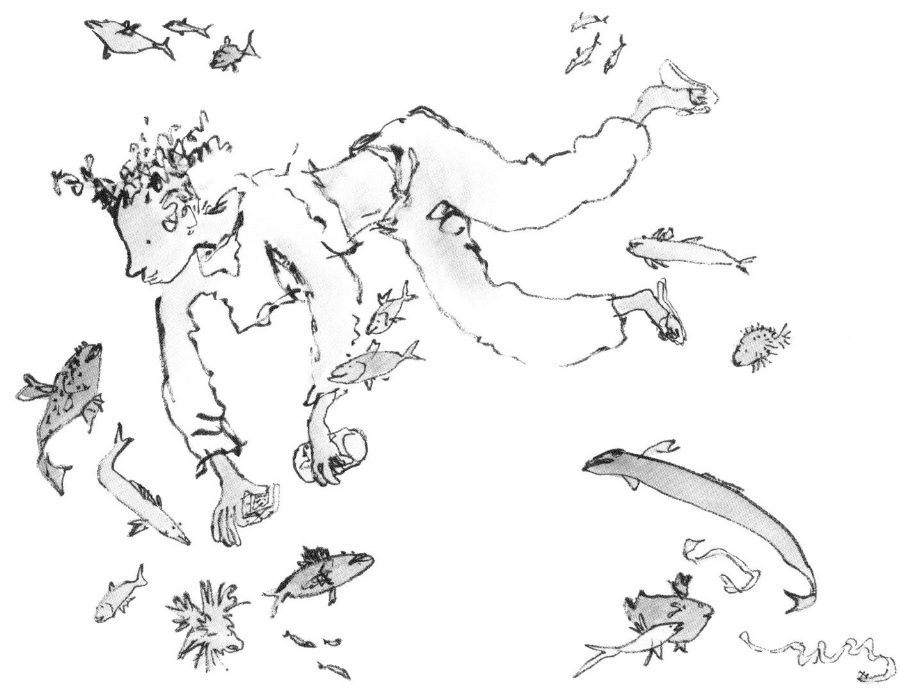

'They are drawn with a brush in a more
naturalistic style than any of the other hospital
pictures so far, which makes it even more possible
for them to behave as though nothing untoward
was happening.'

**QB**

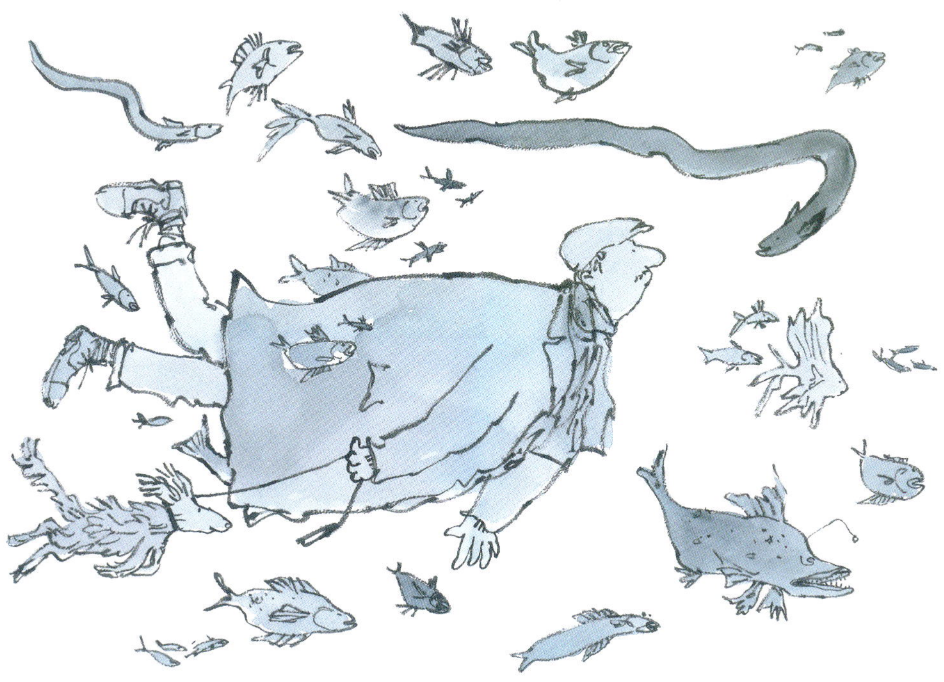

OPPOSITE & ABOVE – *Life Under Water*, 2008

# Angers Maternity Hospital

### *Angers, France*

When Quentin was asked by the University Hospital of Angers to illuminate the walls of their new maternity wing, the unit hadn't been built yet, and he remembers the first meeting with the staff took place in a car park. As he discussed the project with six of the midwives he was struck by their perceptiveness and enthusiasm for the project. Quentin has always loved France: he had a house in La Rochelle for many years, he reads and speaks French fluently, and he would have found these meetings even more pleasurable for being conducted in French.

Without any knowledge of the practice of water birth, he instinctively knew what to draw: 'Visually, I had my answer ready – mothers swimming underwater with their babies…. I already had the idea of swimmers, and that seemed appropriate to the idea of amniotic fluid, to the fact that for a while babies can swim naturally, and even, here in France, to the coincidence that the hospital is on the banks of the River Maine, which has been known to flood from time to time.'

Unlike the swimmers in *Life Under Water,* these mothers and babies wouldn't have any clothes on. This required a different drawing medium: 'A brush seemed to be the right thing for the clothes of the previous swimmers, but not for the naked flesh – for that smoothness a reed-pen seemed the better answer.'

The drawings were to be used in the waiting rooms, midwife stations and delivery suites, 'I thought the mothers would like to look at them during labour and see what they had to look forward to.'

'There were even pictures for sadder spaces, where unsuccessful pregnancies had to be interrupted, and even where relatives could have sight of the small person who had failed to survive.'

Quentin was particularly delighted that some drawings 'were sandblasted onto the fenestration of the entire frontage of the hospital. The technique being particularly extraordinary and the concept creatively brave.'

The style of the drawings is naturalistic; there is no element of caricature or humour here. When Quentin saw them enlarged as murals it occurred to him that 'they had perhaps some kind of odd relationship with seventeenth century rococo decoration, the ribbony seaweed providing the attendant decorative flourishes. At that time the nudity would have been accepted as in order – classical, even seductive. My young women, however, were real, contemporary.'

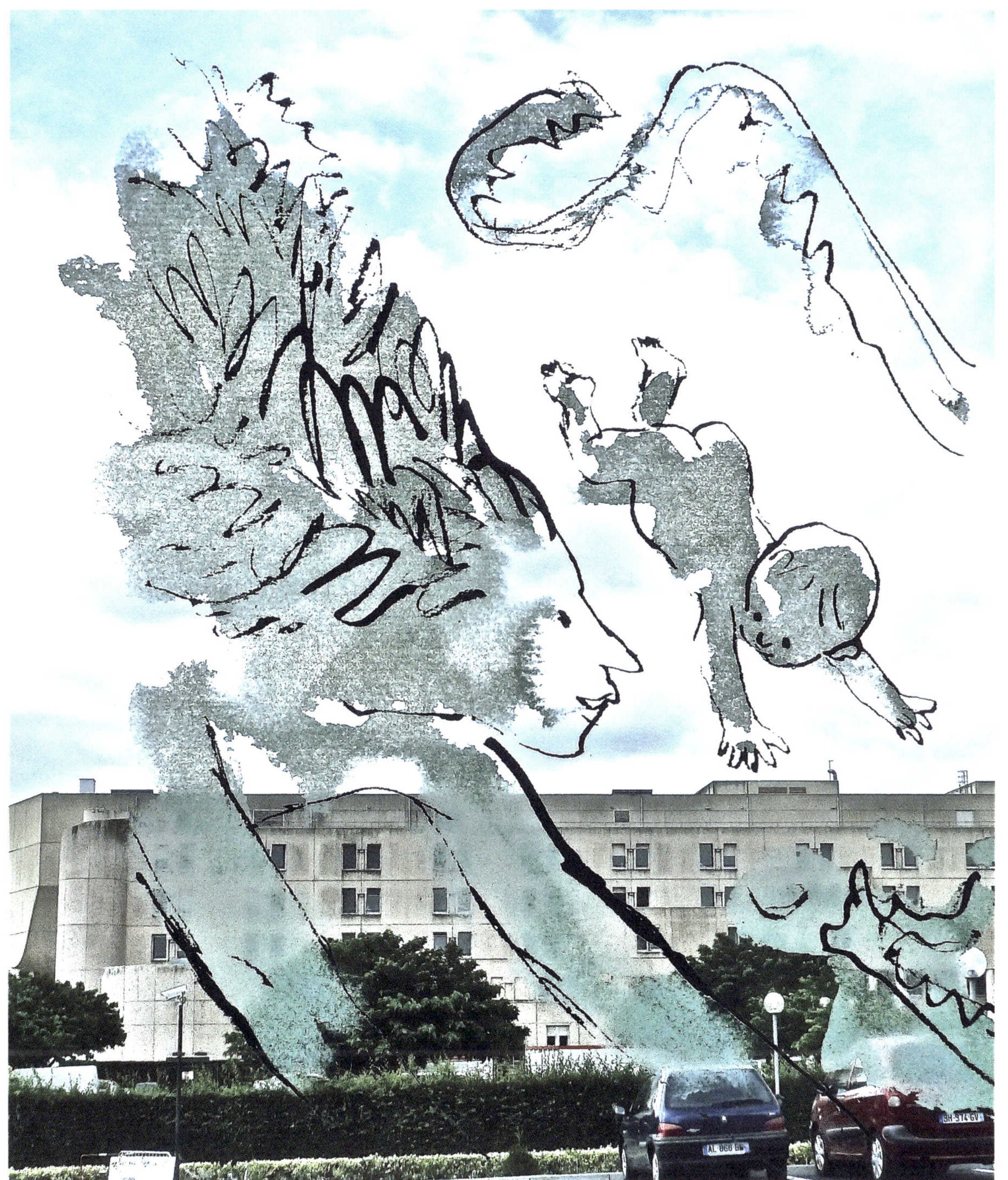

Angers University Hospital, 2011

This naturalistic style might have caused difficulties for an artist who had never drawn from life, but Quentin was able to draw upon his training: 'You produce them from memory – of life-drawing classes and of life – and by trying to find positions and gestures with the drawing implement by imagining them on yourself. "How did you know that?" asked one of the hospital staff; one of the most rewarding things for me that has been said about my work but that is one of the attractions of drawing. Once started it can sometimes take you further than you ever thought you could get.'

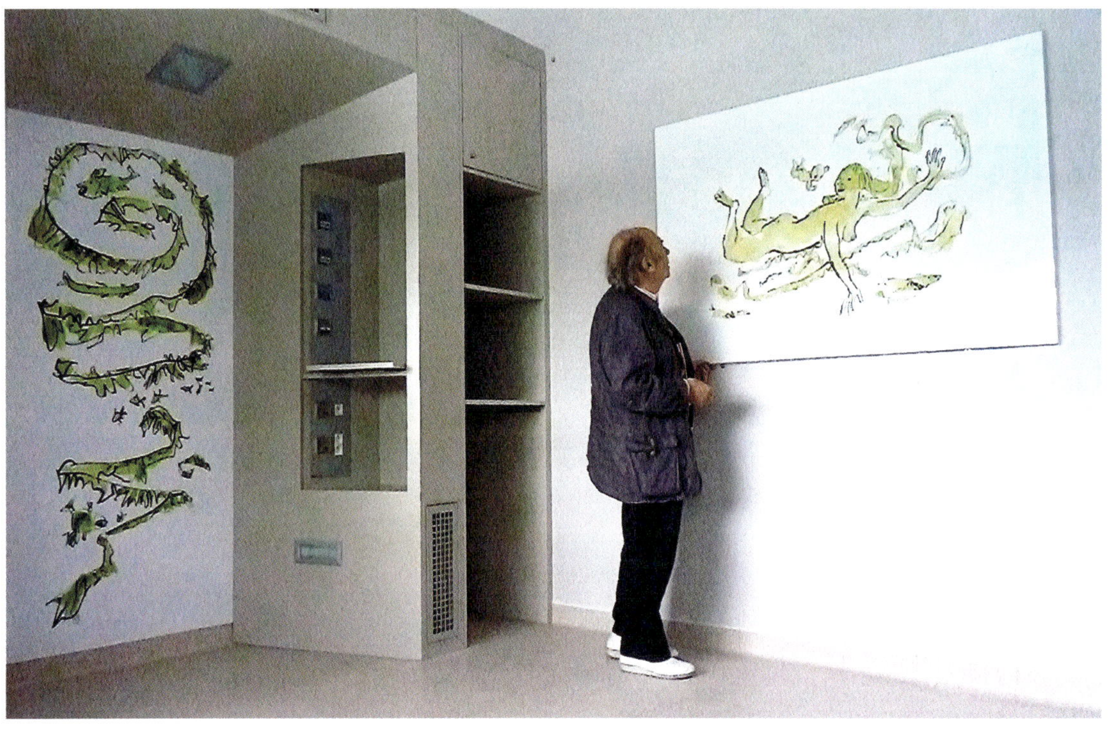

ABOVE & OPPOSITE –
Angers University Hospital, 2011

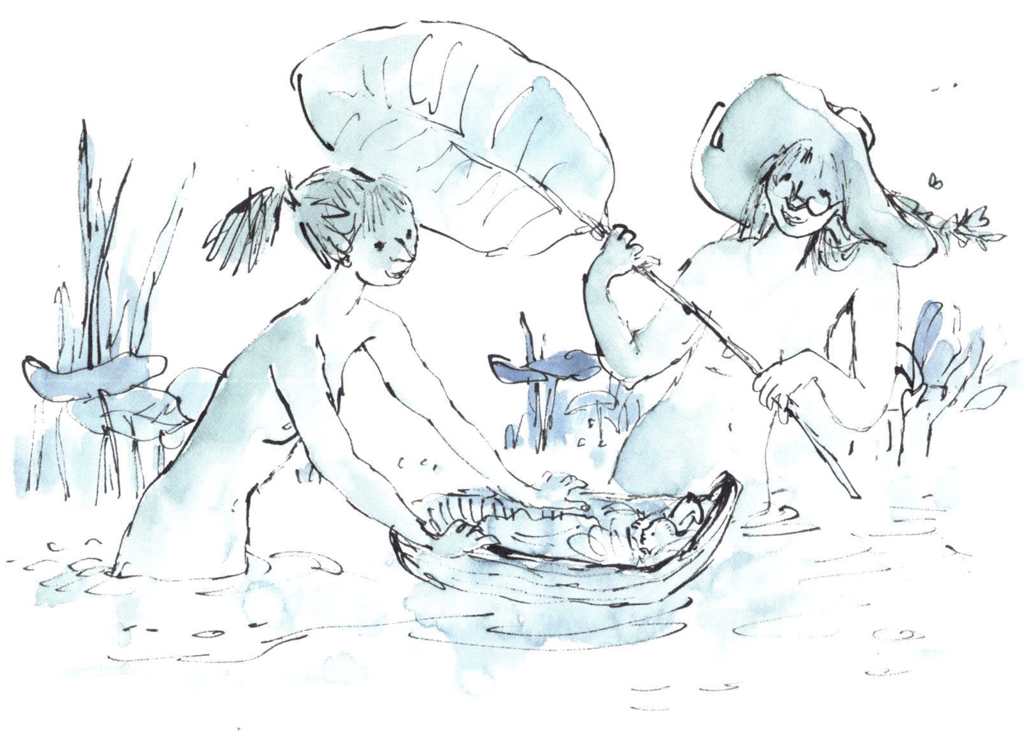

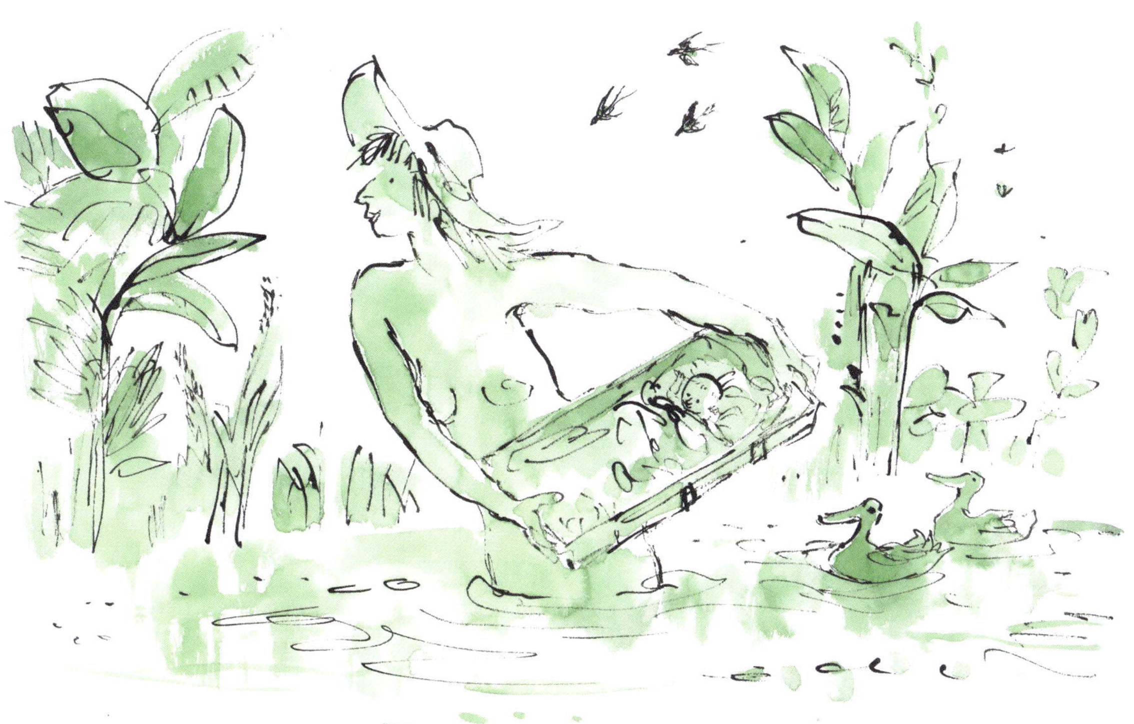

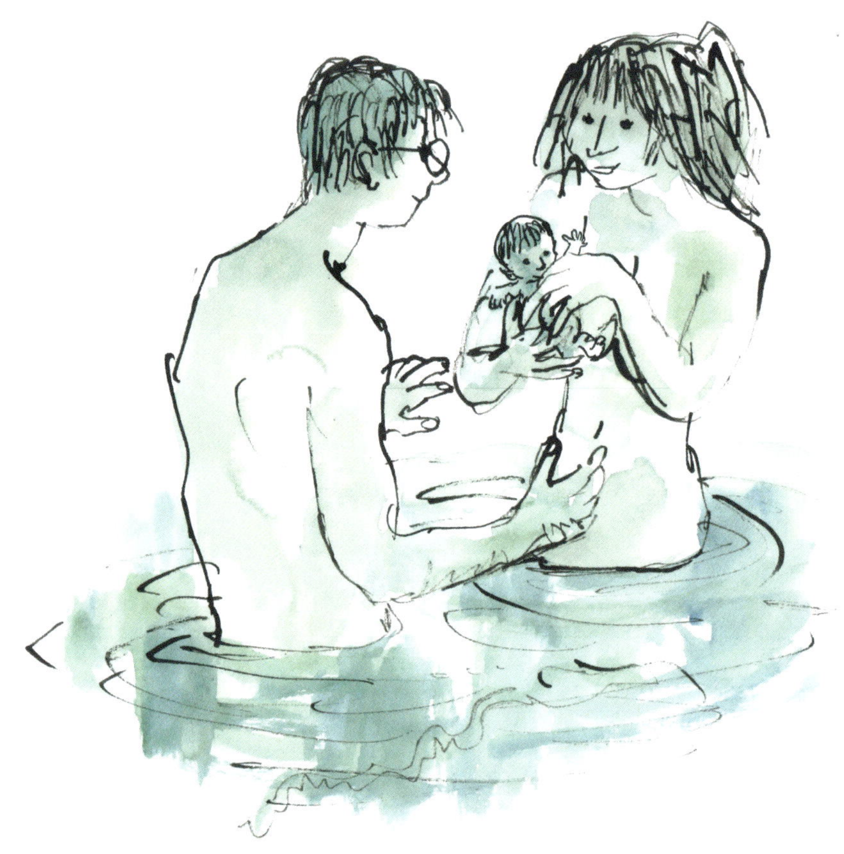


Angers University Hospital, 2011

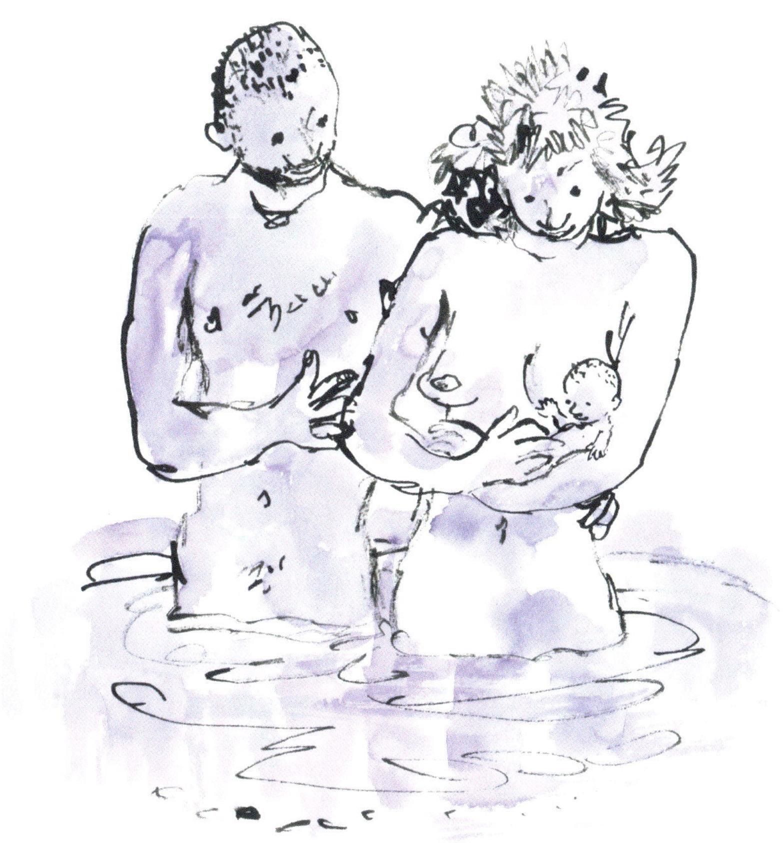

"A brush seemed to be the right thing for the clothes of the previous swimmers, but not for the naked flesh – for that smoothness a reed-pen seemed the better answer."

**QB**

# St Bernard's Hospital

## *Southall*

For St Bernard's Hospital, Quentin thought that a collection of small pictures would suit the space but the framing and hanging of these would be expensive and not durable. Instead his series of drawings of everyday life 'partly, as with other hospital pictures, to keep the spectator in touch with ordinary life' were printed on vinyl wallpaper.

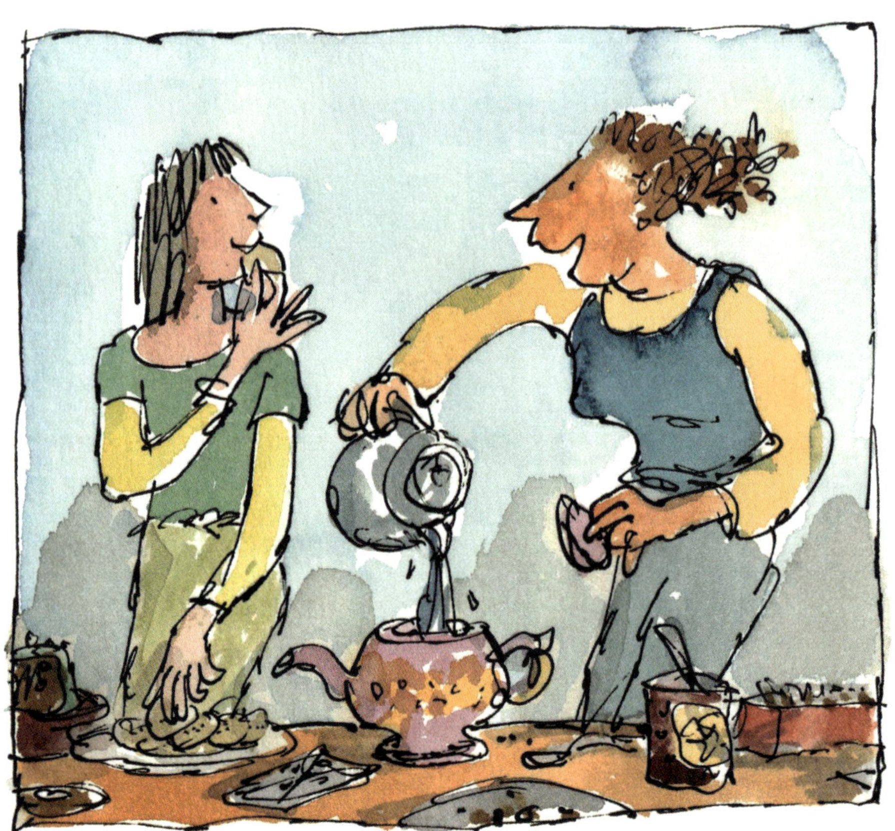

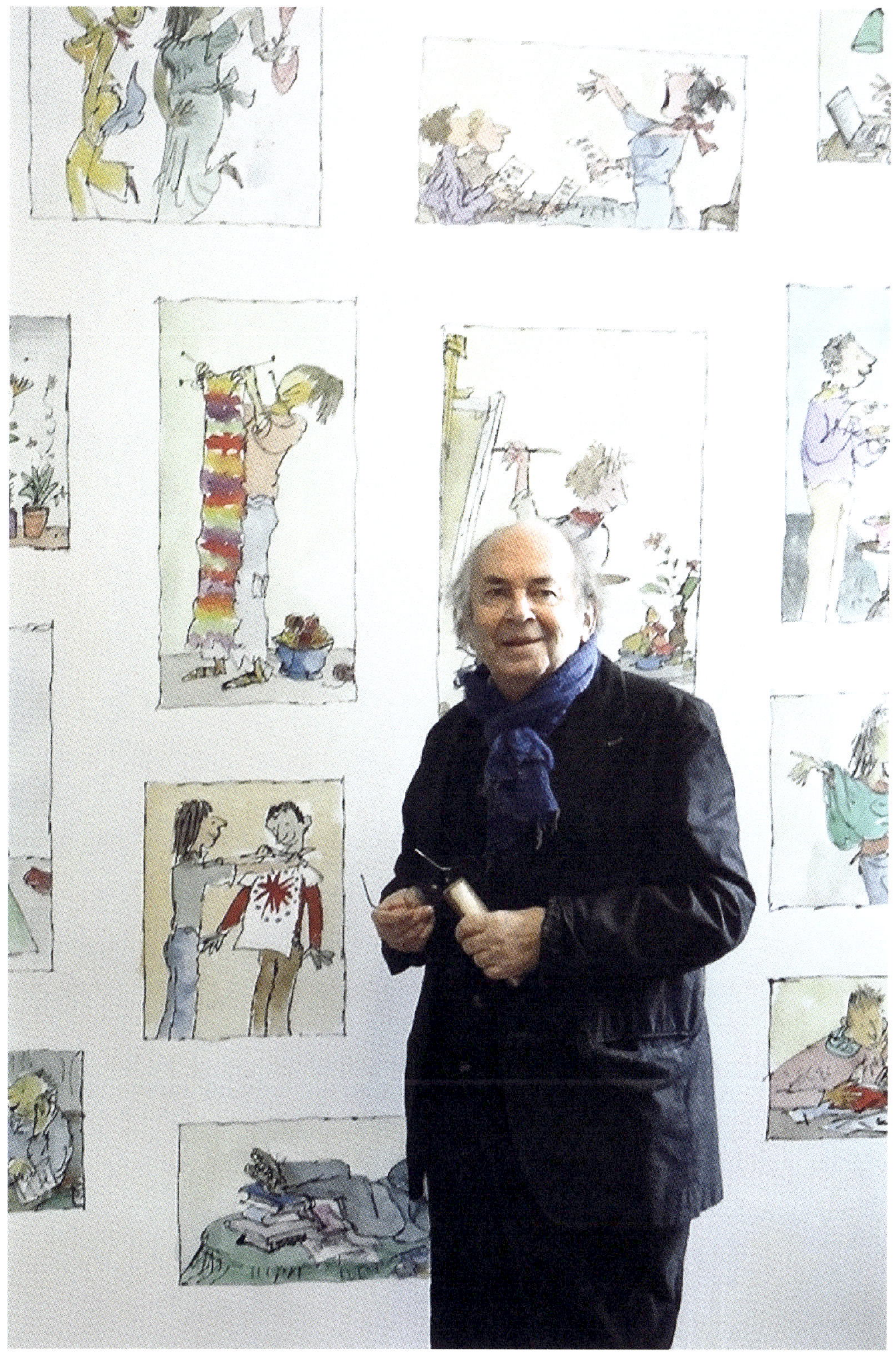

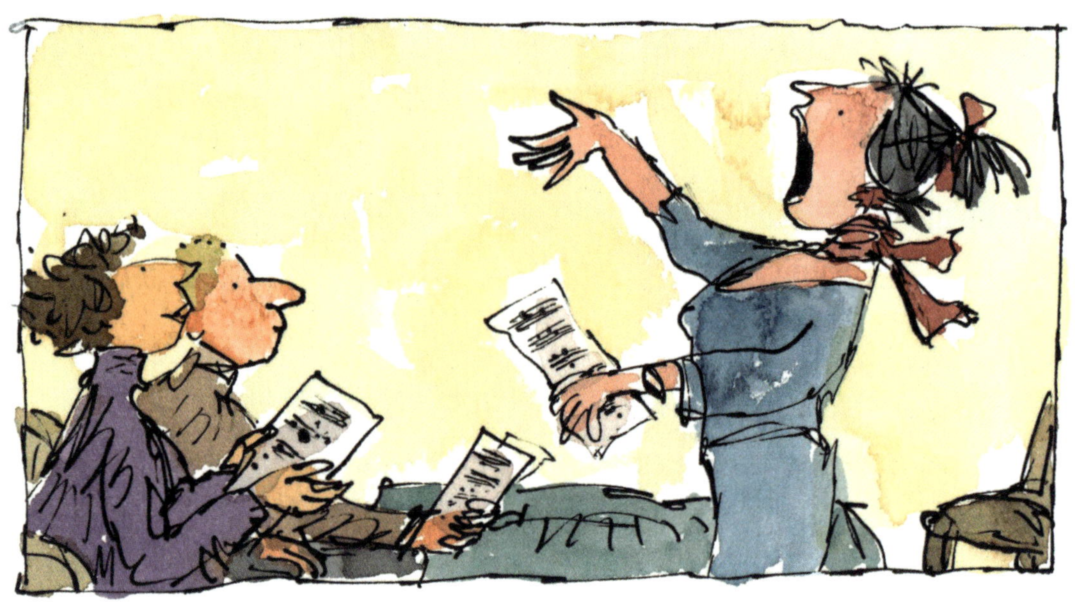

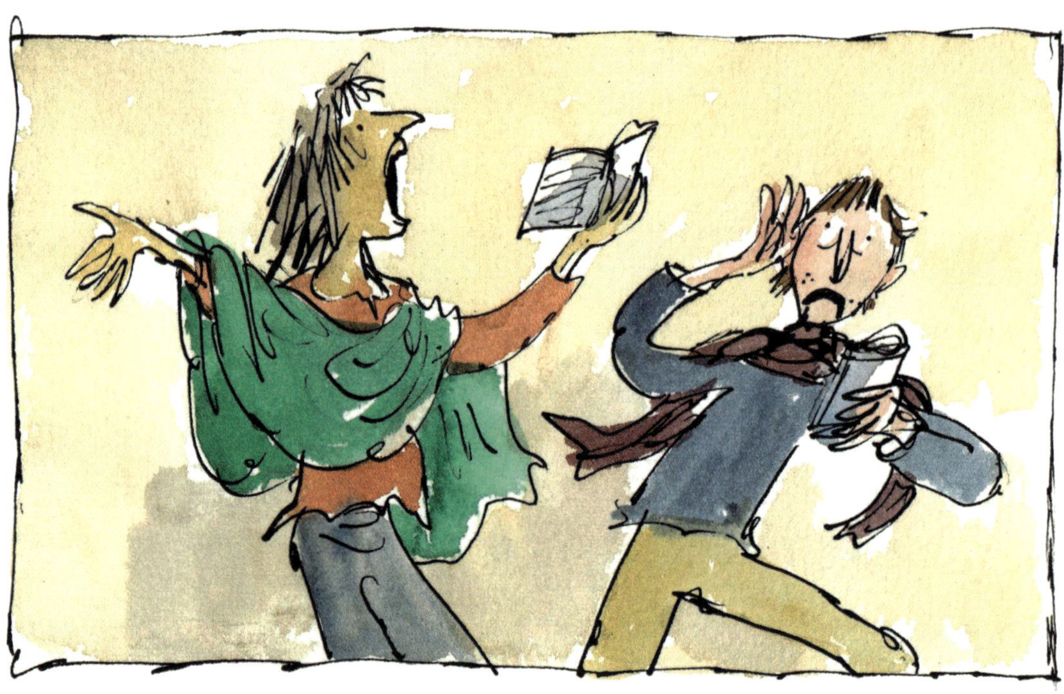

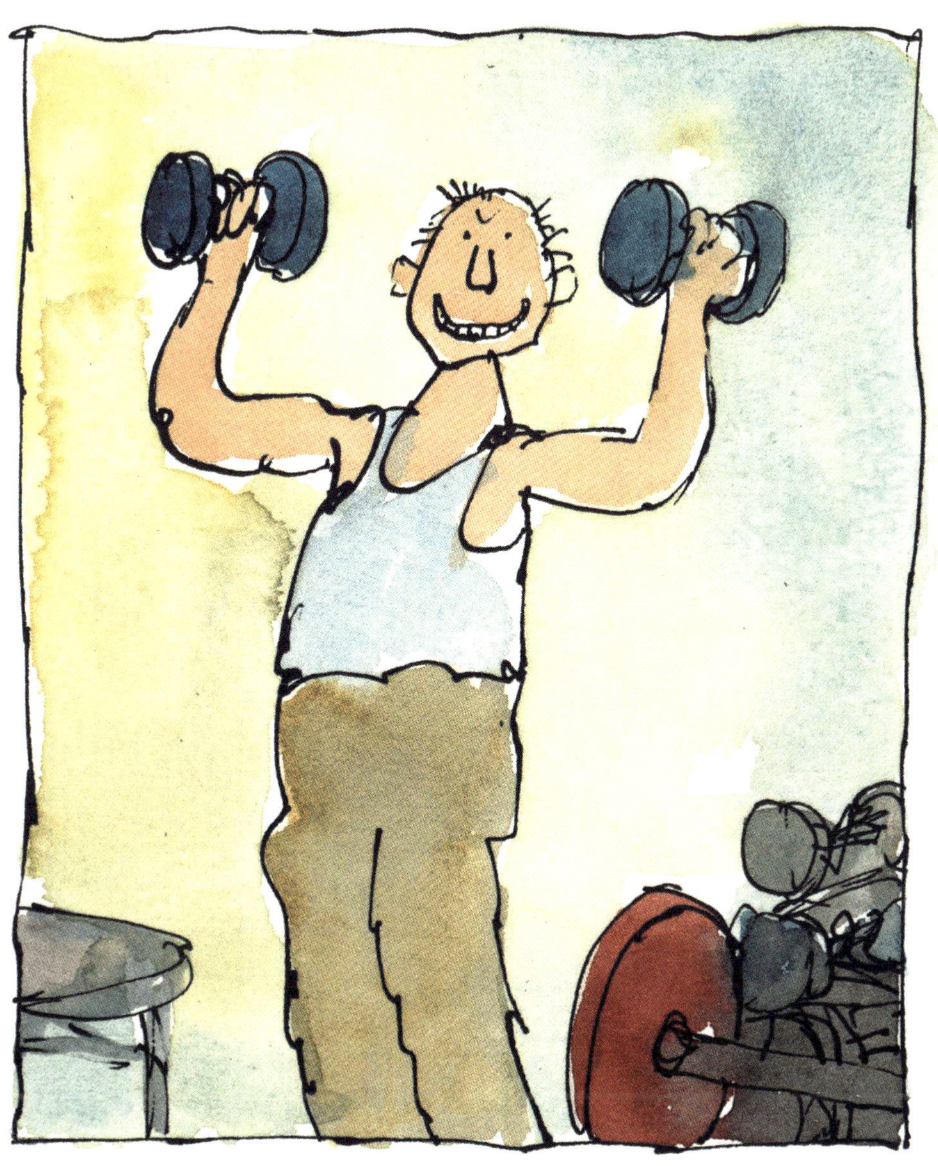

St Bernard's Hospital, 2014

# St George's Hospital

## *Tooting*

The name of the children's ward made the choice of subject matter easy for Quentin.

'There was nothing arduous about drawing a set of ten pictures – one a portrait of the dragon meeting two children, and nine others of (her? him?) going through various hospital experiences. Some were medical – having the tail bandaged, and what were those alarming spots – but there were others, such as reading and drawing; and of course if you have a dragon you have a ride on it.

Burgess Studio organised these images, enlarged and printed on to panels, slightly curved like large sheets of paper, along both sides of a corridor on to which the various consulting rooms opened. I had the reward, on the day of opening, of seeing the consultants emerge looking as pleased as the young patients at what had arrived.'

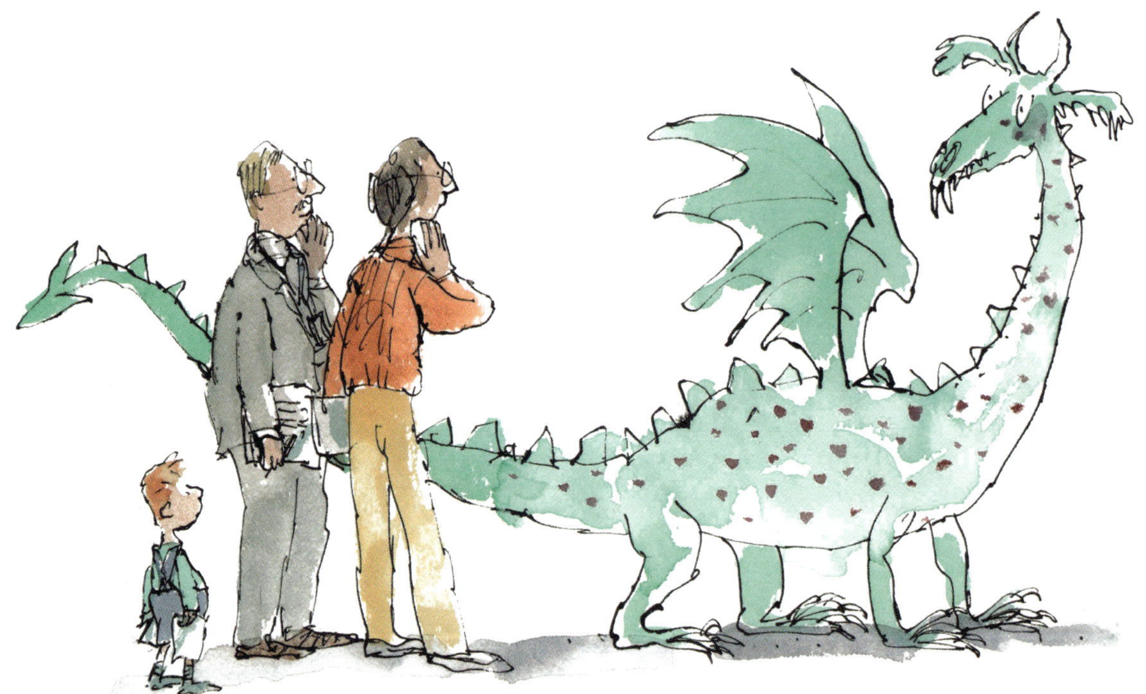

The Dragon Centre, 2014

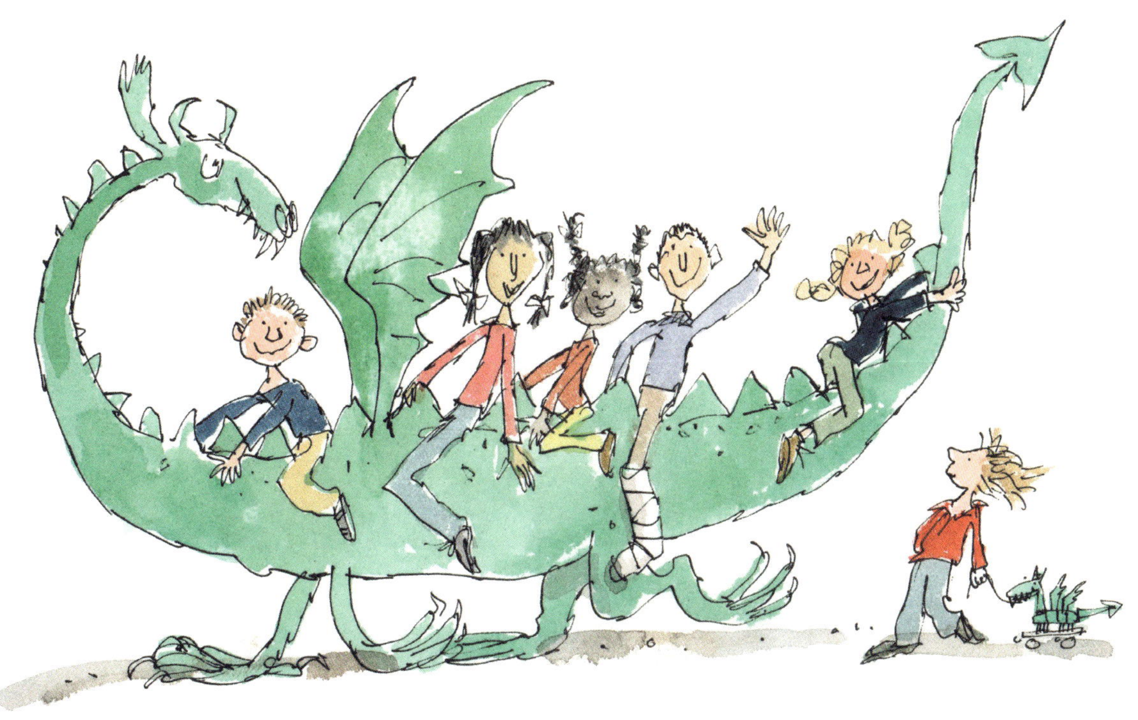

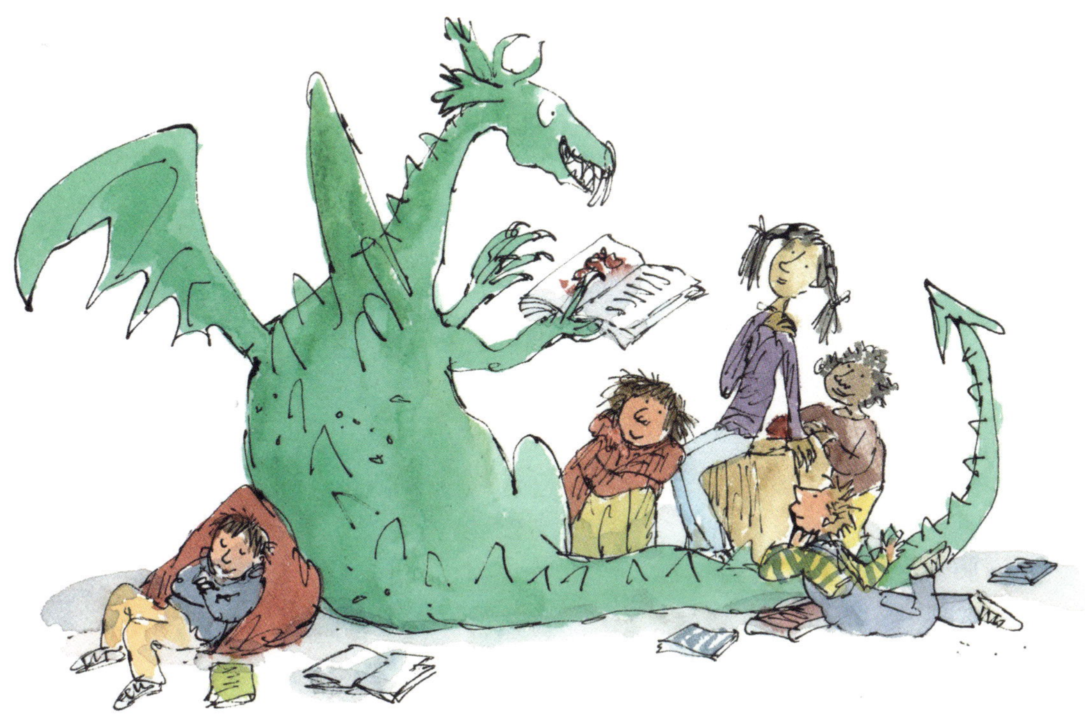

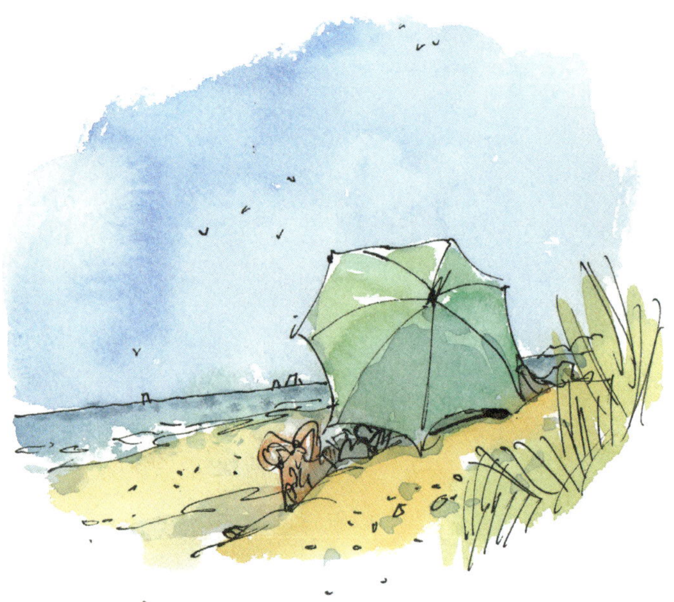

# Great Ormond Street Hospital

## *Bloomsbury*

'I was approached by a young couple (whose) son Elliot, born in Great Ormond Street Hospital, was not to survive; in order that they could be with him for the end of his short life, they found themselves lodged overnight in a room intended for some quite other purpose. Later, aware that other young parents might find themselves in a similar situation (they) asked if Great Ormond Street could find a suitable room; they would pay for its furnishing and decoration, and it would be called Elliot's Room. Having seen some of my other work for hospitals, they asked me if I could create some pictures for it. By this time the hospital projects I had worked on covered many ages and situations, but I was aware that, though I was immediately prepared to respond to this couple's positive and generous gesture, the response would have to be something of a different order. No place here for gambits of cheering up, teasing, activity and optimism. However, as with previous projects I had taken the opportunity to consult both with patients and professionals, here I had the privilege of calling on the reactions of two people with first-hand experience.

The pictures, of course, were more for the parents than for the child and it seemed best for them to be small and framed, a note of domesticity in a room otherwise containing clinical equipment.'

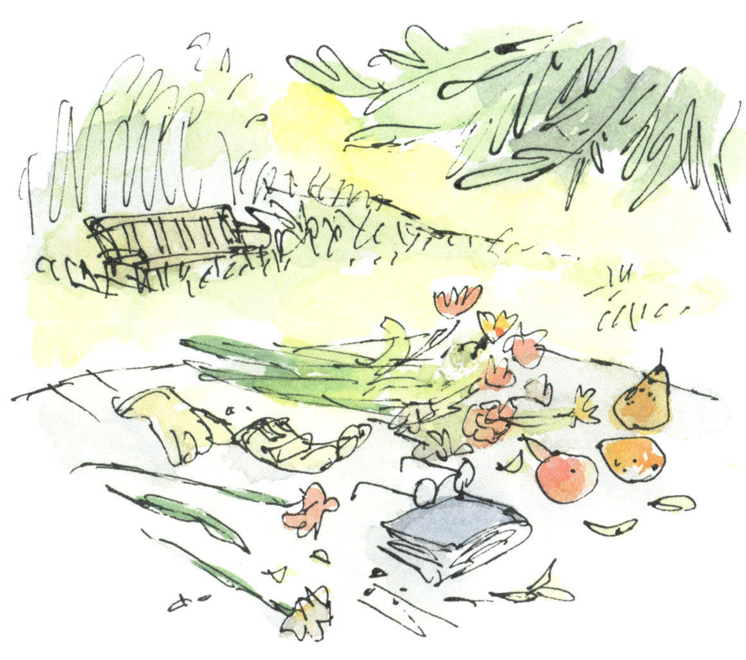

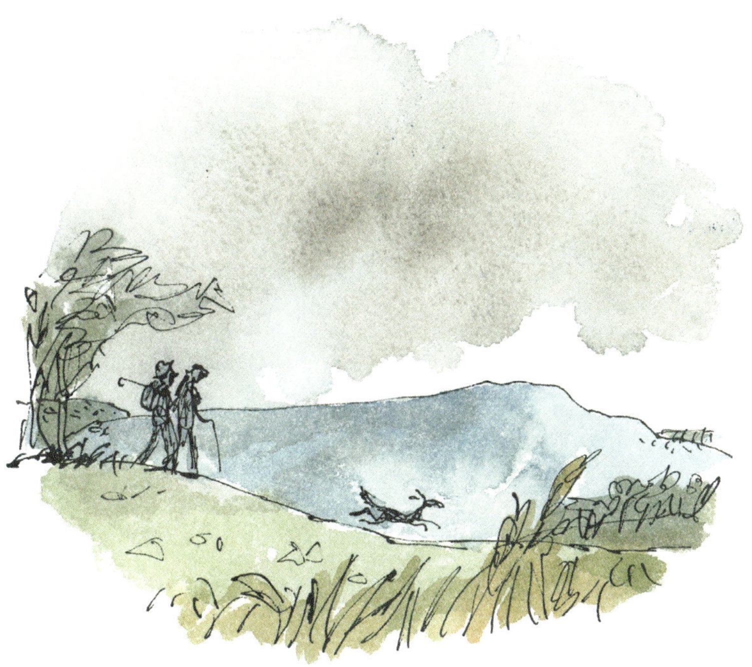

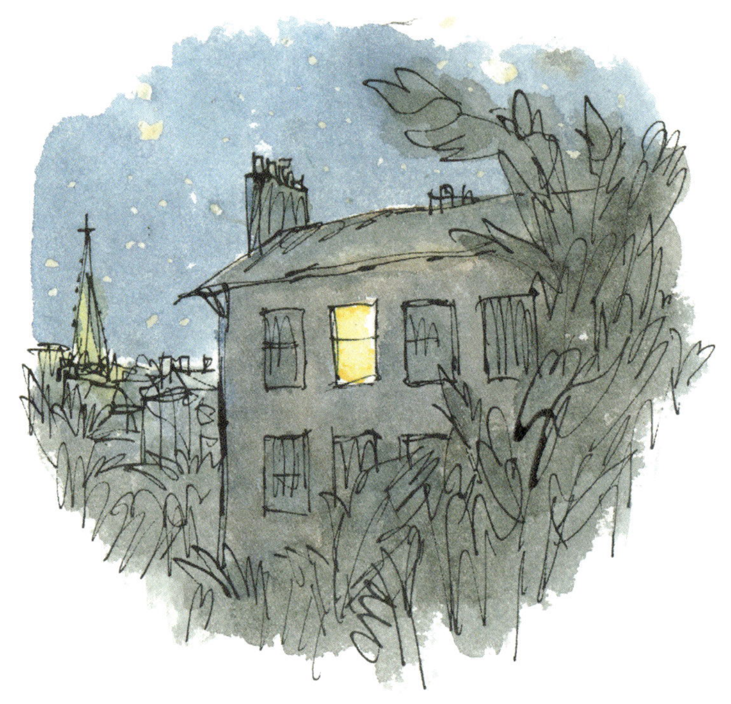

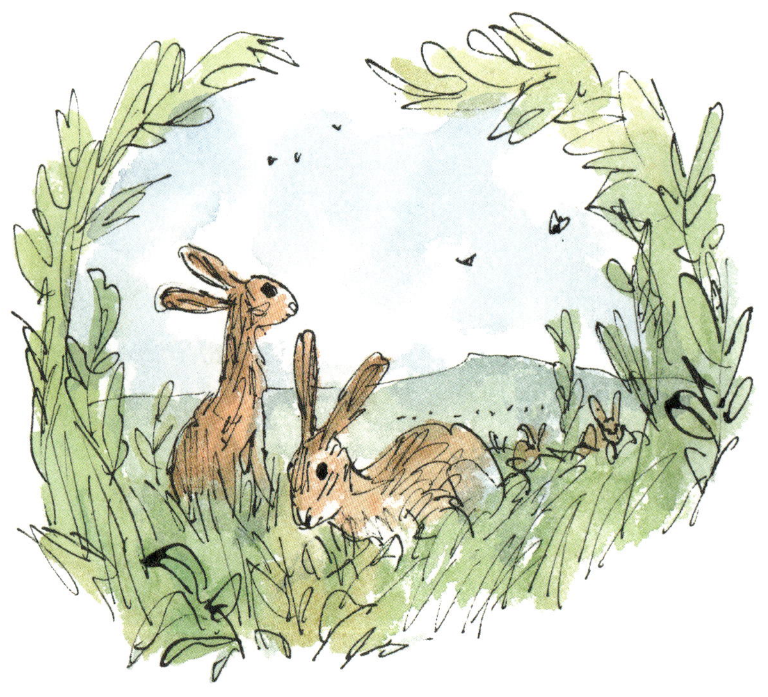

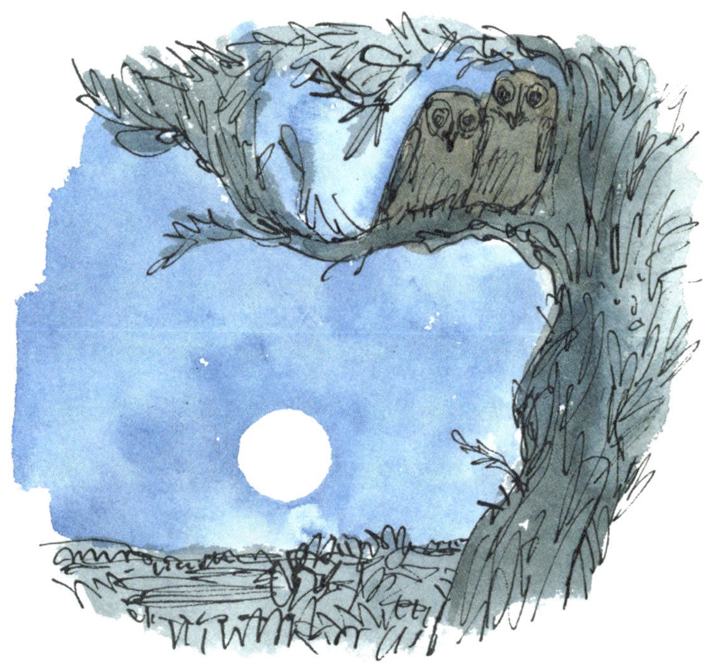

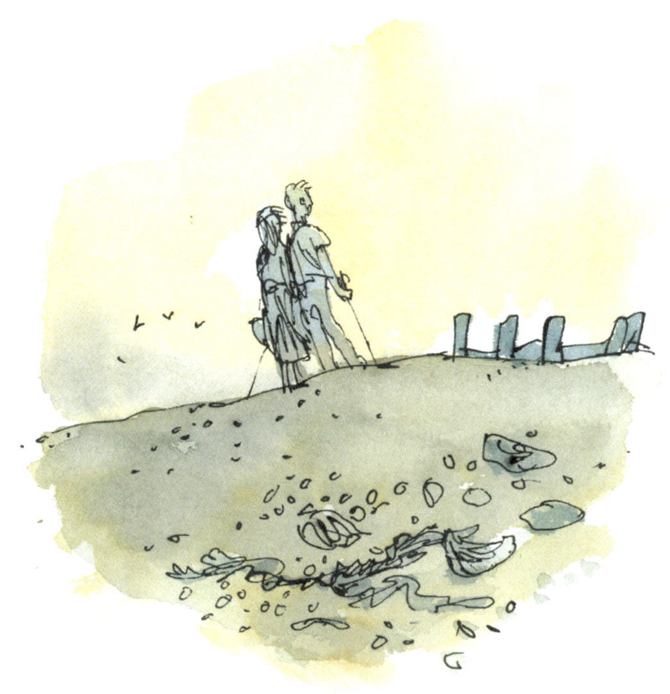

opposite & above – Elliot's Room, 2014

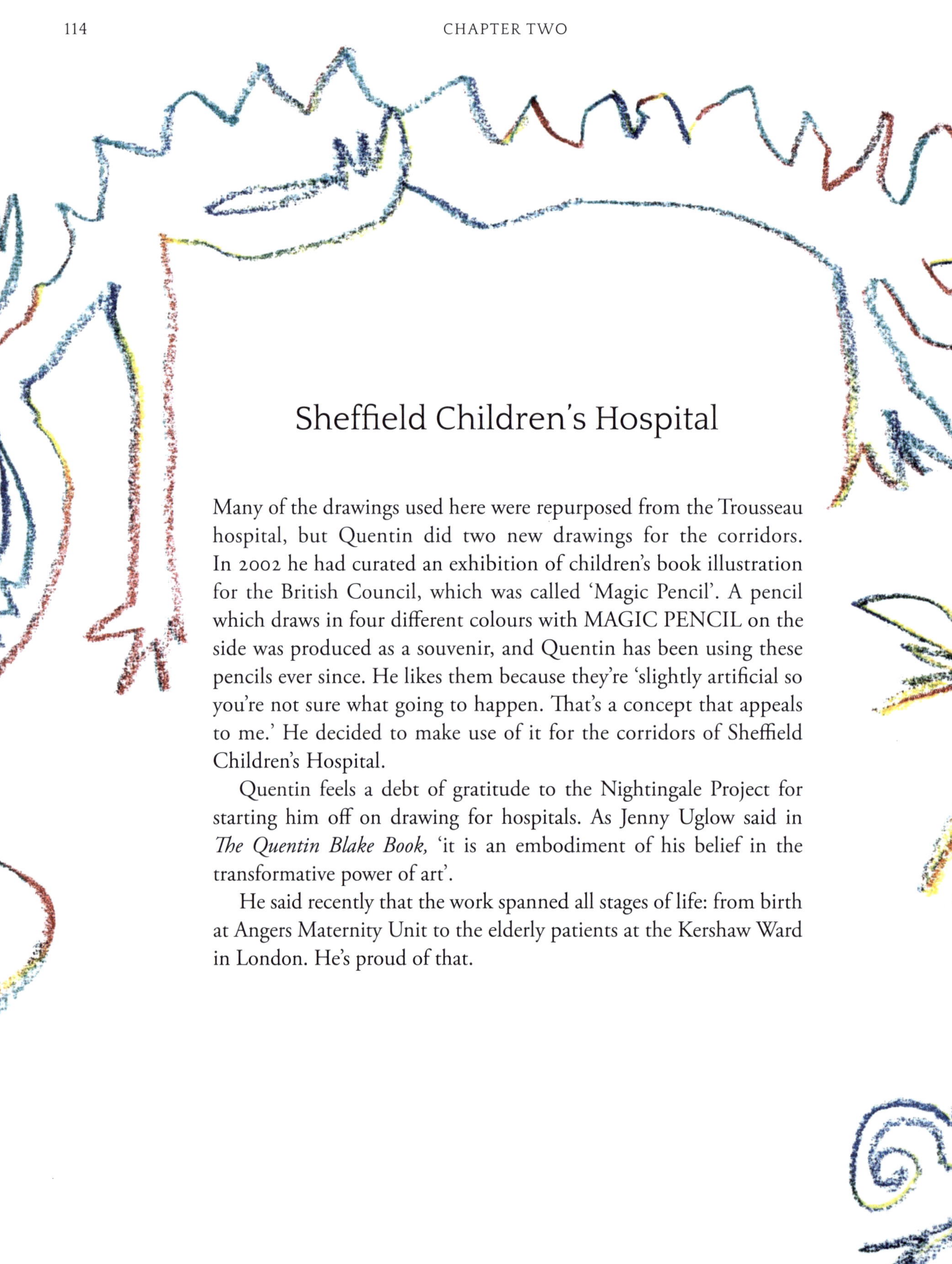

# Sheffield Children's Hospital

Many of the drawings used here were repurposed from the Trousseau hospital, but Quentin did two new drawings for the corridors. In 2002 he had curated an exhibition of children's book illustration for the British Council, which was called 'Magic Pencil'. A pencil which draws in four different colours with MAGIC PENCIL on the side was produced as a souvenir, and Quentin has been using these pencils ever since. He likes them because they're 'slightly artificial so you're not sure what going to happen. That's a concept that appeals to me.' He decided to make use of it for the corridors of Sheffield Children's Hospital.

Quentin feels a debt of gratitude to the Nightingale Project for starting him off on drawing for hospitals. As Jenny Uglow said in *The Quentin Blake Book,* 'it is an embodiment of his belief in the transformative power of art'.

He said recently that the work spanned all stages of life: from birth at Angers Maternity Unit to the elderly patients at the Kershaw Ward in London. He's proud of that.

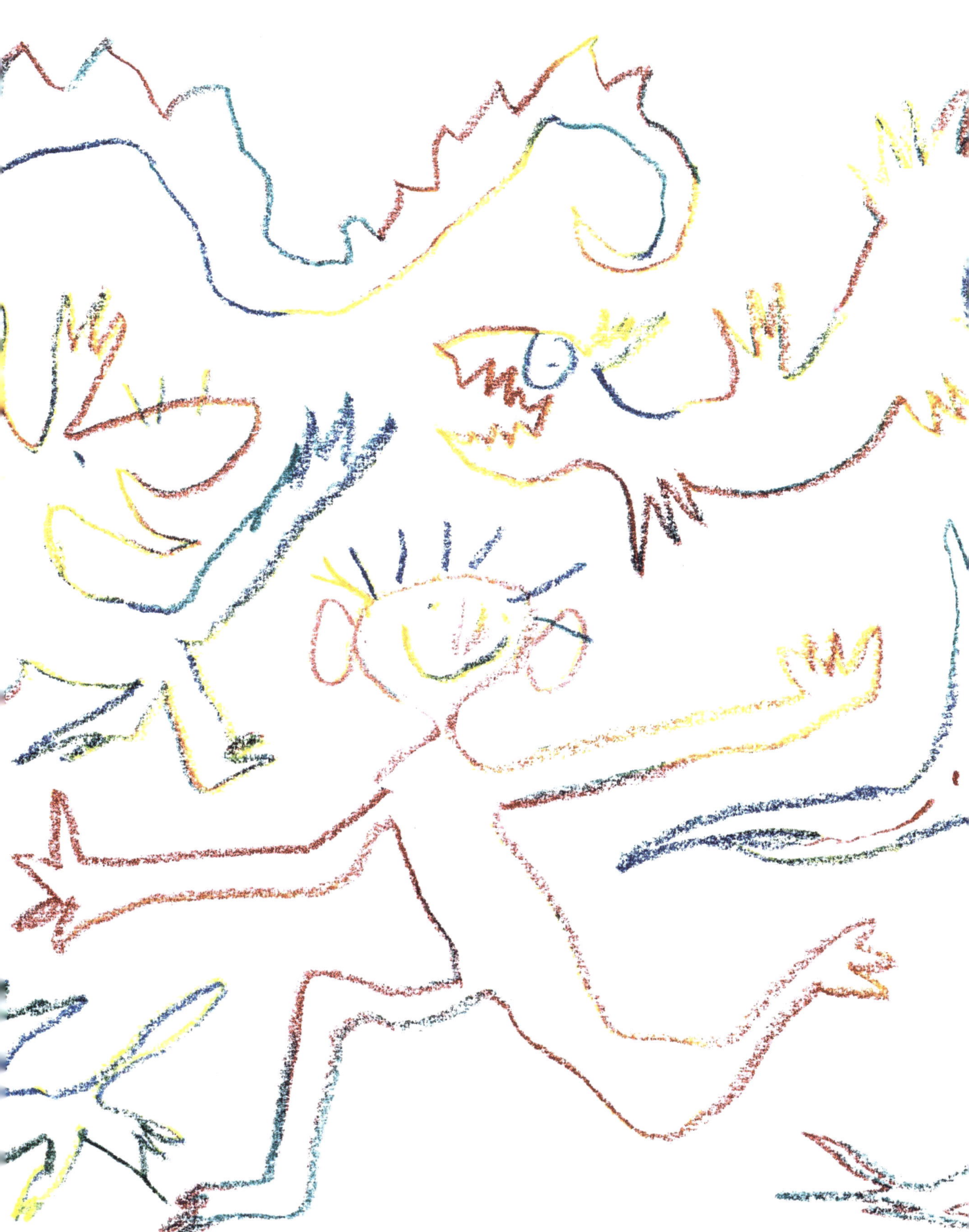

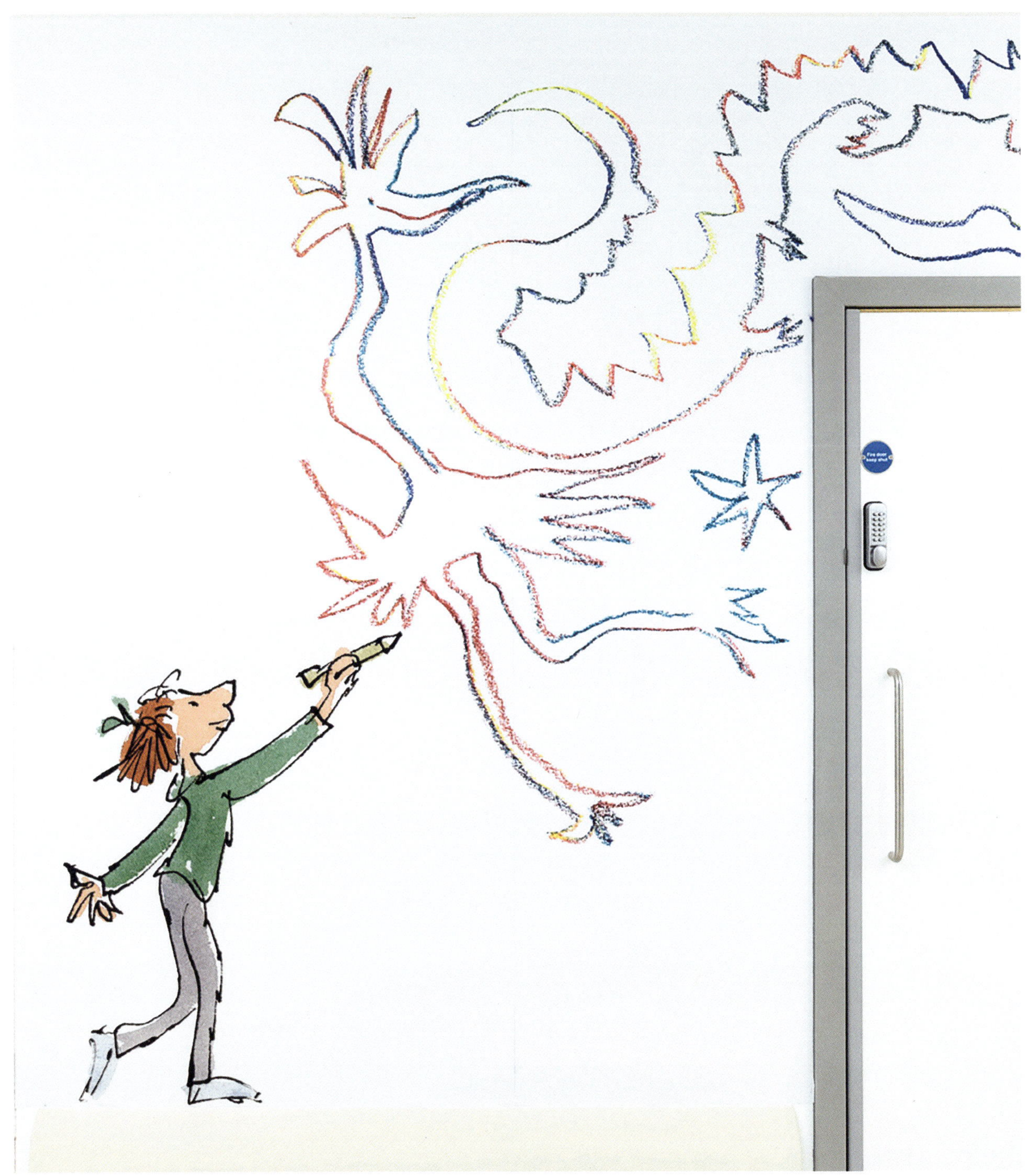

ABOVE & OPPOSITE – Sheffield Children's Hospital, 2019

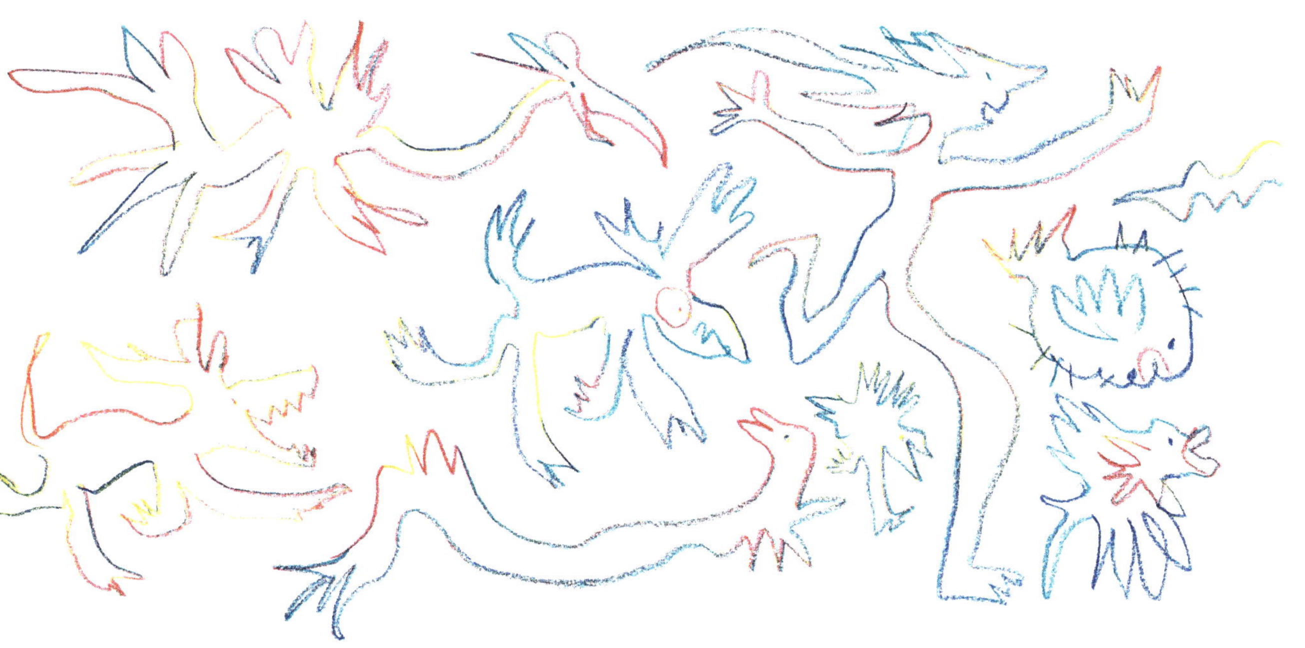

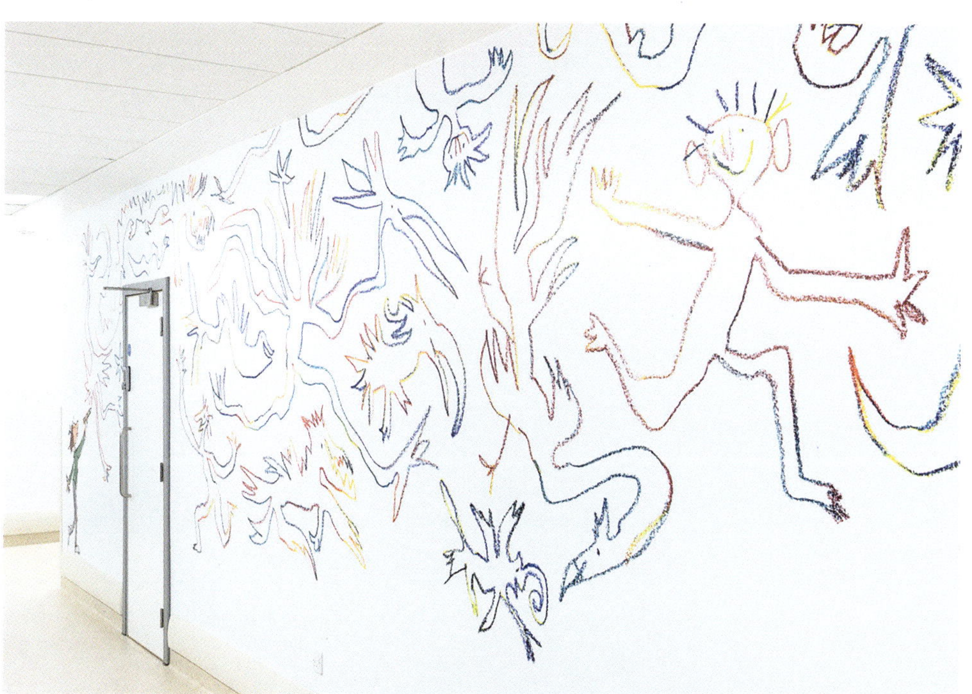

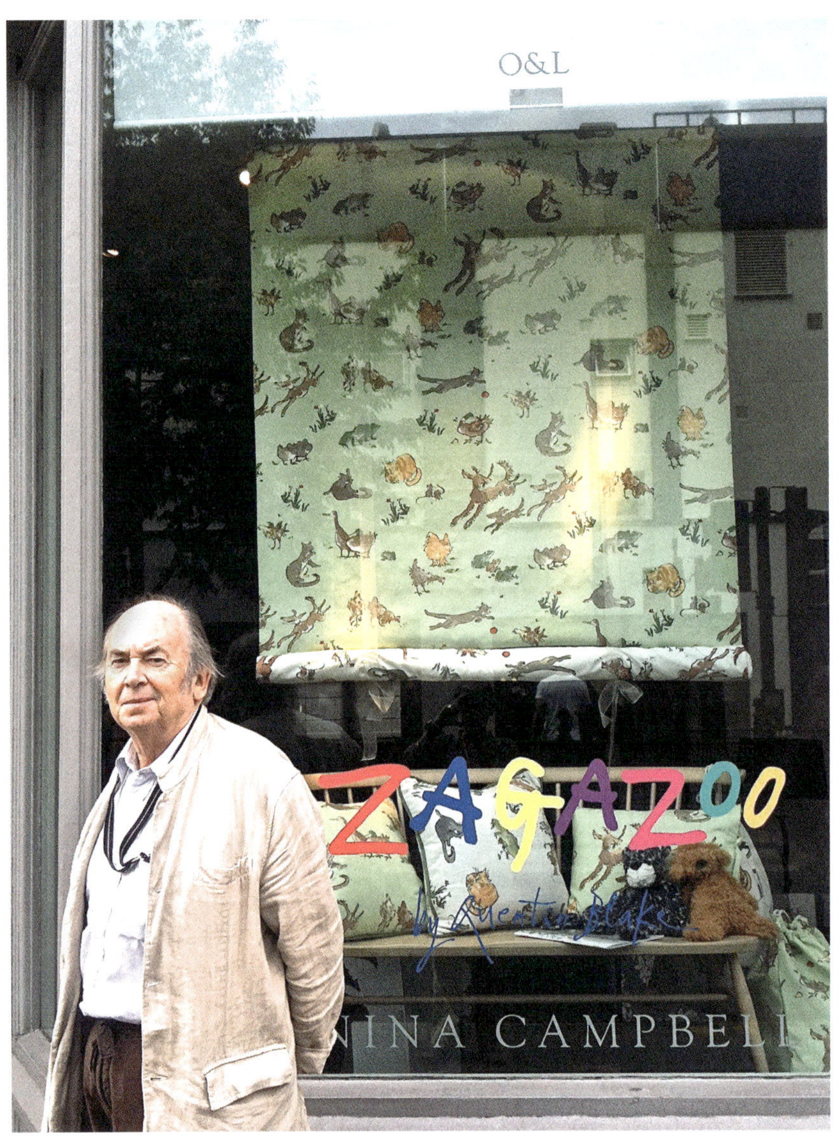



## Osborne & Little

Osborne & Little produced a range of wallpapers and textiles; the designs used illustrations from his books *Cockatoos* and *All Join In*.

*Chapter Three*

# Companies

Quentin has often turned down commercial commissions other than for books, magazines or newspapers, as he felt that they could be construed as advertising. But he has accepted some because of the subject matter and the appeal of the commission, or the person asking him.

**Laurent-Perrier**

'Early in 2016 I was approached by Laurent-Perrier, the champagne company, to find out if I could make drawings of three hotels and a restaurant that were their clients. These images were to be used in press advertisements. I am not normally enthusiastic about advertising, and gave up working for it many years ago. However, it was interesting to be asked to depict architecture, something I am not often asked to but enjoy when I am. There is also the possible embarrassment of promoting a product you don't like or even disapprove of, but this was not the case here.'

As it happens Quentin likes champagne very much and was paid in cases of it.

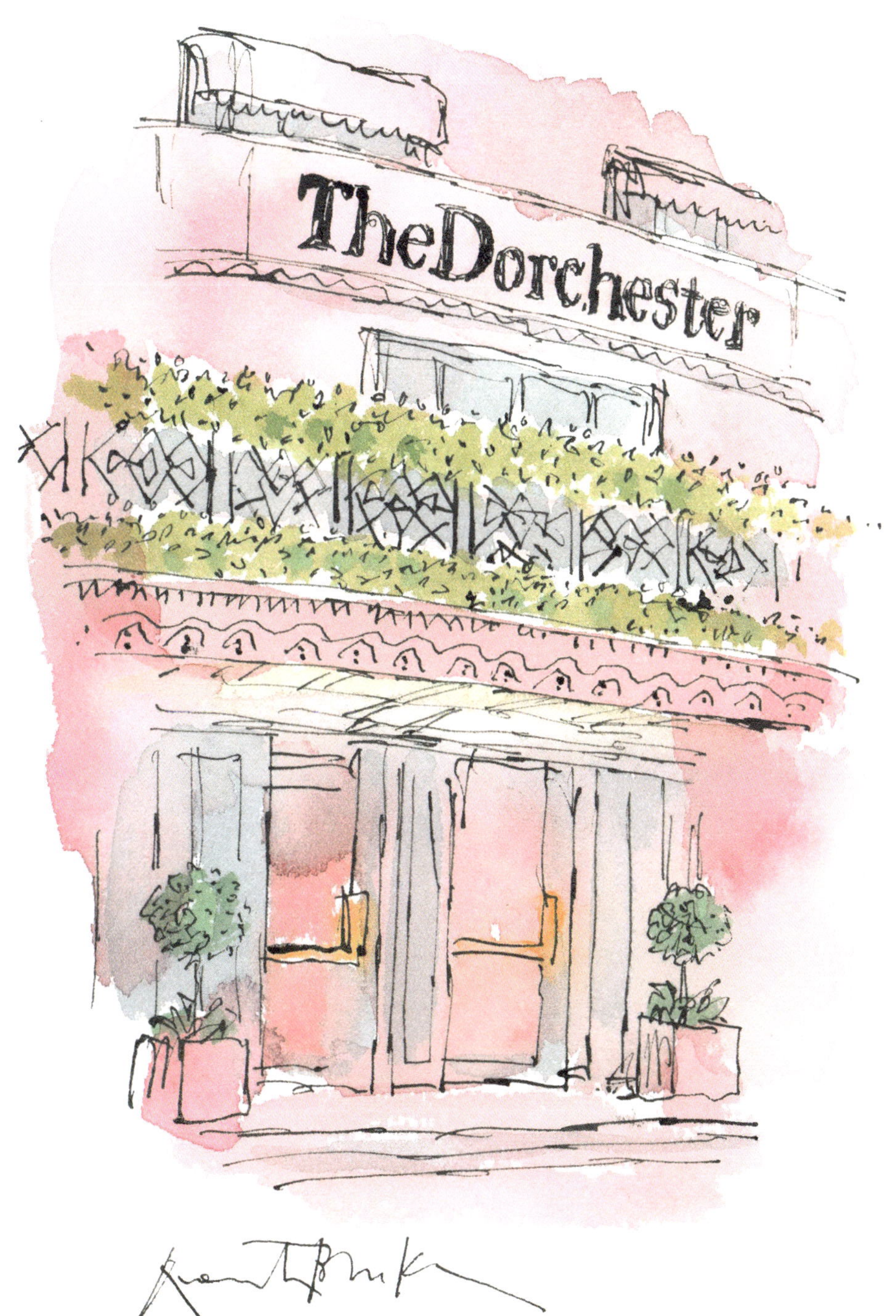
TheDorchester

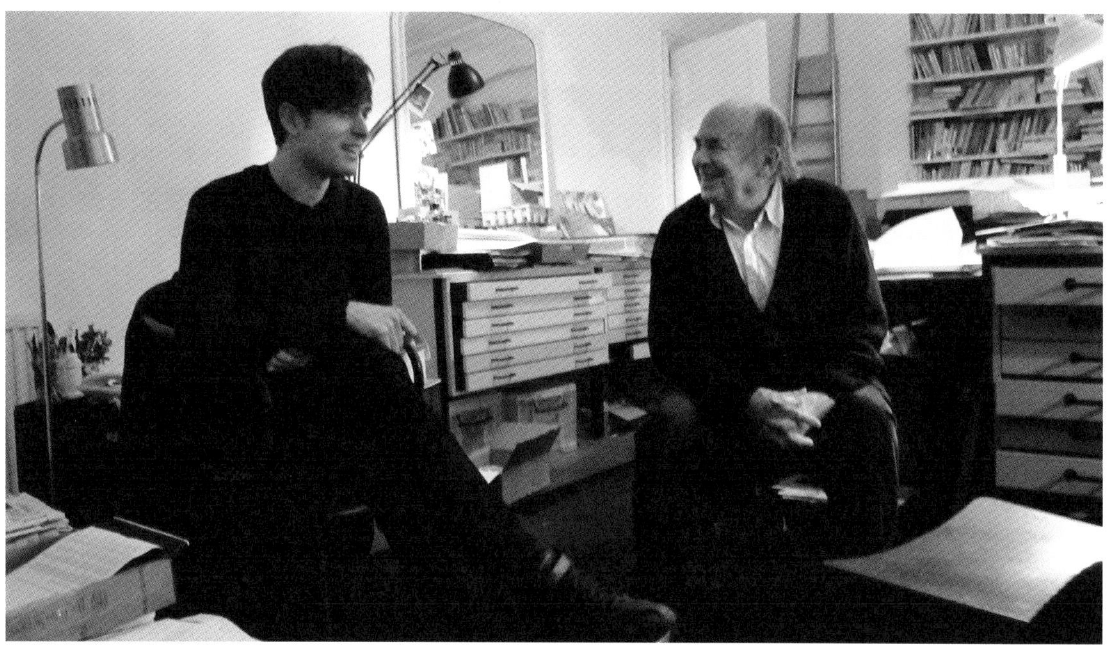

## James Blake

Lexi Burgess's friend, the musician James Blake, asked him who he could suggest to illustrate his new album, *The Colour in Anything*. Lexi suggested Quentin and brought him to the studio, making an unlikely pair: the younger Blake is tall and rangy while the older Blake is small and round.

'I have very little understanding of music, but there was no mistaking the atmosphere of James Blake's. On his previous album I was also able to see a photograph of him walking towards the spectator. I took that characteristic silhouette and transferred it to an imaginary landscape, with crows and women in the trees. Once again, the work was required to appear in different sizes: on the digital recording and on hoardings in London and New York. The vinyl sleeve was followed by the poster for Blake's American tour. I supplied a drawing of Blake at the piano, and a dark scene of various underwater life (one of two of the women seemed to have got down from the trees to join the sharks), which Burgess Studio organized beautifully with light rising from the open top of the grand piano. The poster exists in two sizes, large and enormous.'

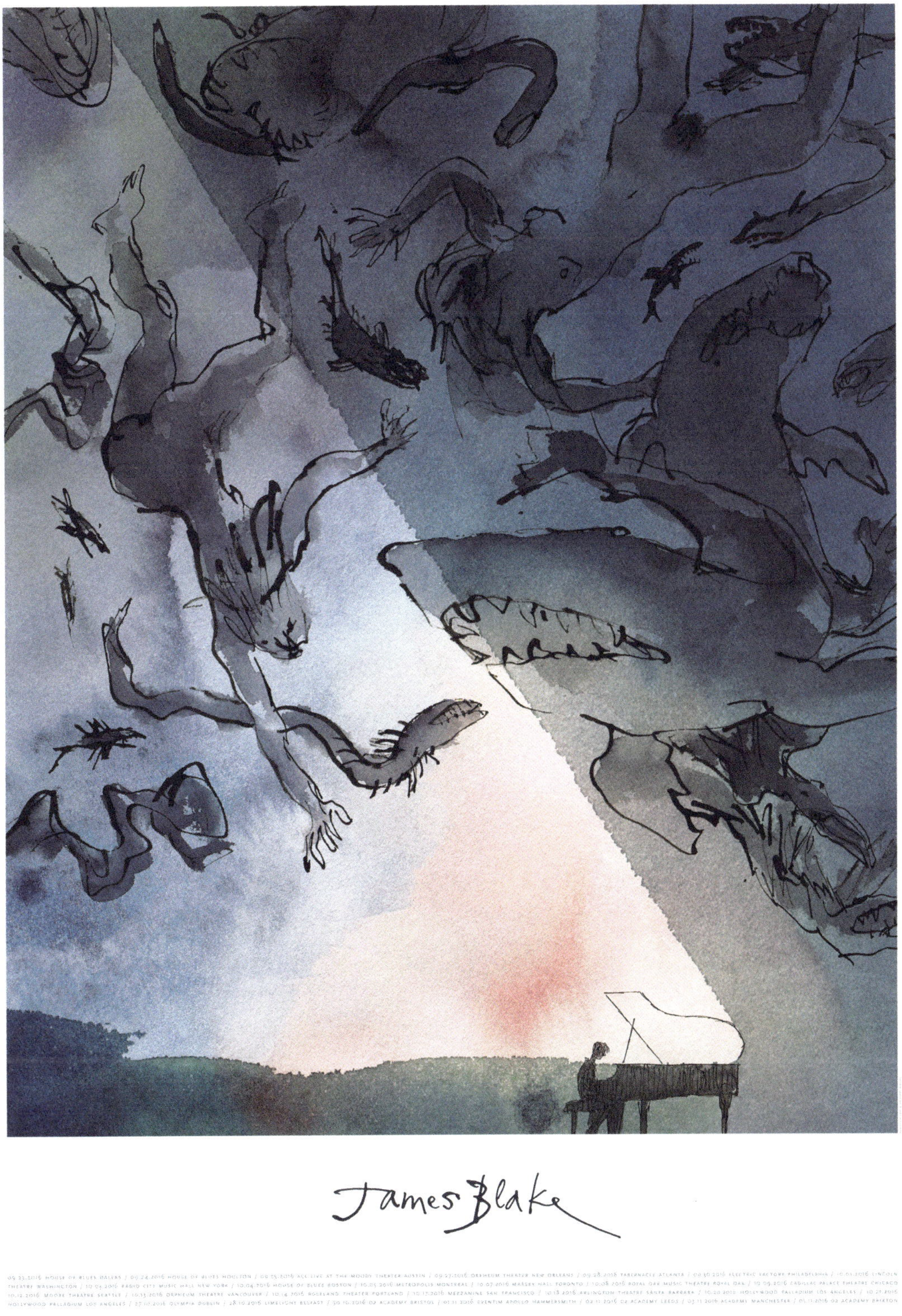

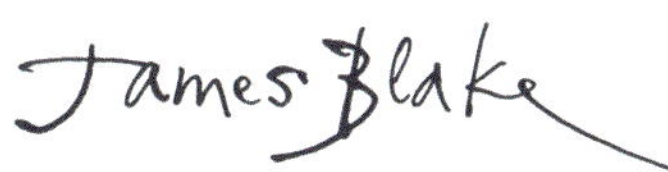
James Blake

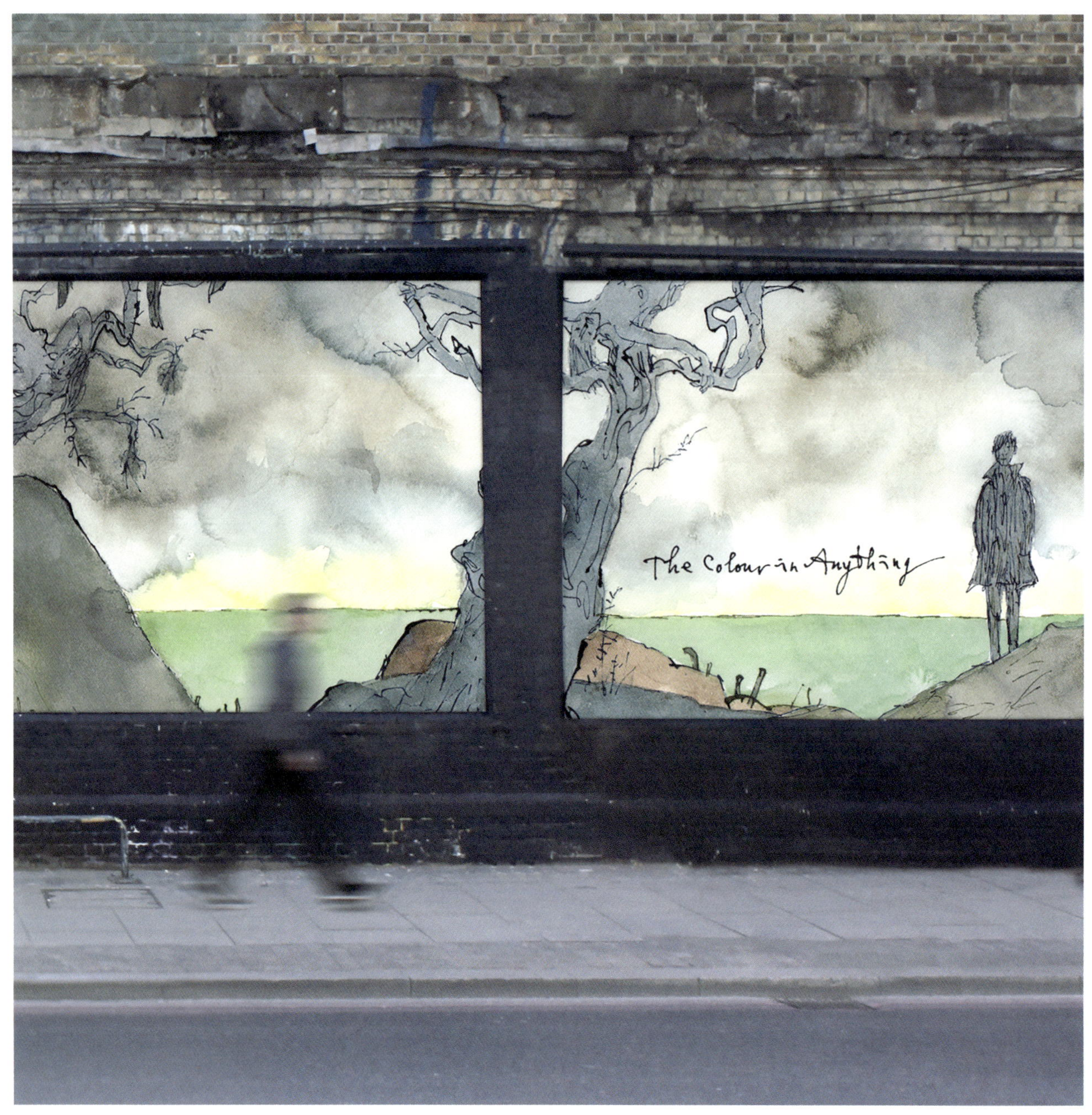


above & opposite – Illustration for James Blake's, *The Colour in Everything*, Vinyl Artwork, 2016

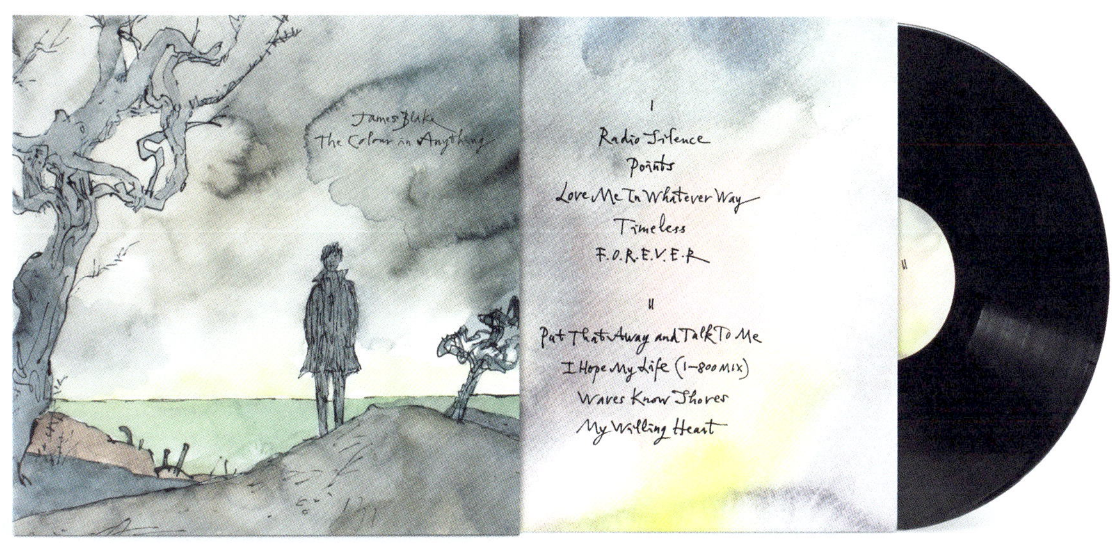
James Blake
The Colour in Anything

I
Radio Silence
Points
Love Me In Whatever Way
Timeless
F.O.R.E.V.E.R

II
Put That Away and Talk To Me
I Hope My Life (1–800 MIX)
Waves Know Shores
My Willing Heart

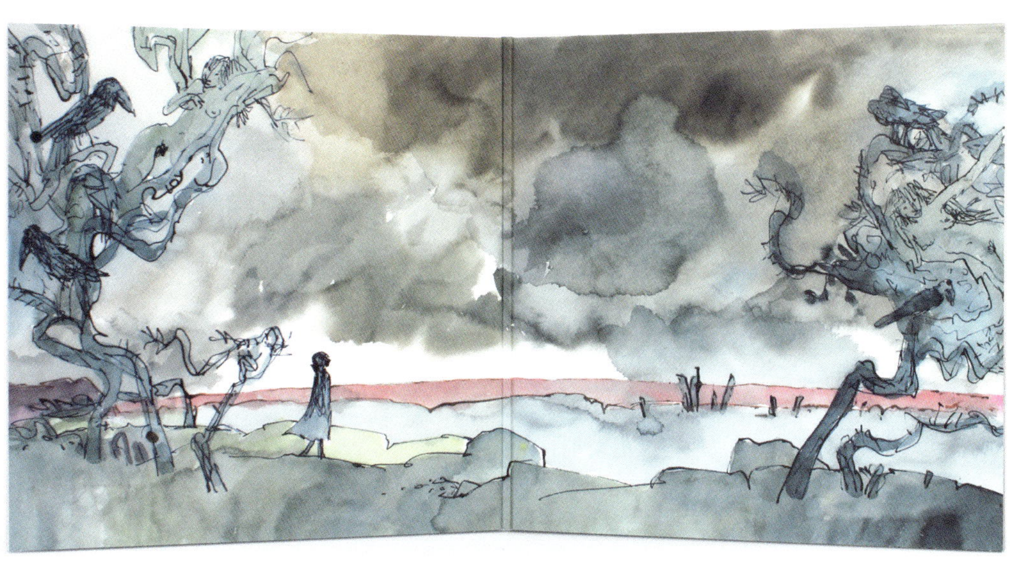

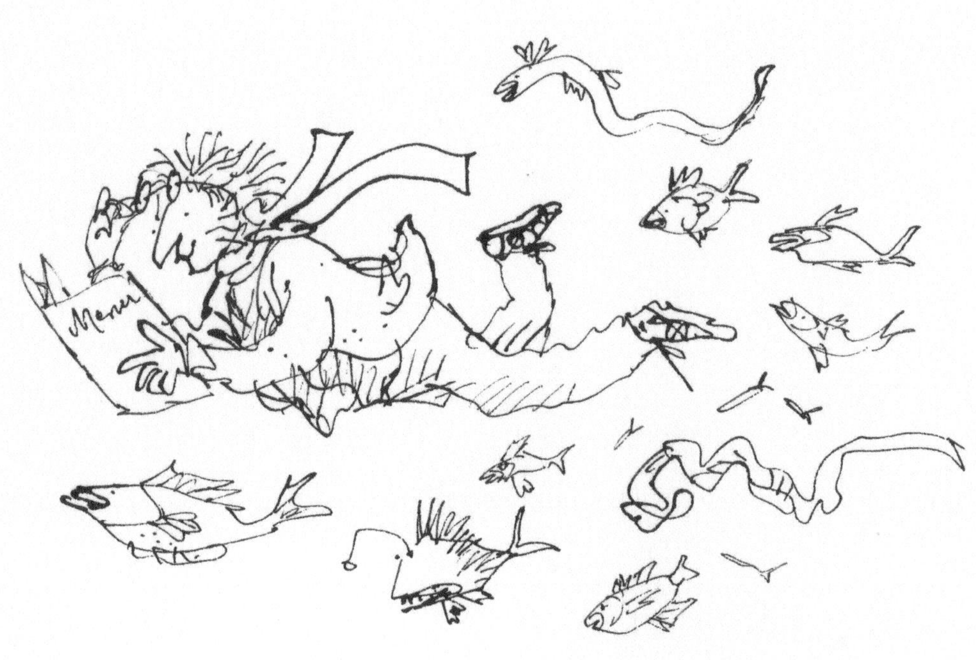

## J. Sheekey's Restaurant

Quentin loves drawing (and eating) fish, and by 2017 he'd had some experience drawing various forms of aquatic life for his hospital series. So when J. Sheekey's in London approached him to provide a set of drawings for the renaming of their oyster bar, he accepted and asked to be paid for the job in free meals.

'Fish and people underwater were already at the tip of my pen and so I was able to depict, swimming and accompanied by fish, five representative individuals. A waiter and a chef were there, as well as a young lady raising a glass of white wine to her lips, and a substantial businessman raising an oyster to his. Sheekey's is in the heart of theatreland, so I drew a lightly bohemian character who I hoped might look as though he was in some way involved in the theatre (actor? director? designer?). At any rate, he was the one chosen to appear on the plates; the only disadvantage, apparently, was that the clients tended to steal them. I have to regard this as some kind of success.'

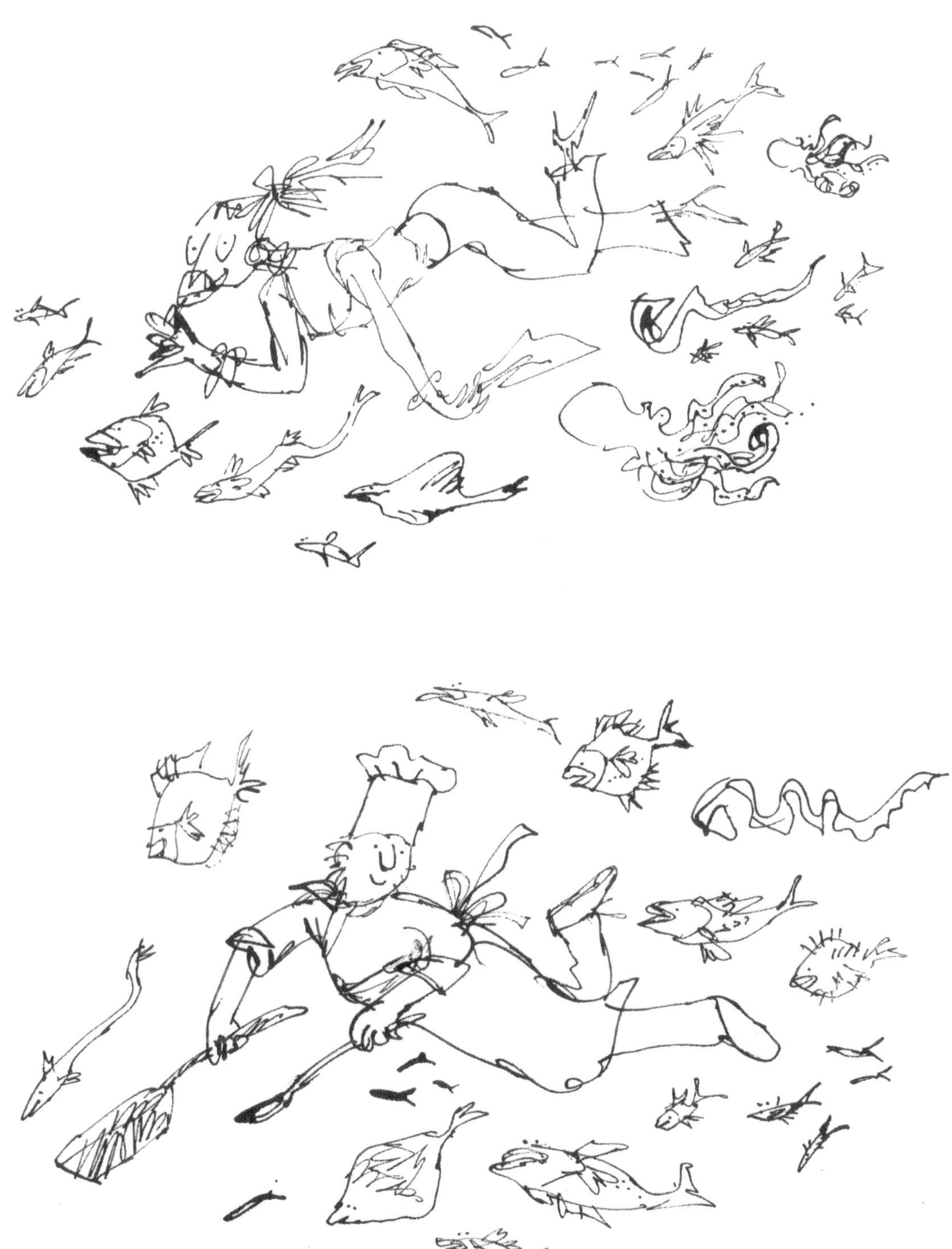

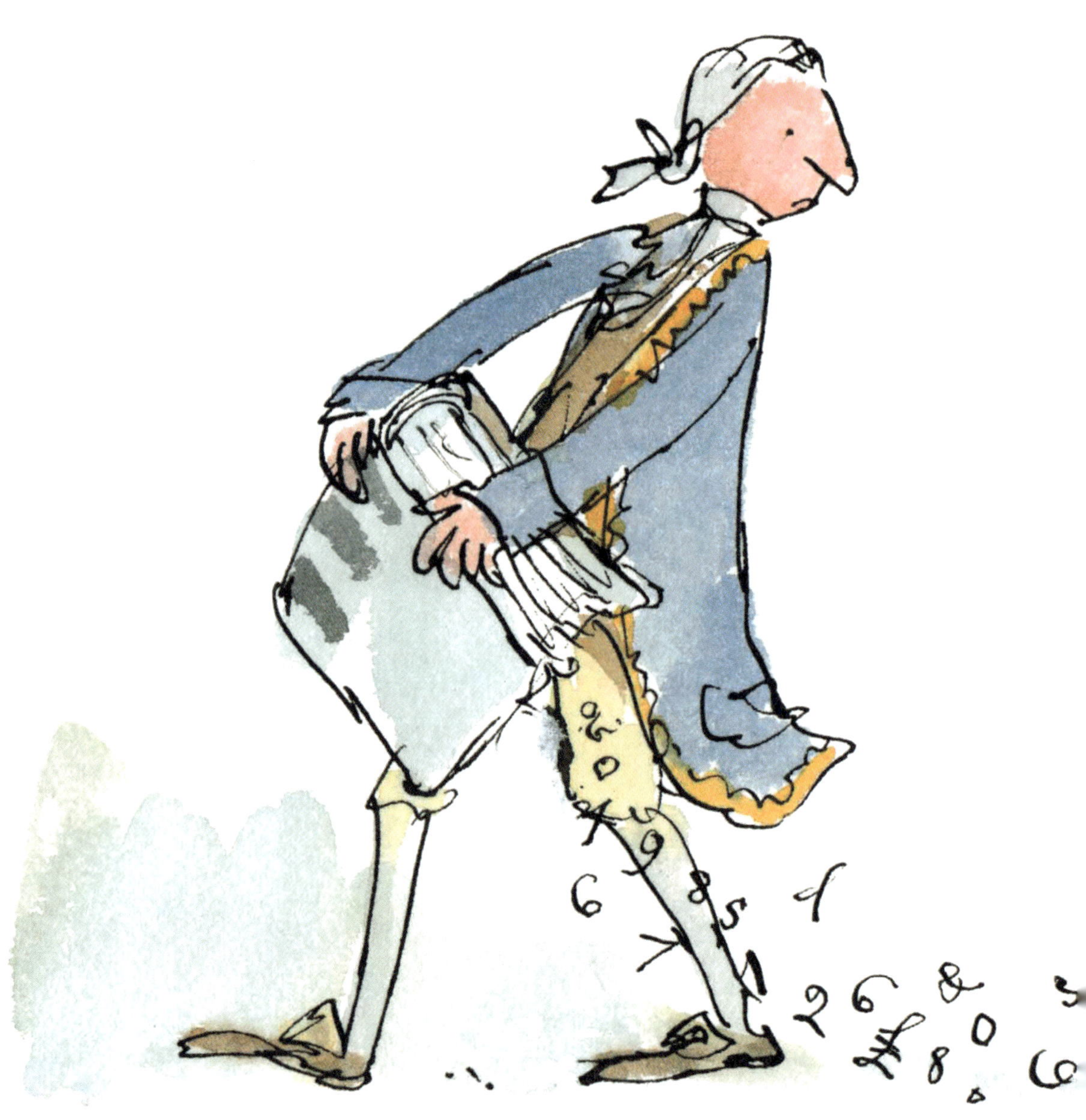

## Hoare's Bank

'It's a private bank and has the interesting distinction of having belonged to the same family since the end of the seventeenth century…. In the main building in Fleet Street each of the various meeting rooms has been given its own identity. I was invited to illustrate one such room. Hoare's Bank still owns all its ledgers, with a distinctive black and white binding in vellum, so I put forward the idea of a Ledger Room.

Though I use the identifiable contemporary binding of the ledgers, the drawings relate to different stages in the history of the firm.'

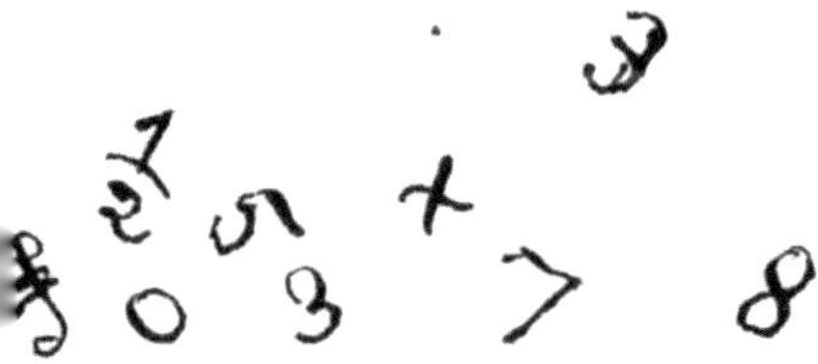

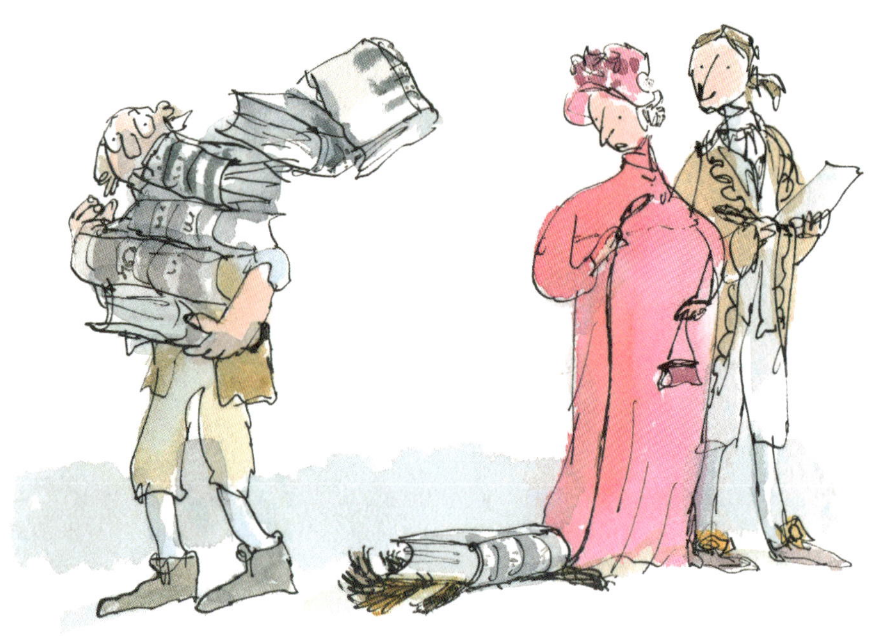

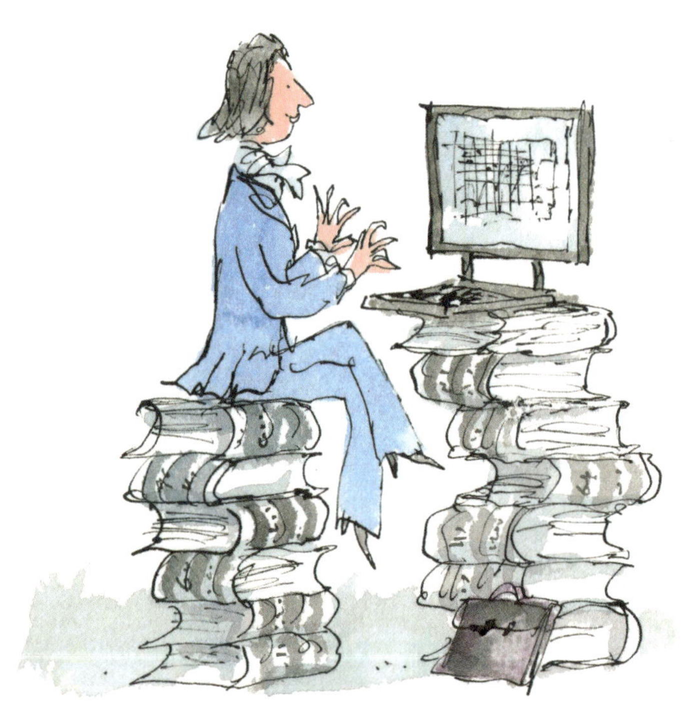

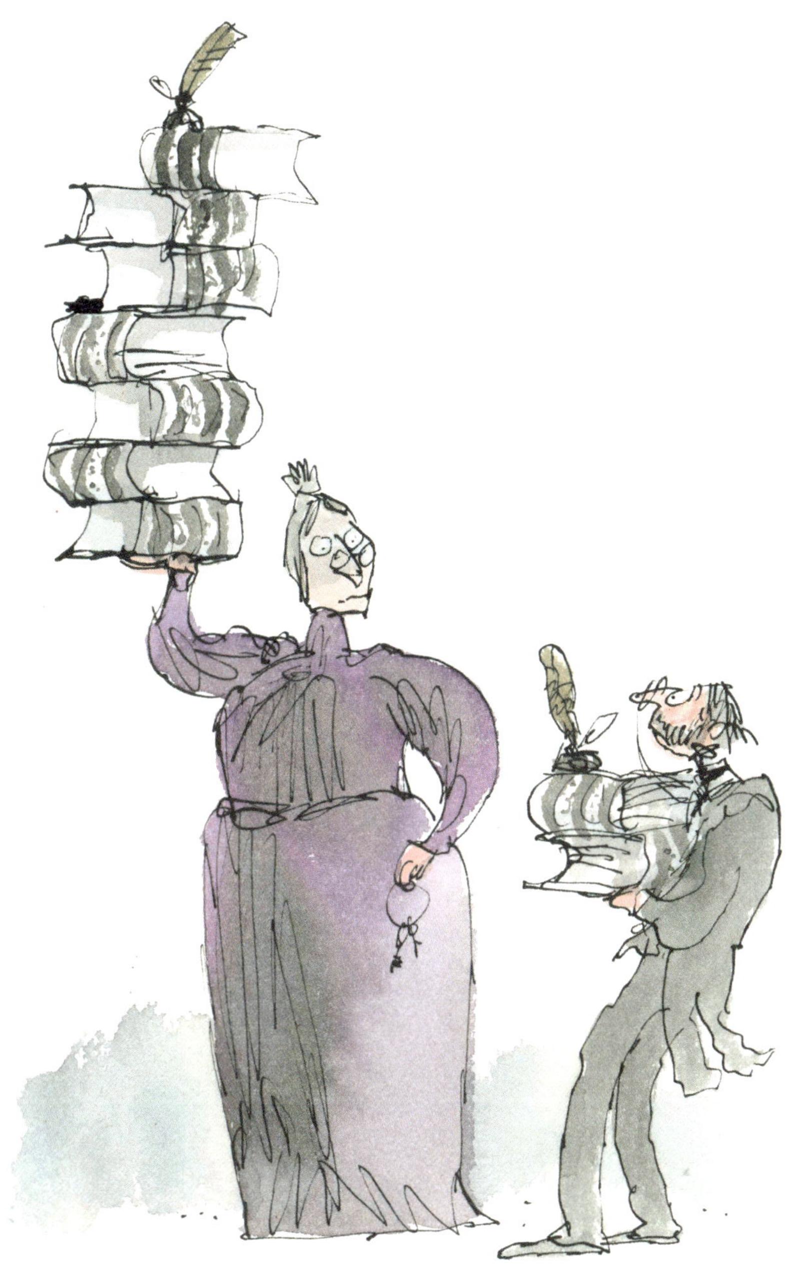

OPPOSITE & ABOVE – *Illustration for Hoare's Bank,* 2014

# Livingstone Whisky

## *The Macbeth Collection*

Lexi Burgess has designed packaging for the collectable whisky market for some time and had become fascinated by the industry. So he set up Livingstone:

'I have always held an ambition to release some whiskies myself. The history of distilling in Scotland can often read like the plot of *Macbeth,* and at some point, I realised the play would be the perfect structure for a whisky collection, with all forty-two characters cast as different whiskies from the length and breadth of Scotland. Having worked with Quentin for twenty years as a designer, of course I wanted him to illustrate the characters. At first he was reluctant; I don't think he could see a way to enjoy drawing lots of men in kilts. But when I suggested they might be birds, rather than people, he said he would think about it. Our conversation took place in his studio in the afternoon, and first thing the following morning he rang to say that he had woken at 4 A.M. and produced a full set of roughs in bed.

As soon as I saw the drawings, created in a fine pen on some ancient notepaper, I knew the collection would be a success. The illustrations were so engaging… I've always loved Quentin's drawings of malevolent characters because they retain their sense of joy. I'm not only convinced that the murderer intends to kill me, but he looks like he's going to have fun doing it. The three witches are the personification of evil; Shakespeare makes it very clear they are having a good time, and Quentin does too, drawing them dancing around the cauldron together.

*Lexi Burgess,* 2024

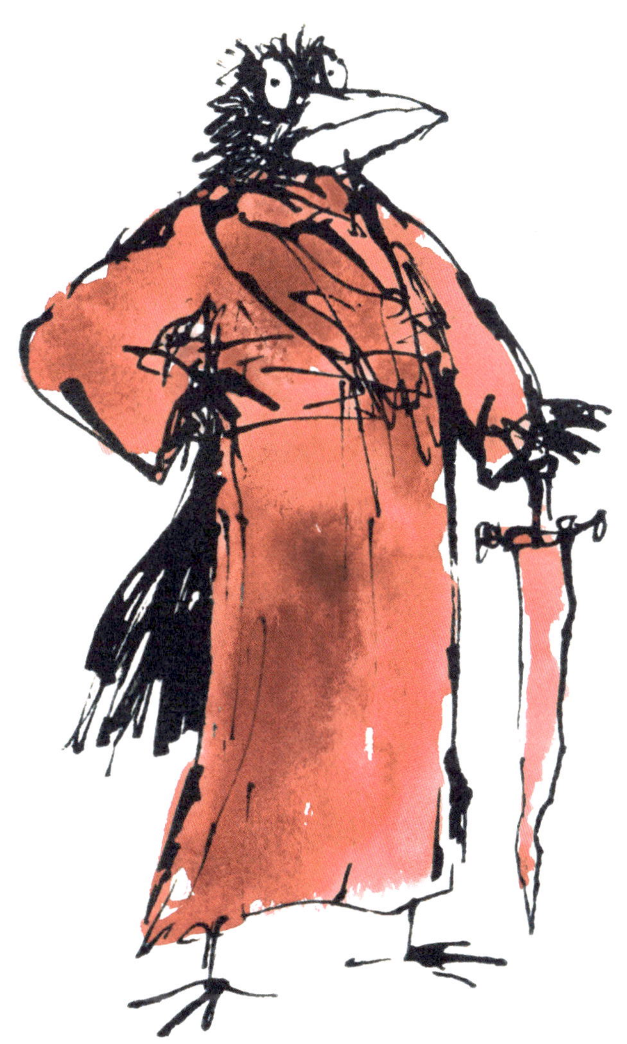

*Macbeth*, The Macbeth Collection, 2022

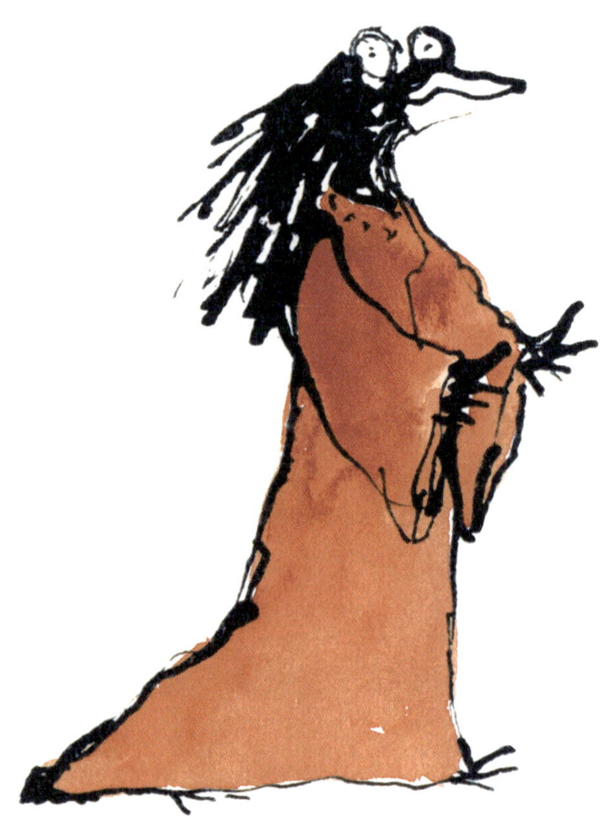

*Lady Macbeth*, The Macbeth Collection, 2022

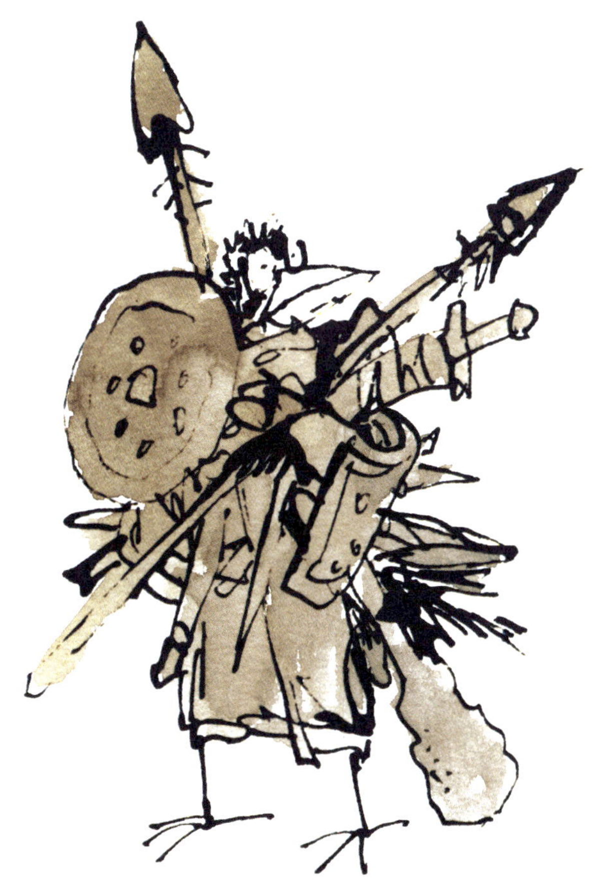

*Seyton*, The Macbeth Collection, 2022

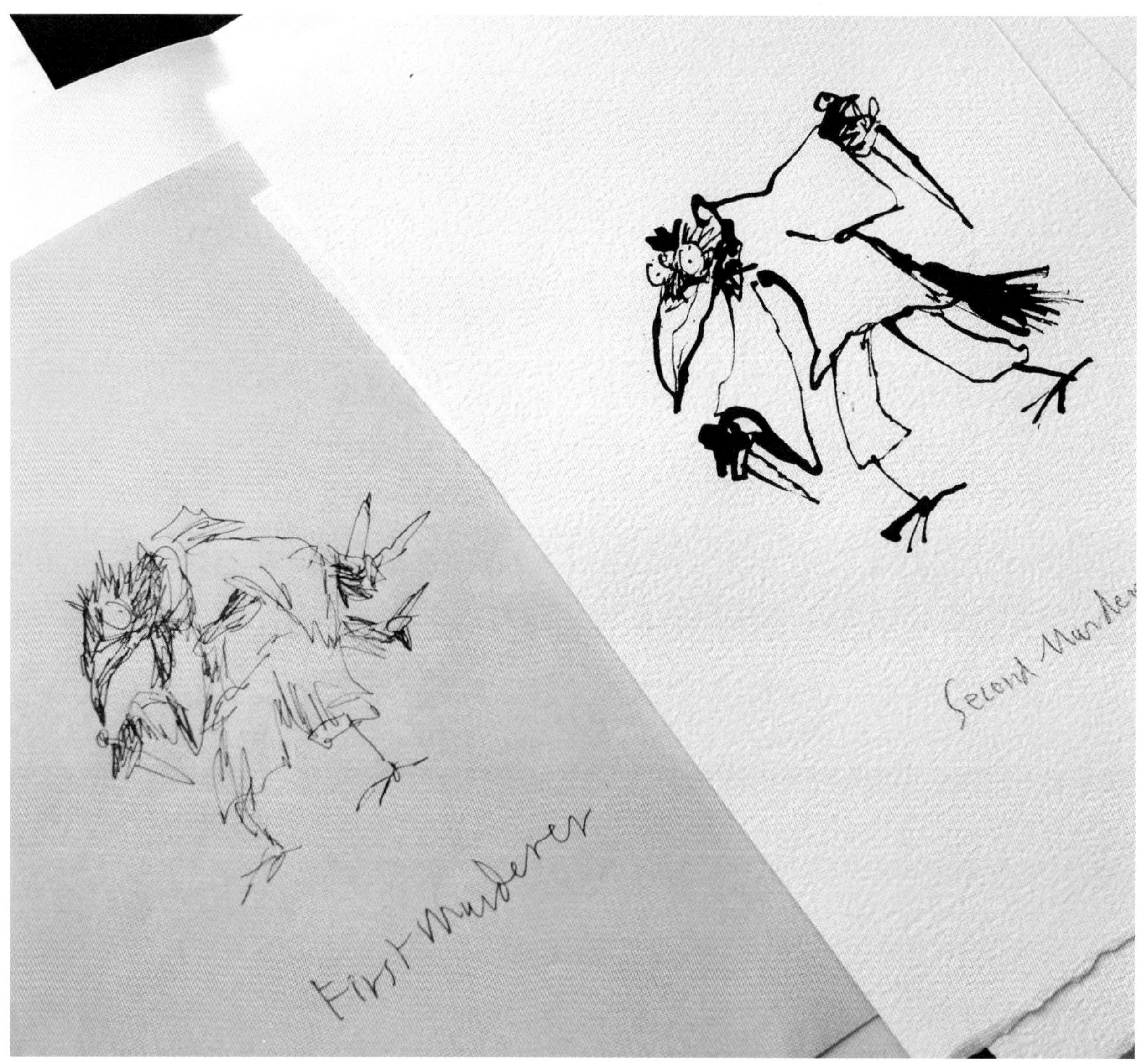
First Murderer
Second Murderer

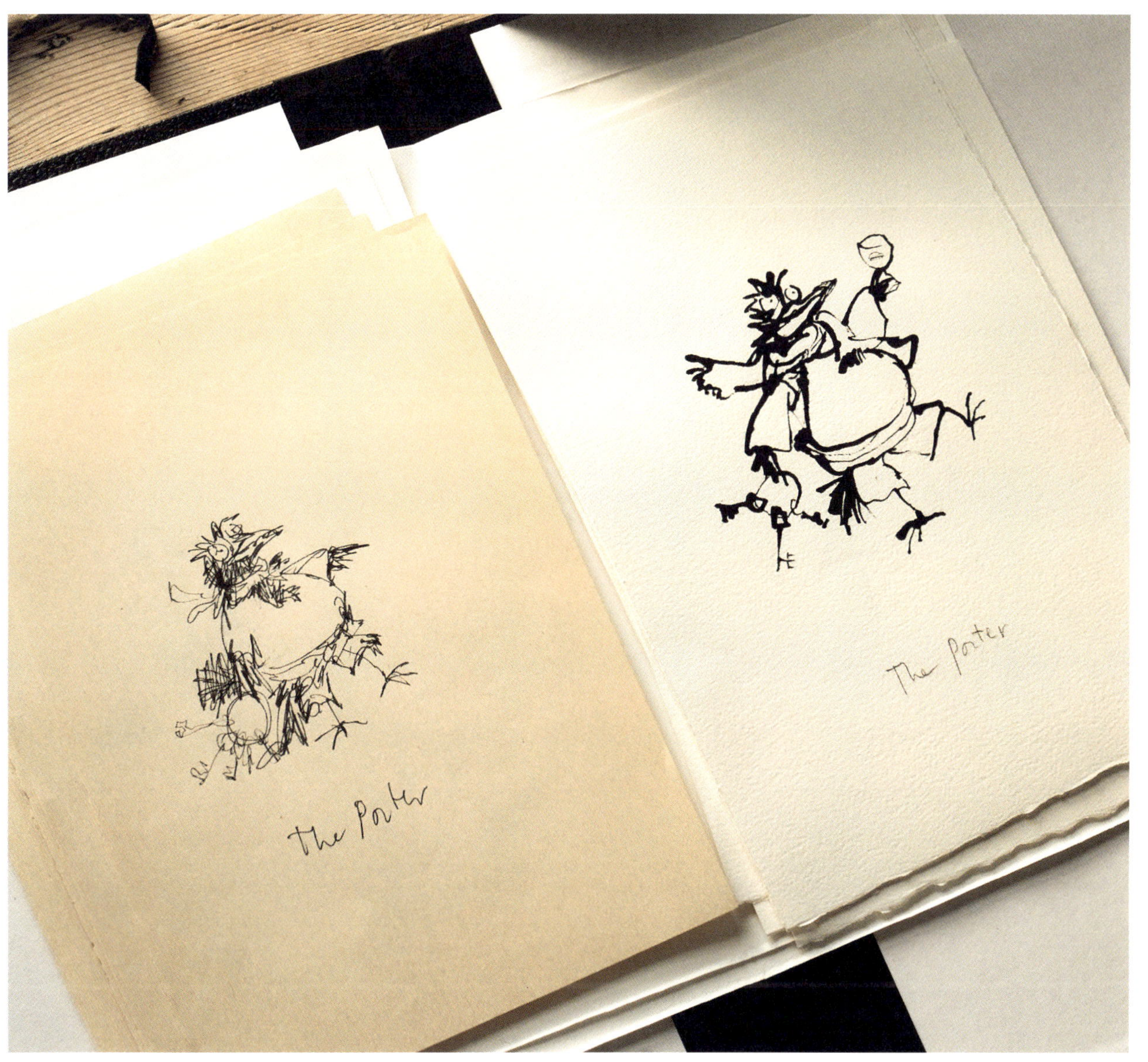

OPPOSITE & ABOVE – *The Macbeth Collection*, Drafts, 2022

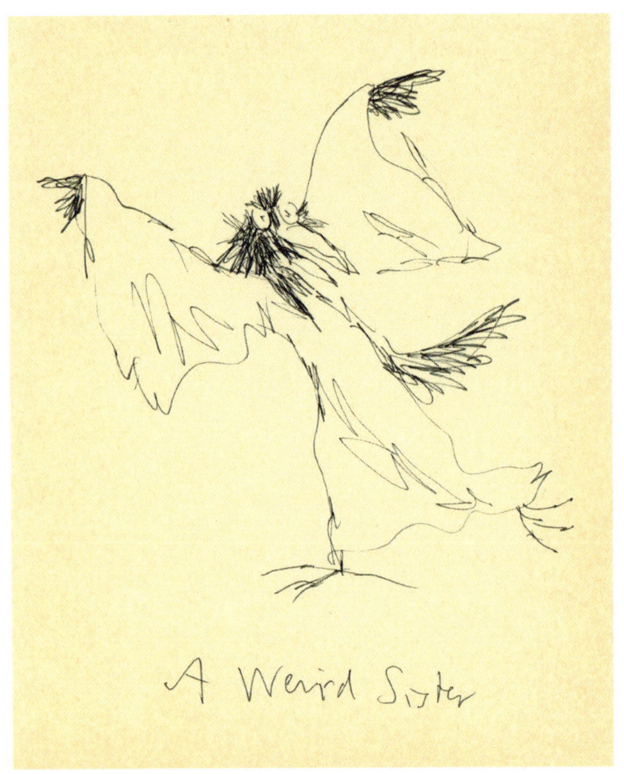


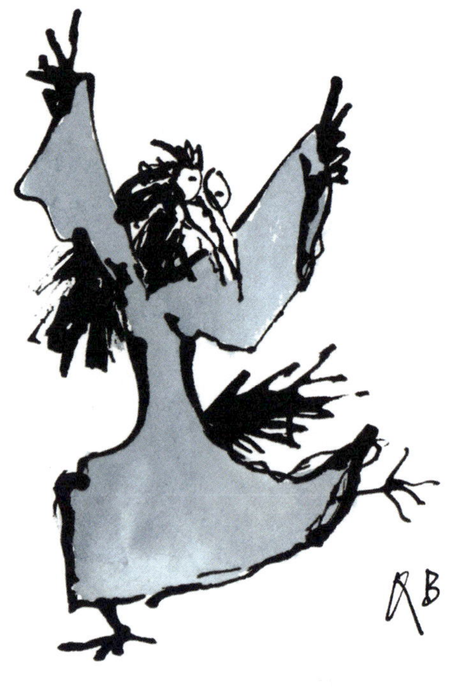

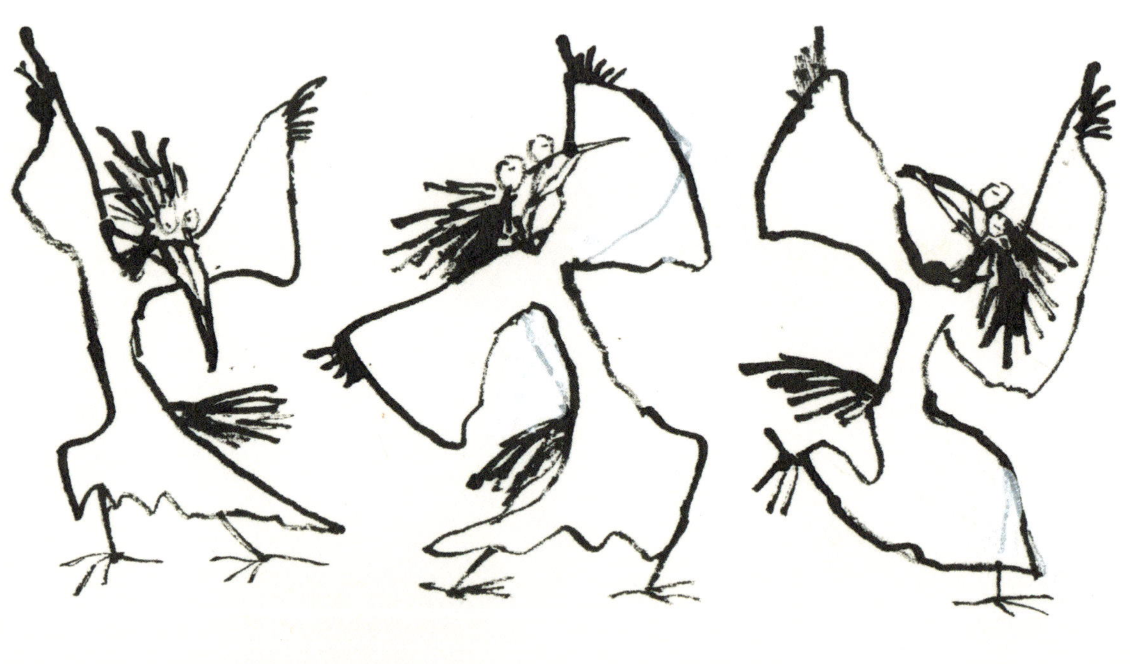

*The Macbeth Collection*, Witches Series, 2022

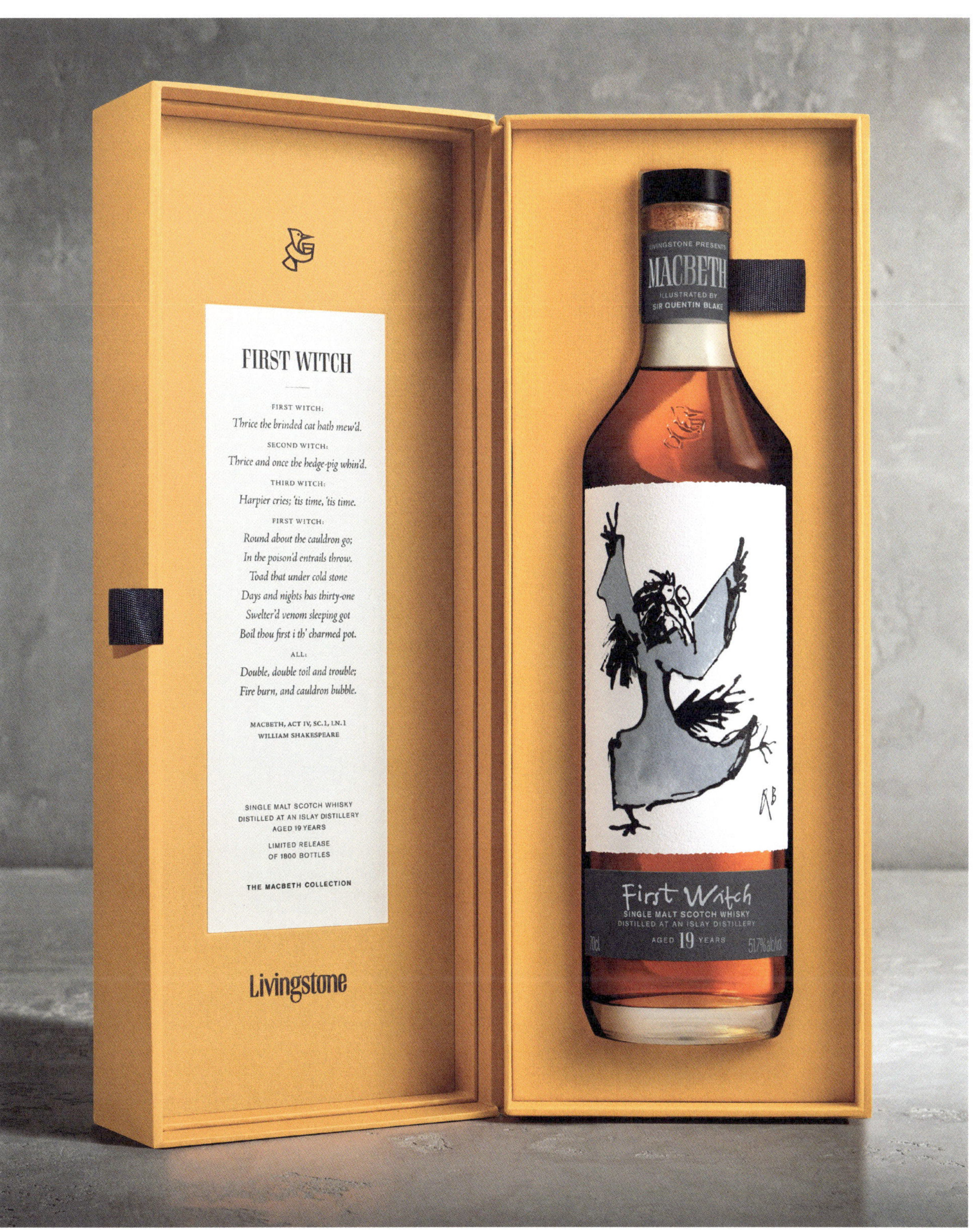


*The Macbeth Collection*, Packaging, 2022

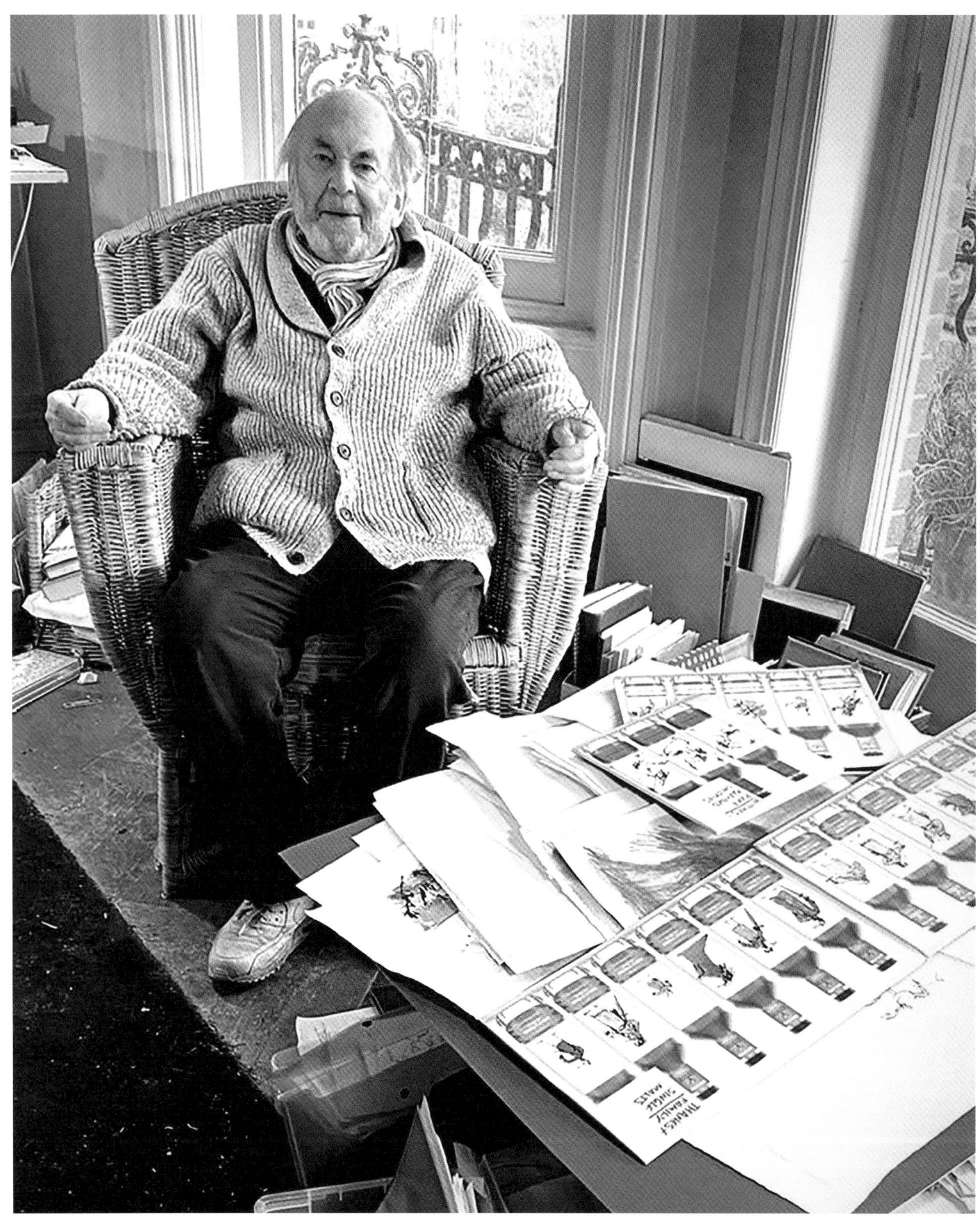

*Quentin working on the Macbeth Collection, 2022*

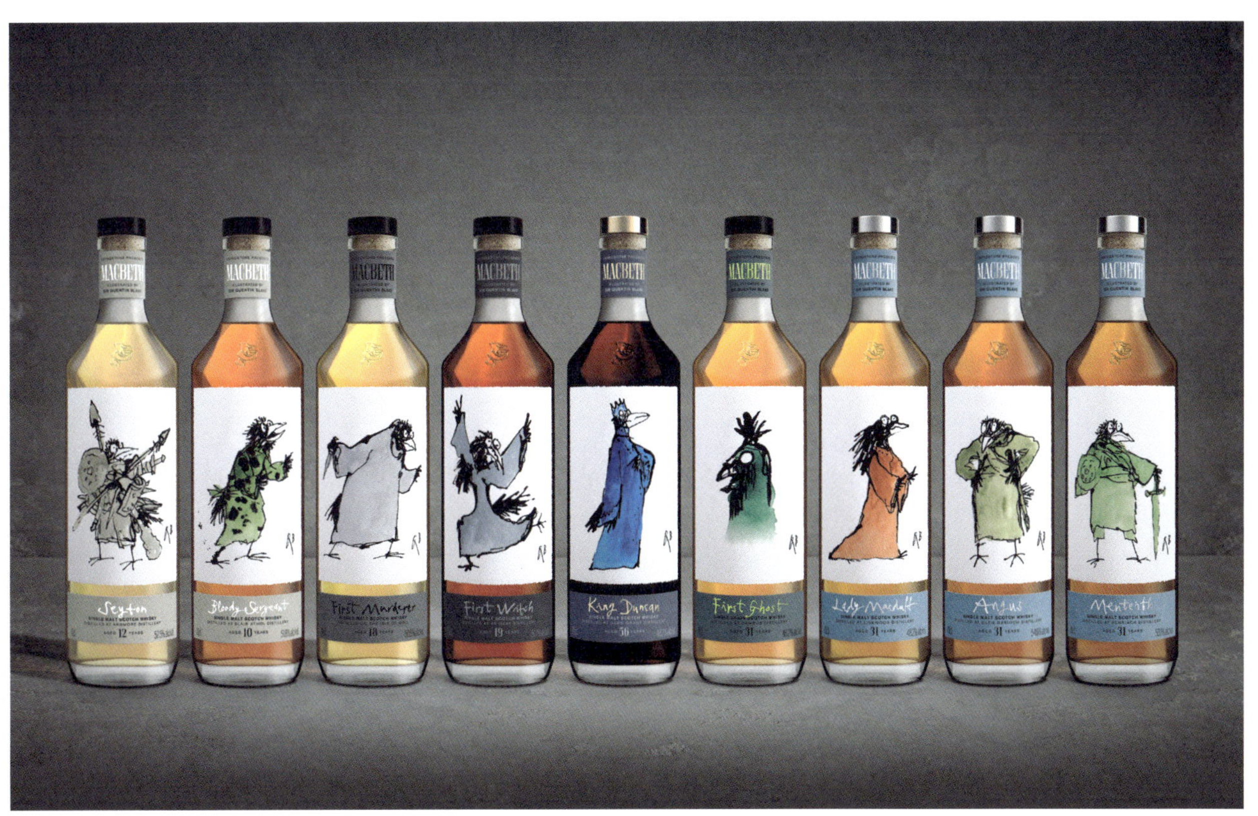

*The Macbeth Collection Act One,* 2022

7

## *Chapter Four*

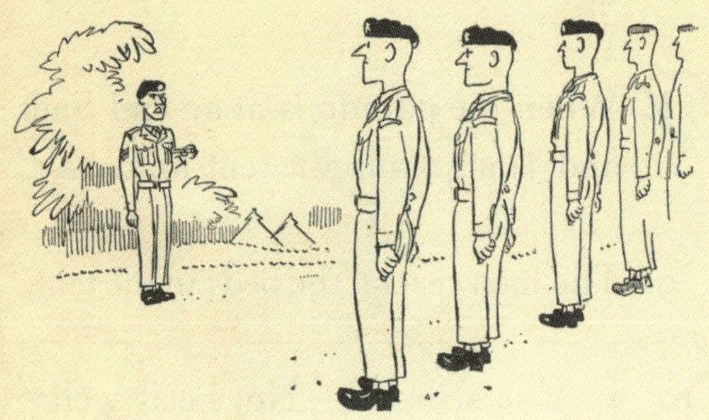

1. Mac is in a tent with Sam and Jim.

2. The tent has six beds in it.

3. The men get out of bed at half past six and get into battle dress.

4. The men in this tent have the best battle dress in camp.

5. At 0715 hrs. Sam has breakfast with his pals.

6. He is on parade till 1200 hrs.

*English Parade,* Royal Army Education Corps, 1954

*Chapter Four*

# Community
# & Charity

At the age of nineteen, Quentin was conscripted for National Service and spent his time in the Royal Army Education Corps.

'I had published a few drawings in the Army magazine, *Soldier,* as well as my drawings in *Punch* and when these were noticed I was sent to spend three weeks at the headquarters of the RAEC re-illustrating a booklet, *English Parade,* used in teaching those soldiers who hadn't yet mastered reading…

It proved to be an early lesson in working to a commission and Quentin understood that a working illustrator had to take his instruction from the client.

'… it was truly a stage in my apprenticeship. Not only did I have to produce a continuous series of related drawings but also, from time to time, I had to take them to show to a lieutenant-colonel for his comment and approval. A few moments of silence as he sat behind in his desk and I stood, at ease, in front of it. Then:

"Very good, Sergeant Blake. But I think… the grass in this one ought to be shorter."

"Yes sir. I'll see to it, sir."

"And I think the creases in these trousers might be a little sharper."

The problem with making grass shorter in drawings is that you can't cut it; you have to do the drawing again. But if there was no chance for artistic rebellion here, there was at least a preparation for encounters with editors and (worse) committees, later on.'

# Christmas Cards

Every summer Quentin would find himself doing artwork for Christmas cards.
Some of them were for sale commercially, but many of them were done pro bono
for organisations and charities he wanted to help. Like all the work in this chapter,
these drawings are Quentin's way of showing his support.

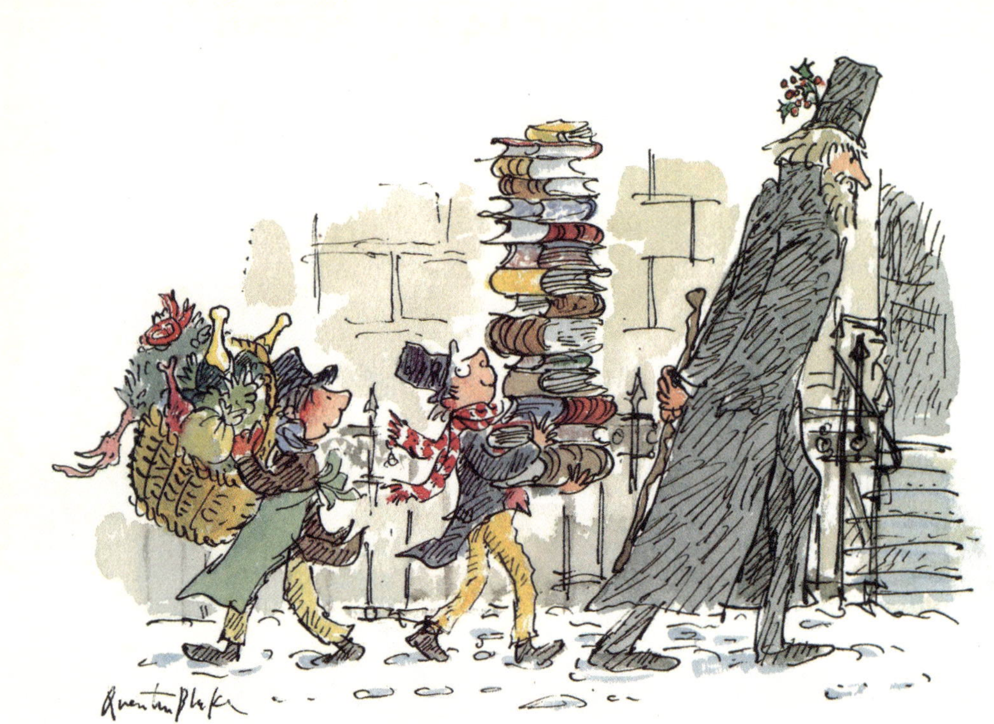

Mr Thomas Carlyle returning his books to St James's Square in a seasonal spirit.

ABOVE – *The London Library*, 1986
OPPOSITE – *The London Library*, 2003

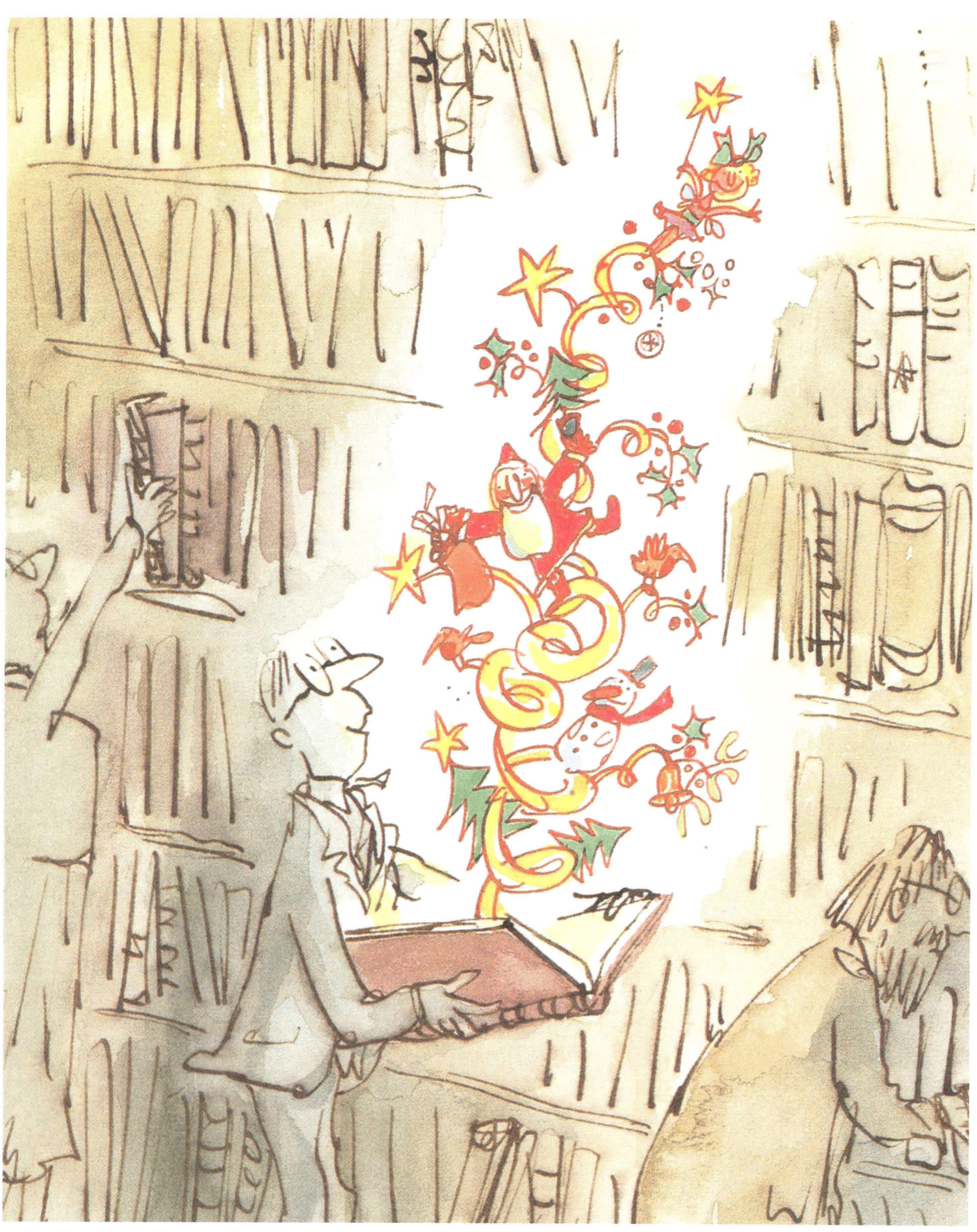

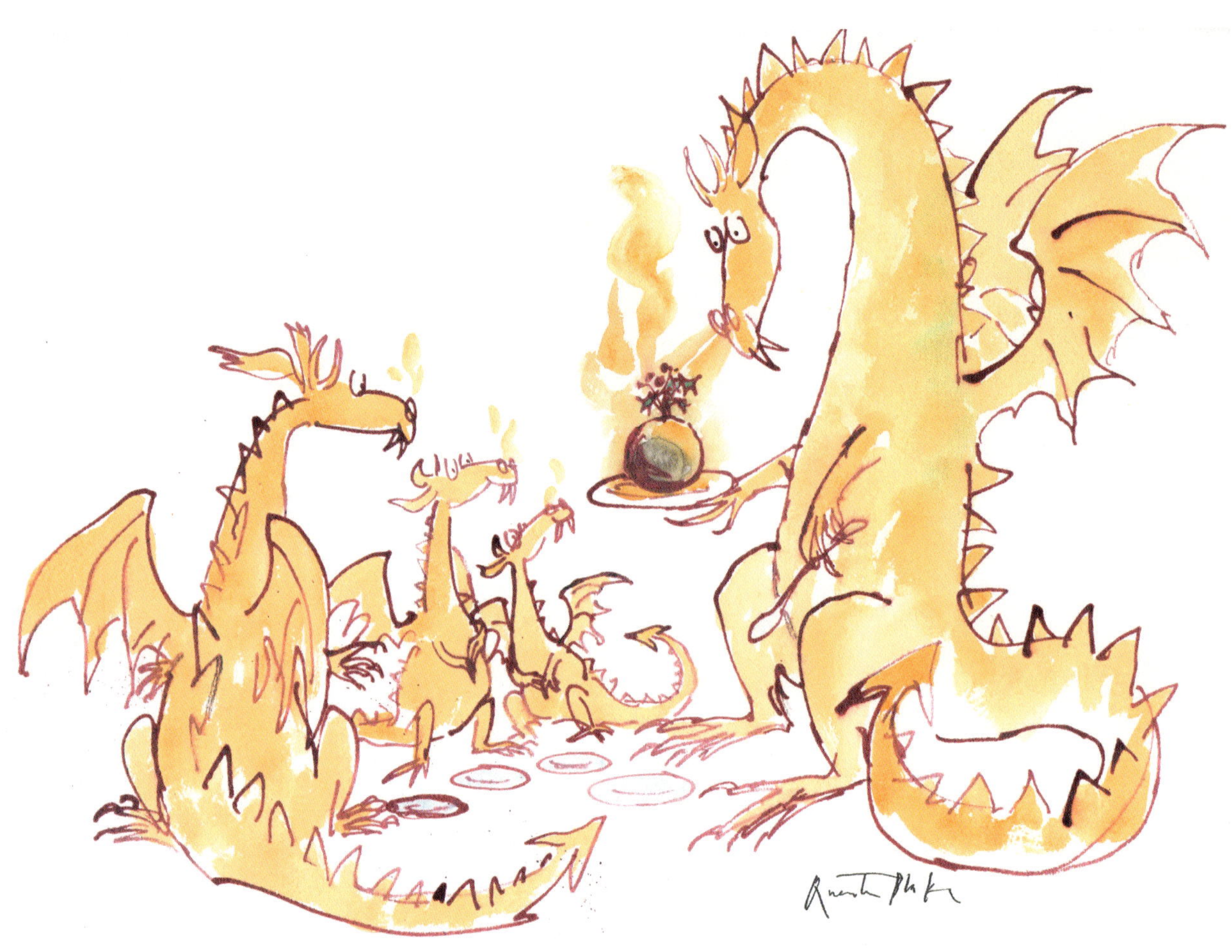

*The Dragon School,* 1992

'It is an unusual year that doesn't include the illustration
of one or two Christmas cards (quite often, it seems, to
be done in the hottest days of August)...'

**QB**

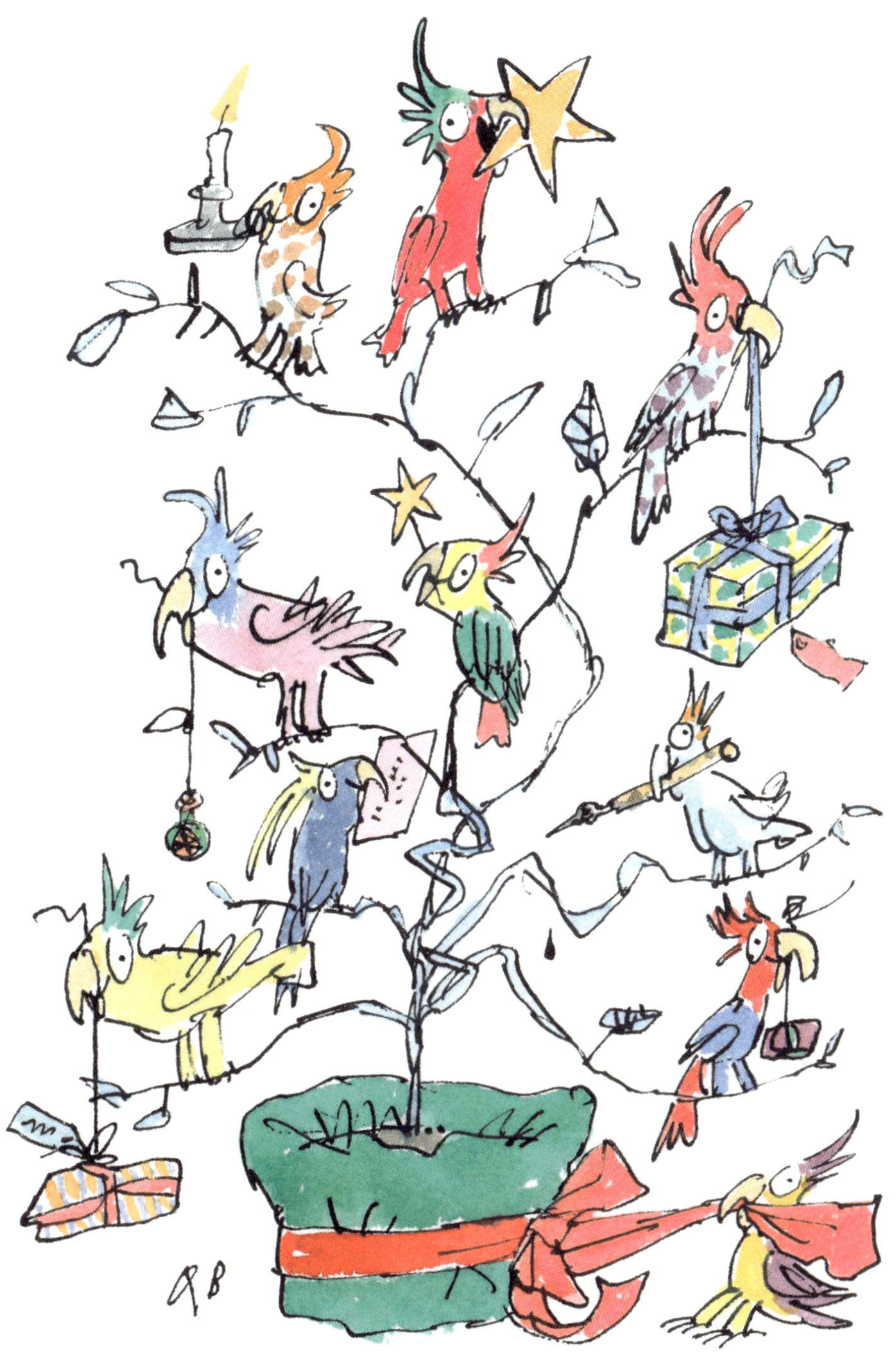

*Royal Society of Authors Christmas Card,* 2000

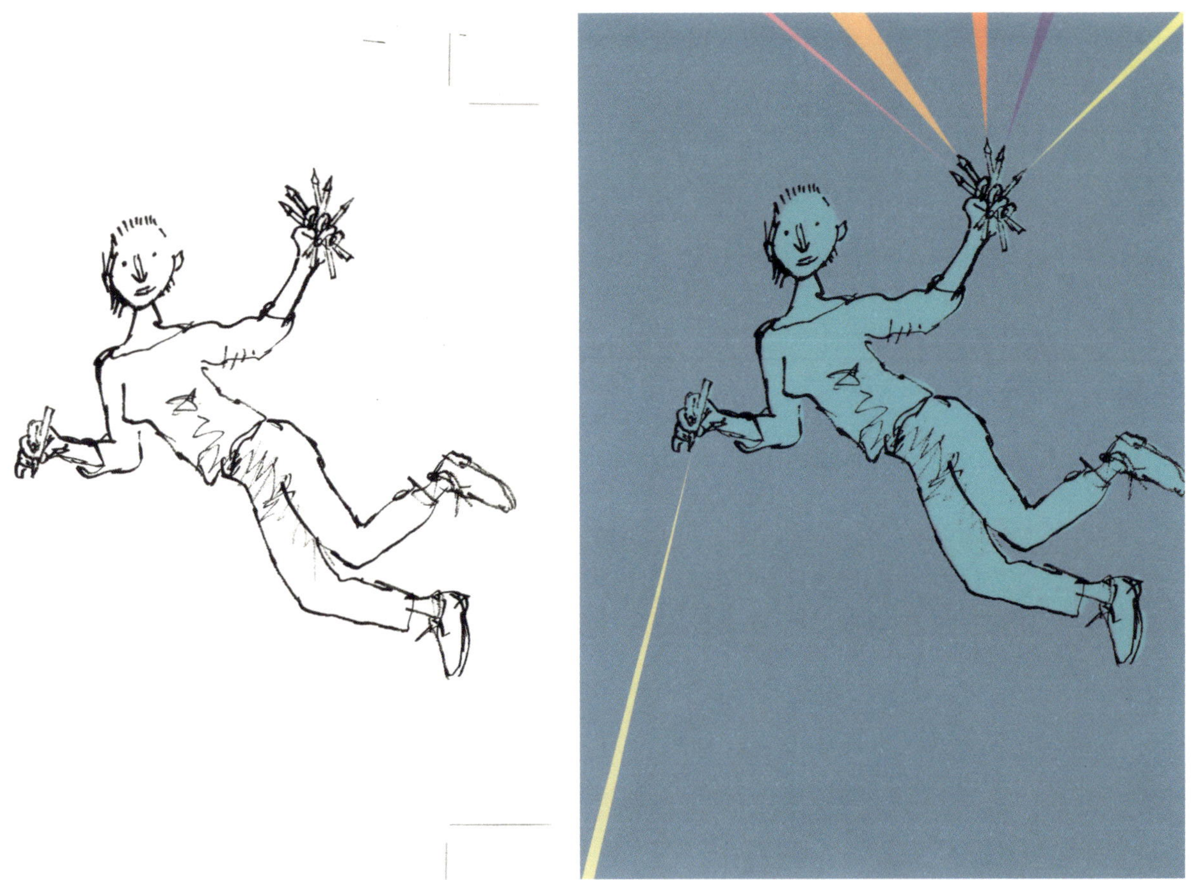

## Royal College of Art

Quentin drew 'The Angel of Art and Design' for the Royal College of Art Christmas Card in 2001, before the colour was added using Photoshop at the college. It is his only computer-generated illustration.

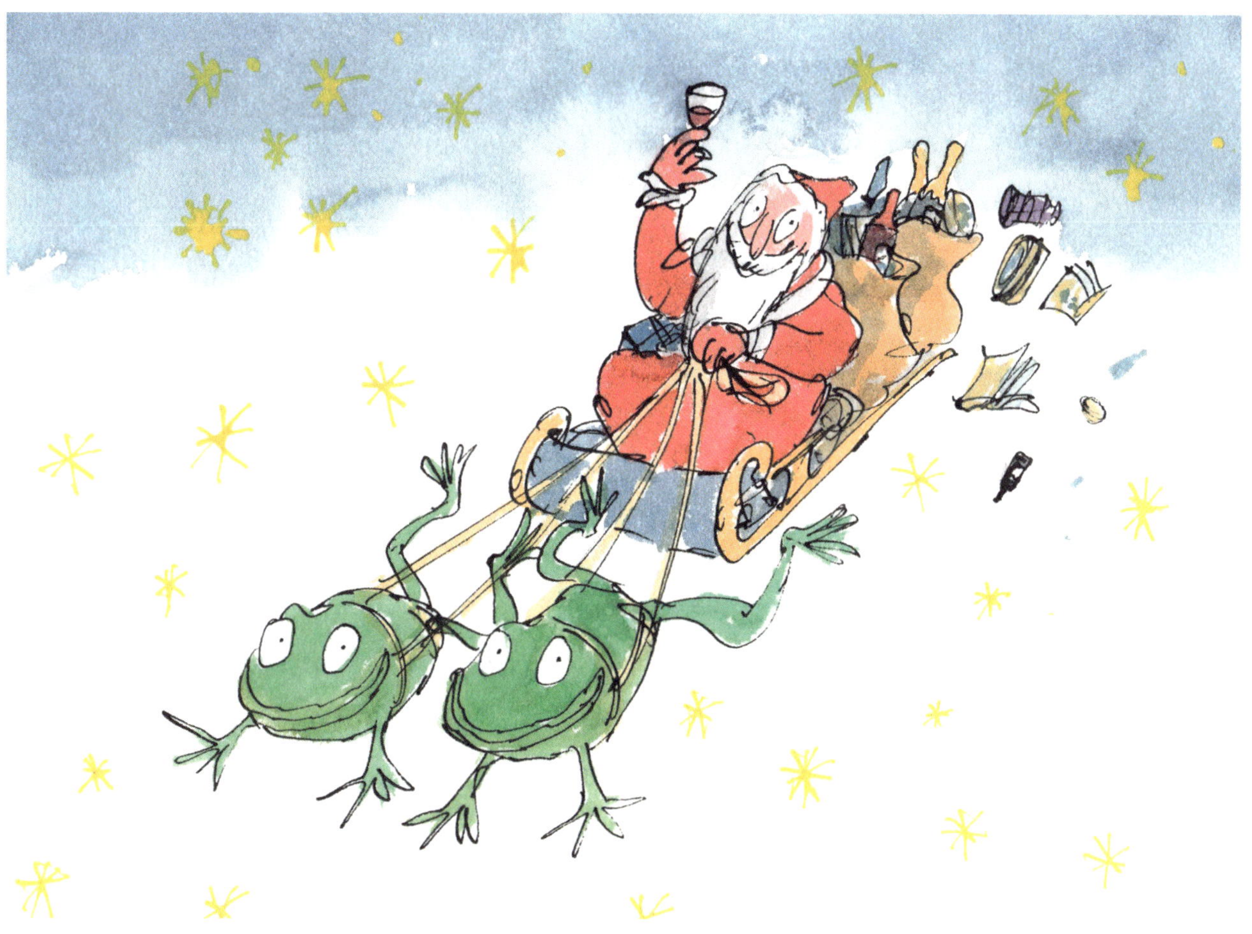

## The French Institute

In these days of sensitivity to negative stereotyping, depicting the French as frogs wouldn't be acceptable, but in 2004 the French Institute were delighted with it.

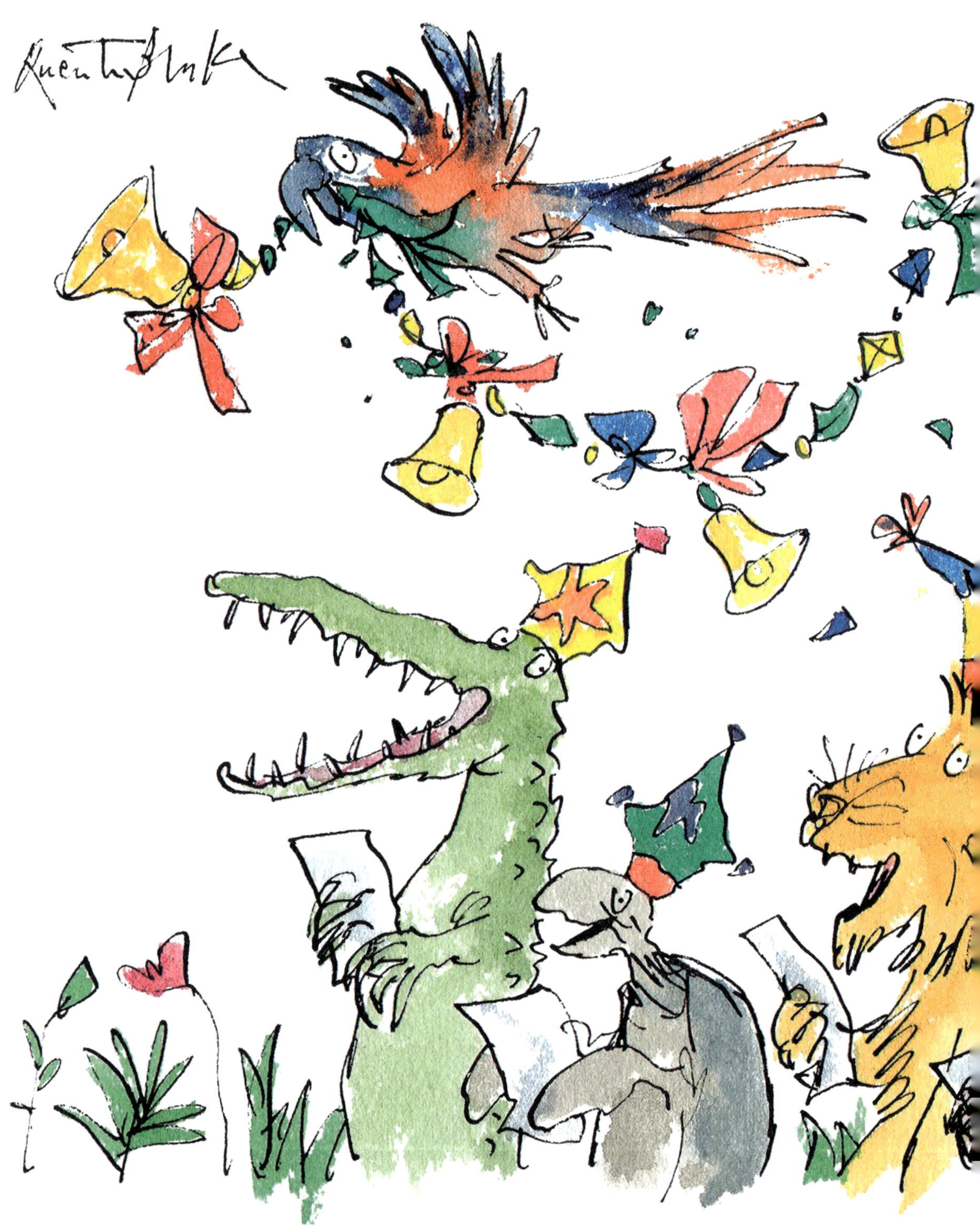

*Flora and Fauna International*, 2006

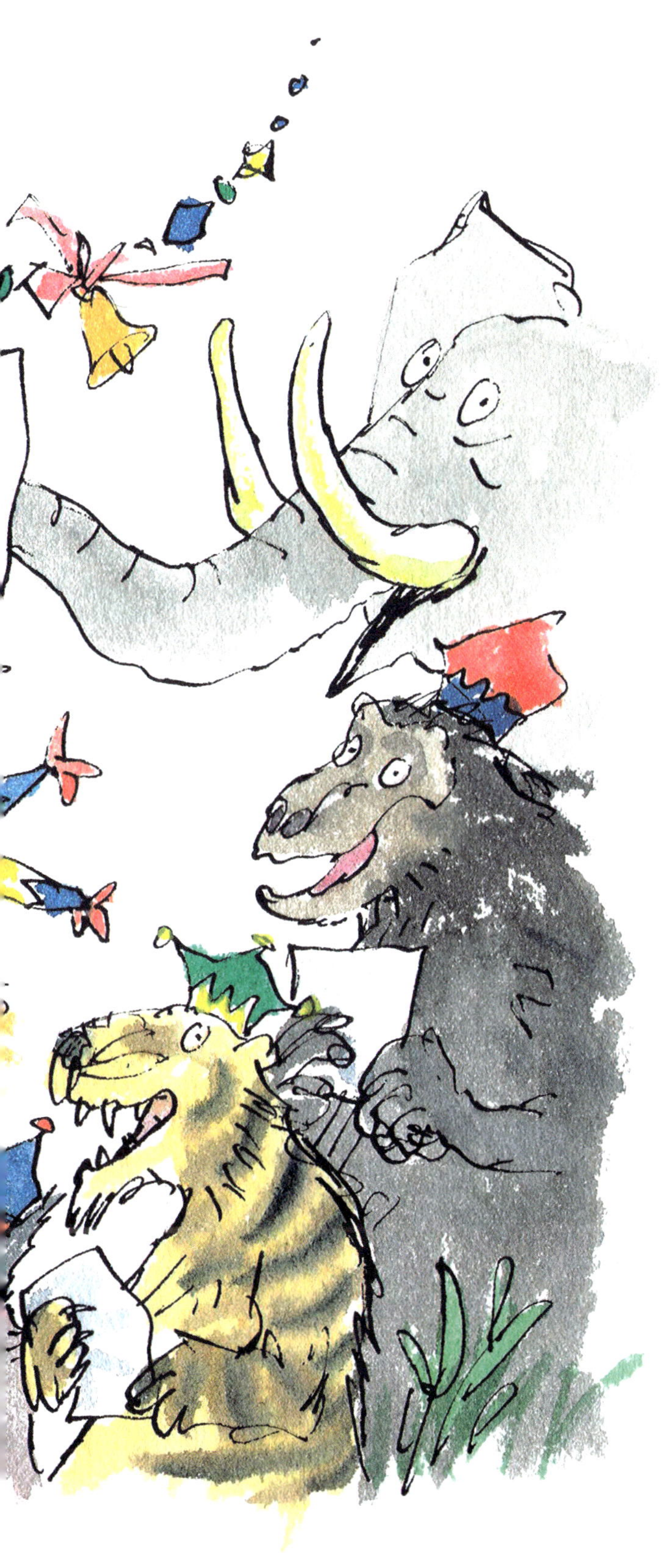

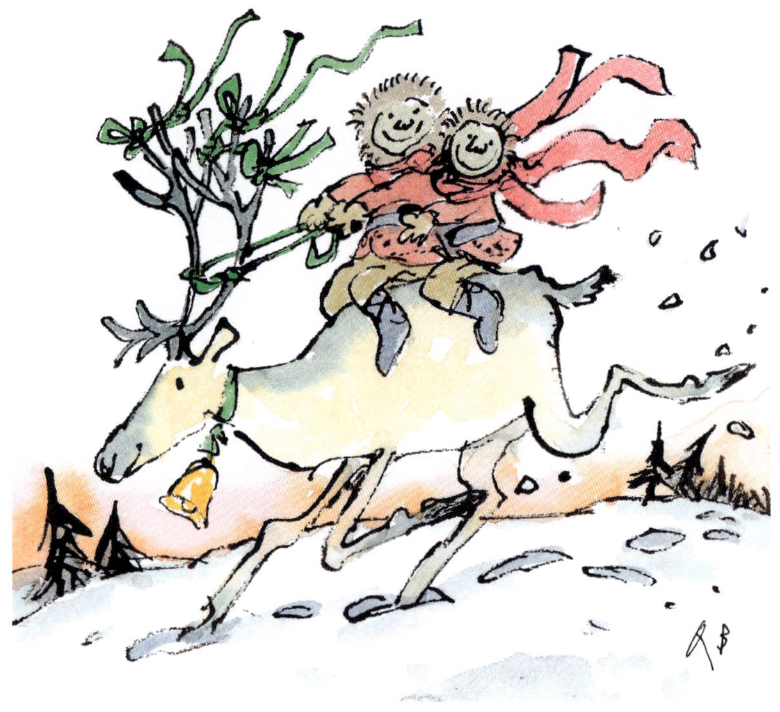

*Survival International,* 2008

## Survival International

'I know nothing about their work at first hand, but I believe passionately in what they are trying to do to minimize some of the effects of our uncaring global culture of greed and relentless growth. Once again my most useful contribution is drawing, and I am pleased that the Christmas cards that I have drawn for them are a useful source of income. I confess that Christmas cards are not an easy task at the best of times and here are not made easier by the fact that these communities will be mostly unaware of Christmas. Thank goodness for reindeer.'

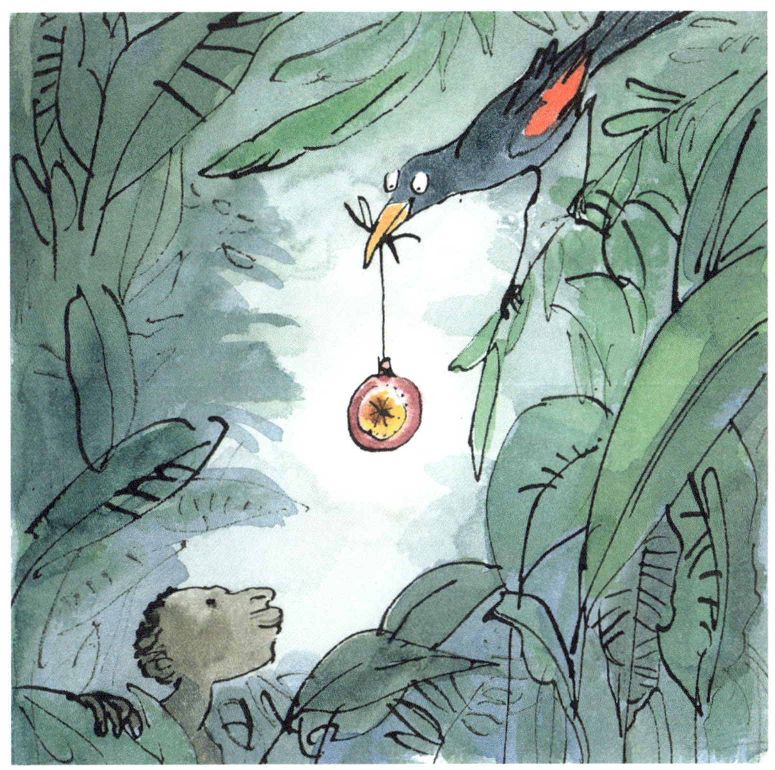

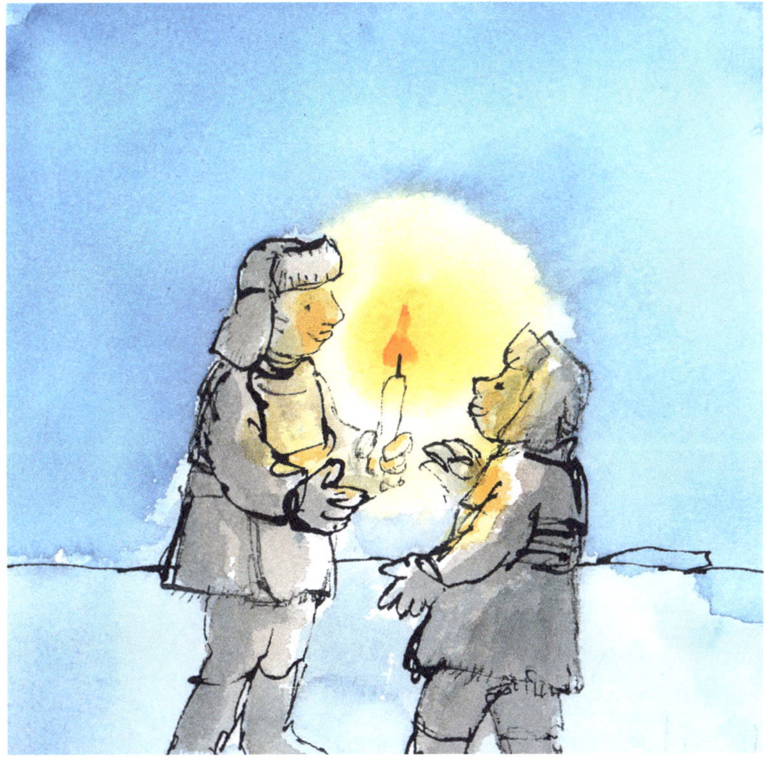

*Survival International*, 2010

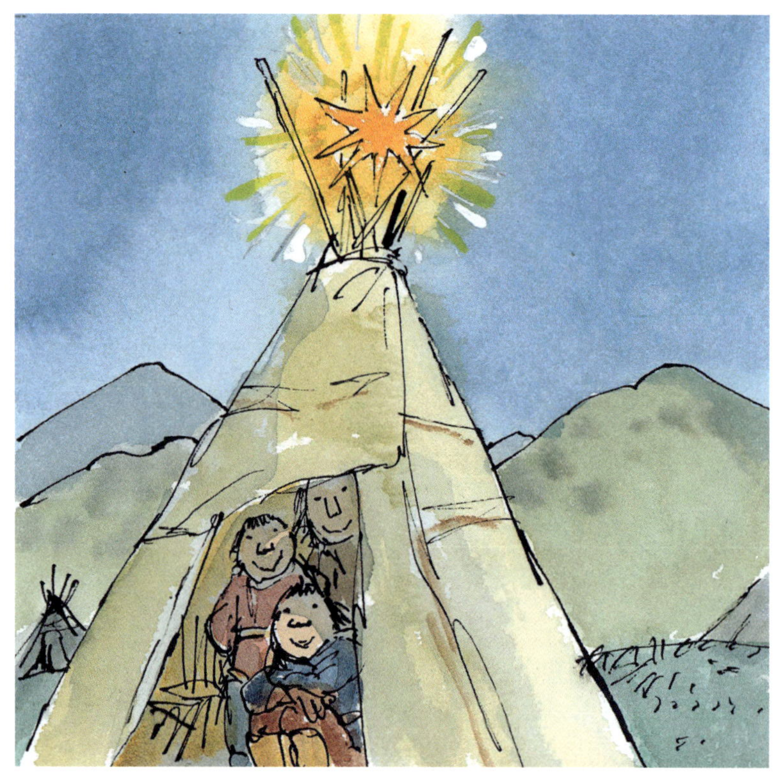

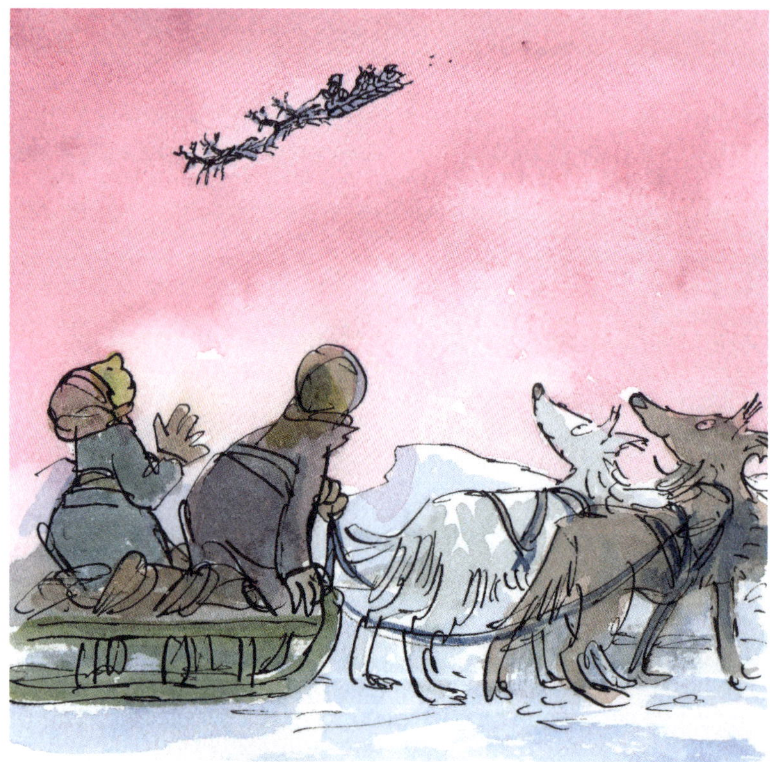

ABOVE – *Survival International*, 2011 & 2012

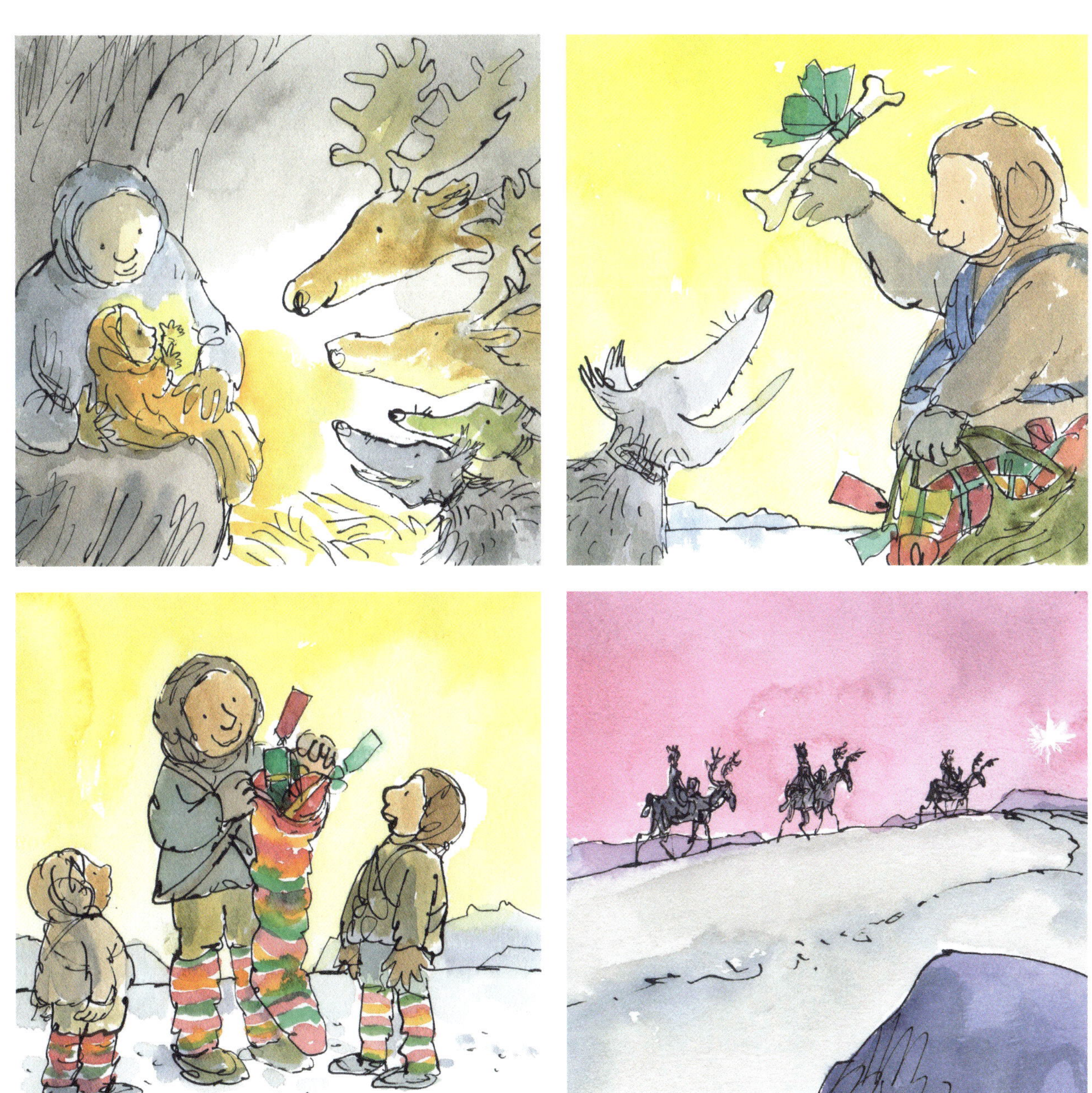

ABOVE – *Survival International,* 2013 & 2014

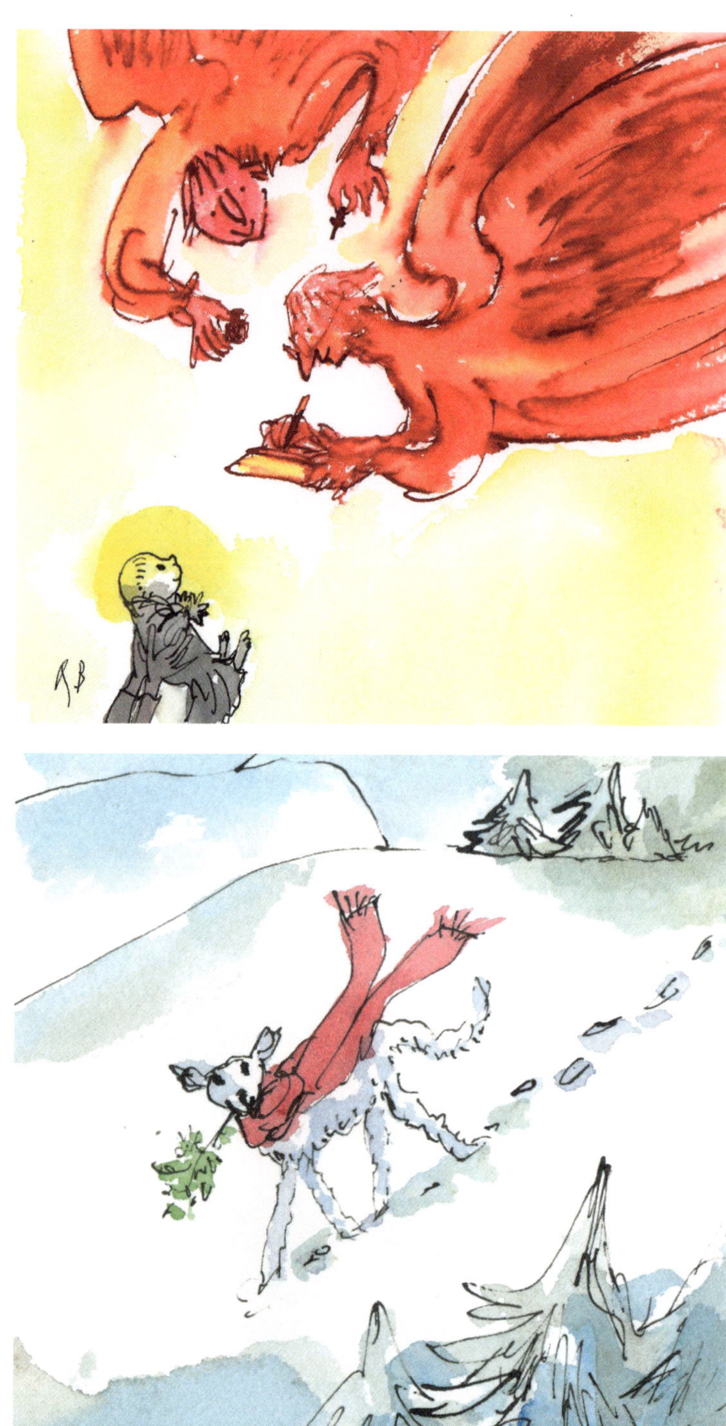

ABOVE – *Dulwich Picture Gallery*, 2008
BELOW – *The Foundling Museum Christmas Card*, 2020

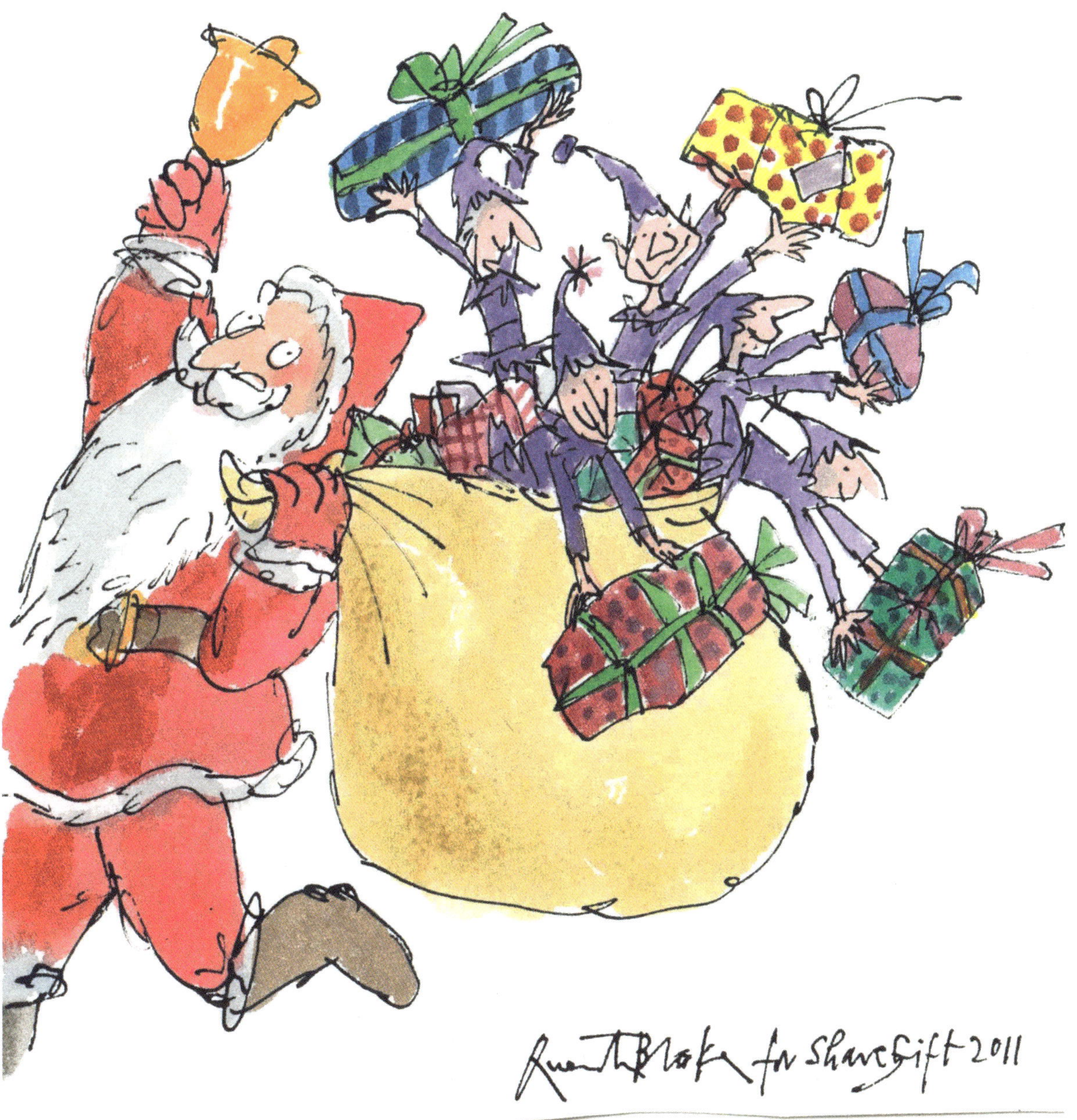


*Sharegift Christmas Card,* 2009

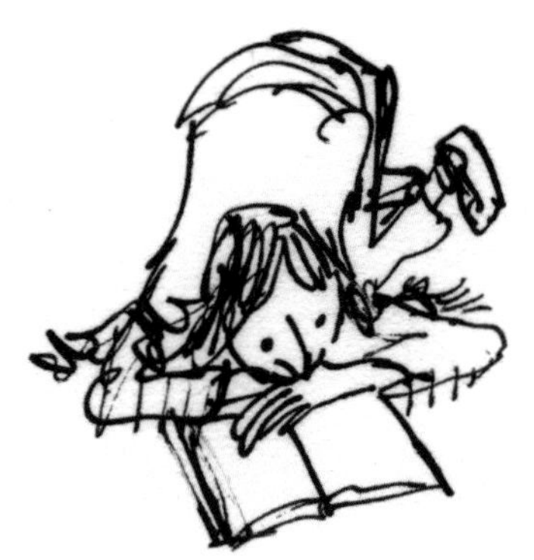

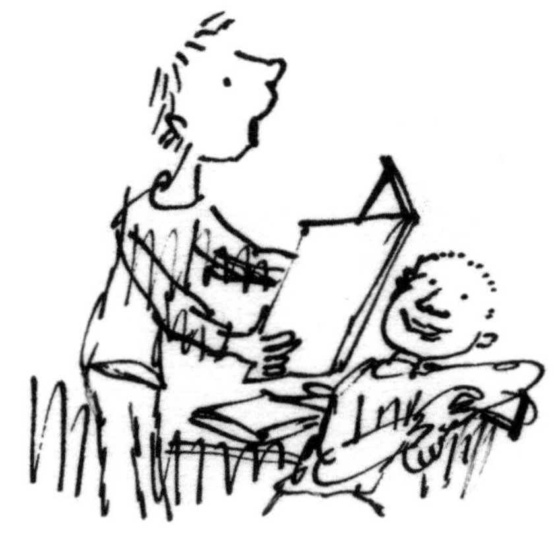

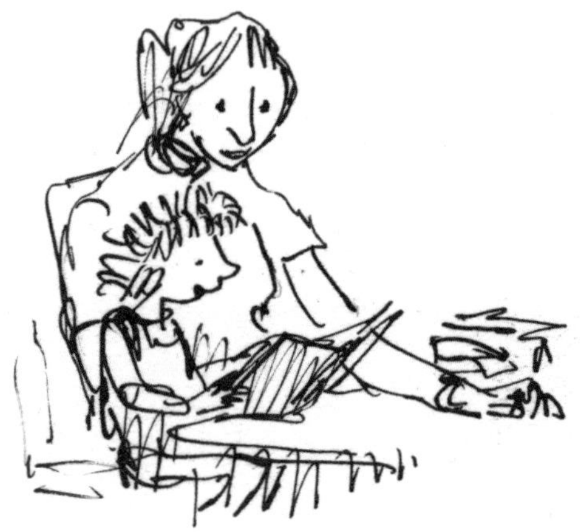

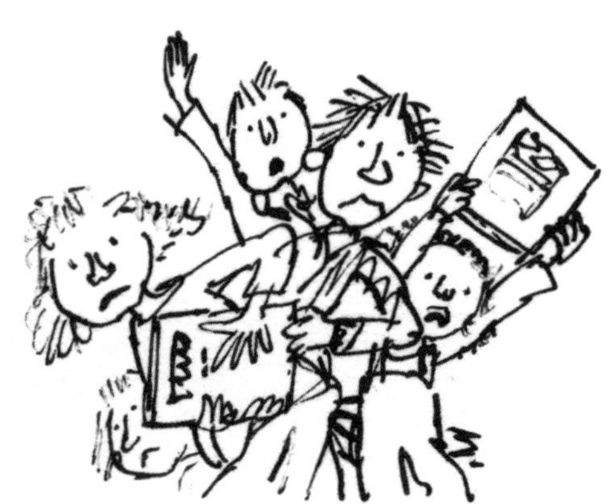

### The Dyslexia Association and The Centre for Literacy in Primary Education

'I have been called upon on several occasions to draw children reading – nervously, for the Dyslexia Association; enthusiastically for the Centre for Literacy in Primary Education.'

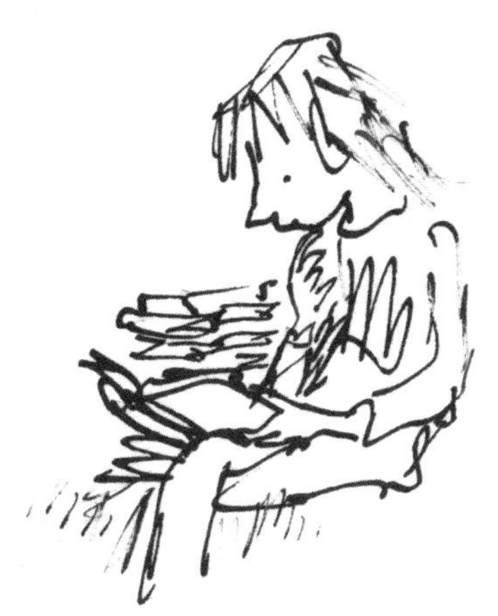
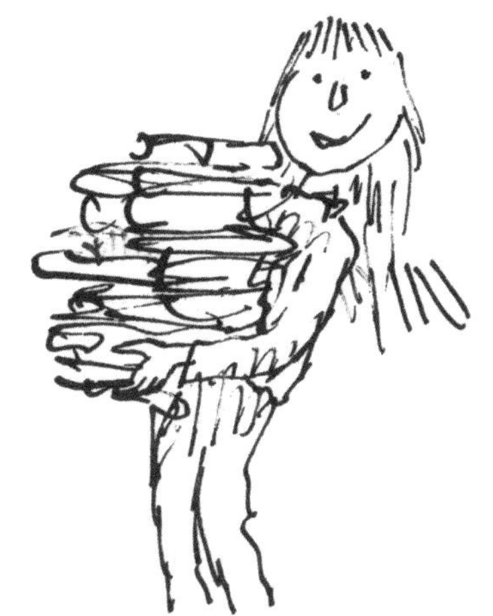
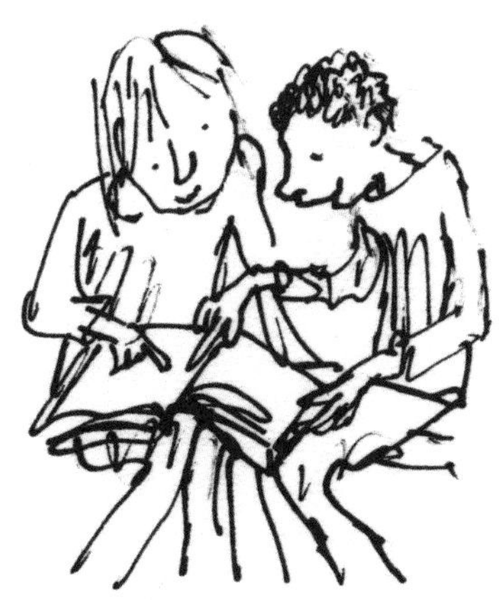
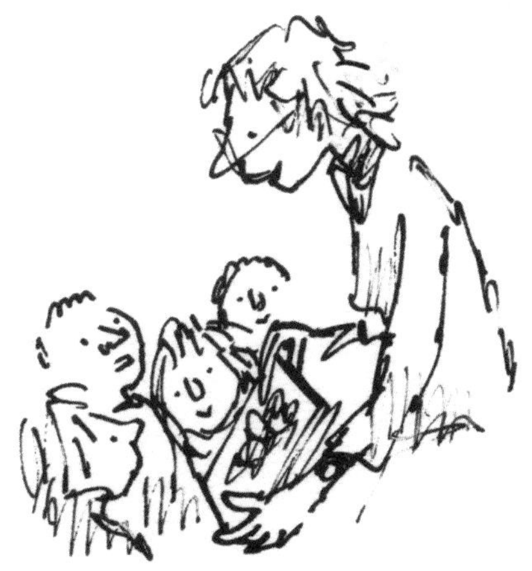

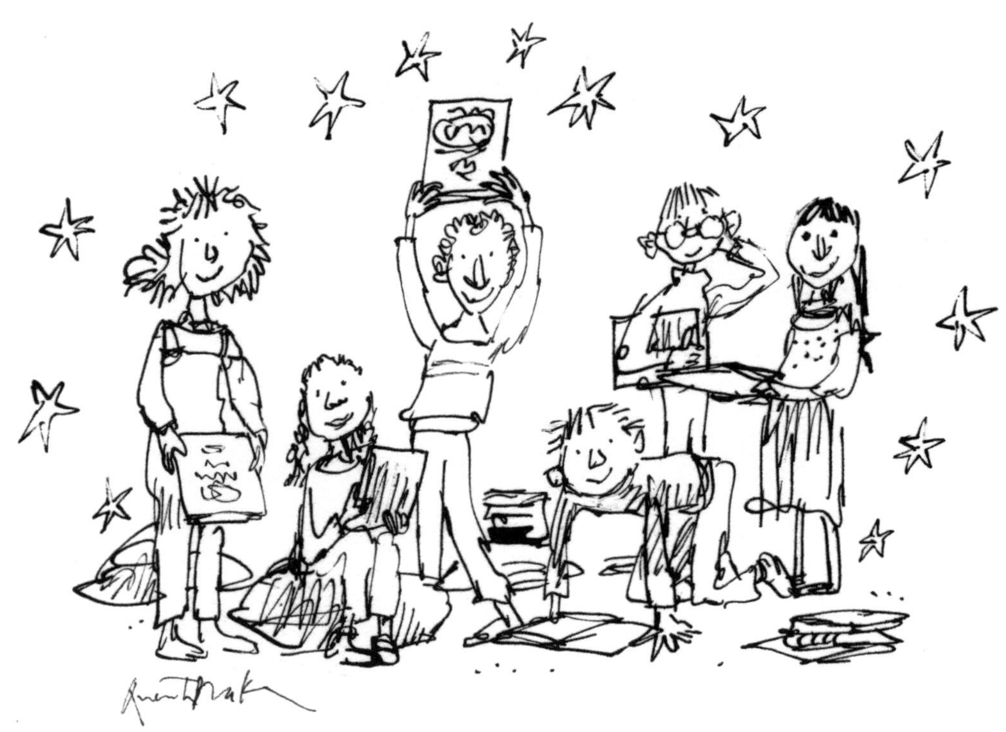

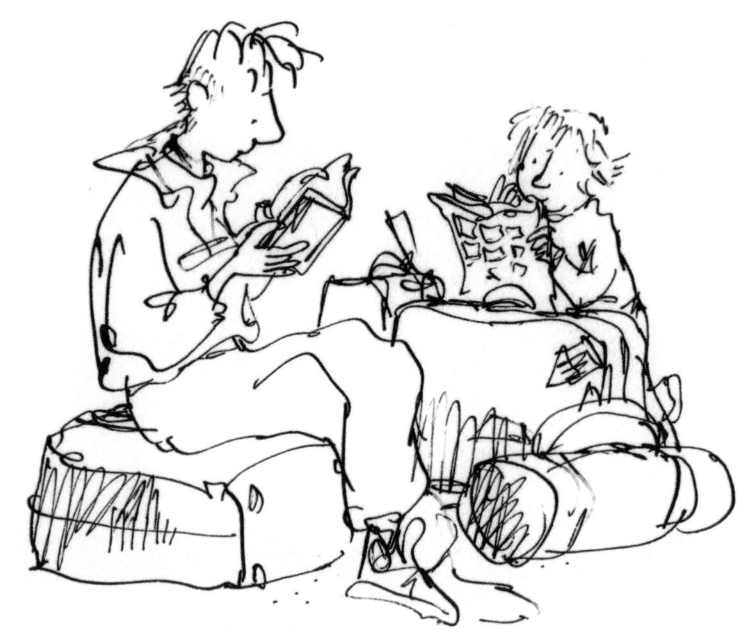

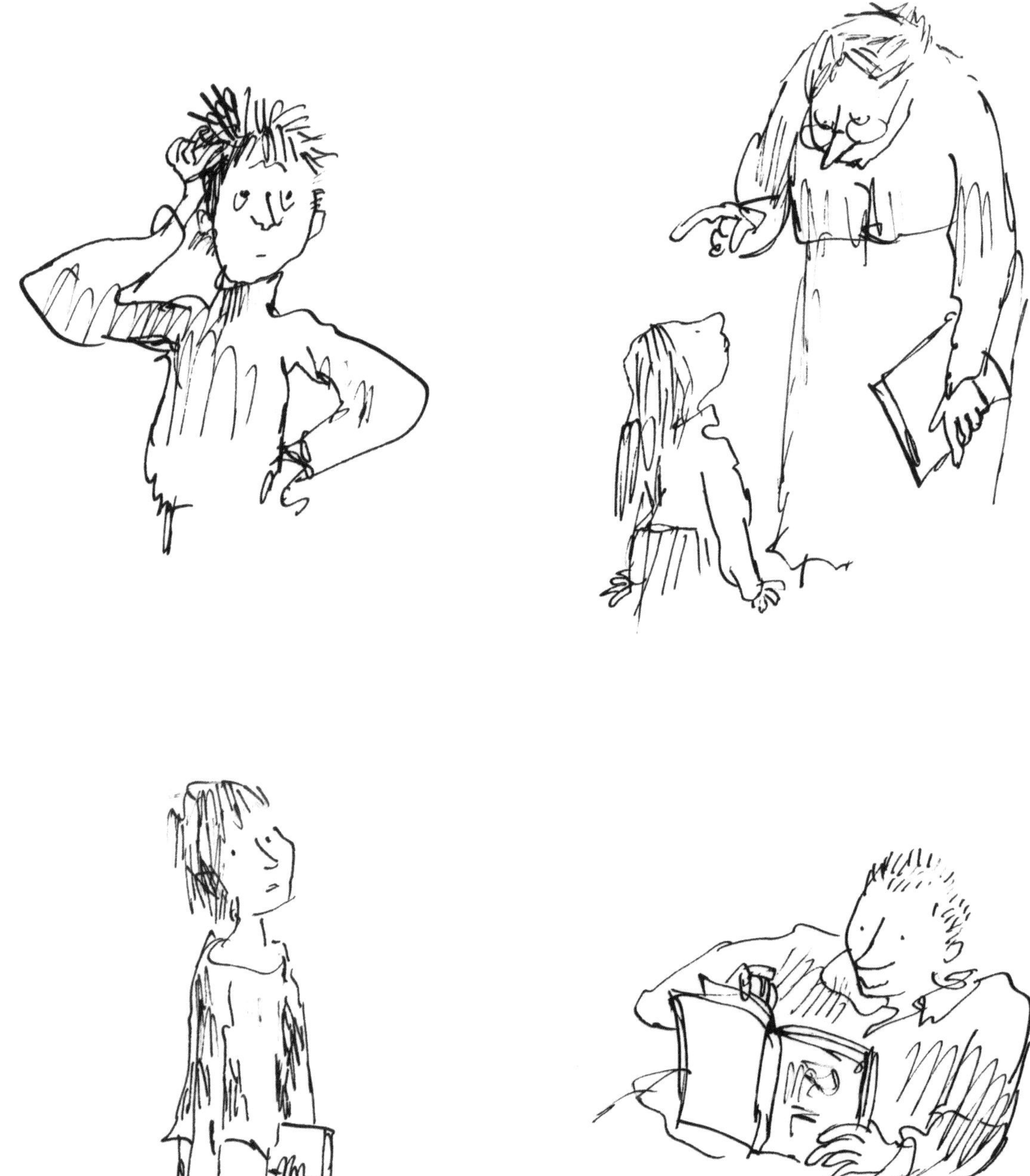

OPPOSITE & ABOVE – *The Centre for Literacy in Primary Education*, 1996

**A Baker's Dozen, exhibition poster, 1999**

'The Bury St Edmunds Art Gallery in Suffolk invited me to help curate an exhibition of children's book illustrators.' They wanted to show 'not only an exhibition of originals, but also preliminary work, roughs and sketches, which will introduce the spectator to the various approaches and ways of thinking of each artist. I like this, because it matches my wish to emphasise the skill and expertise that go into drawing and writing for children.'

Quentin called the show 'A Baker's Dozen' as there were thirteen artists included in the show.

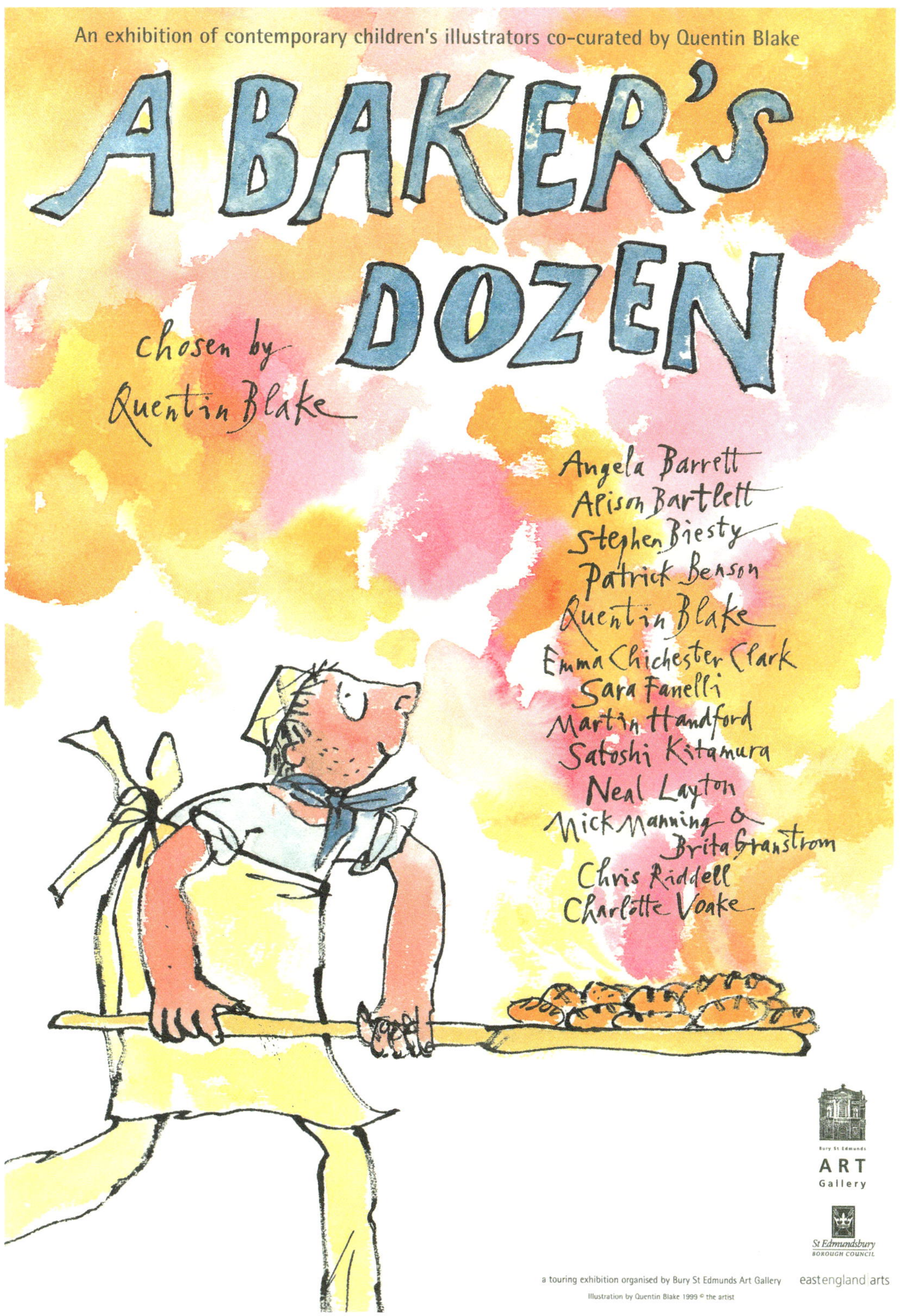
An exhibition of contemporary children's illustrators co-curated by Quentin Blake
A BAKER'S DOZEN
chosen by Quentin Blake
Angela Barrett
Alison Bartlett
Stephen Biesty
Patrick Benson
Quentin Blake
Emma Chichester Clark
Sara Fanelli
Martin Handford
Satoshi Kitamura
Neal Layton
Nick Manning &
Brita Granstrom
Chris Riddell
Charlotte Voake
ART
Gallery
St Edmundsbury
BOROUGH COUNCIL
a touring exhibition organised by Bury St Edmunds Art Gallery    eastengland arts
Illustration by Quentin Blake 1999 © the artist

# Campaign for Drawing

There are some charities, close to Quentin's heart, which he has been involved in for many years.

'I was in at the start… This was set up in 2000 with a grant from the Guild of St George (established in his own lifetime by John Ruskin) to encourage people to draw – not only children but people of every age. What was revelatory to me about it (if not exactly surprising) is that not a great deal of encouragement is necessary, and it is almost more a question of giving an assurance that you are allowed to draw, though an amateur, just as you are allowed to sing. The Big Draw, in October, is its main occasion and that is repeated in hundreds of sites across the country.

…I suggested that you can't have something called 'The Big Draw' without doing a Big Drawing. Someone else suggested that we should do it in a tunnel – the one that leads from South Kensington Underground Station towards the South Kensington museums.

September 2000. We're in the tunnel. Lined with lavatory tiles, not very well lit, and about a quarter of a mile long, it isn't the most attractive of places. But there is a lot of paper already up on the walls, thanks to London Transport, and free artist's materials, thanks to Crayola…'

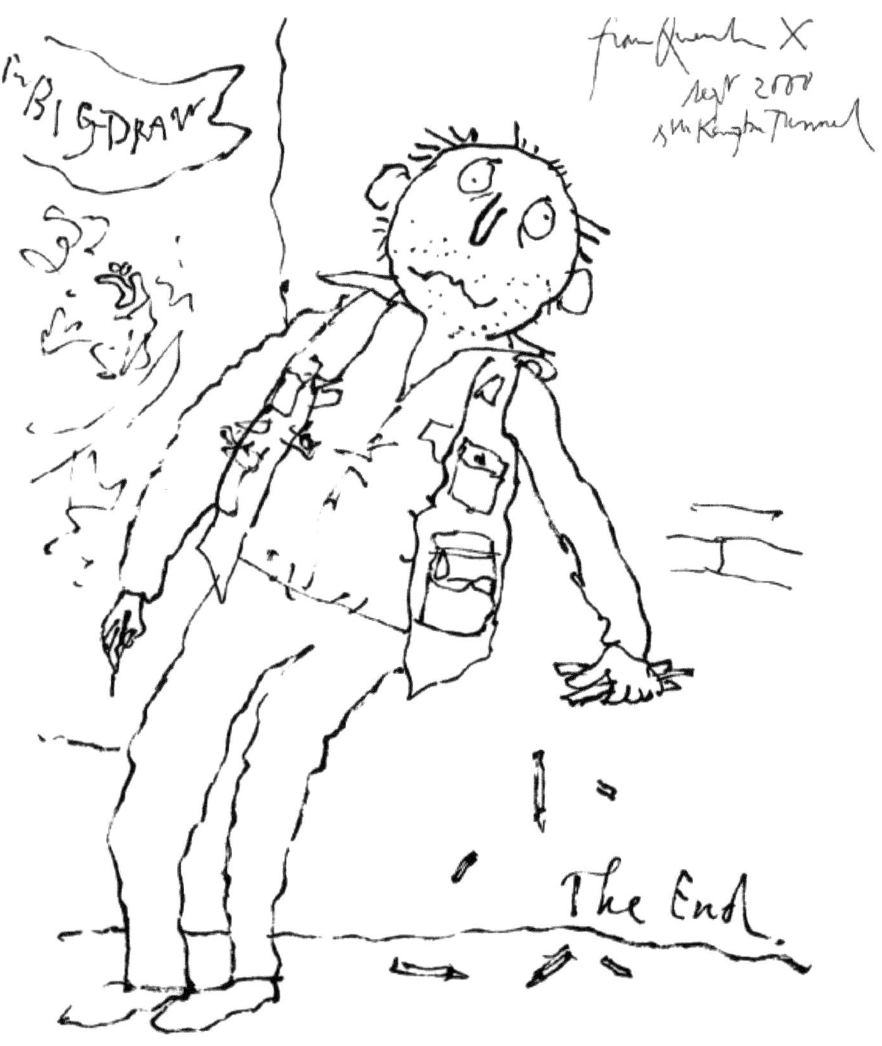


*The Big Draw's Big Splash,* Self-Portrait for the Campaign for Drawing, 2000

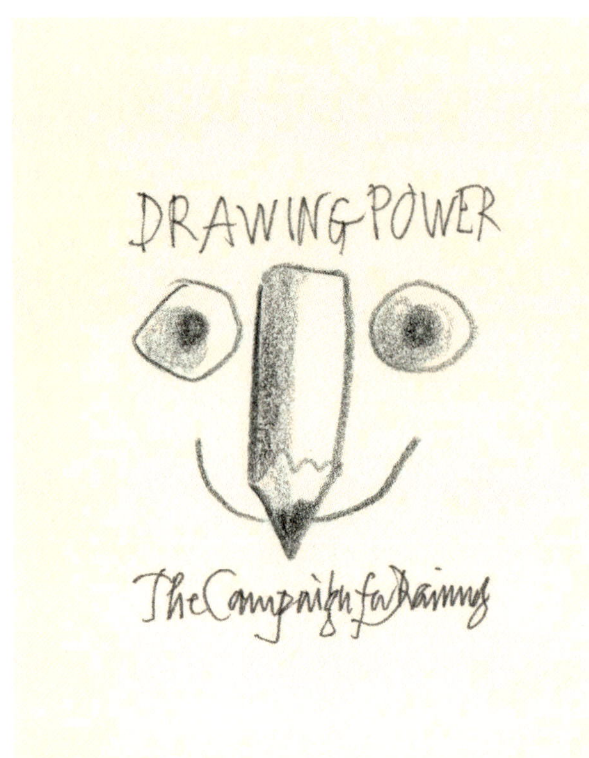


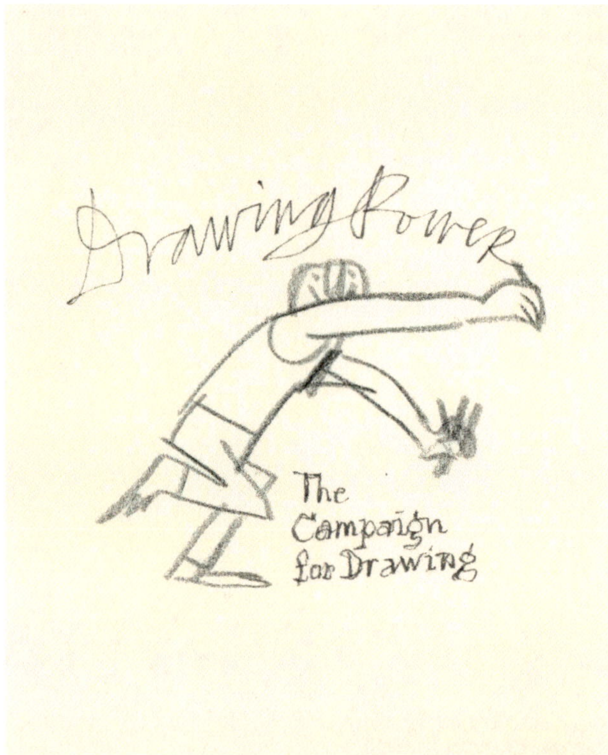


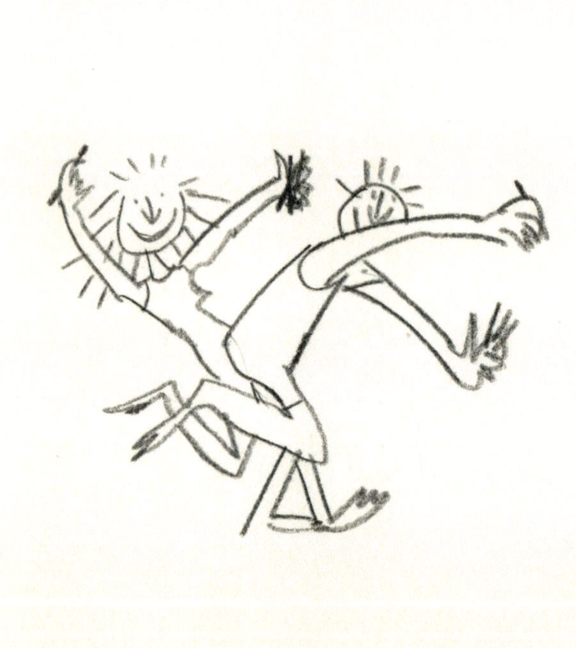

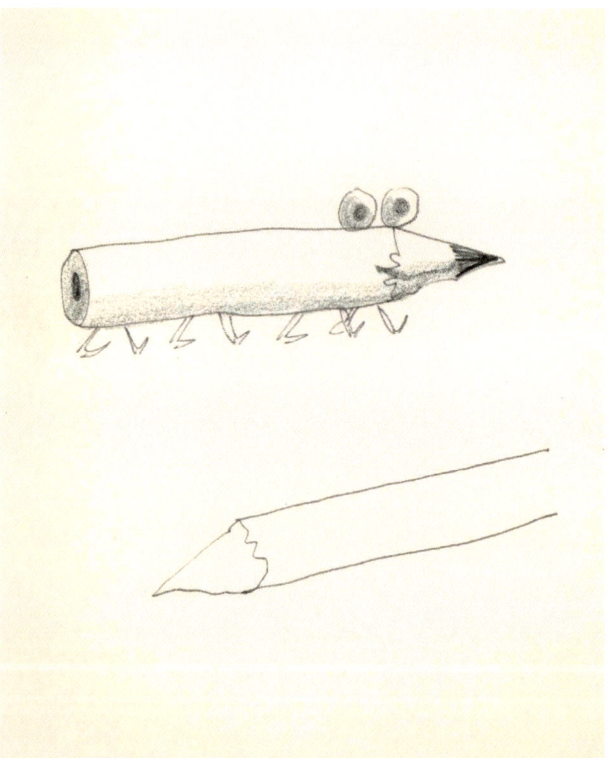

*The Big Draw*, Roughs for the Logo, 2000

*'Drawing Power' Logo*, 2000

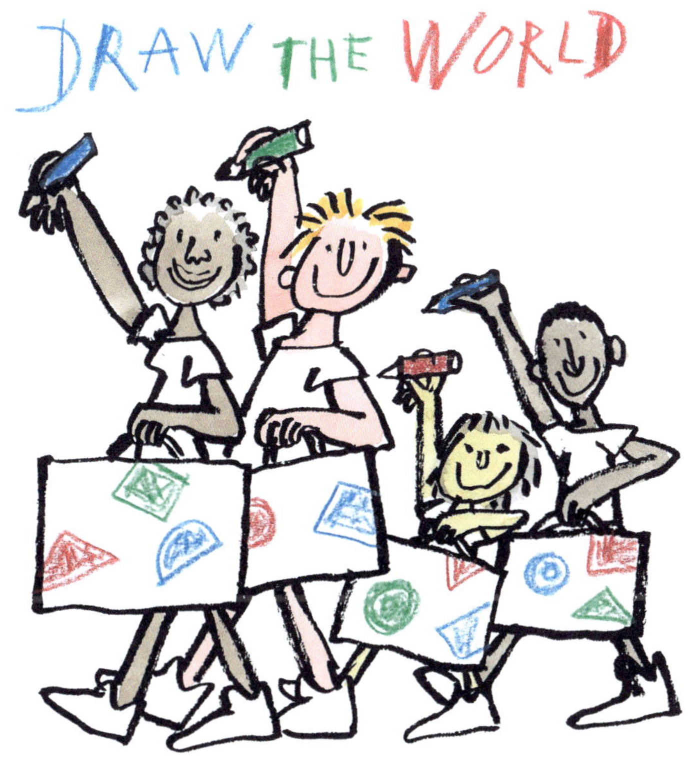


*'Draw the World' Logo*, 2001

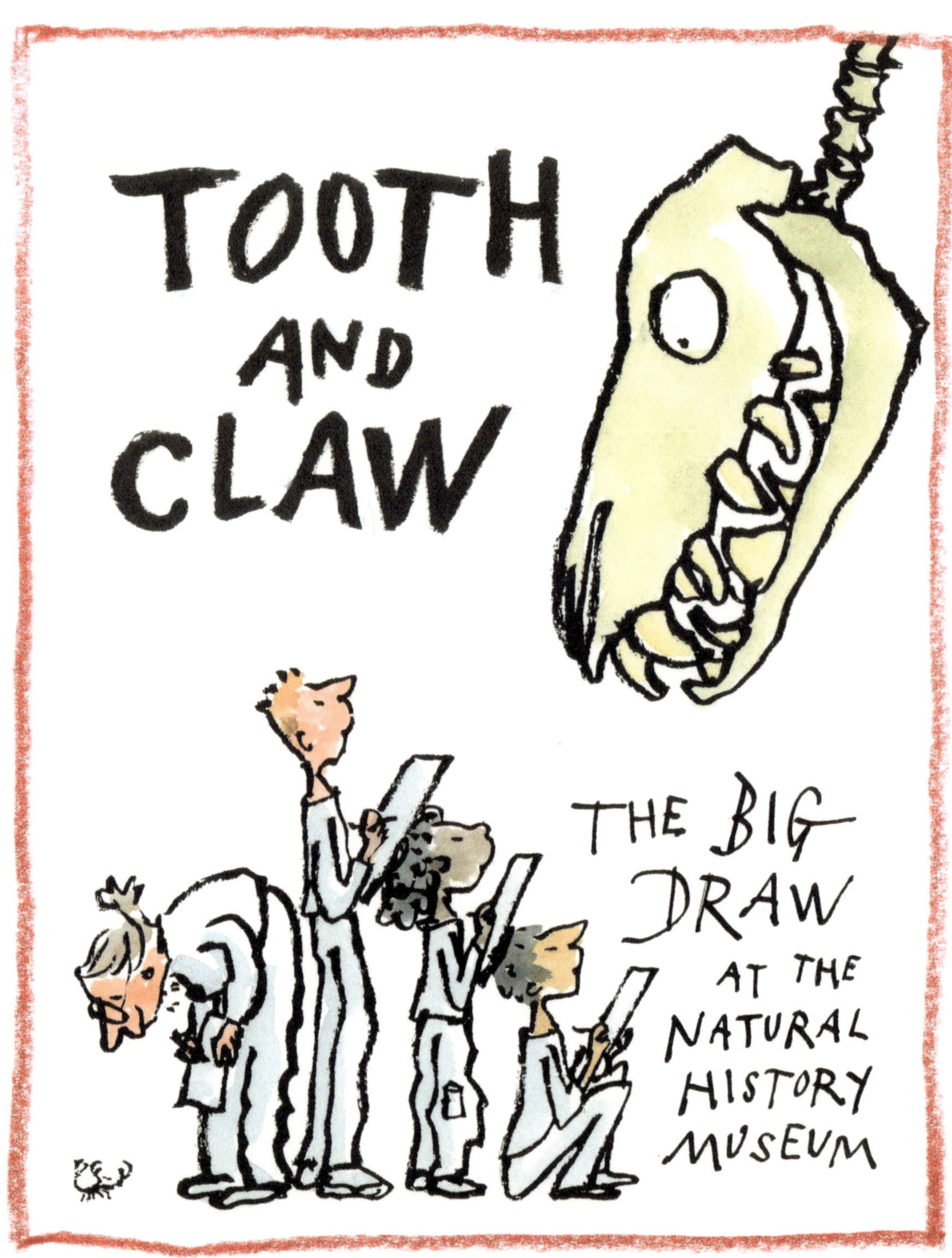


*Tooth and Claw,* Logo for the Big Draw at the Natural History Museum, 2002

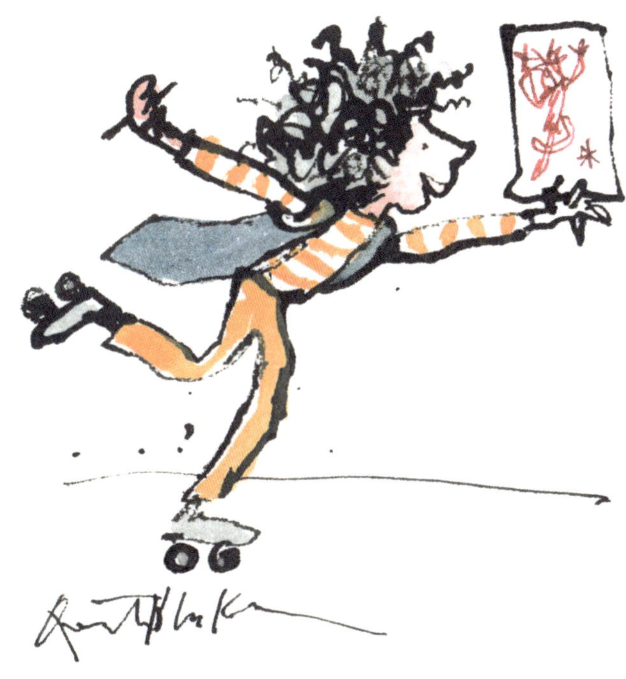

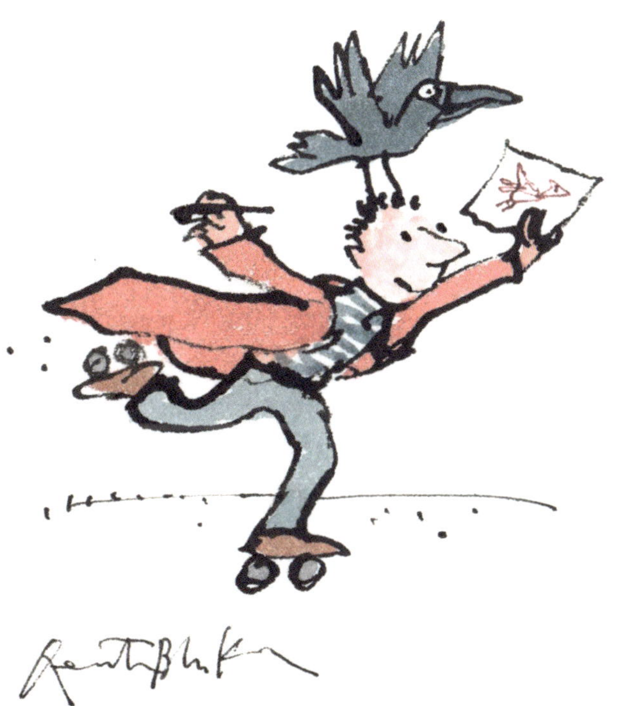

*The Big Draw Anniversary Auction,* 2009

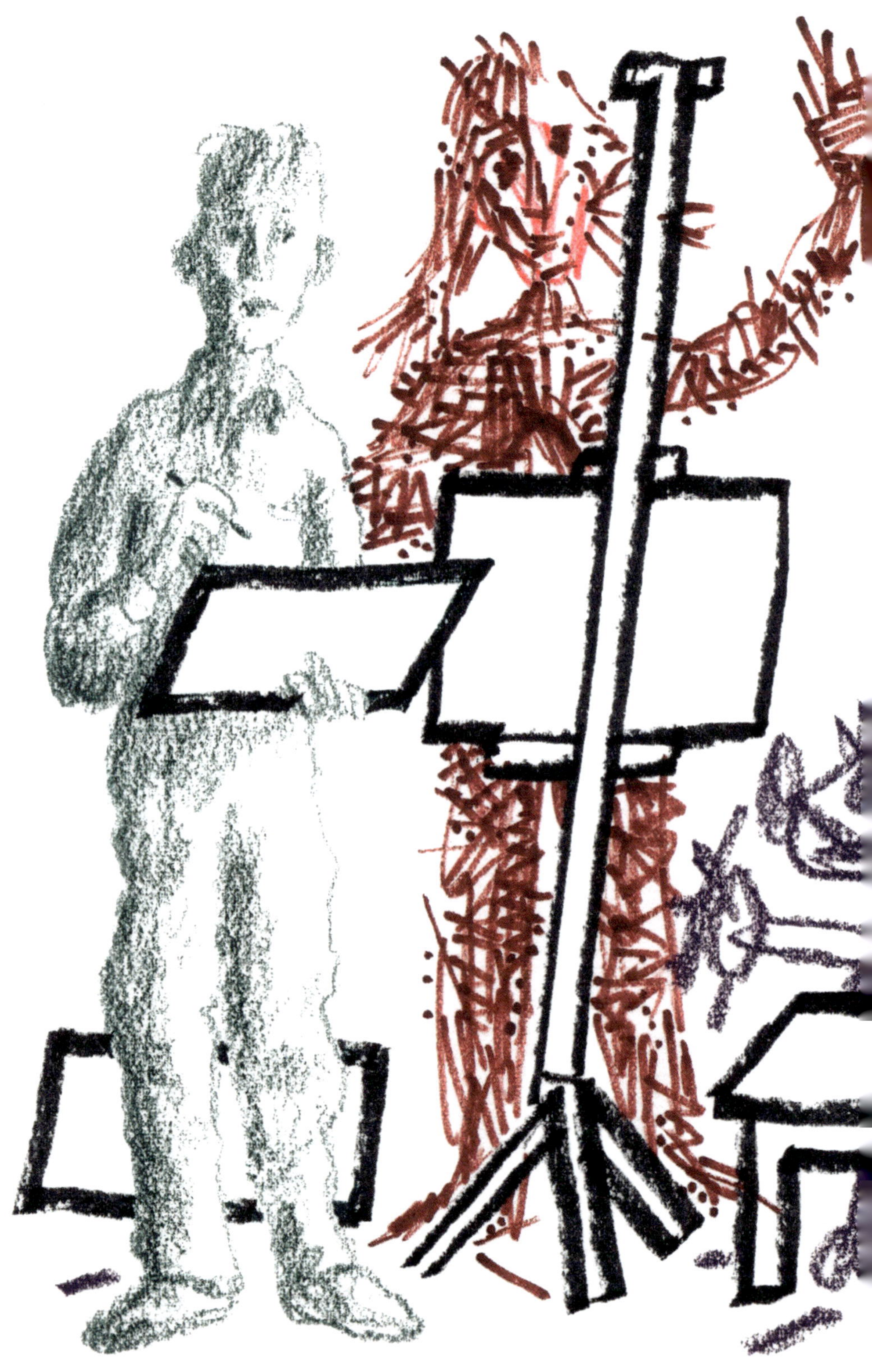

*Illustration for Article on Drawing in* The Guardian, 2000

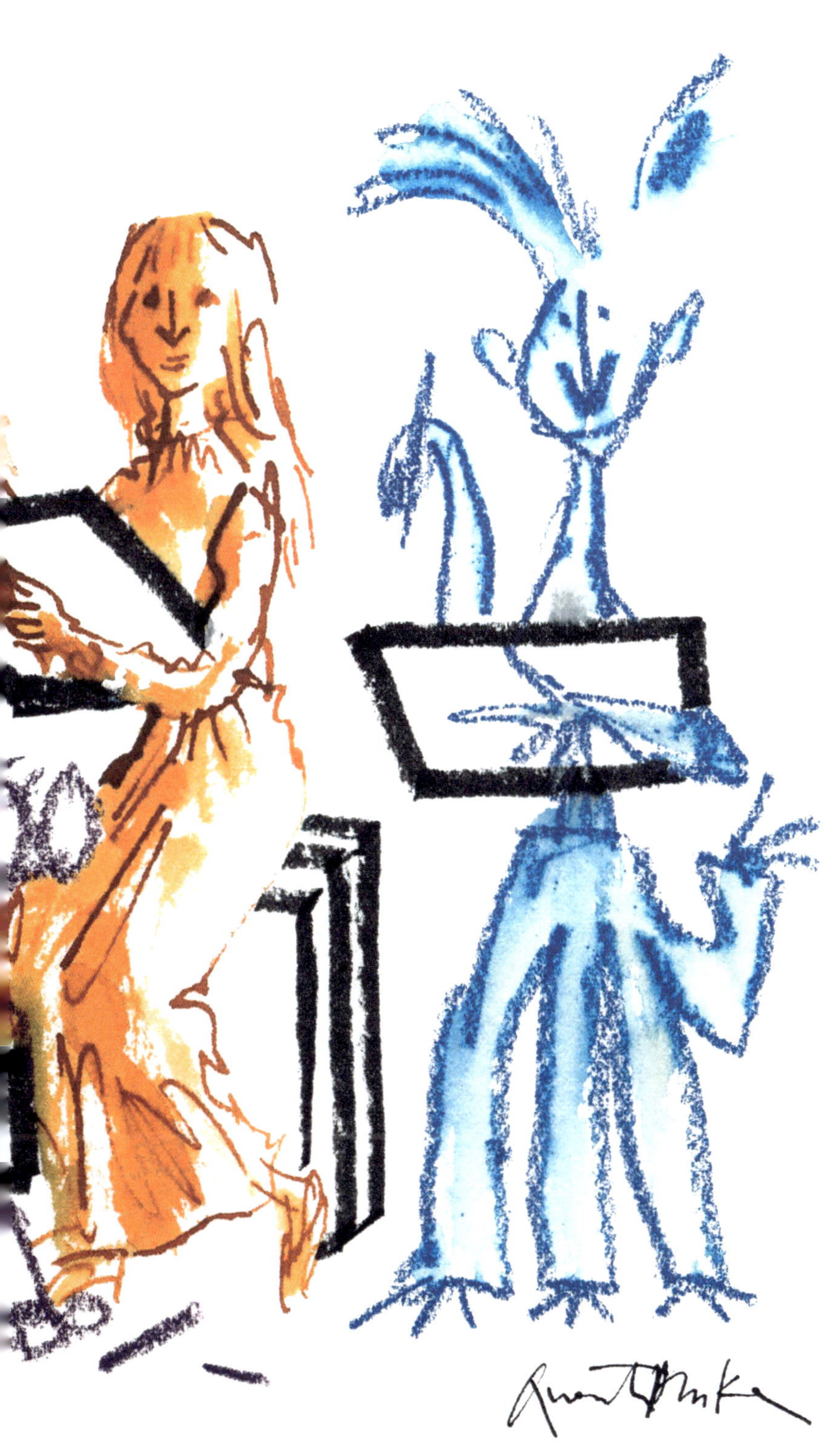

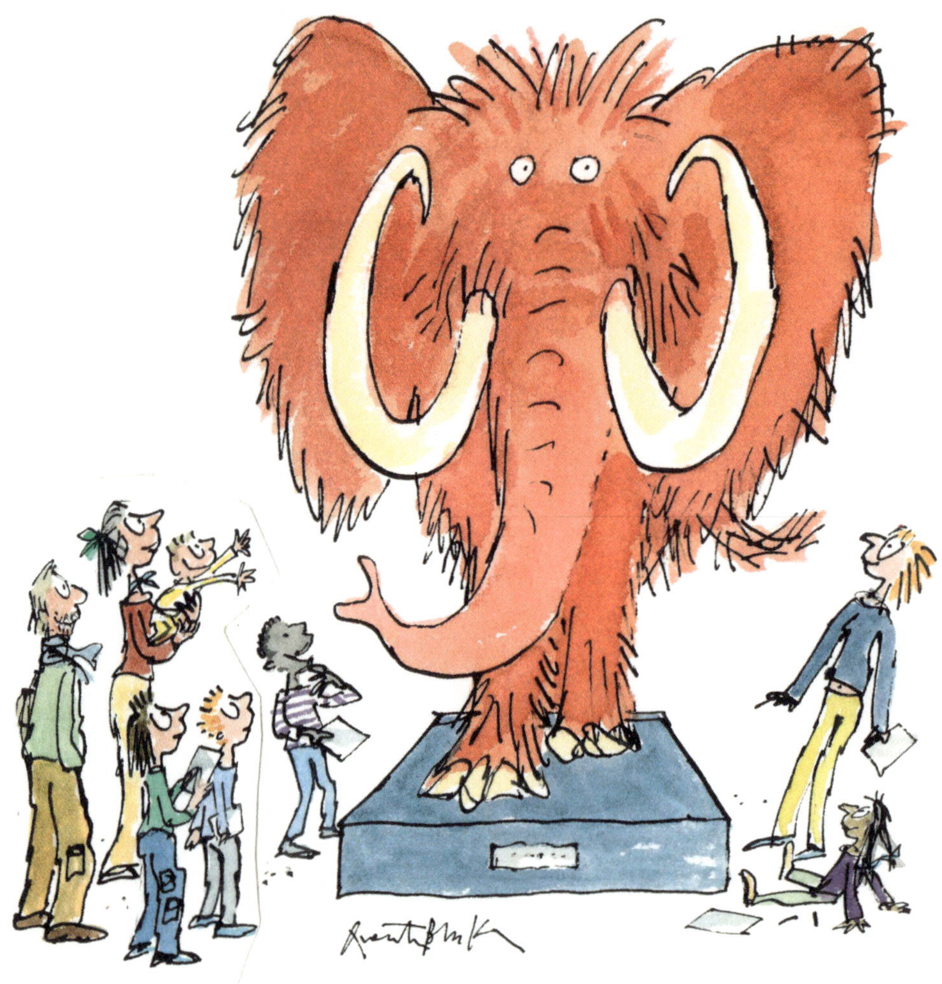

*Kids in Museums Logo,* 2001

### 'Kids in Museums' Campaign

Quentin revisited the project several times; the changes in the subject matter of his artwork reflect the growing awareness of inclusivity.

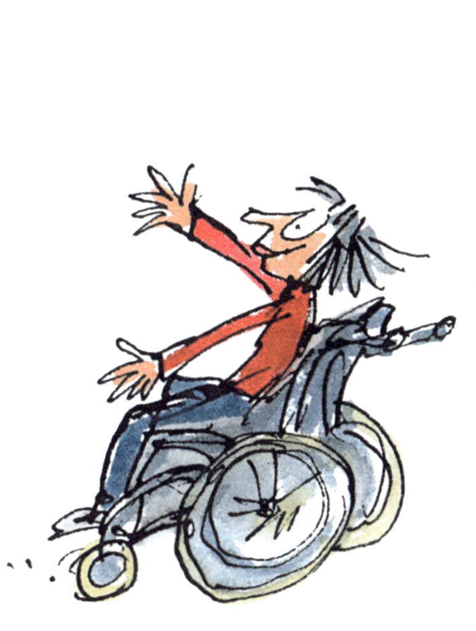

*Kids in Museums,* Campaign, 2001

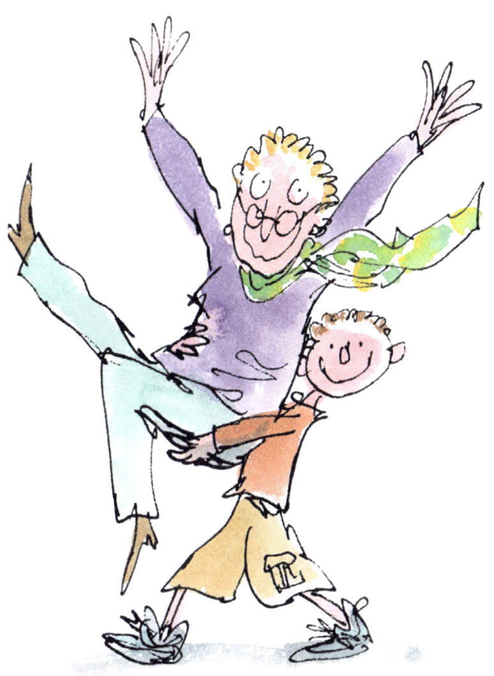

*Take your Granny to the Museum,* 2008

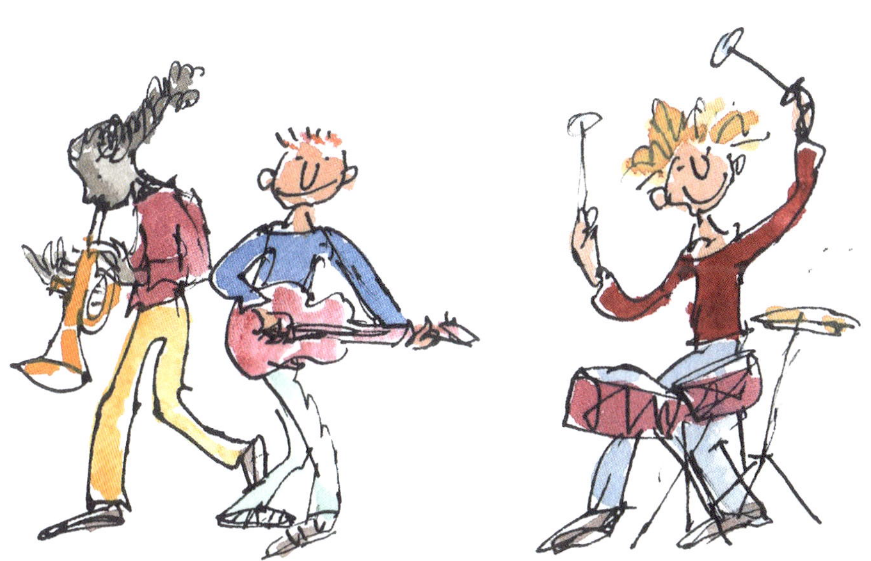

*Gigs in Museums Logo,* 2016

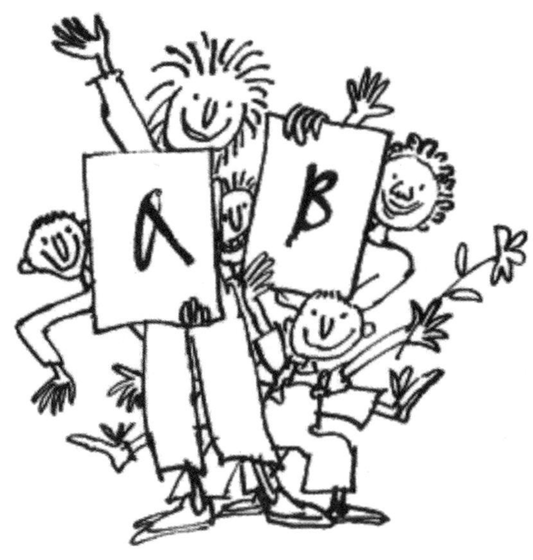

## The Quentin Blake Europe School

Berlin has several schools known as Europe schools which are bilingual. In 2003 the Staatliche Europaschule 13 decided it would prefer to have a name and voted to name their school after Quentin. He was there for the naming day and visited the school on a few other occasions; on these visits he would often do impromptu drawings:

'…what has been most rewarding, as often in this kind of situation, is that the occasion of my visit is the wonderful pretext for a surge of the children's drawing, painting, writing and performance. I don't think I have ever seen so many hand-drawn cockatoos together at one time.'

Some years later, when Quentin felt less inclined to make the journey to Berlin, he offered to do something more permanent for the school. Two drawings were enlarged to create mural panels: one where the children eat and another where they relax. As with some of the artworks he created for the Nightingale Project, he made 'use of decorative trees, so that we don't have to bother with perspective and we get a good view of the children's various activities.'

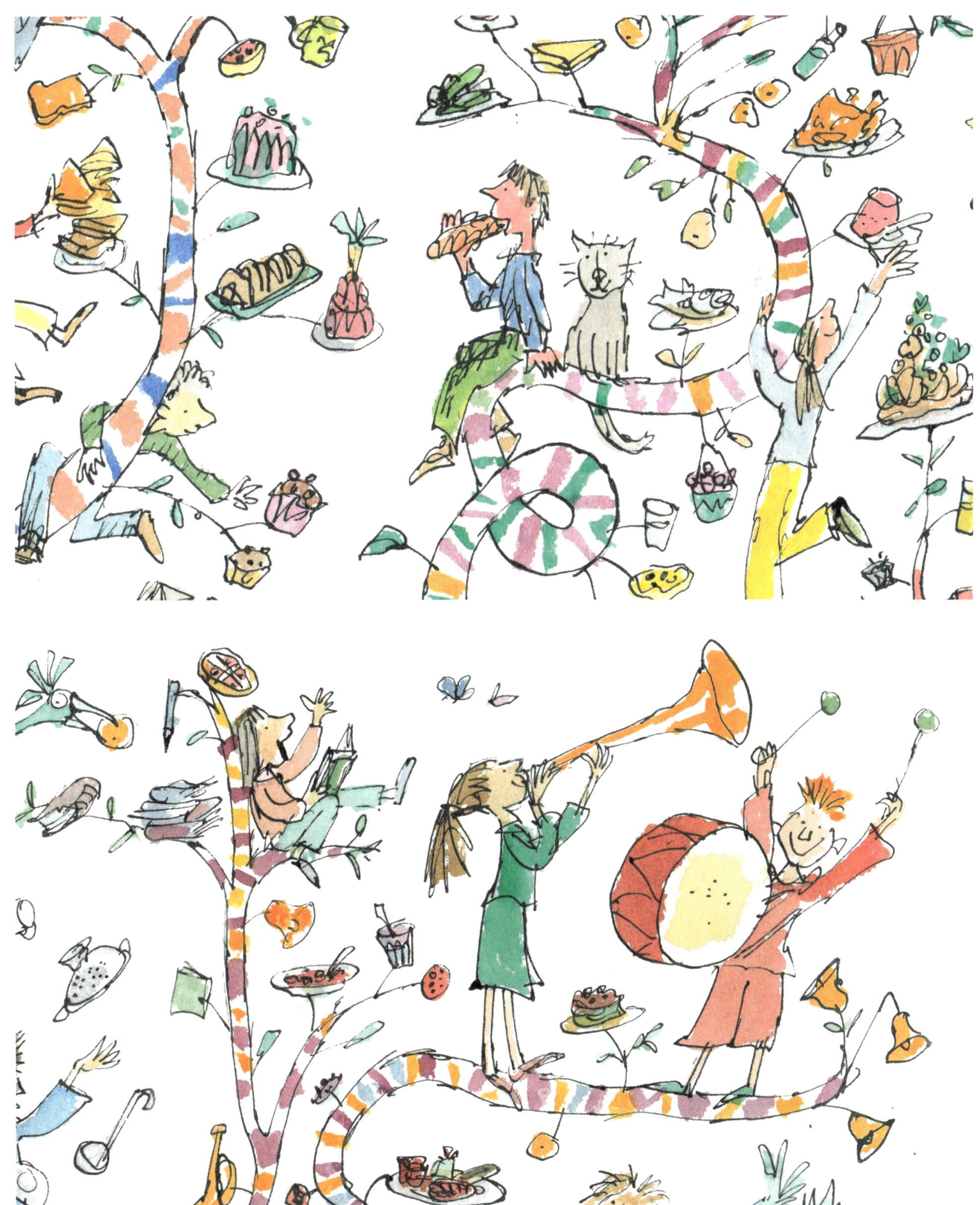

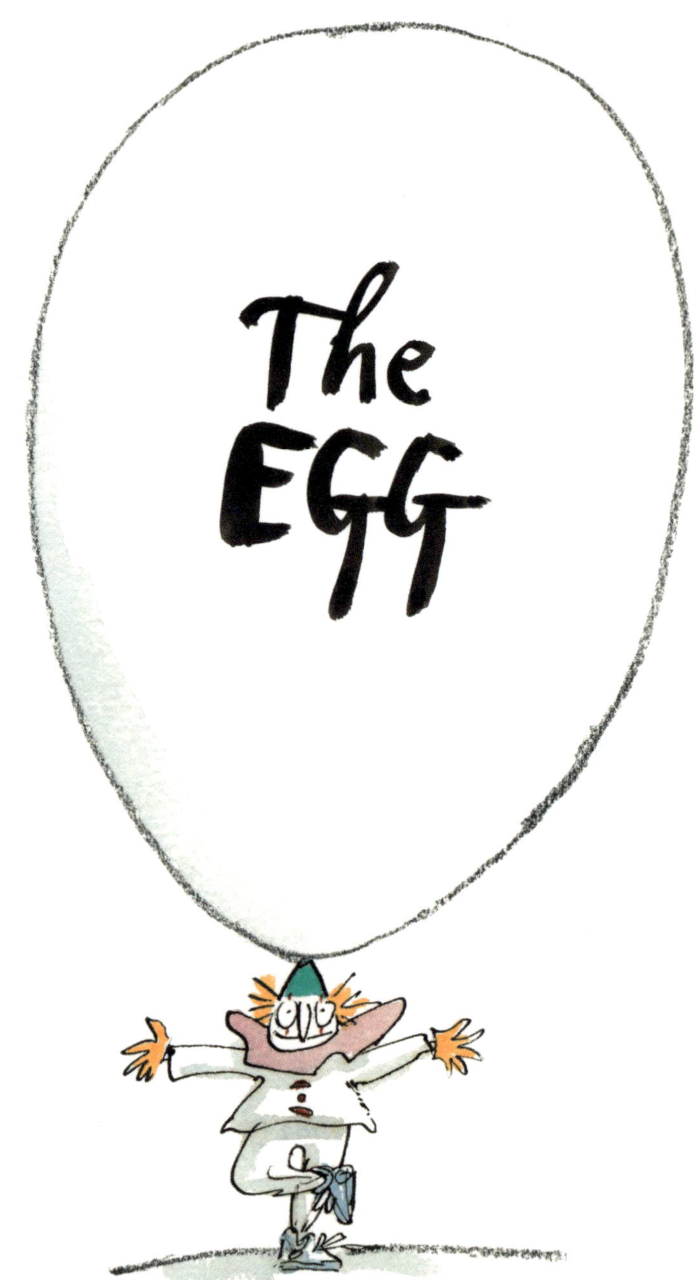

# The EGG

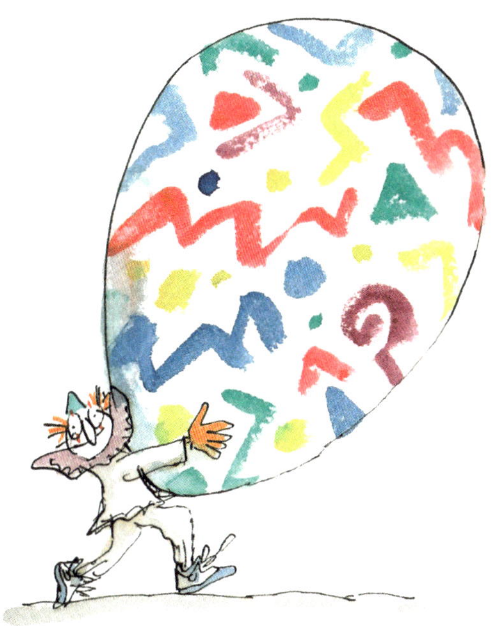

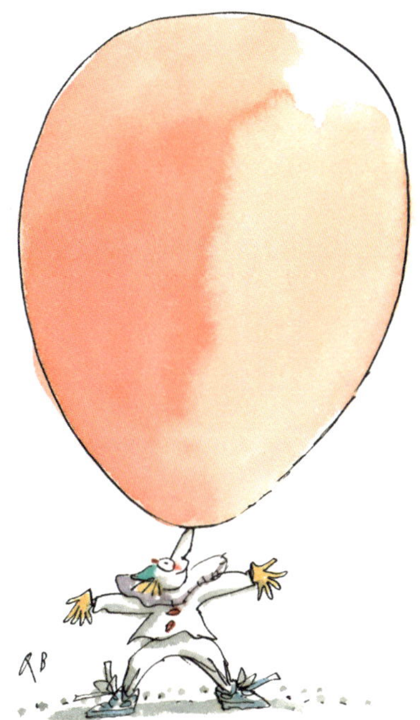

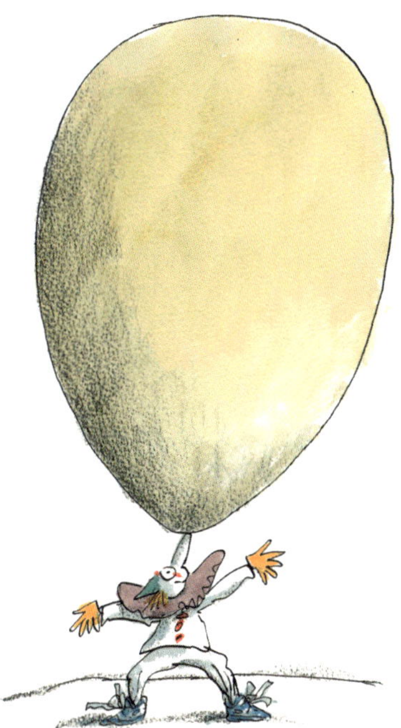

*Poster for The Egg Theatre*, Bath, 2006

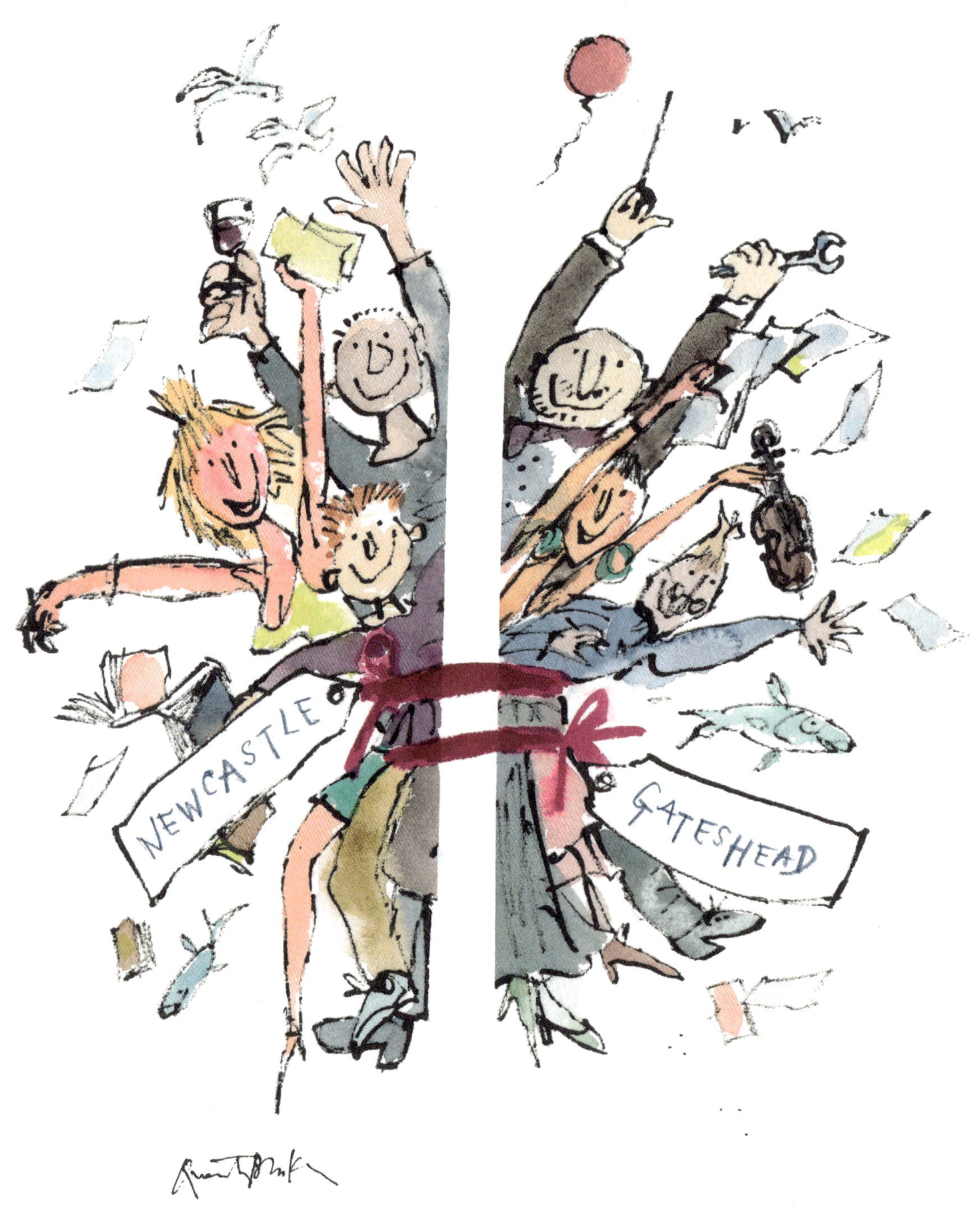


*Banner for Five TV 'Newcastle Gateshead' Promotion*, 2005

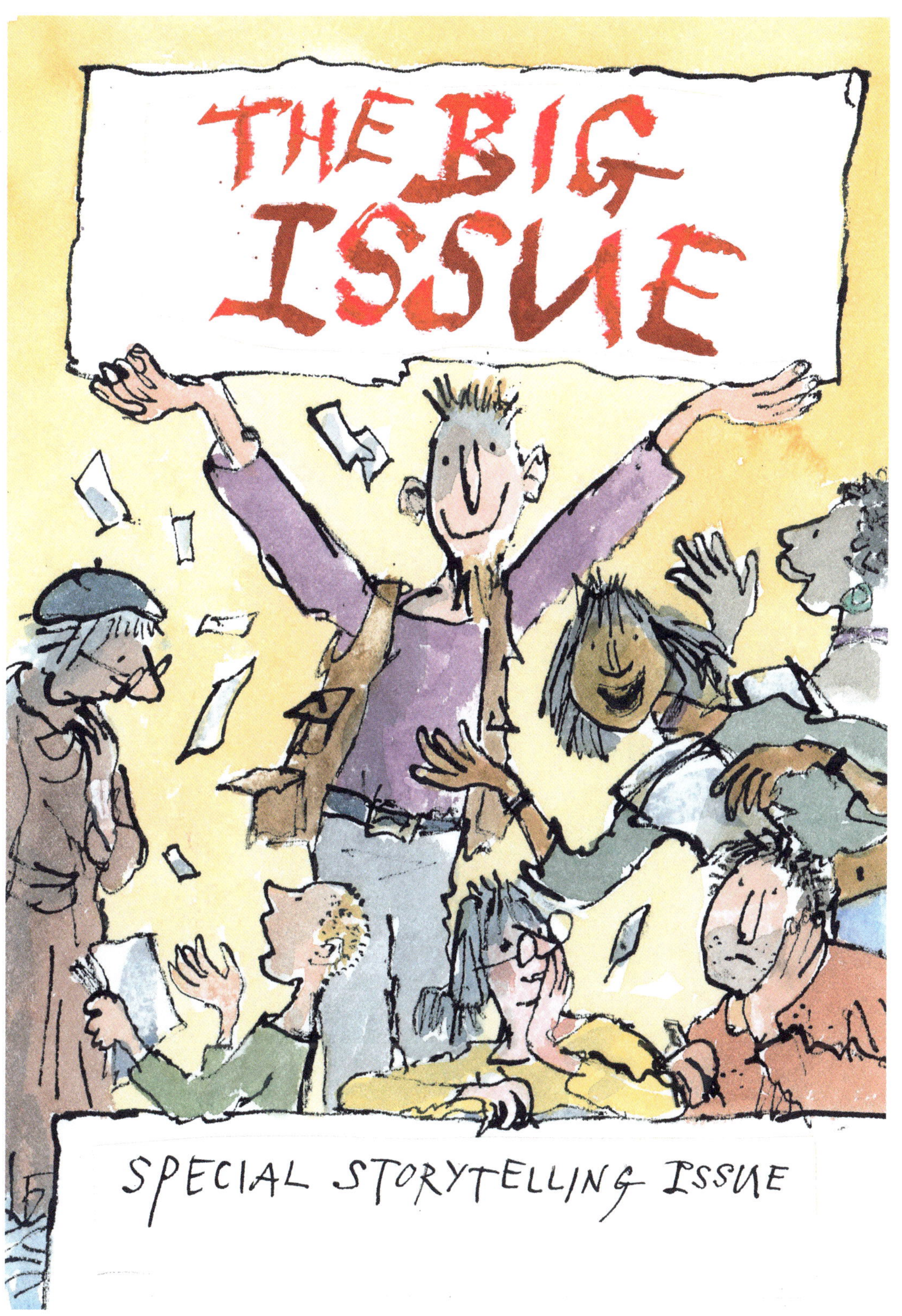


*Cover for* The Big Issue, *Storytelling Issue,* 2006

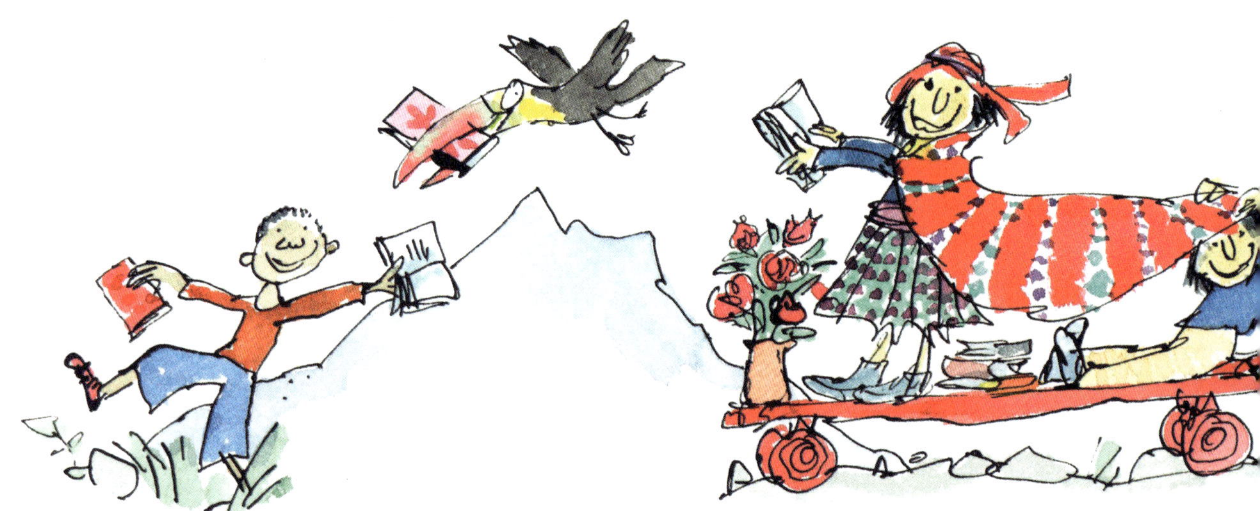

## Book Buses

In 2007 Tom Maschler, Quentin's editor of thirty years at Jonathan Cape, asked Quentin to illustrate a bus.

'The Book Bus travels around Zambia visiting schools and orphanages. It's a peripatetic library run by volunteers and which organises visits by artists and writers. In 2009 the project extended to another bus in Ecuador, the inspiring initiative of the parents of a group of gap-year students who had lost their lives in an accident there in 2008.'

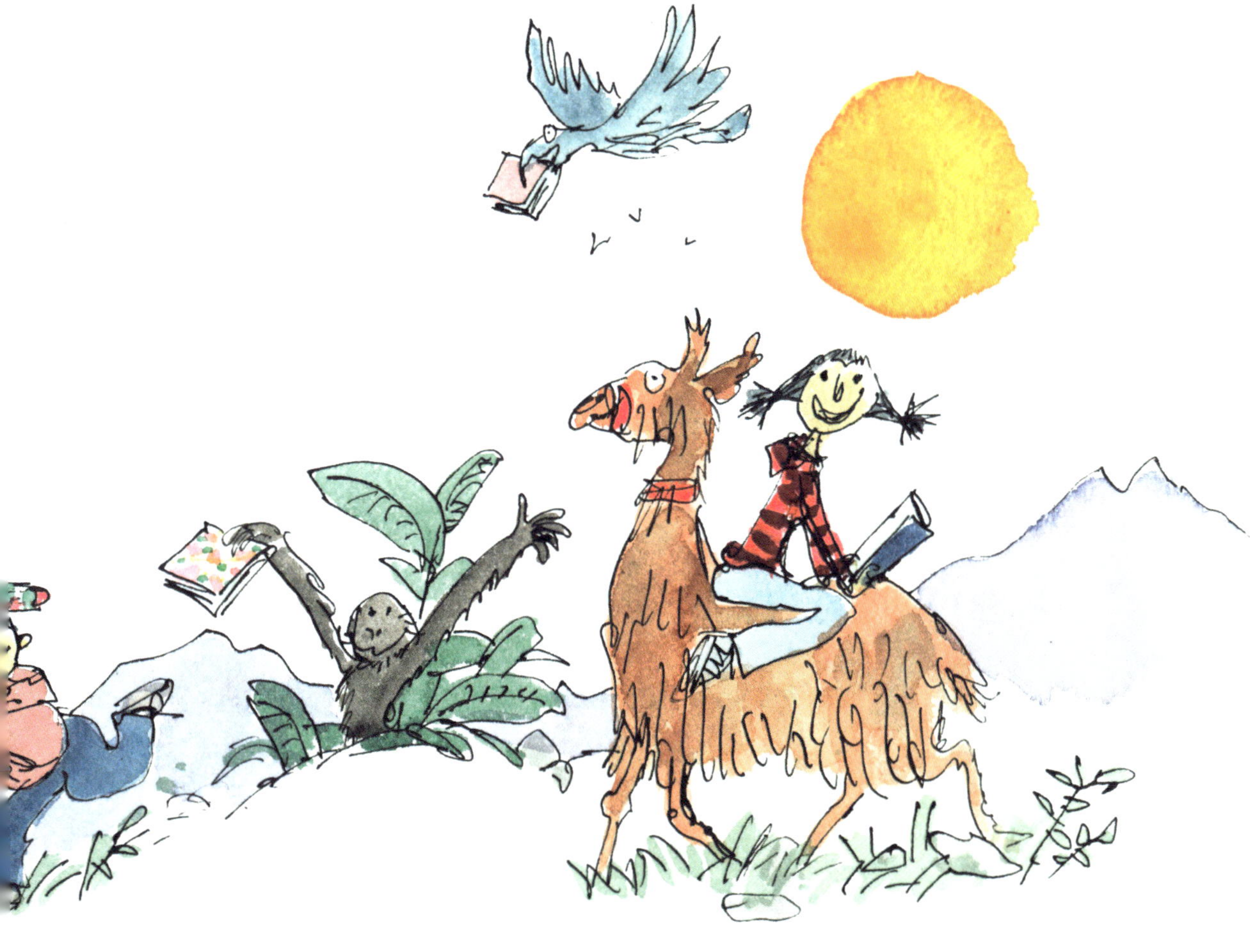

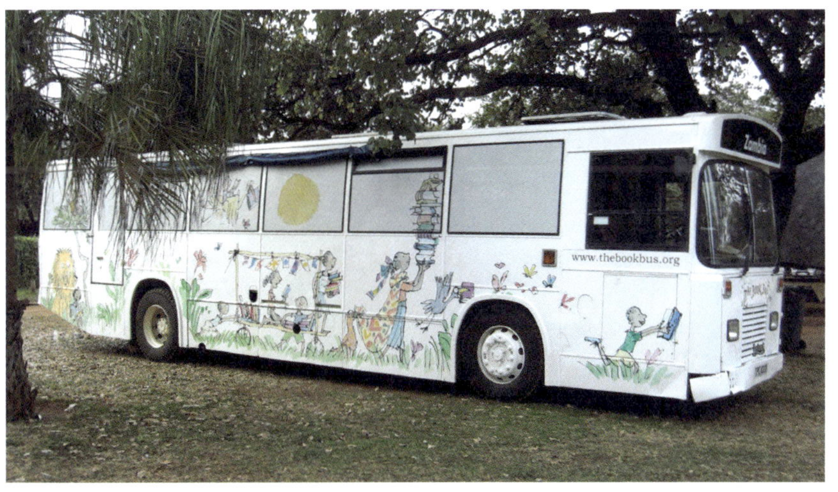

In 2018 Quentin's old school in Sidcup, the Lamorbey Church of England Primary School, bought a London bus to use as a library and they asked him if he would come to the opening:

'I explained that I really no longer make visits, but I am always happy to draw – so would they like some drawings on the side of the bus? They would, and I was able to fill the panels formerly occupied by advertisements with pictures of an assortment of young readers.'

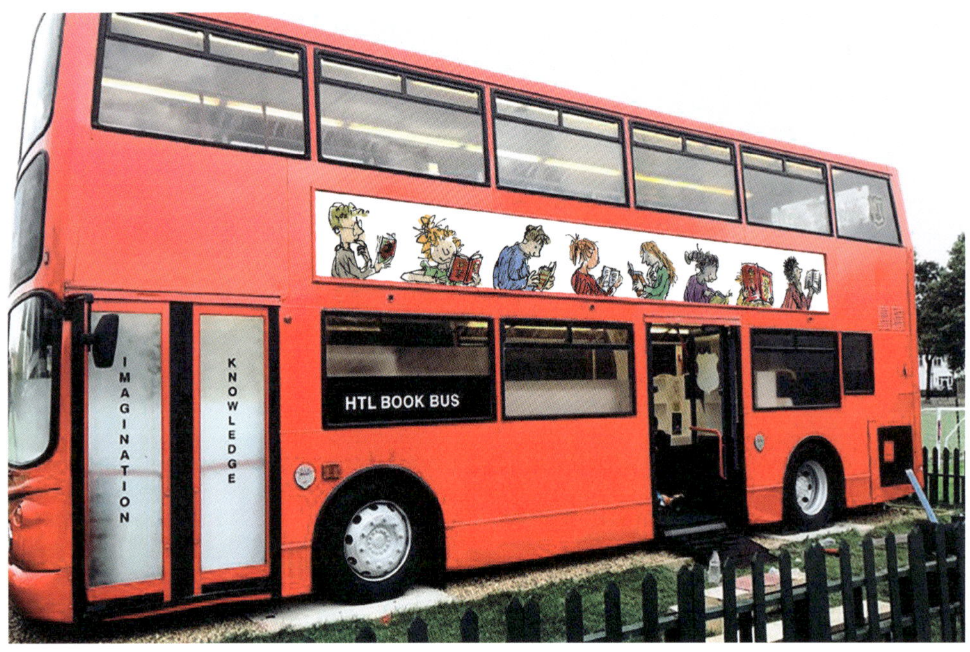



ABOVE & ALL OPPOSITE – *Lamorbey School Book Bus Visual and Illustrations,* 2017

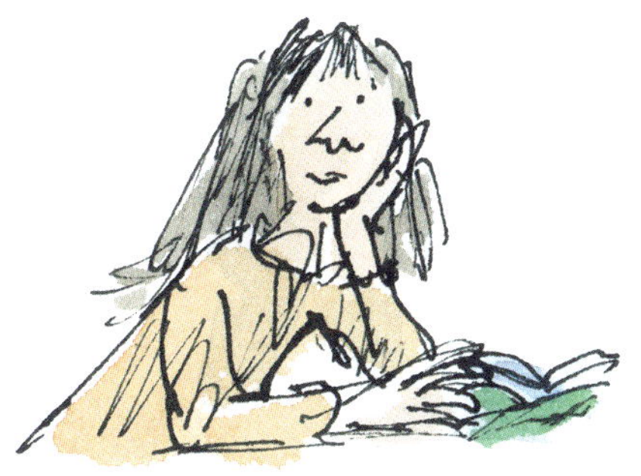
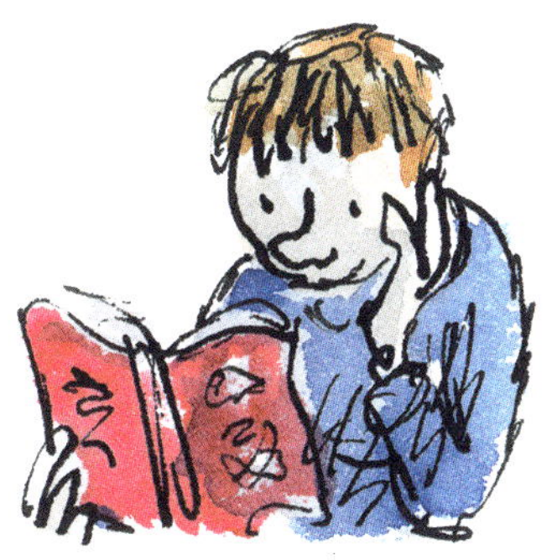

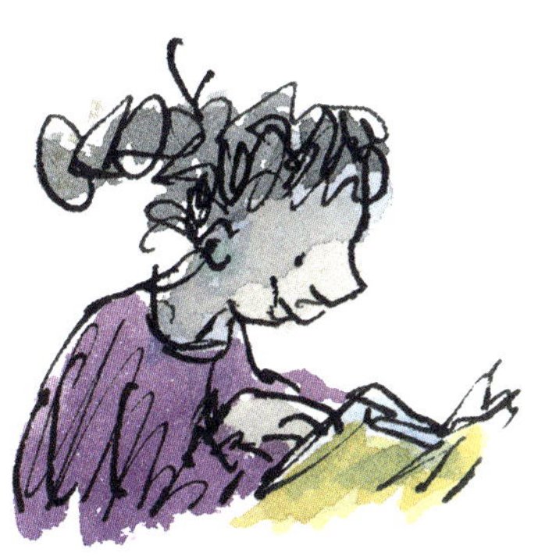
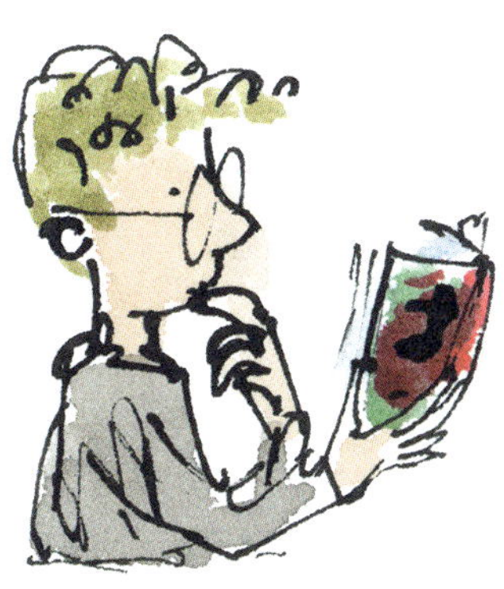
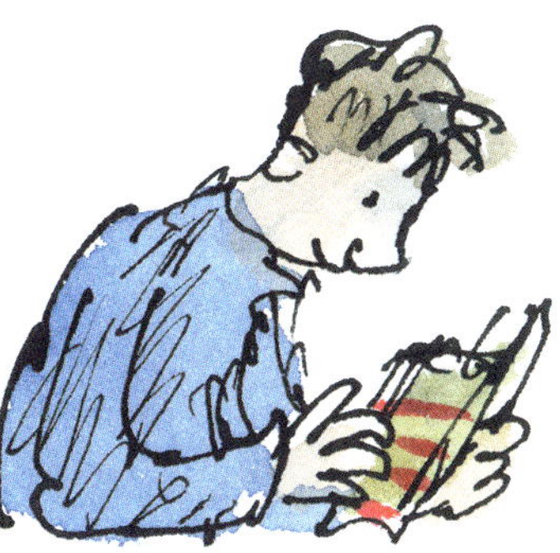
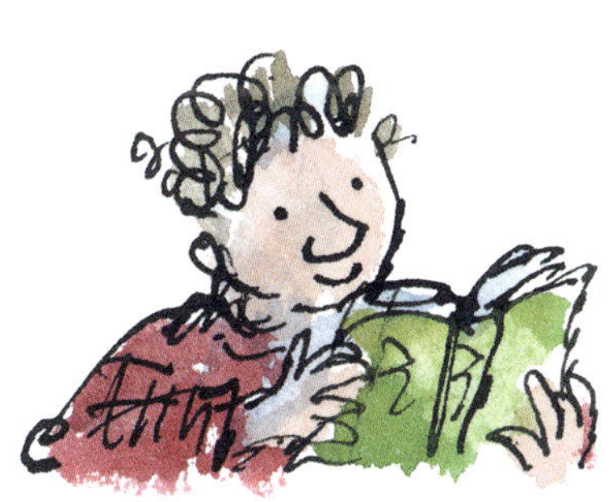
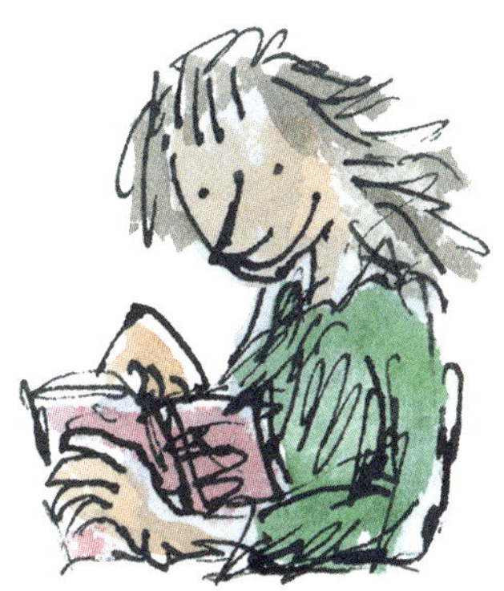
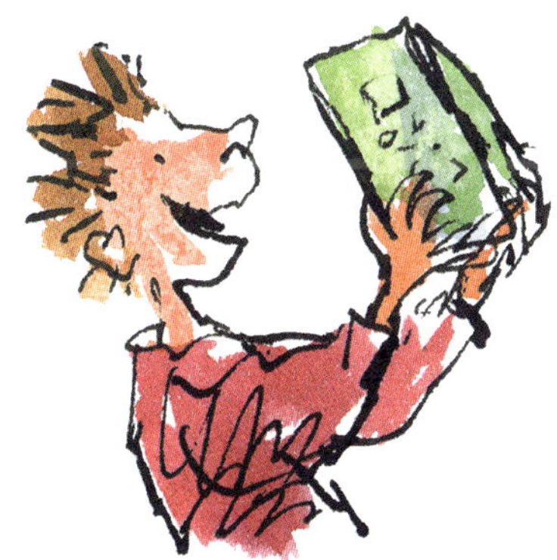

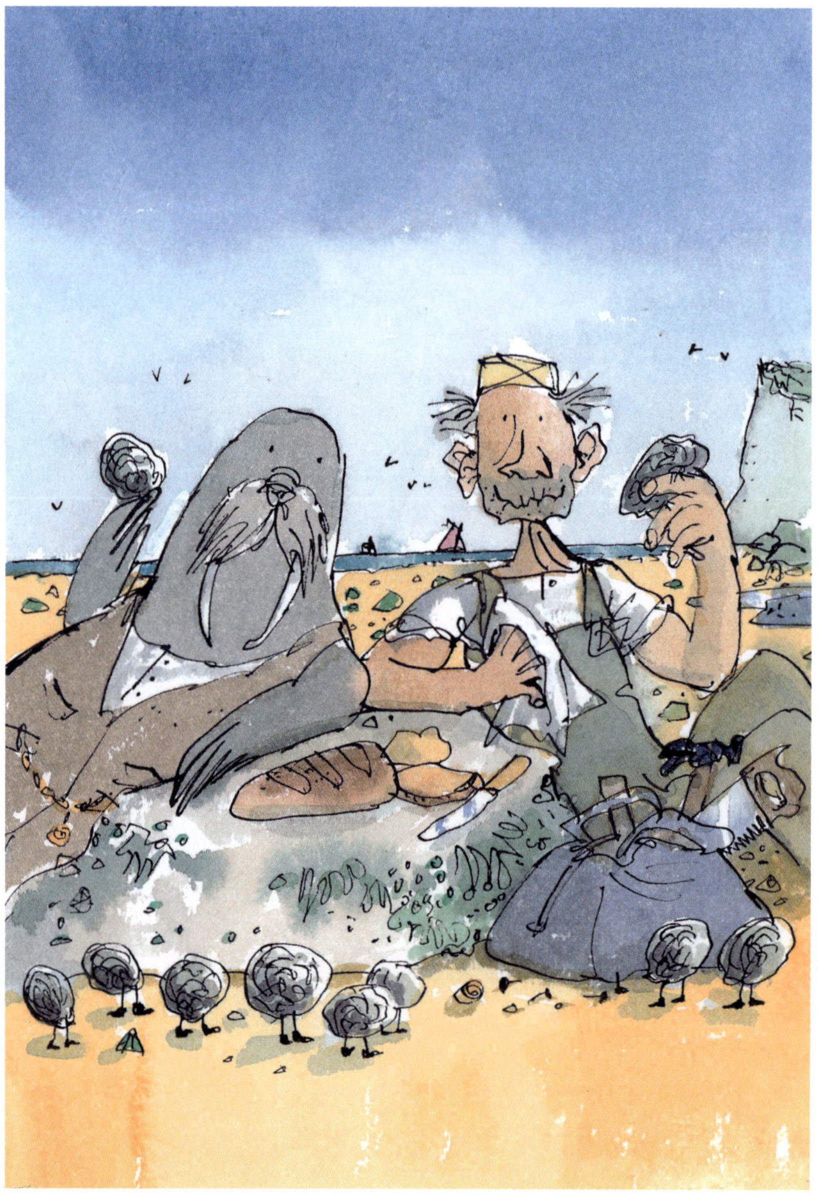

## The Children's Trust

Cover artwork for *The Walrus and the Carpenter and Other Favourite Poems,* an anthology in aid of The Children's Trust, a charity for children with brain injury and multiple learning disabilities.

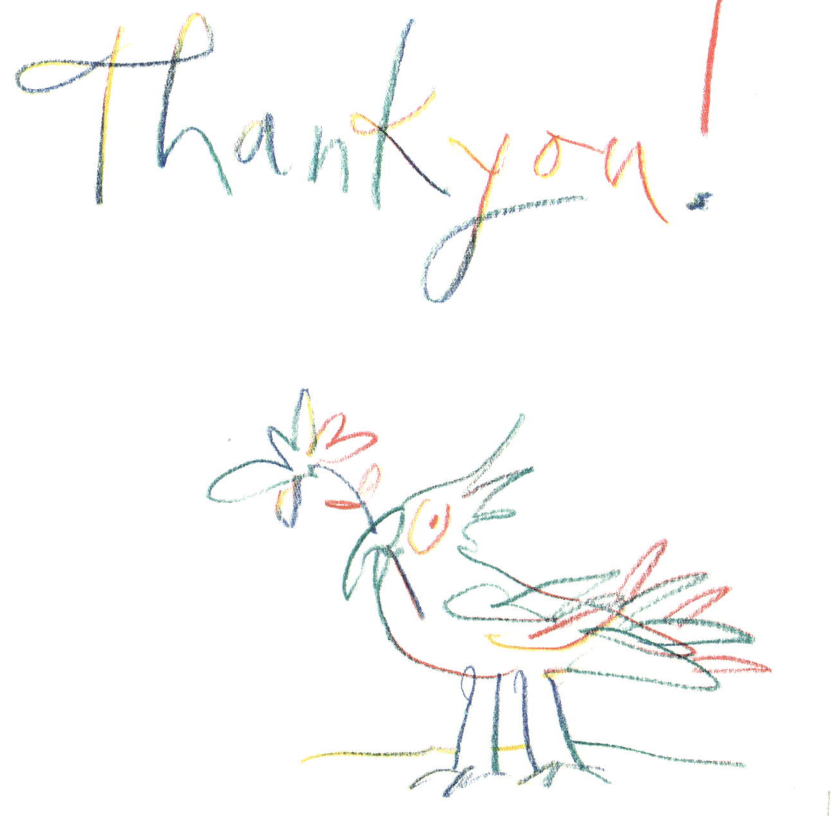


**'Thank You' Card**

Quentin drew this using a Magic Pencil as a standard reply letter for schoolchildren who wrote to him.

# HAY FEVER

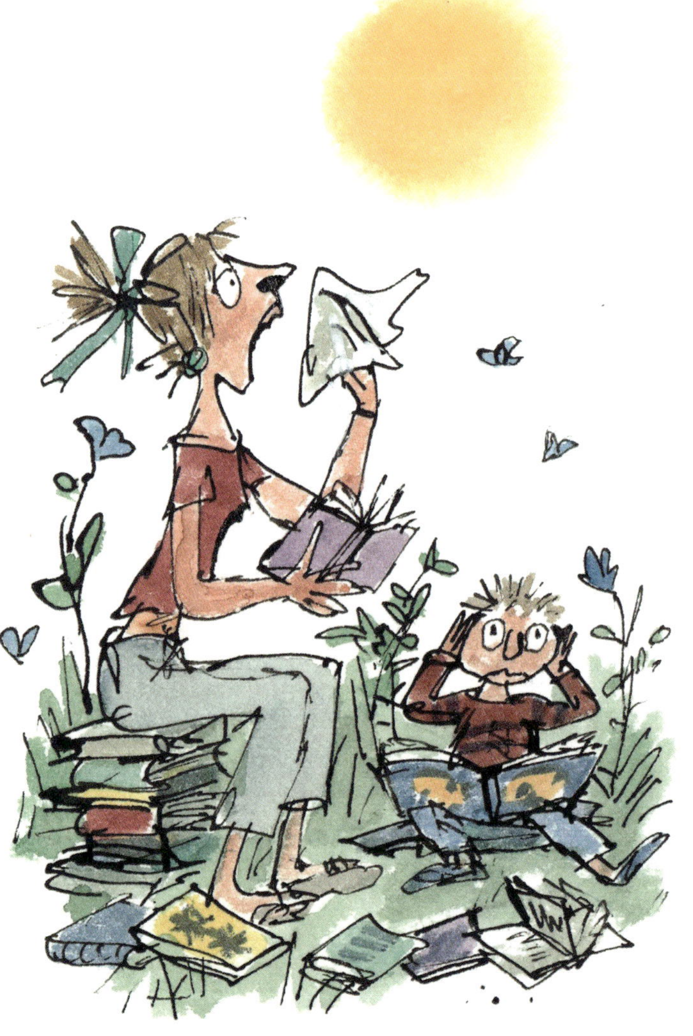

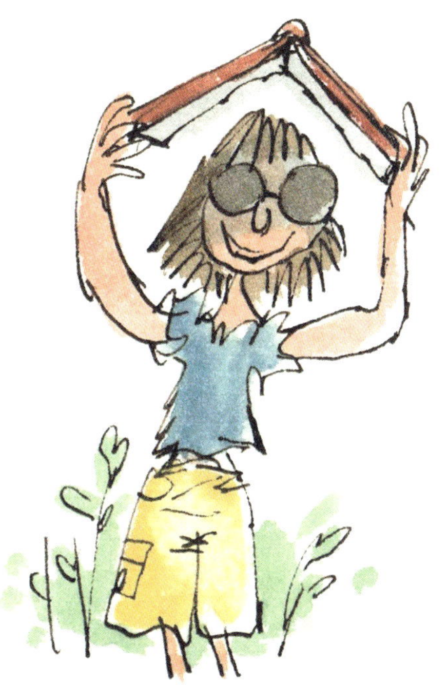

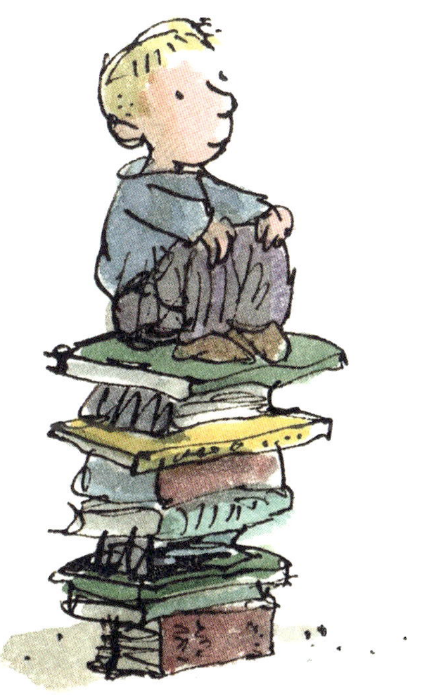

OPPOSITE & ABOVE – *Illustrations and Lettering for the Hay Festival Brochure,* 2017

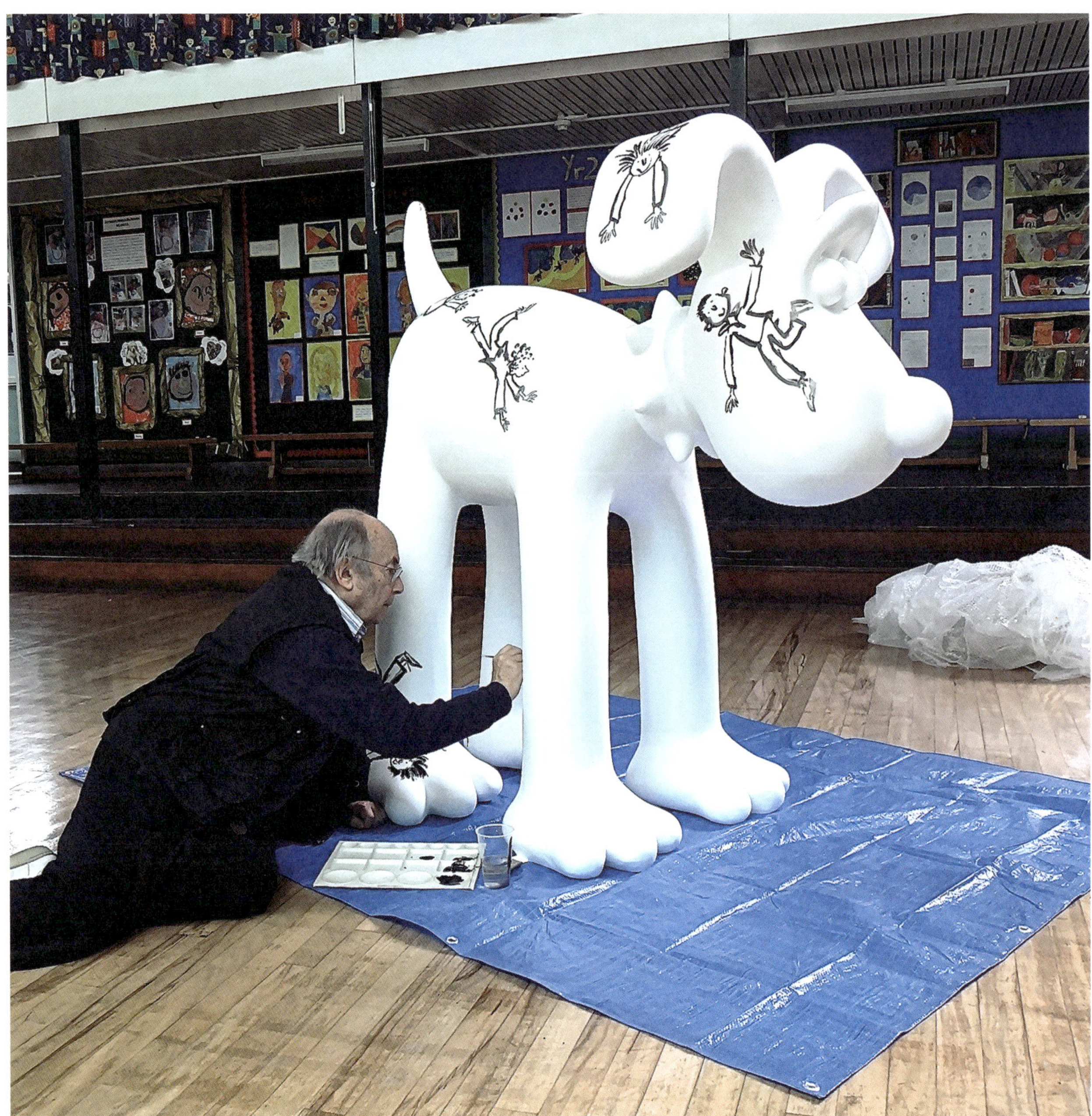

## Gromit Unleashed

Eighty fibreglass sculptures of Gromit were placed on the streets of Bristol and then auctioned to raise funds for Wallace & Gromit's Grand Appeal, a charity dedicated to the Bristol Children's Hospital.

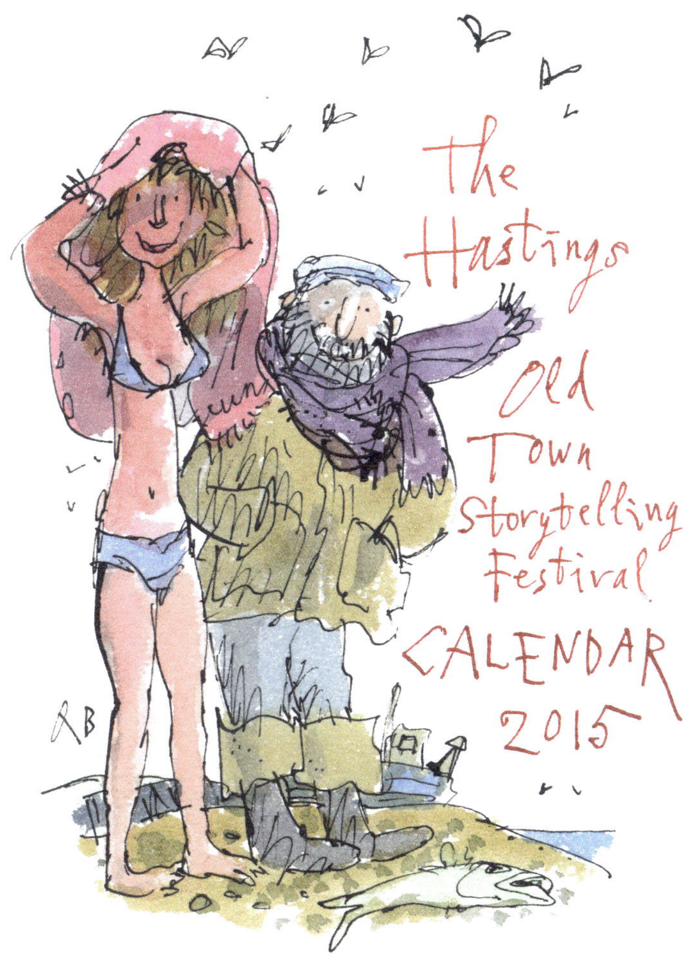


## Hastings

For many years, Quentin had a house in Hastings Old Town. When the Jerwood Hastings opened in 2012 (later to become Hastings Contemporary), its director, Liz Gilmore, embraced him as a local artist and Quentin has had several exhibitions there. It also meant that the wider Hastings community realised that they had the peerless illustrator on their doorstep. The local Storytelling Festival asked him to do some drawings for their calendar and the Hastings Library wanted a 'decorative feature'.

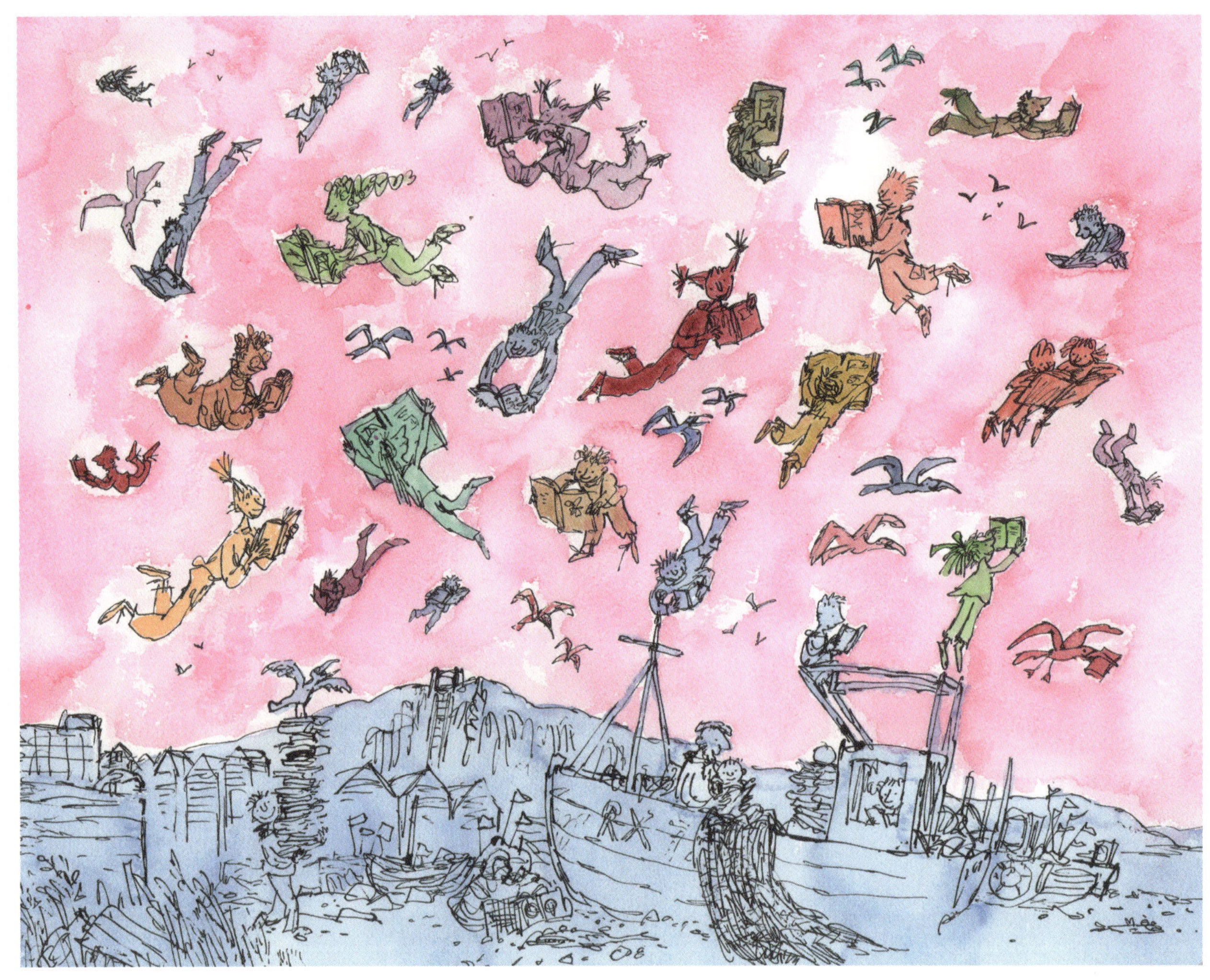

ABOVE – Library Banner, 2015<br>
OPPOSITE – A Warm Winter Scarf, 2023

'To make it belong particularly to Hastings I wanted to show something of the fishing beach, with a fishing boat in the foreground. Some years ago I did the cover of a brochure for the Bologna Children's Book Fair, where I showed children flying about on their books, and I made use of the idea again here. This time the sky was full of young readers, as well as one or two surprised-looking seagulls… The picture is not real life, but I hope it genuinely says something about the effect of books, especially on young people.'

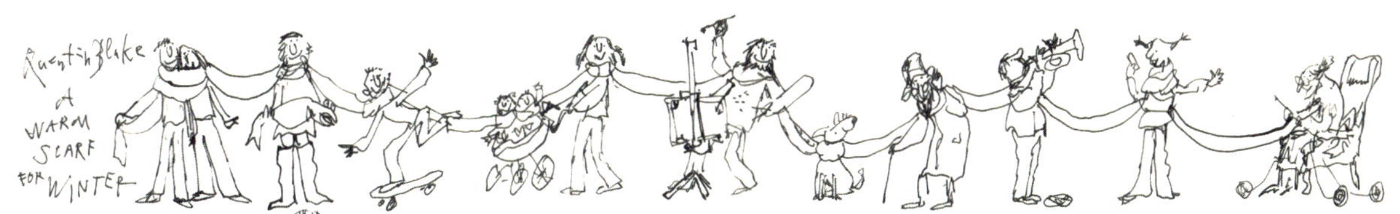

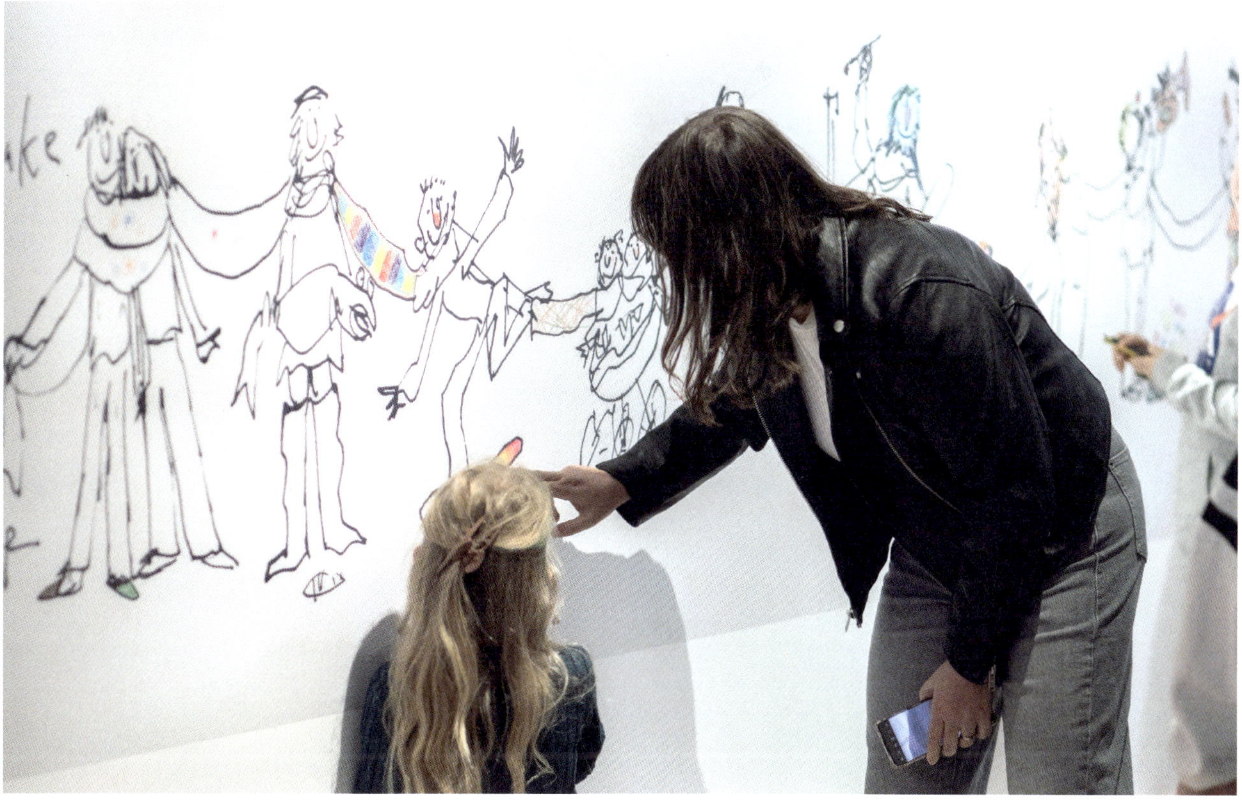

In October 2023 Quentin drew the outline for *A Warm Winter Scarf* – a mural for Hastings Contemporary, which was left blank so that visitors to the gallery could colour it in. When the scarf was completed, it was replaced with a new one.

# The Dal Babu Projects

Dal Babu is a retired Chief Superintendent of the Metropolitan Police who works tirelessly to help prevent knife crime and gang warfare among young people in London. In 2001 he launched a crime reduction programme in the King's Cross area.

Dal remembers that 'there was a huge problem with young people from the area fighting and this resulted in serious injuries and a death.… Many of the young people who were involved had missed school and had trouble reading. But they recognised Quentin's illustrations of the BFG and Matilda.'

He invited Quentin to Albany Street Police Station to draw for some of the children and young people. Quentin works fast so he can draw live, in real time. He did A2 drawings of the BFG, Matilda and The Enormous Crocodile as well as a lion, a boy, a chicken and an old lady. He talked to young people about staying safe.

'… It was amazing getting some of the children who had been fighting in the same room; they were mesmerized by Quentin's illustrations.… After Quentin's visit we saw a drop of 184 calls about youth fighting in 6 months to 4 calls in the following 6 months… With Quentin they felt like normal kids – law enforcement didn't work.'

Some years later Dal arranged for Quentin to visit St Francis de Sales school in Tottenham. The main hall was teaming with five hundred children from the school and from St Paul's All Hallows School in Harrow. They were nine to twelve-year-olds and they were accompanied by teachers, carers and parents. Quentin used an overhead projector to draw on so that his work could be seen on a huge screen. He drew The Twits, Miss Honey, the BFG and Sophie and talked about good and bad characters, and that it's the expressions rather than the features of a character which tell you whether they are unpleasant people or not. After Quentin's visit the children drew posters on the theme of young people and safety which were displayed in Harrow and Tottenham including at Harrow police stations.

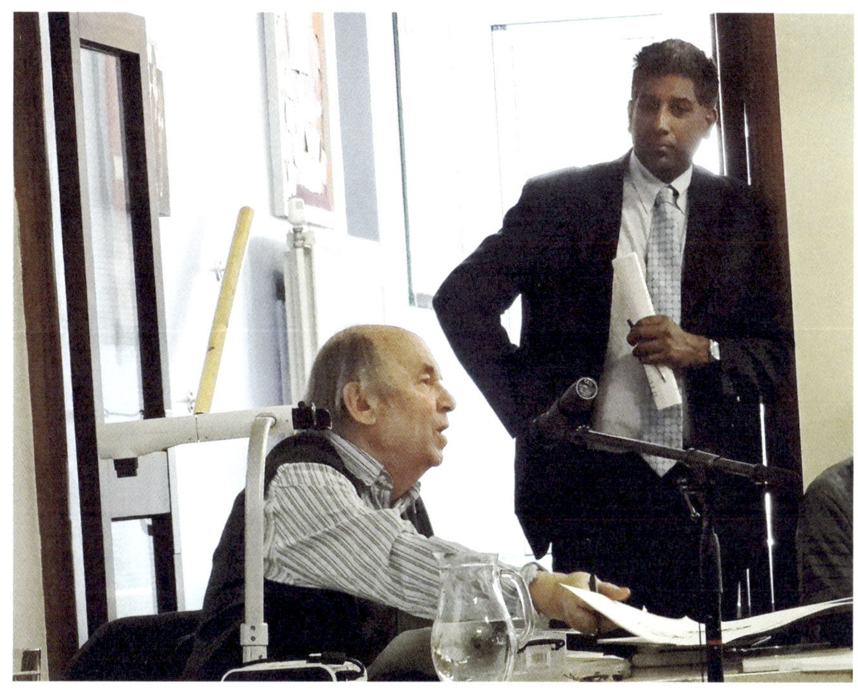

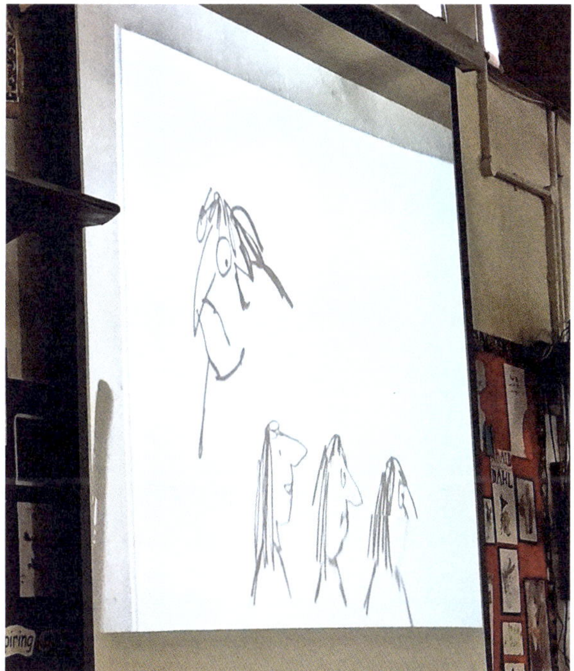

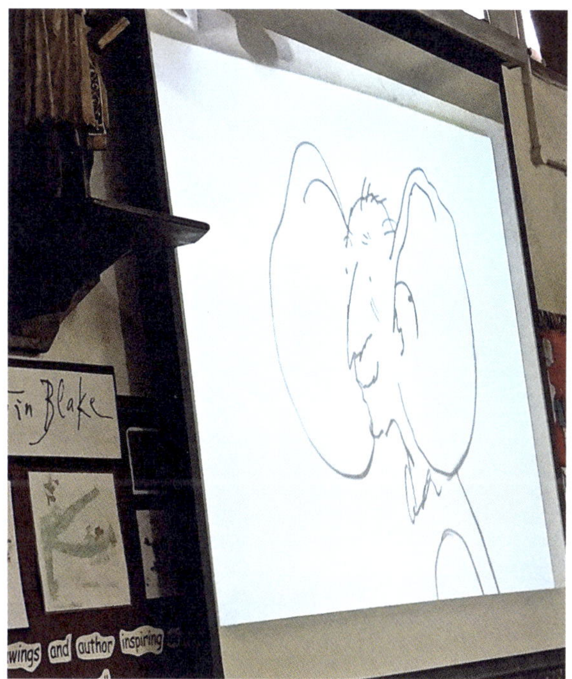


Quentin and Dal at St Francis de Sales School, 2014

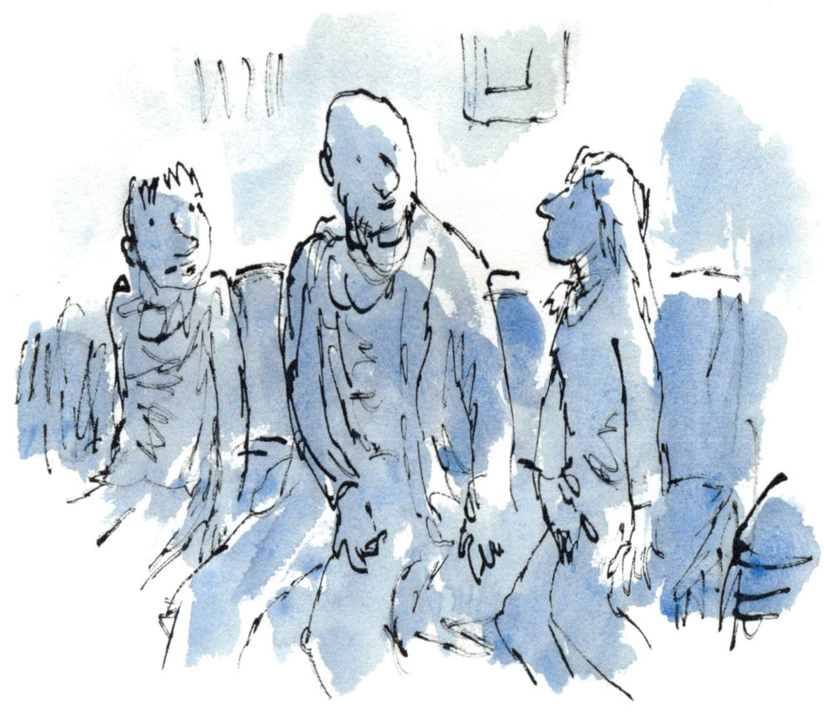

## *HM Prisons*

In 2023 Dal had become a member of the Parole Board for HM Prisons and asked Quentin if he would do a series of drawings for the visitors' rooms where families meet with the prisoner. But the prison services thought they weren't what they needed; Quentin understood that they were 'too aspirational' and started again.

'I started looking at family scenes and, more specifically, the relationship between children and their parents, especially those in prison. The task immediately became a real pleasure.'

He did a series of ten drawings and the Prison services reproduced five of them. By the time the drawings were officially unveiled at Brixton Prison in August 2024 the prints were already hanging in every prison in the UK. As Dal said, 'it wouldn't have happened without Quentin.'

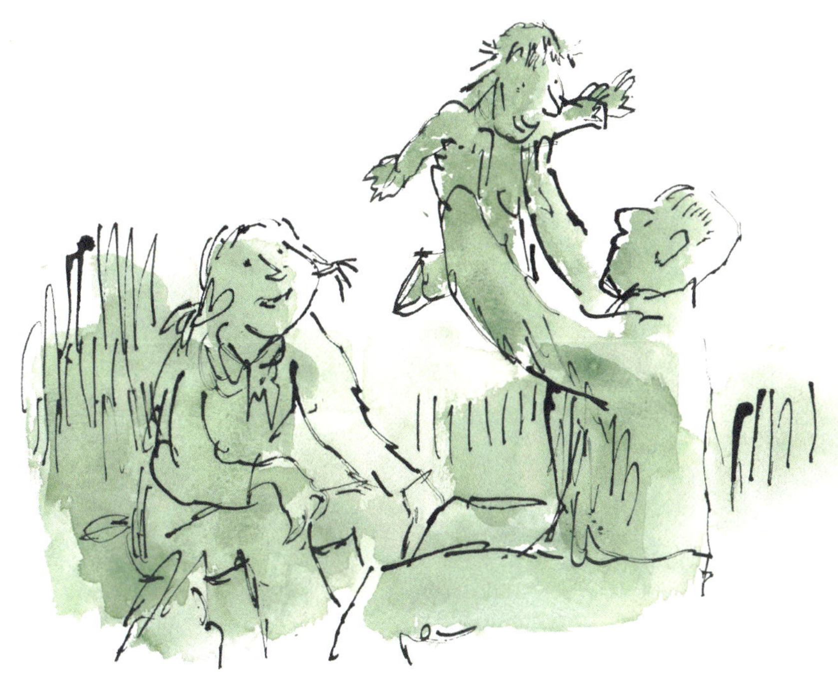

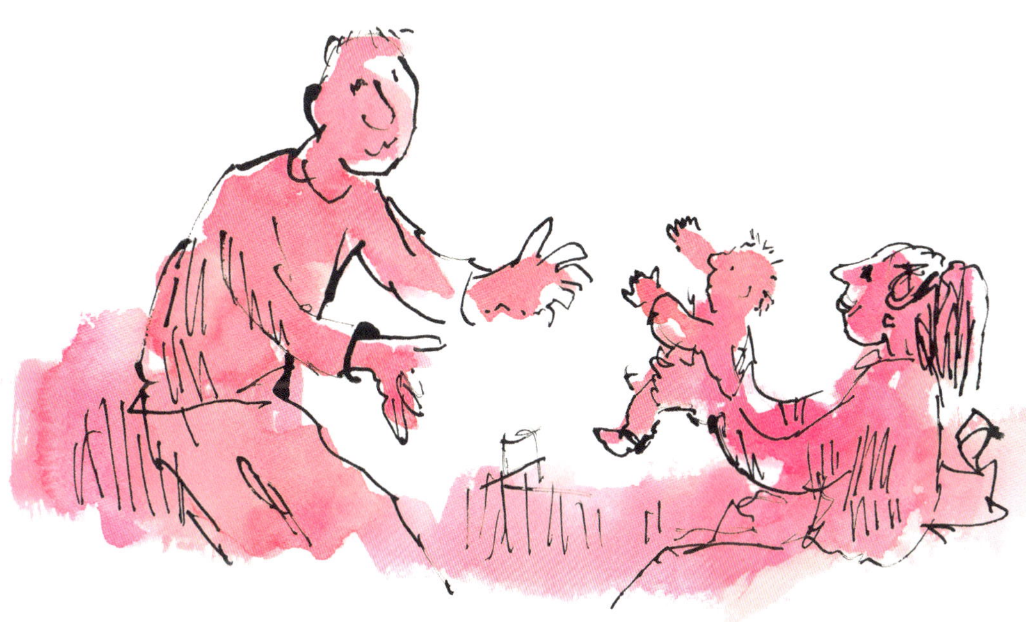

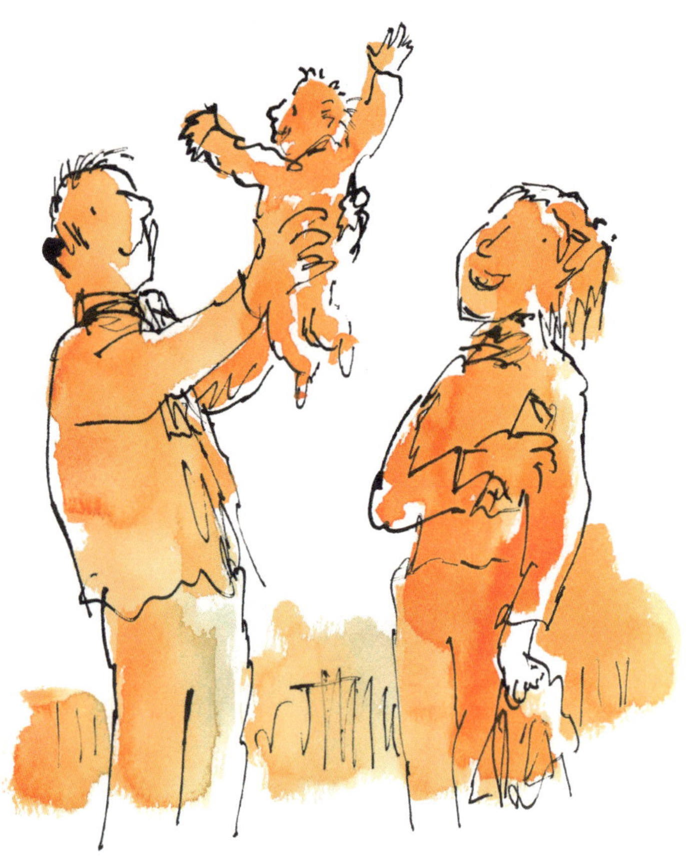

## *Cafcass*

Dal is also on the board of Cafcass, who represent and advocate for children and young people in the family court. He thought that they would also benefit from some of Quentin's drawings and Quentin agreed they should be given the remaining five drawings from the prisons series. The prints are used as starting points for conversations with children in the organisation's family rooms all over the country. The CEO of Cafcass, Jacky Tiotto, wrote to Quentin thanking him for the pictures and to explain the profound effect they had on the children:

'We have to start a conversation with children about what their lives are like…. They have to trust a complete stranger and share intimate and sometimes painful things. Your pictures are going to help to start that trust and connection. That is worth more than you may have known when you drew them.'

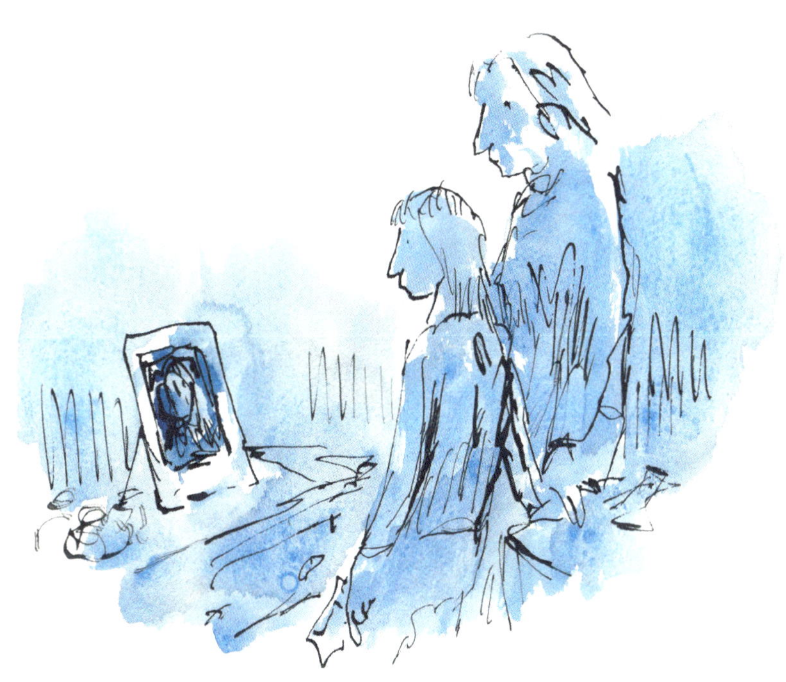

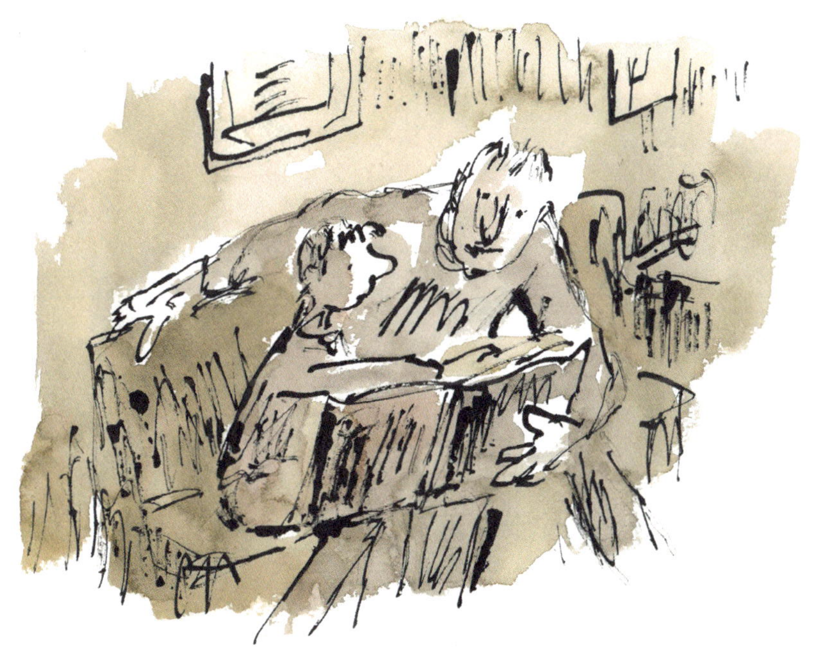

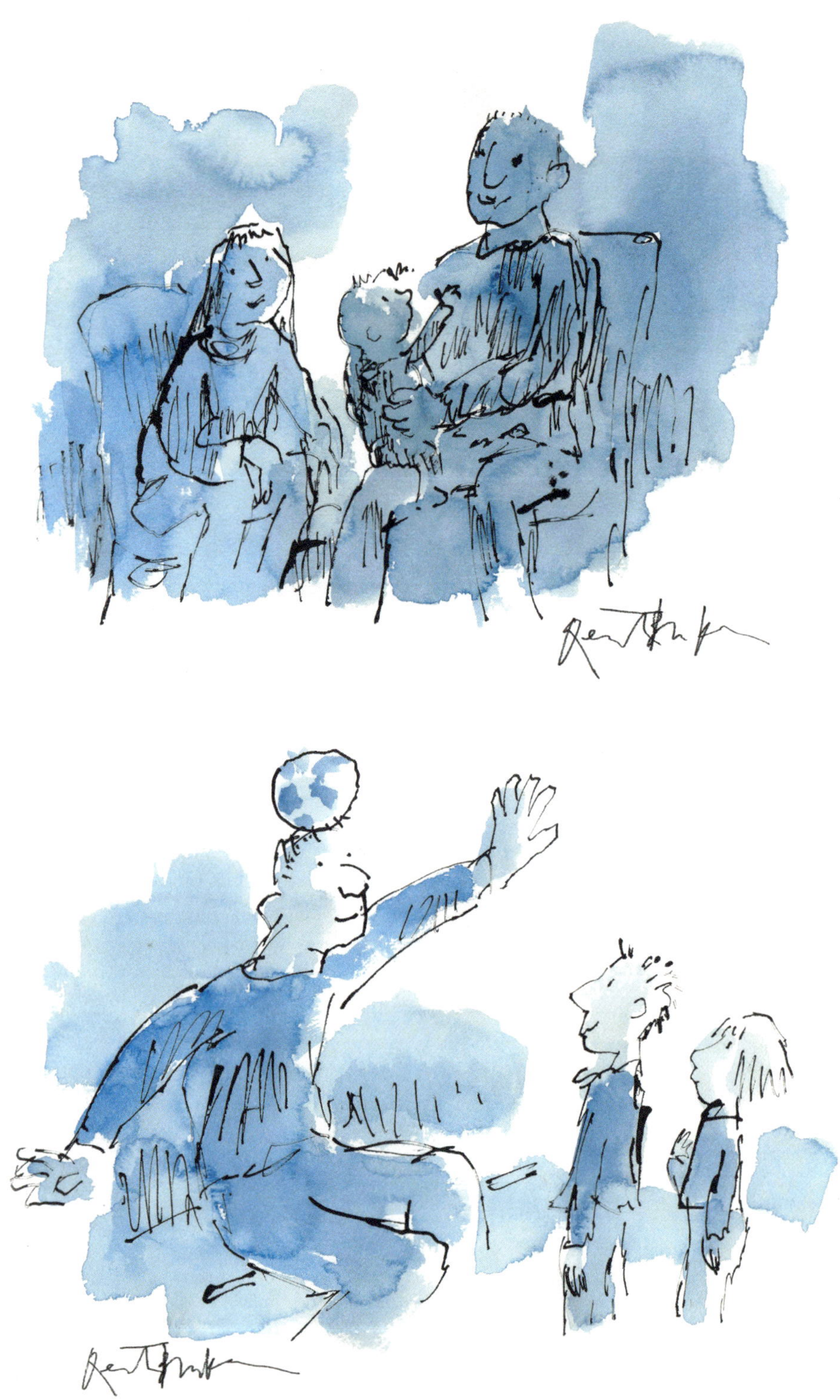

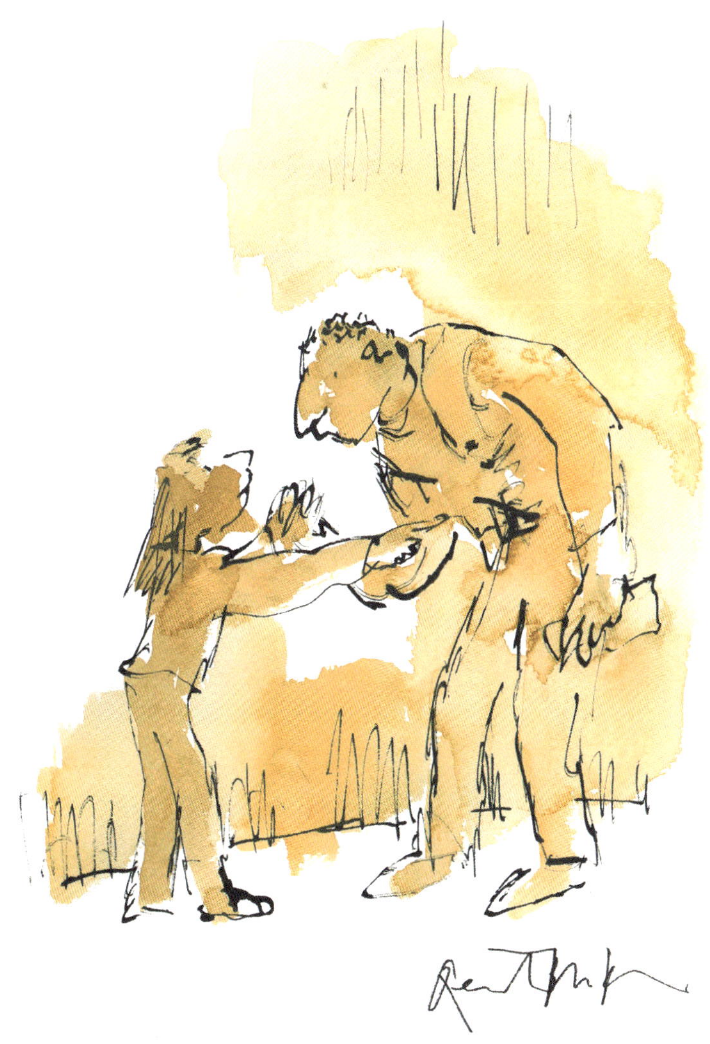

## *Approved Premises*

There are a hundred approved post-release premises that support men and women who have just come out of prison. The Chief Inspector of Probation wrote to Dal saying, 'I recently visited an approved premises for women released from prison and they have attempted to make the place welcoming by adding artwork etc. It immediately occurred to me that Quentin's artwork might be placed in this environment.'

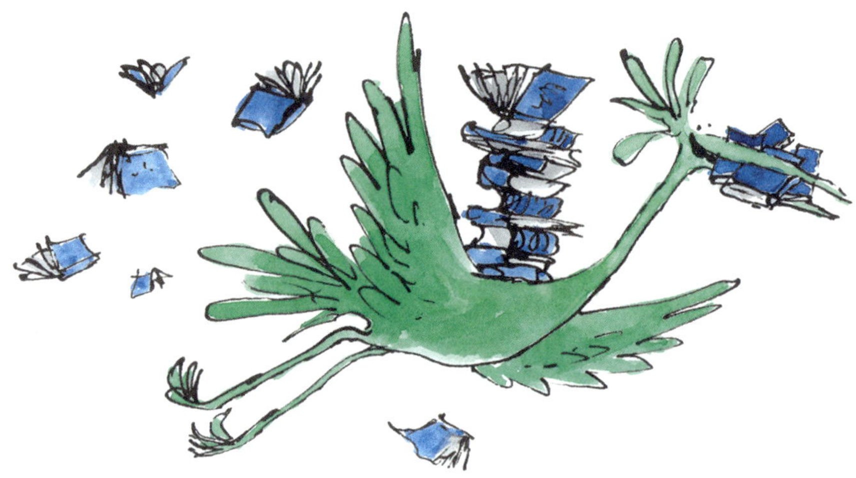

### Bibliothèque Quentin Blake, Wall Hanging

The French Institute is a twenty-minute walk from Quentin's home and studio in South Kensington. The Institute, and the area surrounding it, is like a little piece of France with its French food and book shops.

Every November the Institute had a festival of cultural and literary activities. 'Somehow I got involved at the start and ever since I have been its patron. I have also given talks and engaged in live drawings matches with visiting French artists, friends such as Bruno Heitz, Philippe Dumas and Joann Sfar.'

When the Institute decided to refurbish their children's library, they asked if they could name it after him:

'Would I consider giving my name to the reopened junior library? Not a doubt in my mind about the response. I treasure the two medals I have been awarded by France, but this is an honour that is unique.

I wanted to express my appreciation by creating a wall hanging for the library, of assorted children.'

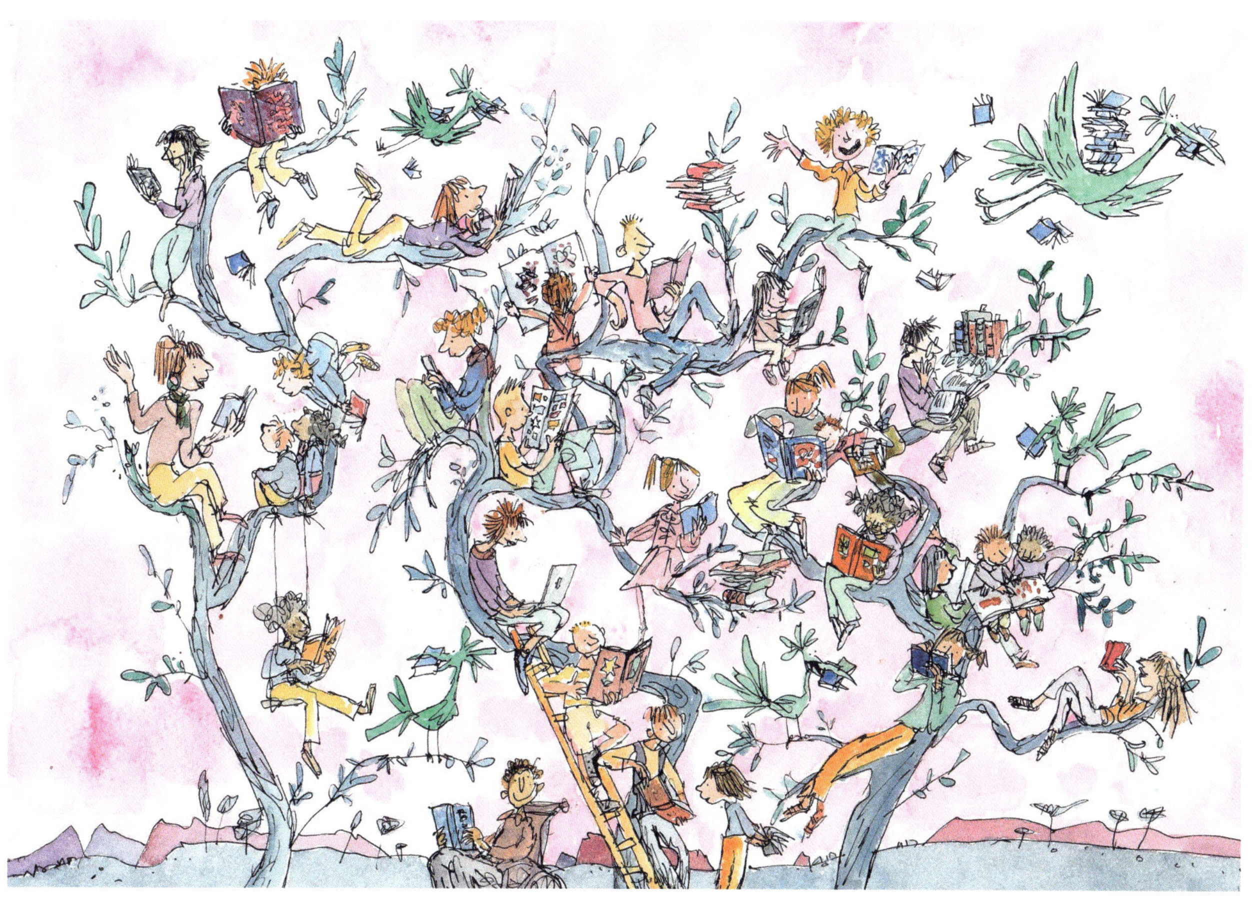

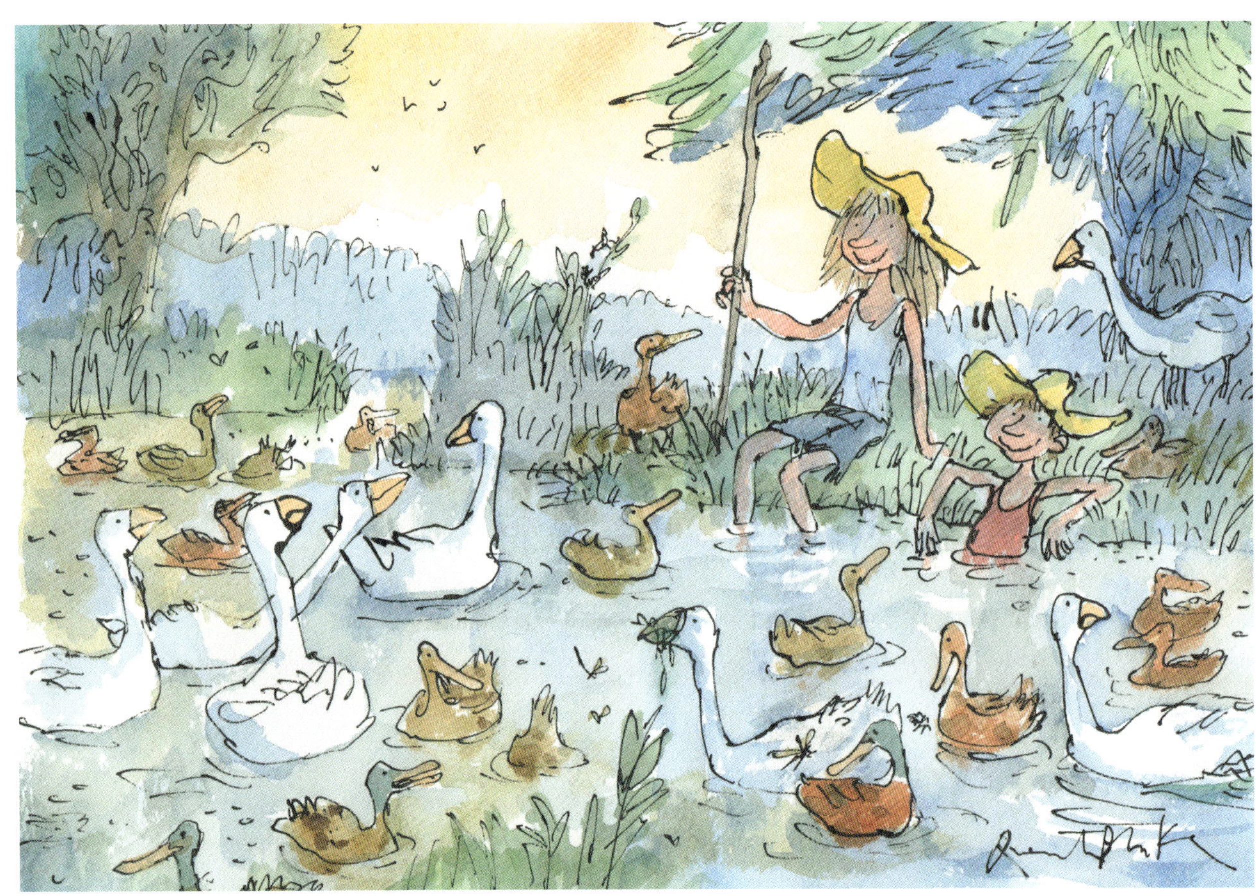

## Farms for City Children

Farms for City Children was started by Michael and Clare Morpurgo. They arrange for groups of children from city schools to visit farms in the West Country and Wales, owned by the charity, where they spend a week working on the farm and experiencing rural life. Quentin has done illustrations for two anthologies, *Muck and Magic* and *More Muck and Magic,* as well as cards and tea towels to help raise funds for the charity.

LOVE MUD!

LEARN WILD!

LEARN WILD!

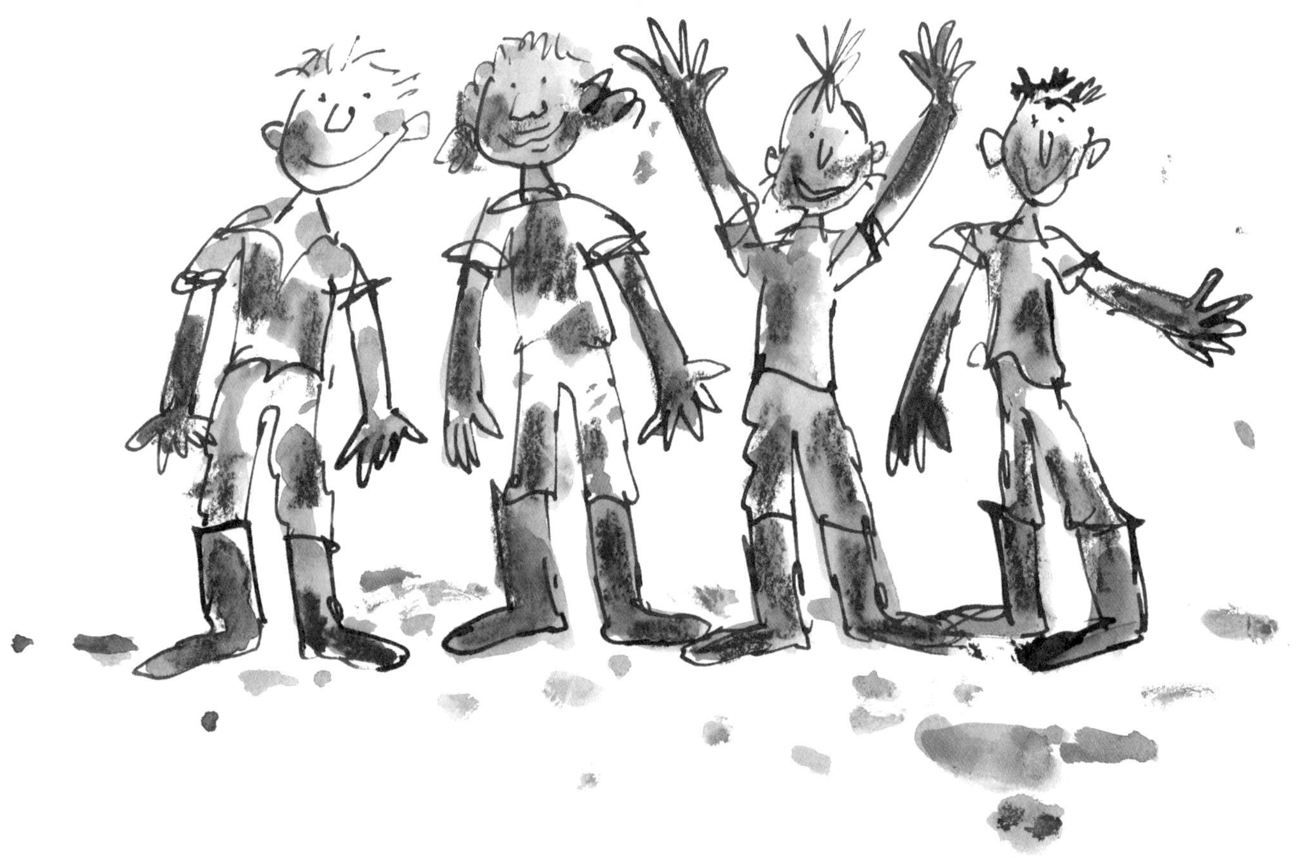

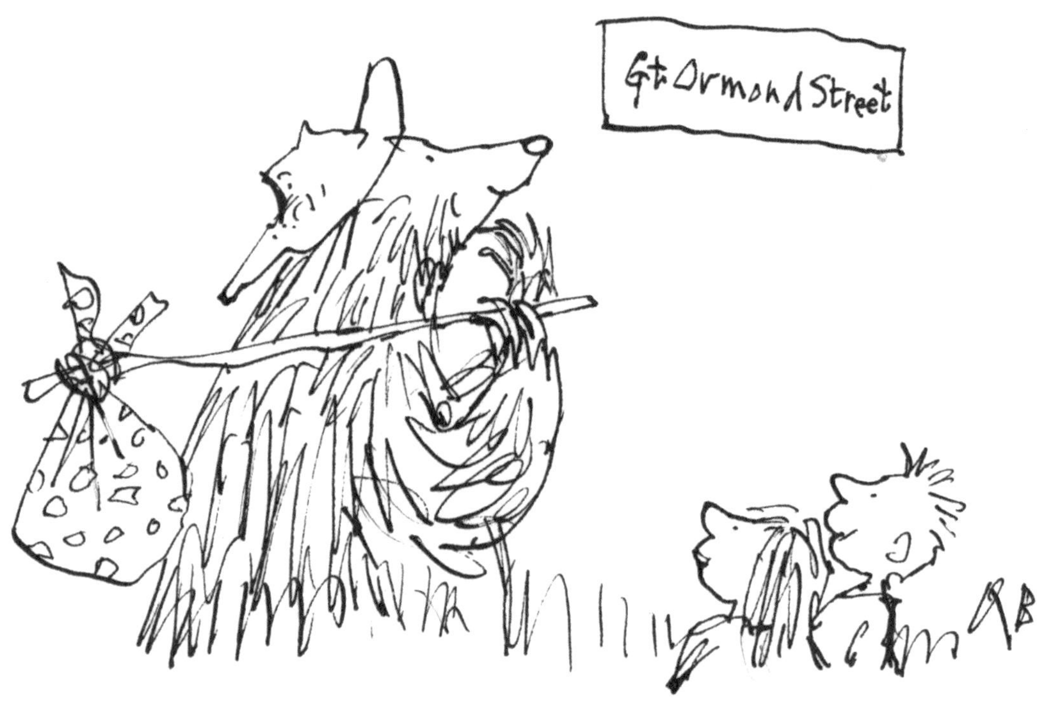


## Bear with Me Sketchbook

Between October 2012 and November 2013, a sketchbook was sent to thirty illustrators in the UK; each one continued the story of an adventurous bear. The book was then auctioned to raise money for Great Ormond Street Hospital. Quentin illustrated the cover and wrote the foreword:

'I am very pleased to have the opportunity to write a few words at the beginning of this book. Not everyone realises the amount of good a travelling bear – I mean a storybook bear – is able to bring about. The one I know best (which was in a book by John Yeoman called *The Hermit and the Bear*) was so clumsy it seemed sometimes that he was more trouble than he was worth; but he was full benevolence. And of course, though they are full of benevolence and beneficence, bears often do need some support. Here they get it from an extraordinary group of gifted artists. With some of them I know and admire their work already, but I've also been delighted to be introduced to some fascinating illustrators who are new to me. It's clearly been a most successful journey. And it's all in favour of the wonderful Great Ormond Street Hospital!'

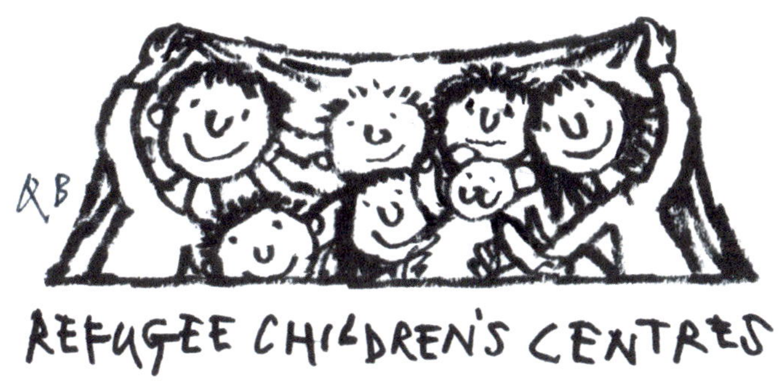

*Logo for Refugee Children's Centres campaign*, 2016

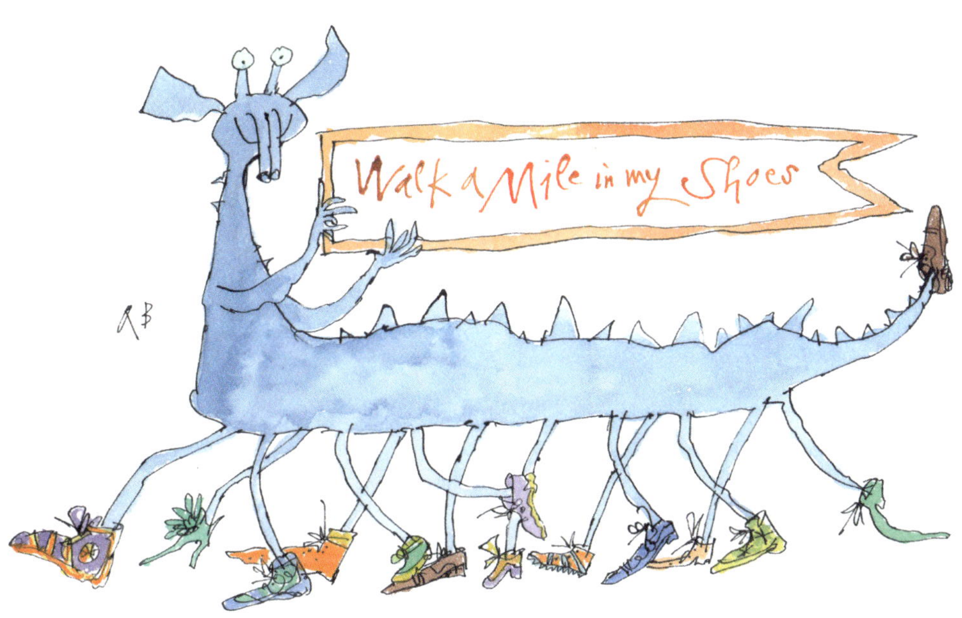


*Walk a Mile in My Shoes*, Illustration for Association for Young People with ME, 2016

## A Book with Hundreds of Authors

All the books Quentin has worked on are a straightforward commission to illustrate a text written by a single author. But there is one exception: a book that that involved working with hundreds of French children. Some years ago a group of French school teachers near Quentin's house in La Rochelle had the idea of creating a book based on the suggestions of school children in the region.

'I am conscious that it is slightly mad to take on anything else at this moment and I am also aware that the idea is attractive and I am touched that they are asking a foreign visitor to join them. How can I say no? I don't.

But what is this book to be about? It is to be *sur l'humanisme:* not, as I first imagine, about humanism, but about humanitarian issues – bullying, racism, pollution, war. How do I start off such a project for all the children who are to be my collaborators?… I need both a boy and a girl, but I also need some way in which they can encounter a scenario of distress. As we are near the sea I decide I can put them in a boat, and when I come to do a handful of rough drawings I give it the utmost versatility I can imagine – a boat that can go on sea or on land, and even fly. The teachers select three of these drawings, take them into their classrooms and begin to explore their possibilities. When the results of their discussions and writings come back it become clear that almost everyone has gone for the opportunity to fly.'

Children from French-speaking schools all over the world took part in creating the story; the teachers sifted through the enormous number of ideas and, from their selection, Quentin put together a rough version of the book. After two more meetings with several hundred children in La Rochelle and Rochefort Quentin had the makings of a book. He approached a small publisher who specializes in 'contemporary issues such as ecology and children's rights. It is run by one man, Alain Serres, who initially responds with a note of caution – a book by children, as he points out, isn't necessarily a book for children. But this, we agree, is a book by me, even though I have 1,800 collaborators.'

Alain reworked the text to make it more fluent and came up with the title, *Un Bateau dans le Ciel.* All that remained was for Quentin to draw the forty illustrations: 'I have become so involved that nothing will do but a focus as intense as I can manage. In June, in France, I get the pictures finished; by September, brilliantly, Alain Serres produces the final book. Everything has happened within the space of a school year.'

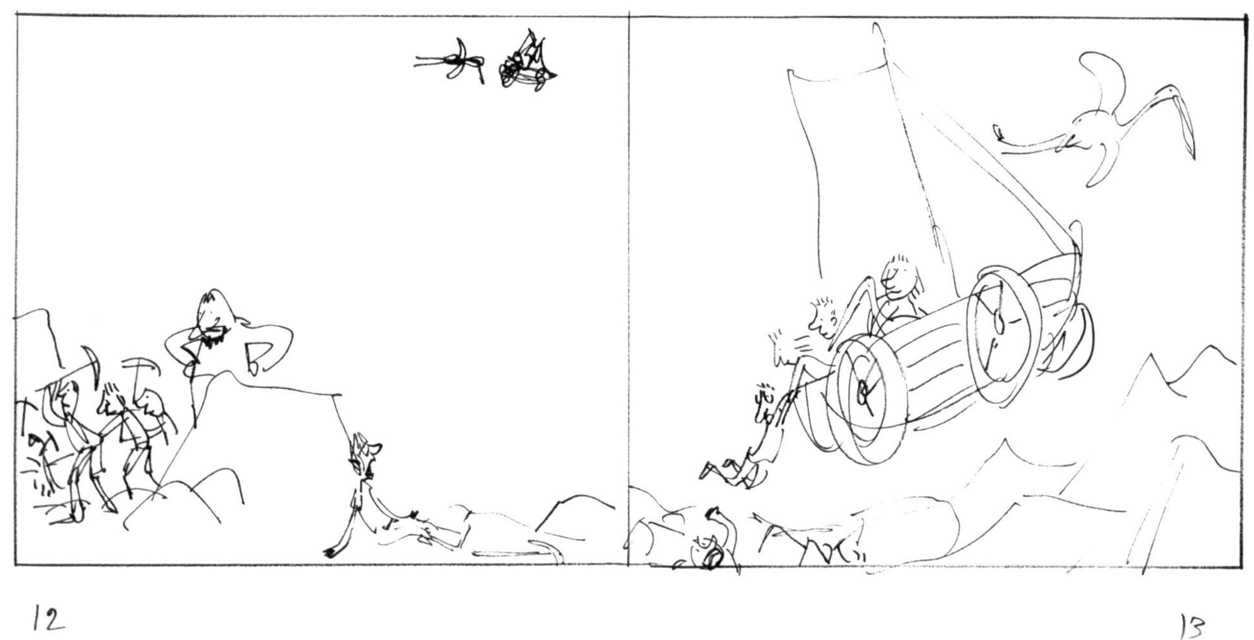

12    13

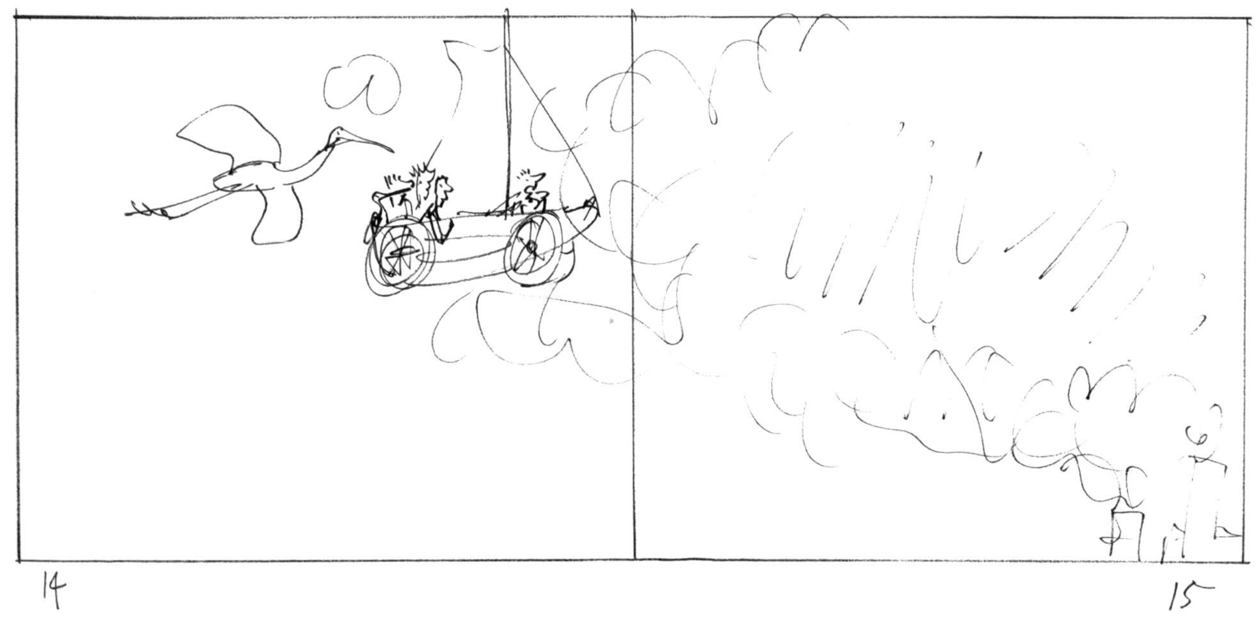

14    15

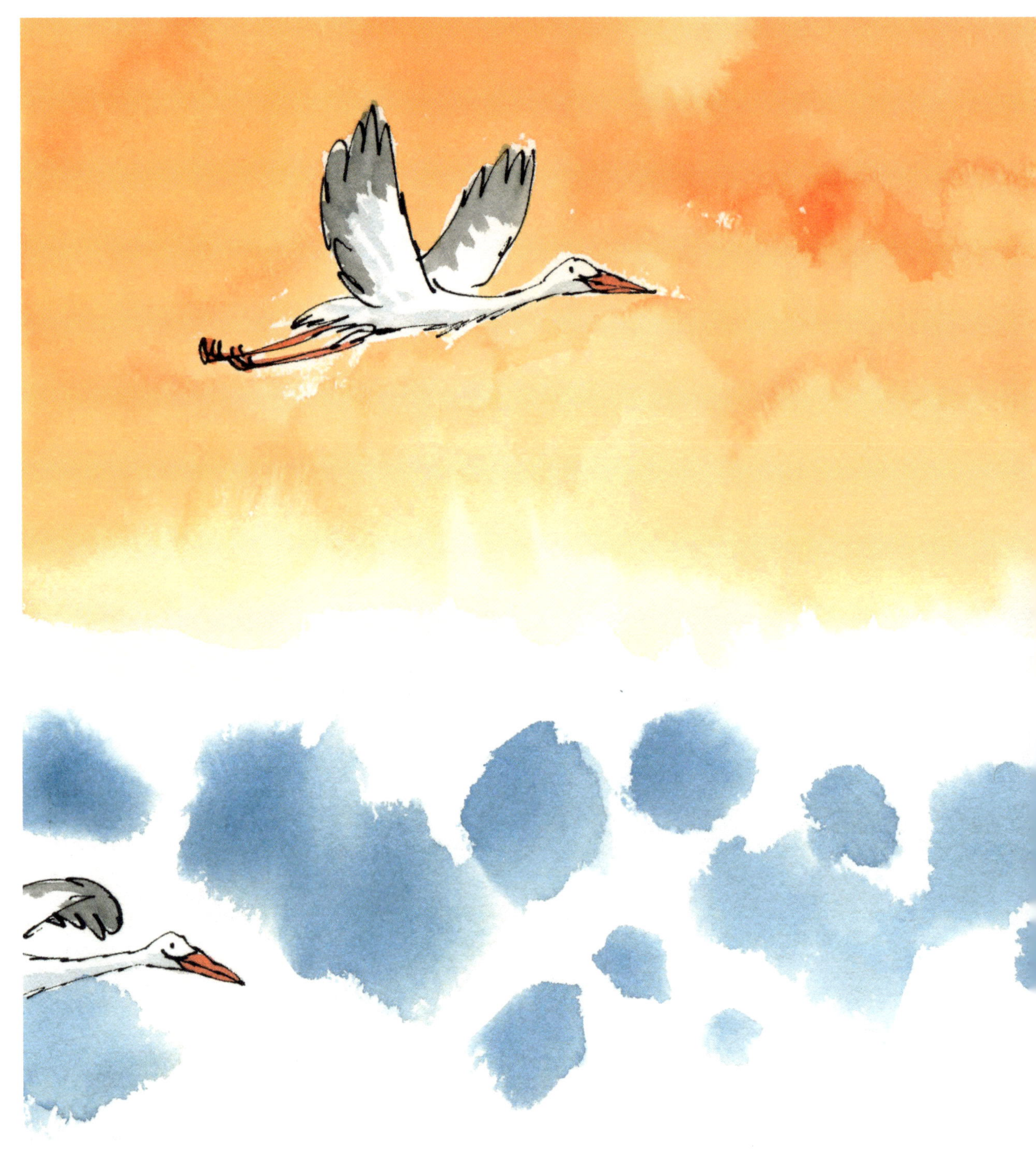

*Un Bateau Dans le Ciel*, Book Cover, 2016

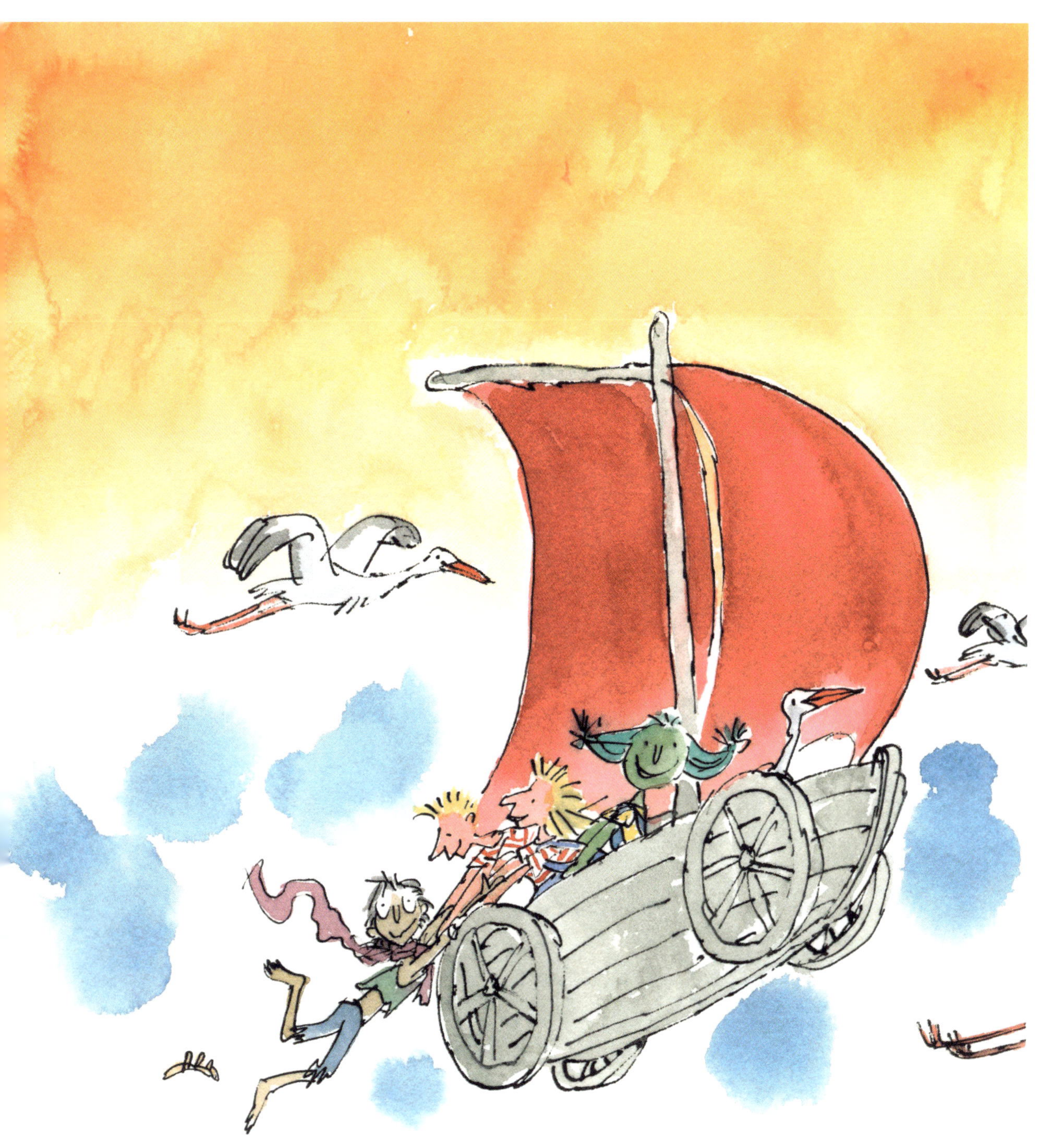

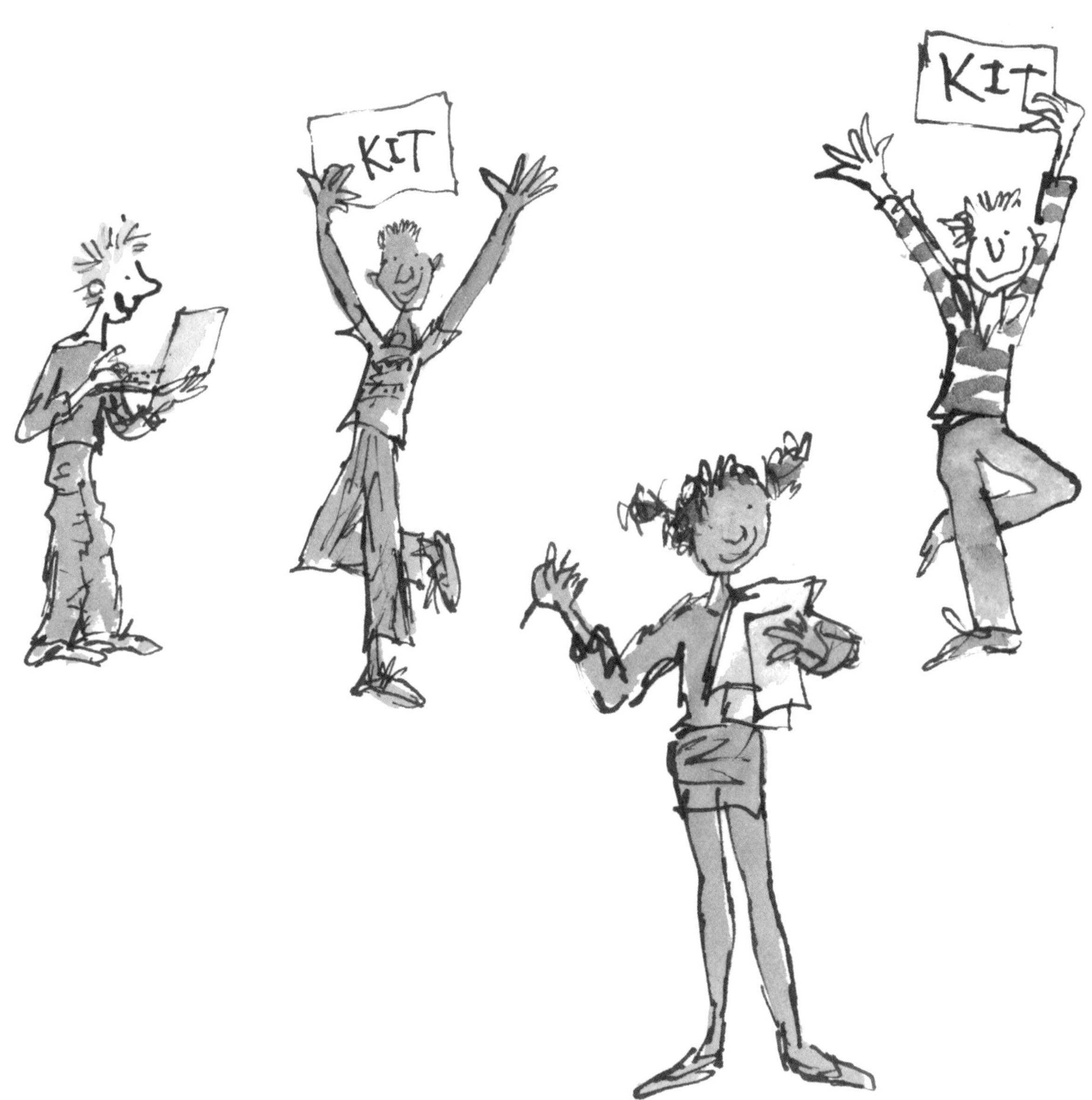


### Kensington Aldridge Academy

KAA sits in the shadow of Grenfell Tower and serves a deprived area of west London. Quentin was asked if he would do a drawing for the Intrepidus Trust, a campaign to raise funds for extracurricular activities. He did seven, which were then auctioned.

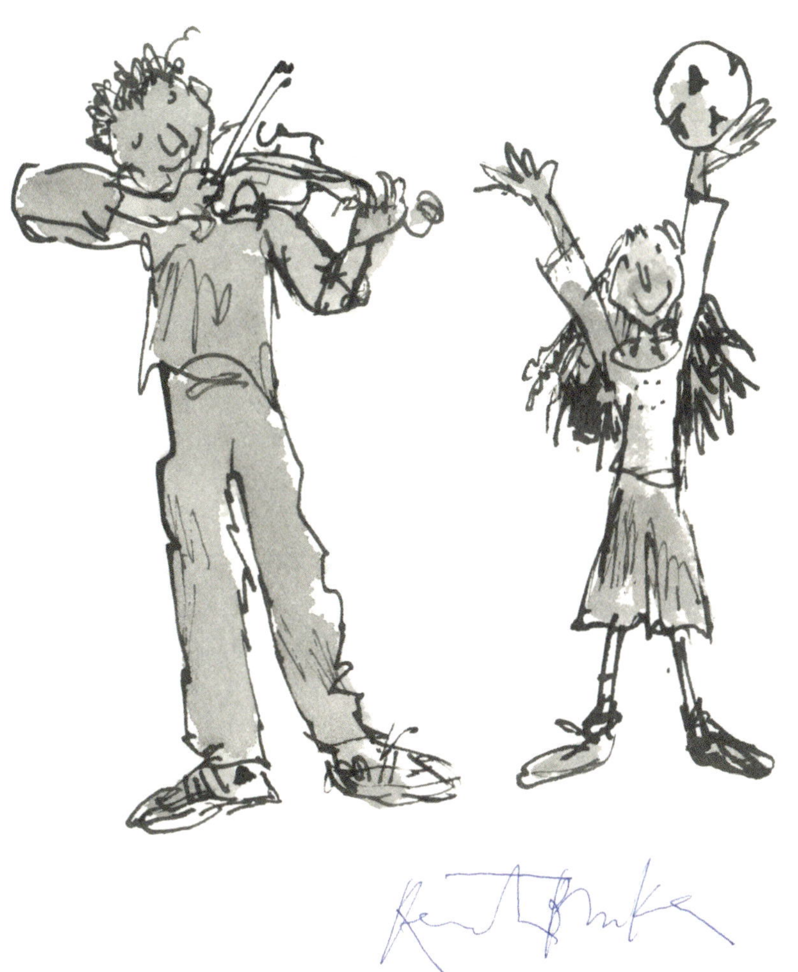

**Roald Dahl's Marvellous Children's Charity**

The charity trains and provides specialist nurses for children with complex, lifelong conditions.

'It has two presidents: one is very active, Felicity Dahl, and the other who is me, does very little except when called on to draw something.... An unusual venture was a series of fifty Dream Jars (inspired by *The BFG*) which appeared in various sites across London and Birmingham, Cardiff, Glasgow and Cheshire, real jam jars about two and half feet in height, each containing a three-dimensional creation of the dream of some well-known celebrity… my dream was that I could fly, and three separate pictures found me encountering a Roly-Poly Bird, helicopters and a giant peach – three Dahl airborne moments.'

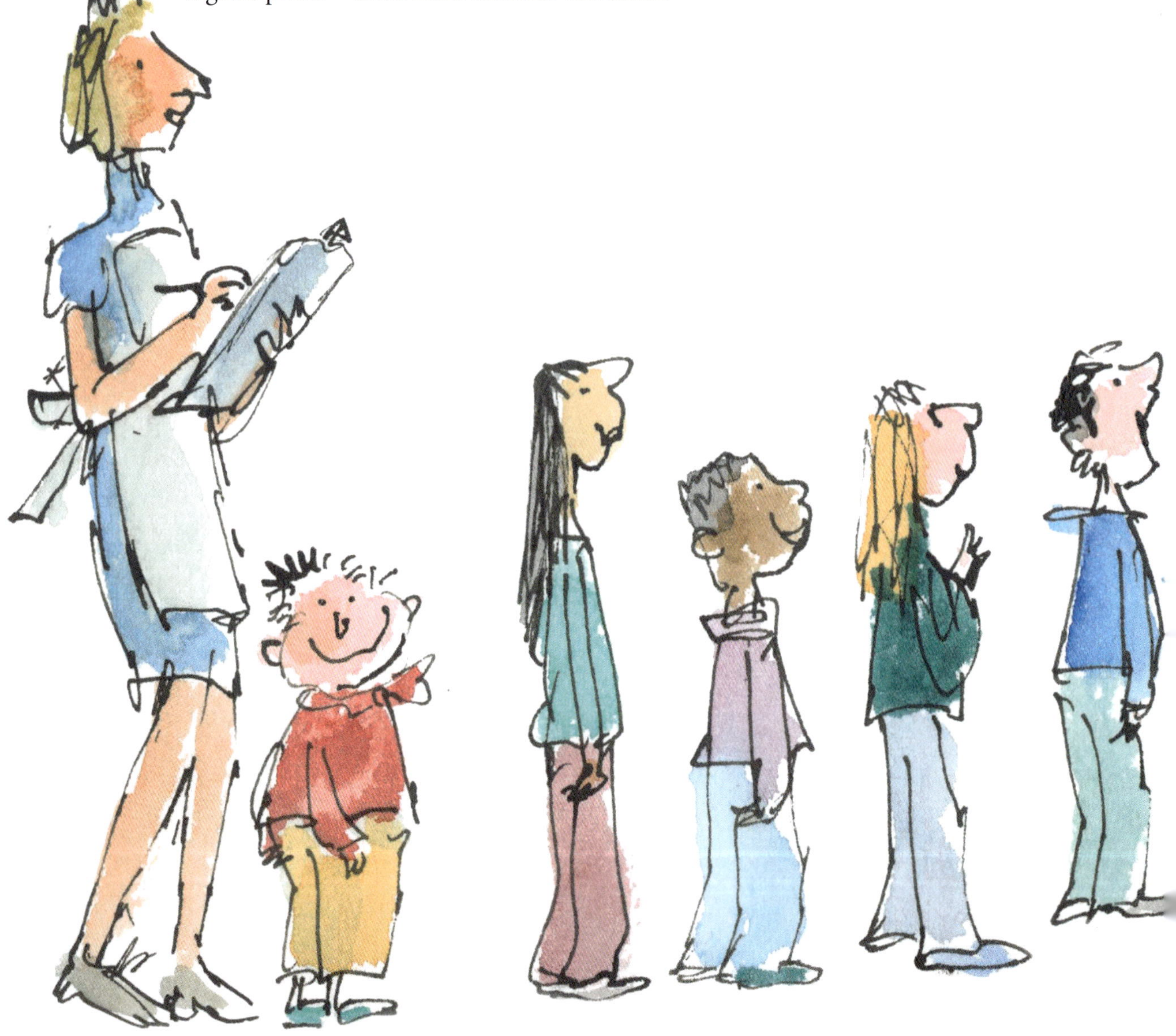

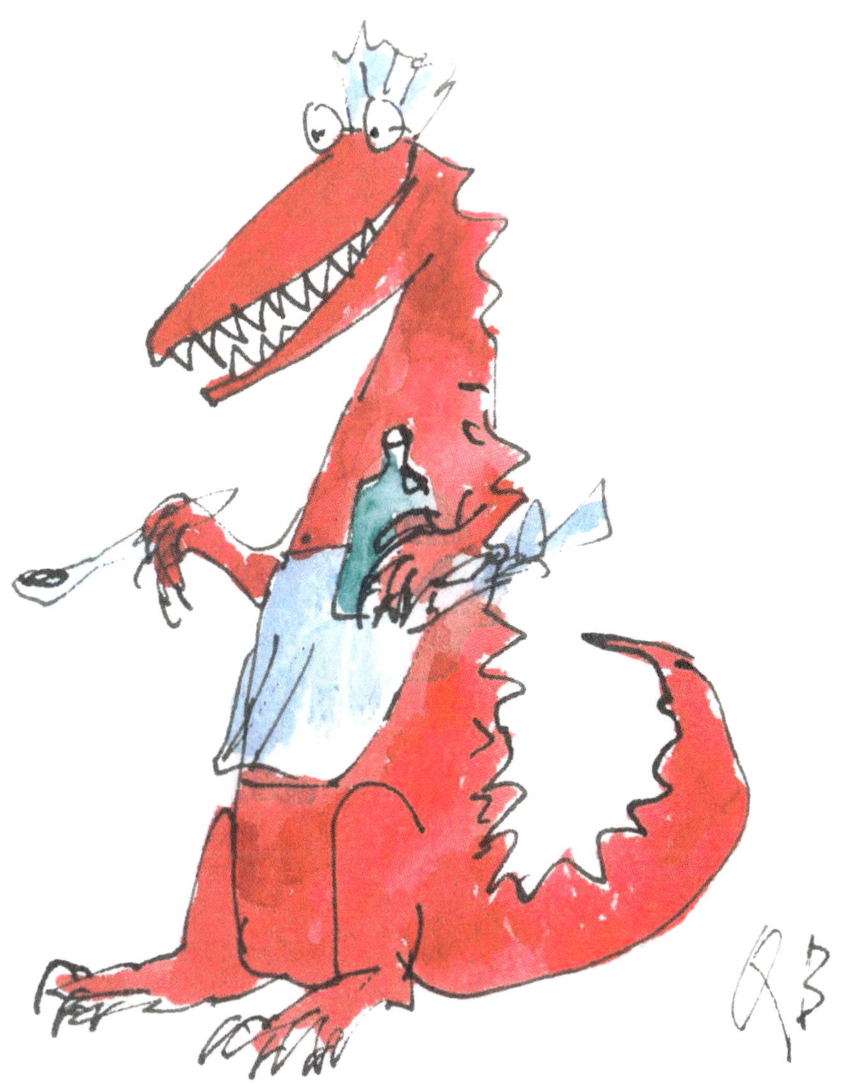

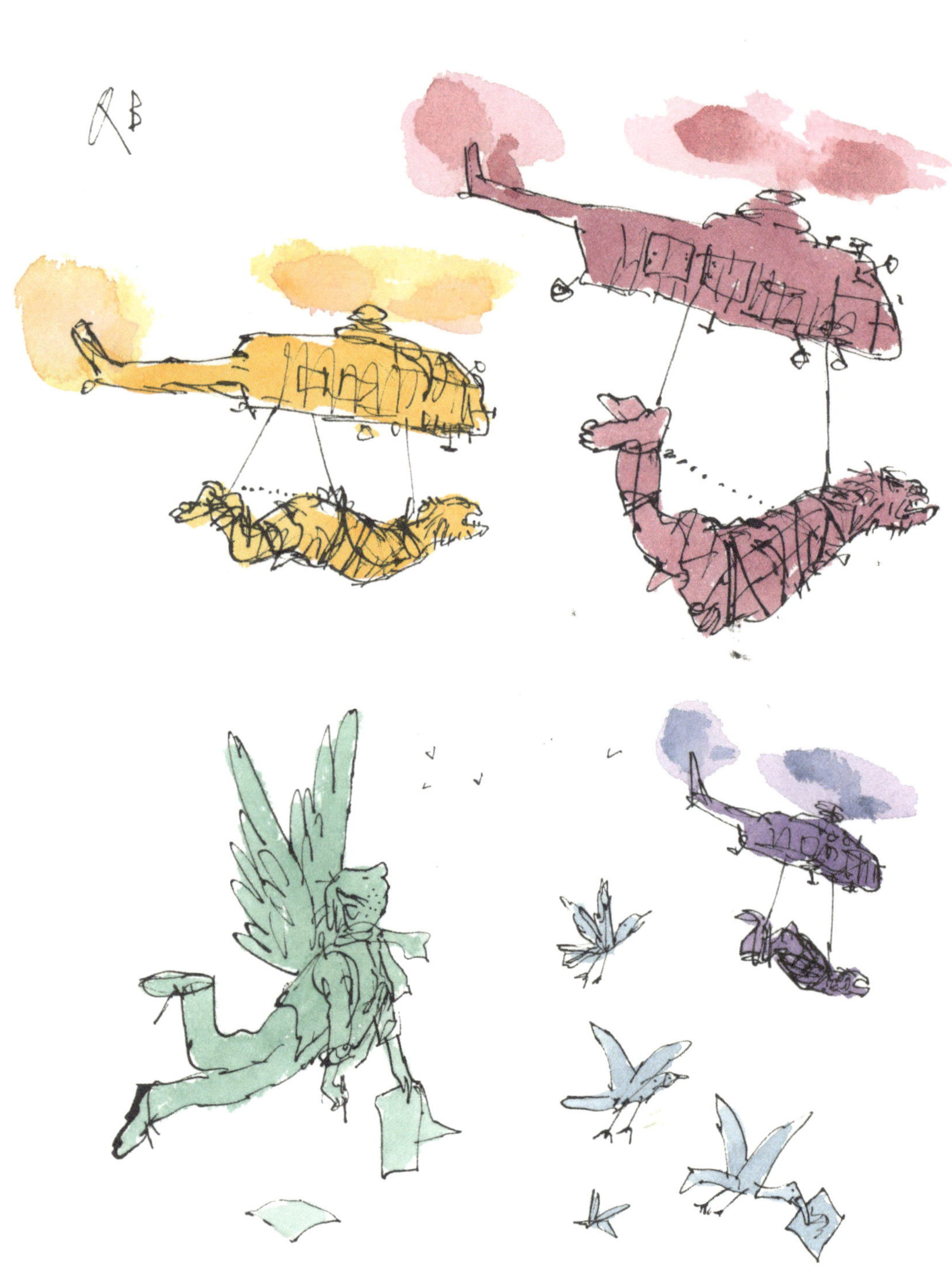

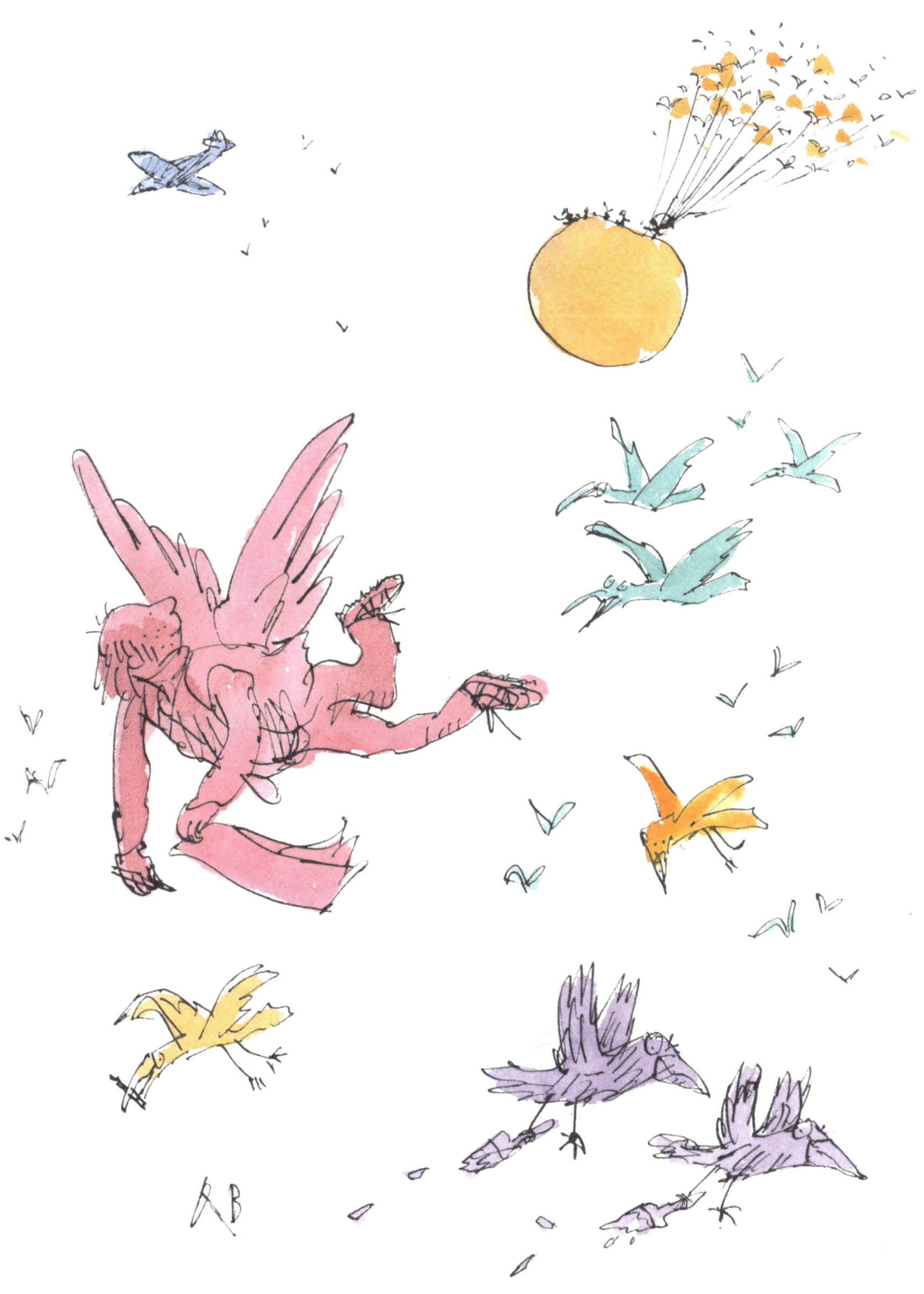

*Roald Dahl Marvellous Charity Dream Jars*, 2016

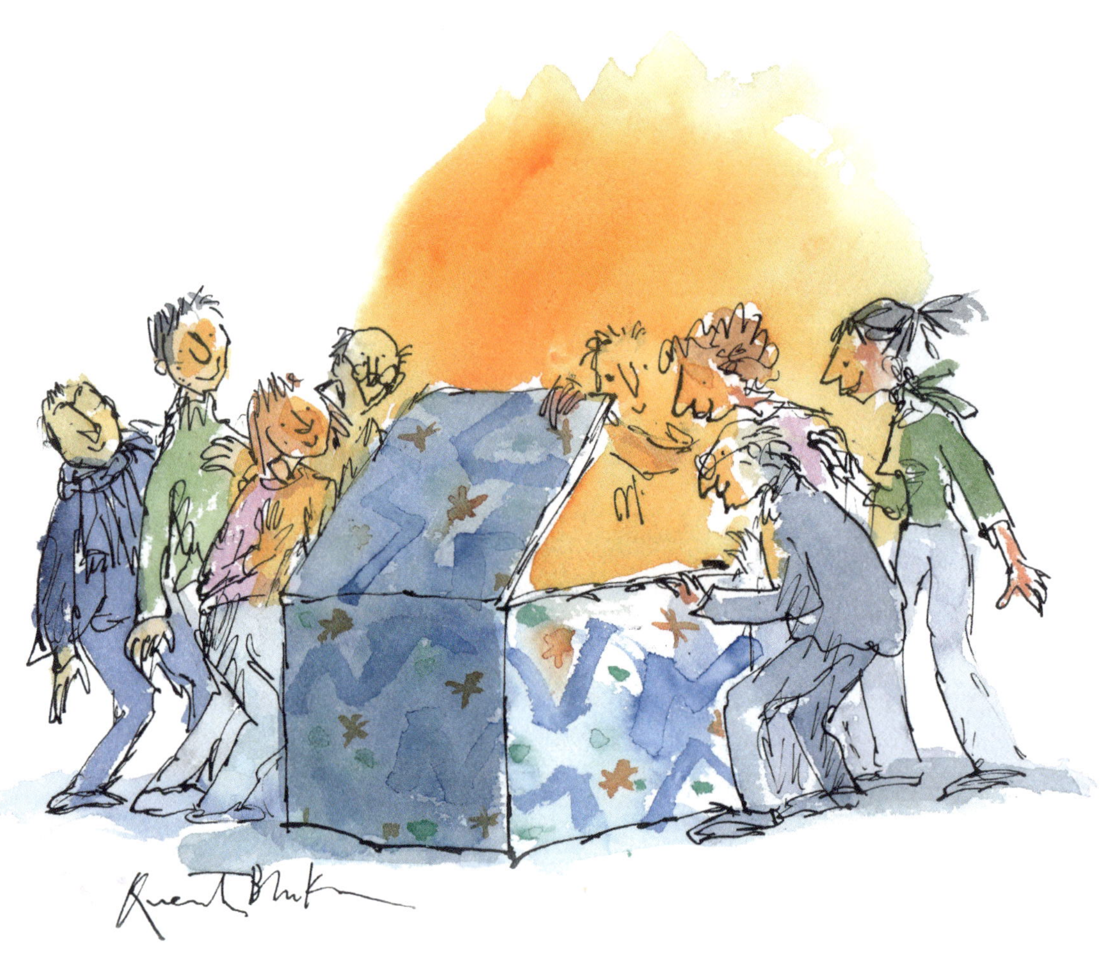

*Open University 50th Anniversary Drawing*, 2018

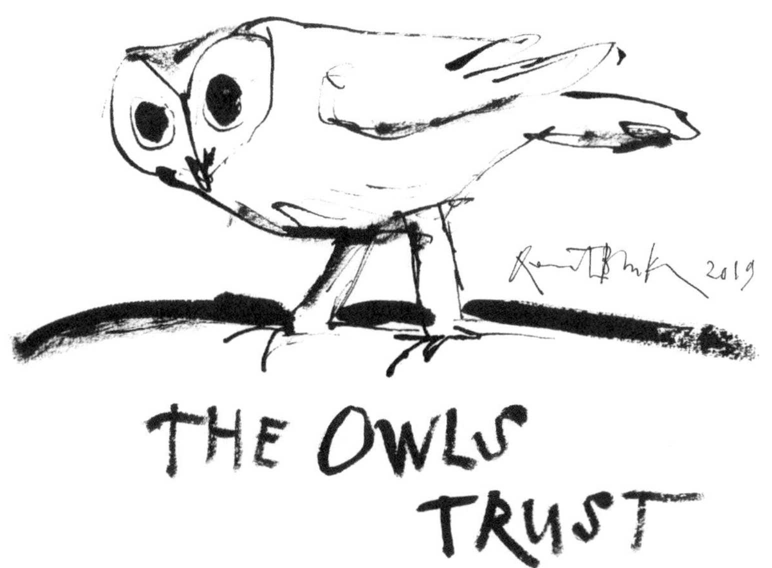


*The Owl's Trust Signage*, 2019

# The Lockdown Projects

In 2020, during the pandemic, Quentin's office was closed and there were fewer demands on his time.

'It seemed like a time when a few straightforward jokes might not come amiss; as I know that people have been putting rainbows in their windows to express solidarity, I took the liberty of borrowing them. You will see that I have supposed that they are real and portable, and I hope optimistic too.'

There were ten drawings in the series, which were auctioned in aid of NHS Charities Together. Three of the illustrations also appeared on mugs, which were sold in aid of the charity.

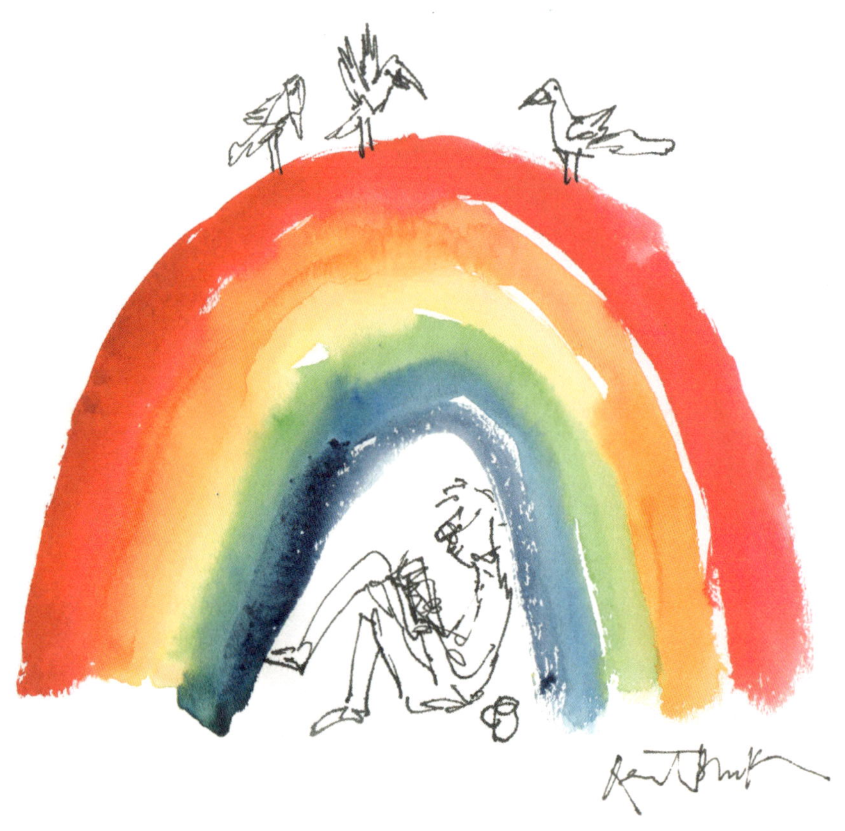

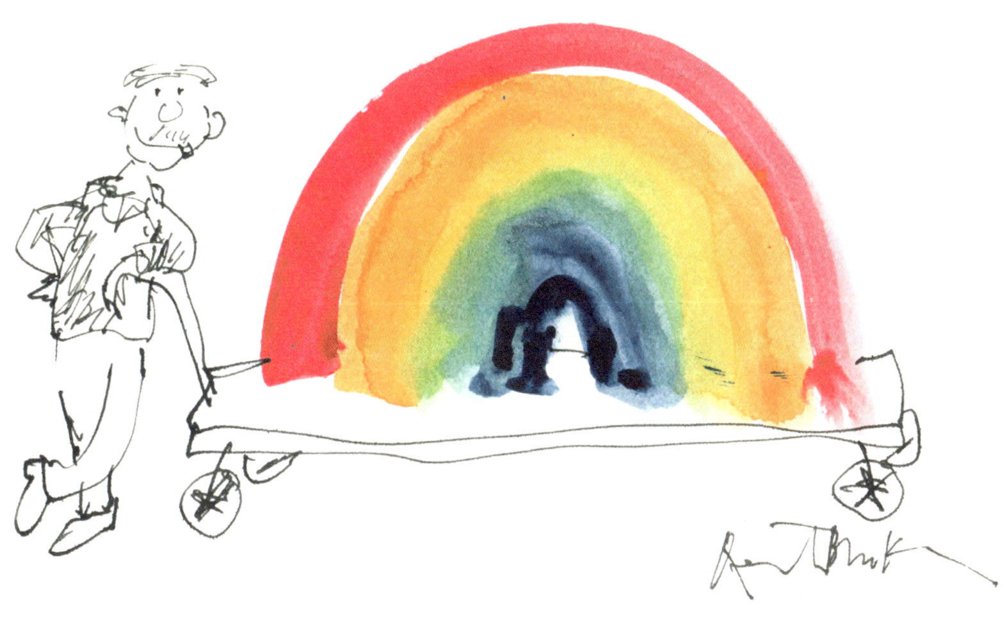

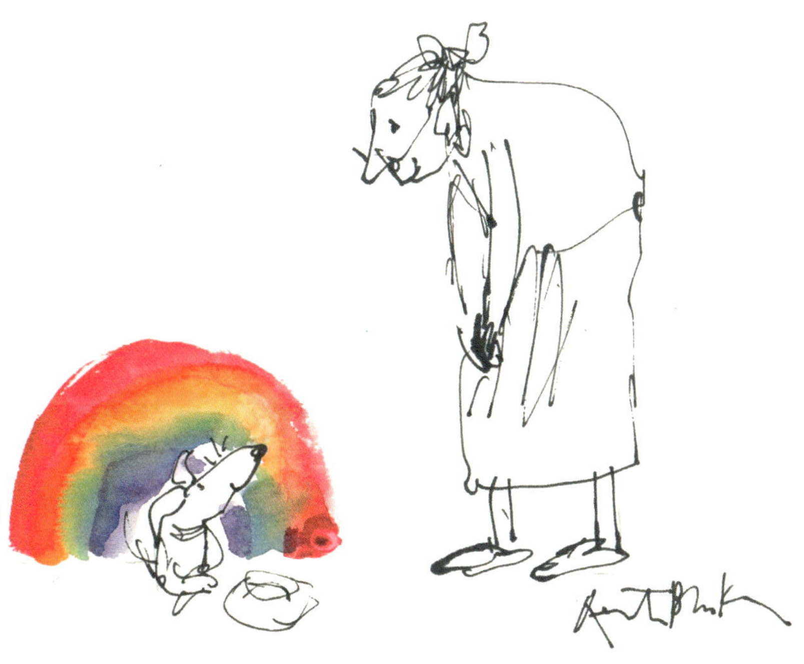

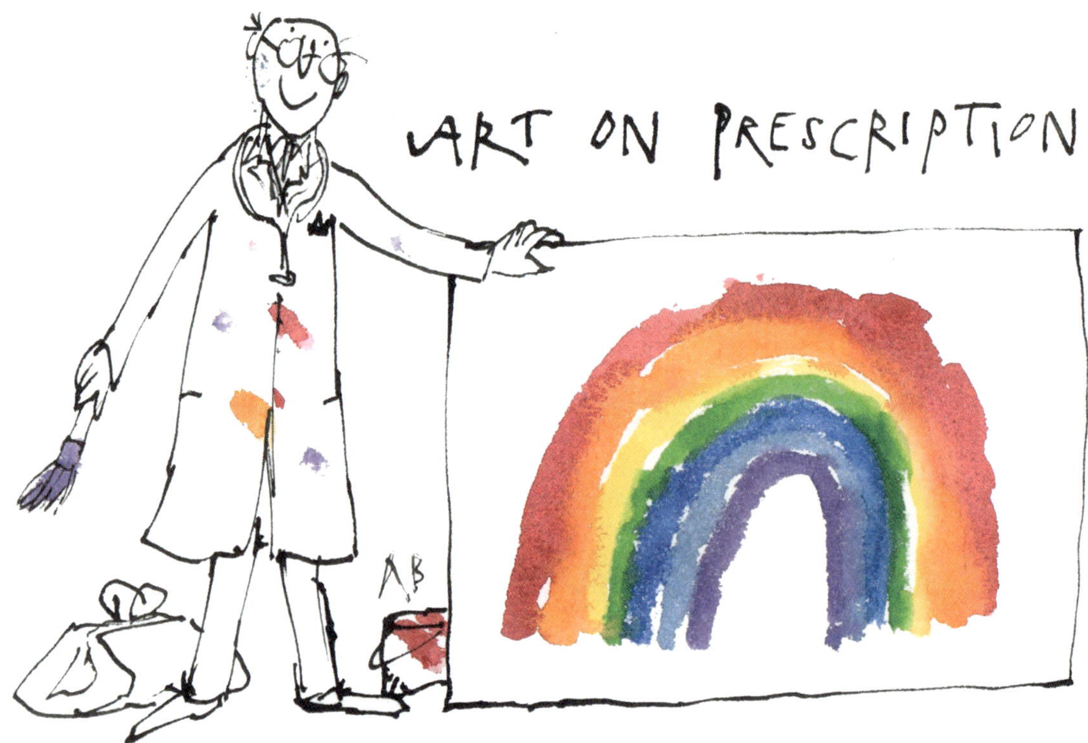



## Art on Prescription

Set up in Hastings in June 2019, Art on Prescription work with the NHS to provide creative activities to help self-expression and social engagement. When they launched their lockdown project to reduce social isolation, they asked Quentin to draw a logo for their website. The sickly tattooed man was rejected, but they used the doctor in white coat.

# ART ON PRESCRIPTION

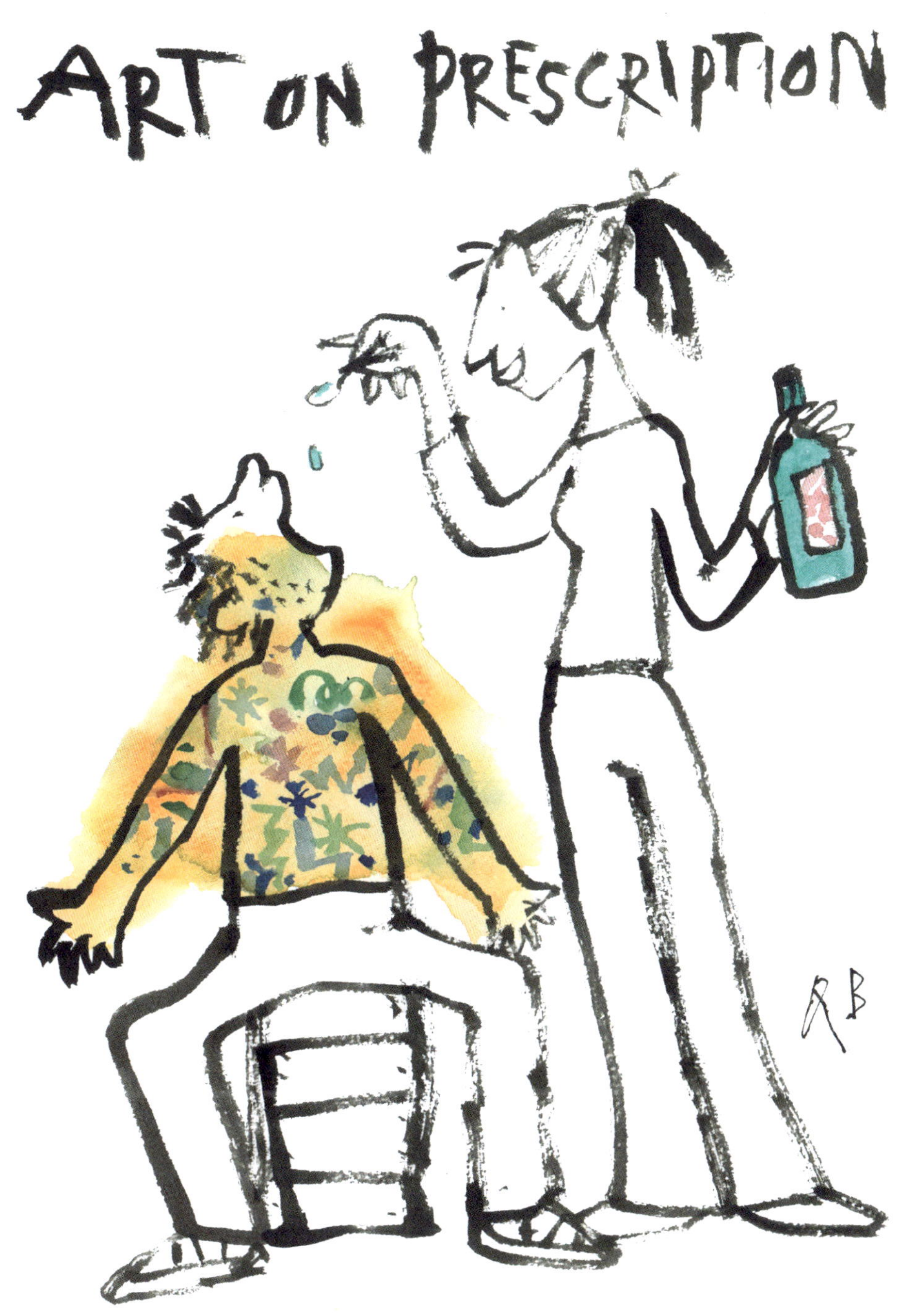

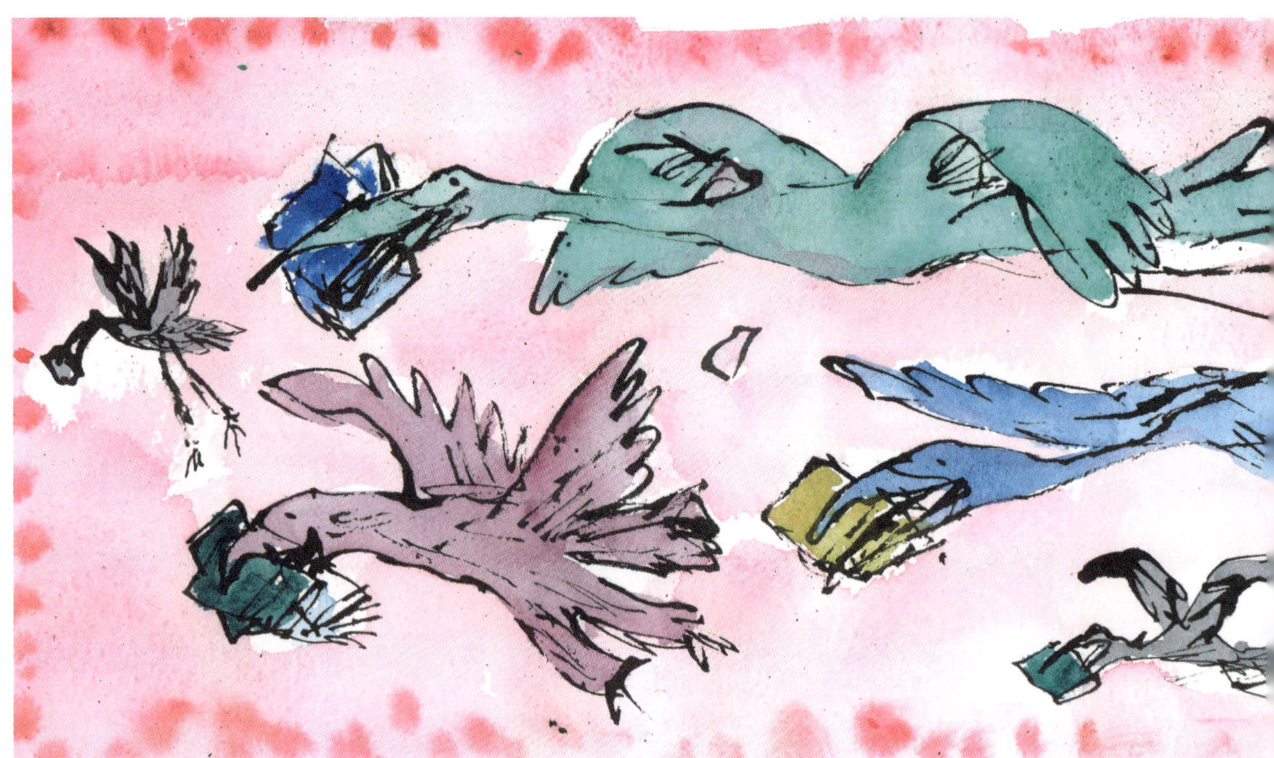

## *IBBY*

International Board on Books for Young People (IBBY) is a not-for-profit organisation working globally to build local libraries and improve the quality of books published. They provide bibliotherapy to refugee children, children displaced by natural disaster, and unaccompanied minors. In 2020 they invited ten illustrators to create limited-edition scarves.

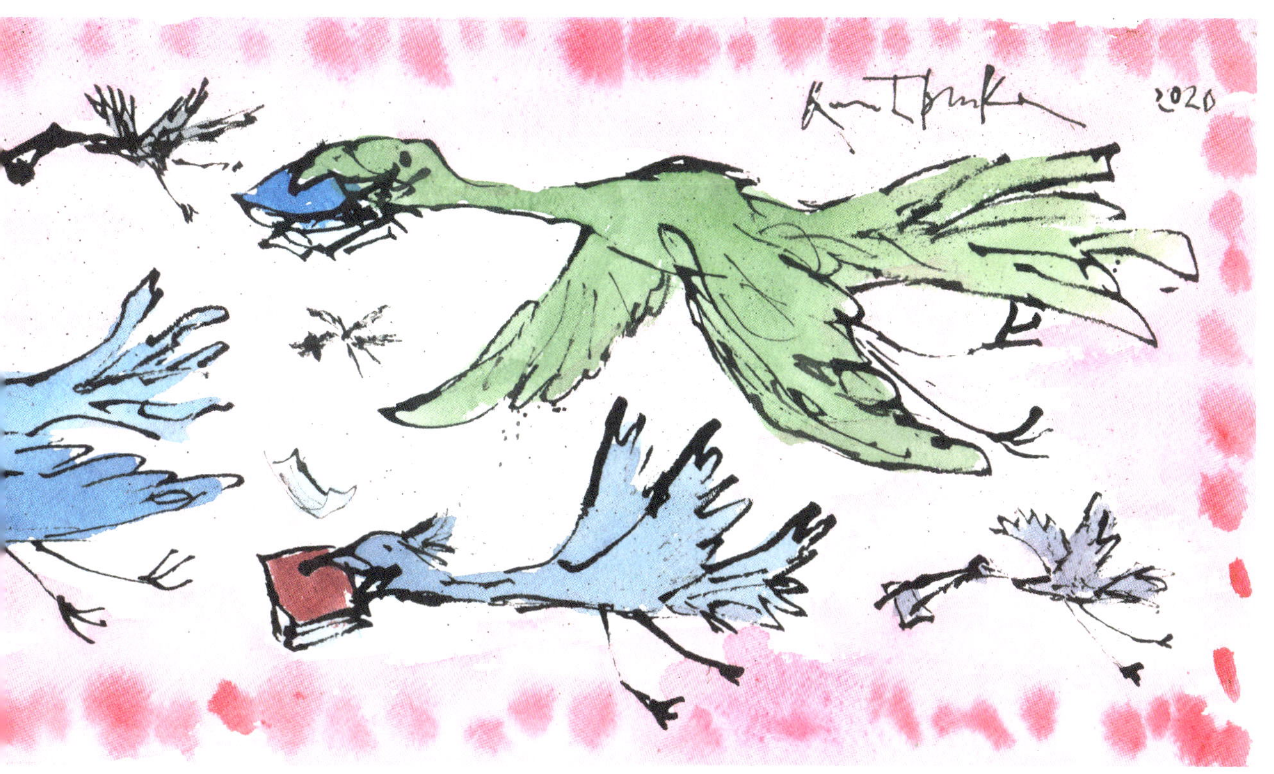

# Comic Relief

In 2008 Comic Relief asked Quentin to do a logo and fonts for Red Nose Day, which were eventually not used by the charity. Then, during lockdown in 2020, they asked Quentin if he would donate some drawings for an auction so that Comic Relief could help support charities in urgent need of funds to respond to the impact of the pandemic.

He produced a series of fifteen drawings called 'Imaginary Friends'.

'When I was asked to make the drawings I naturally thought of all those people isolated by lockdown, and I realised that I voluntarily spend quite a lot of time on my own, with pen in hand drawing imaginary friends (well not always friends actually).'

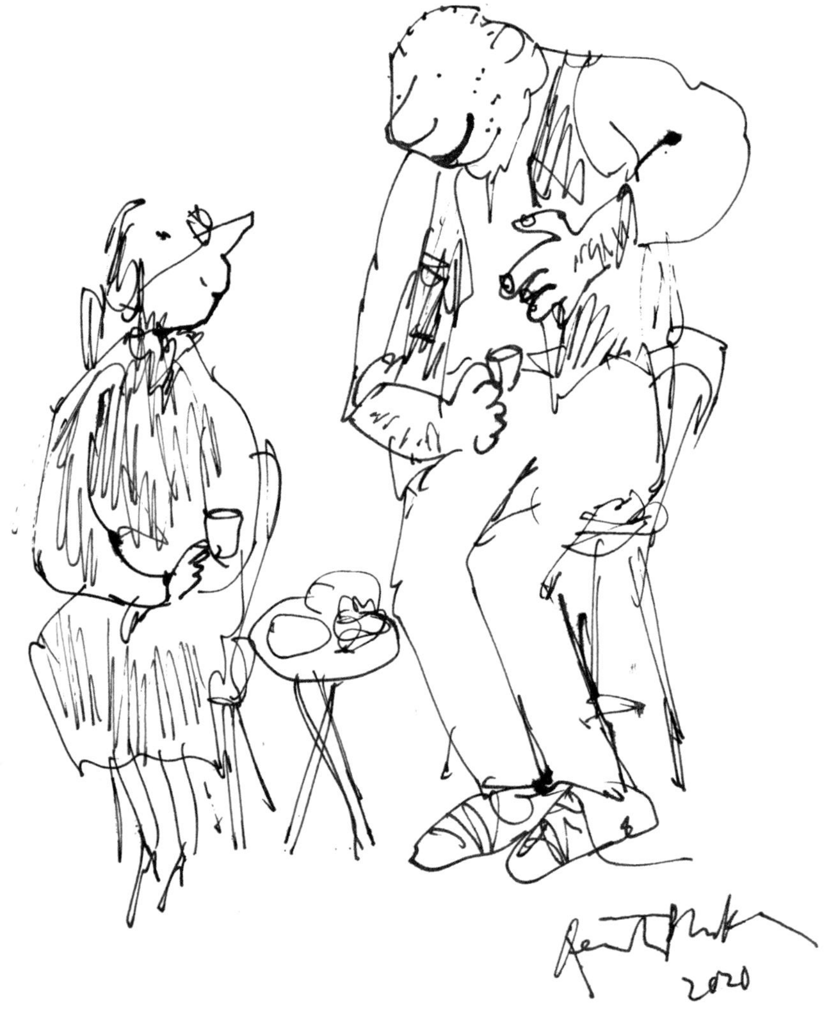

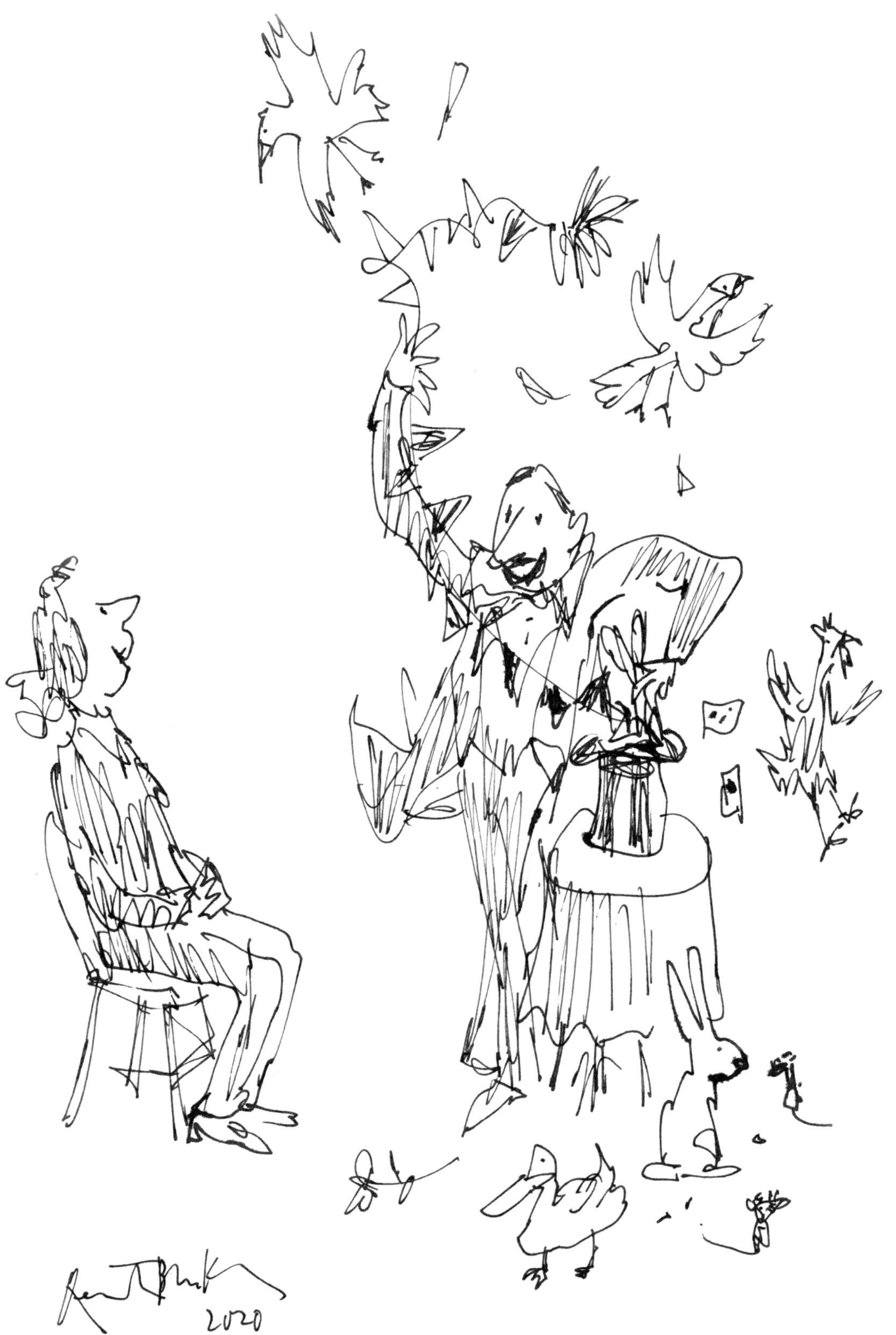

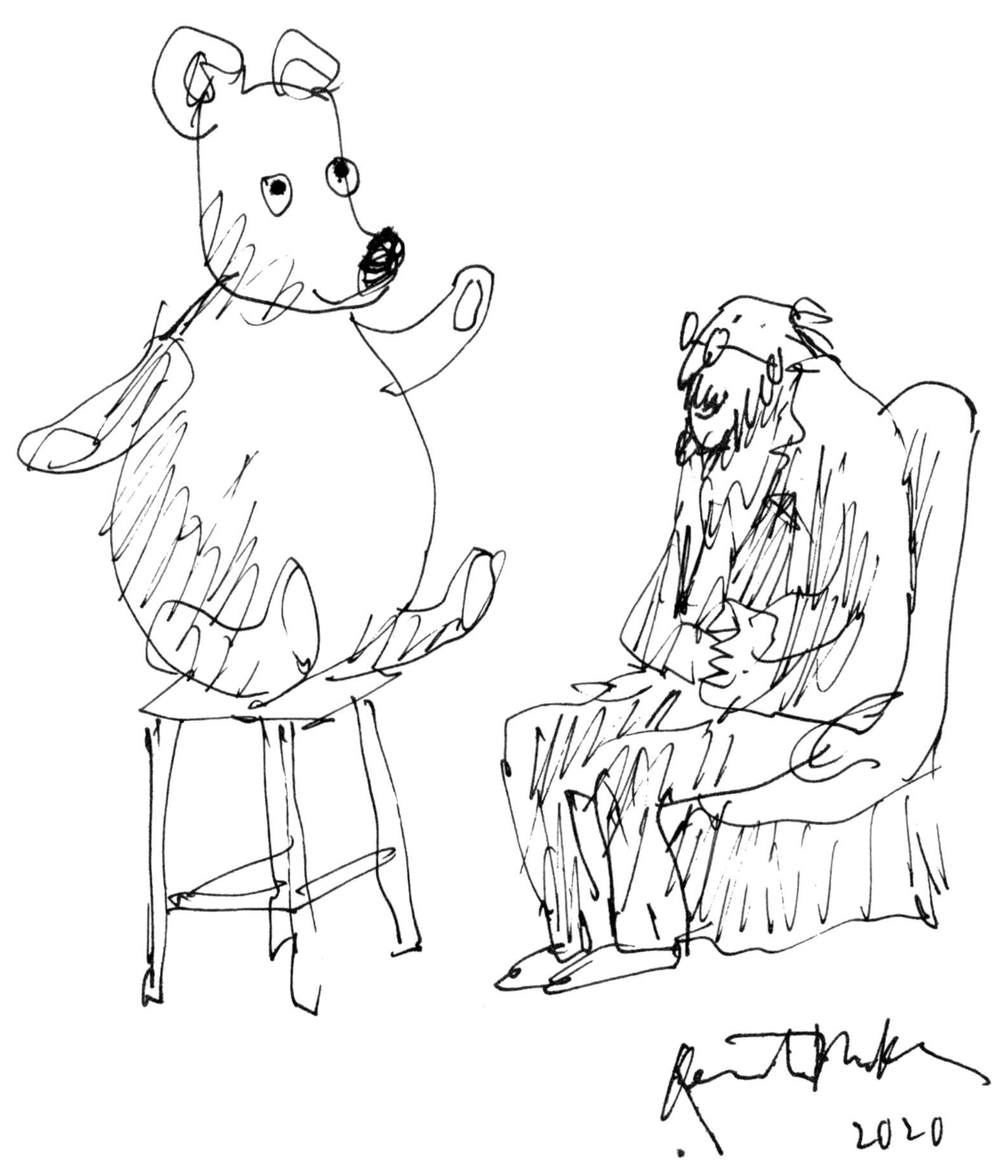

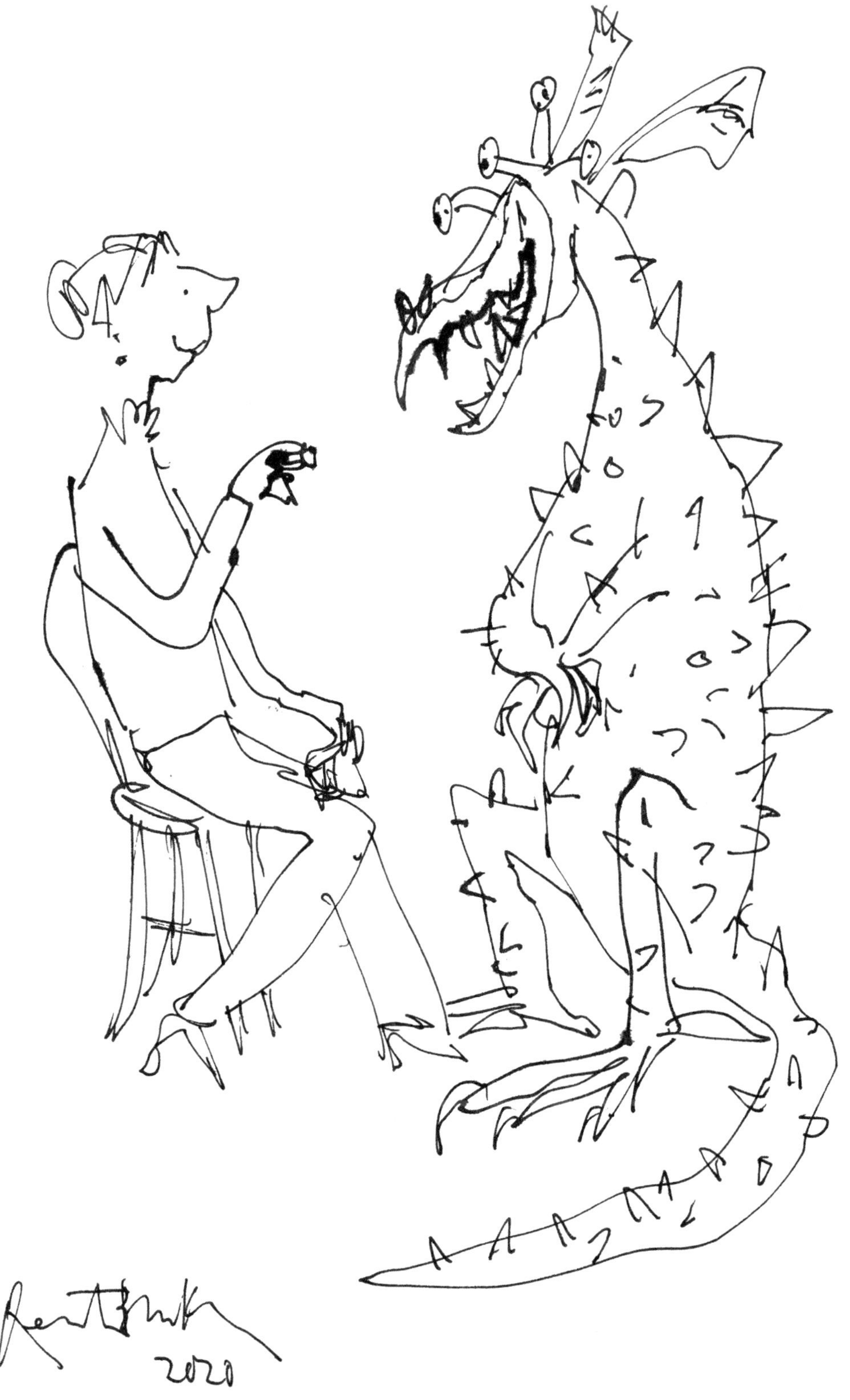

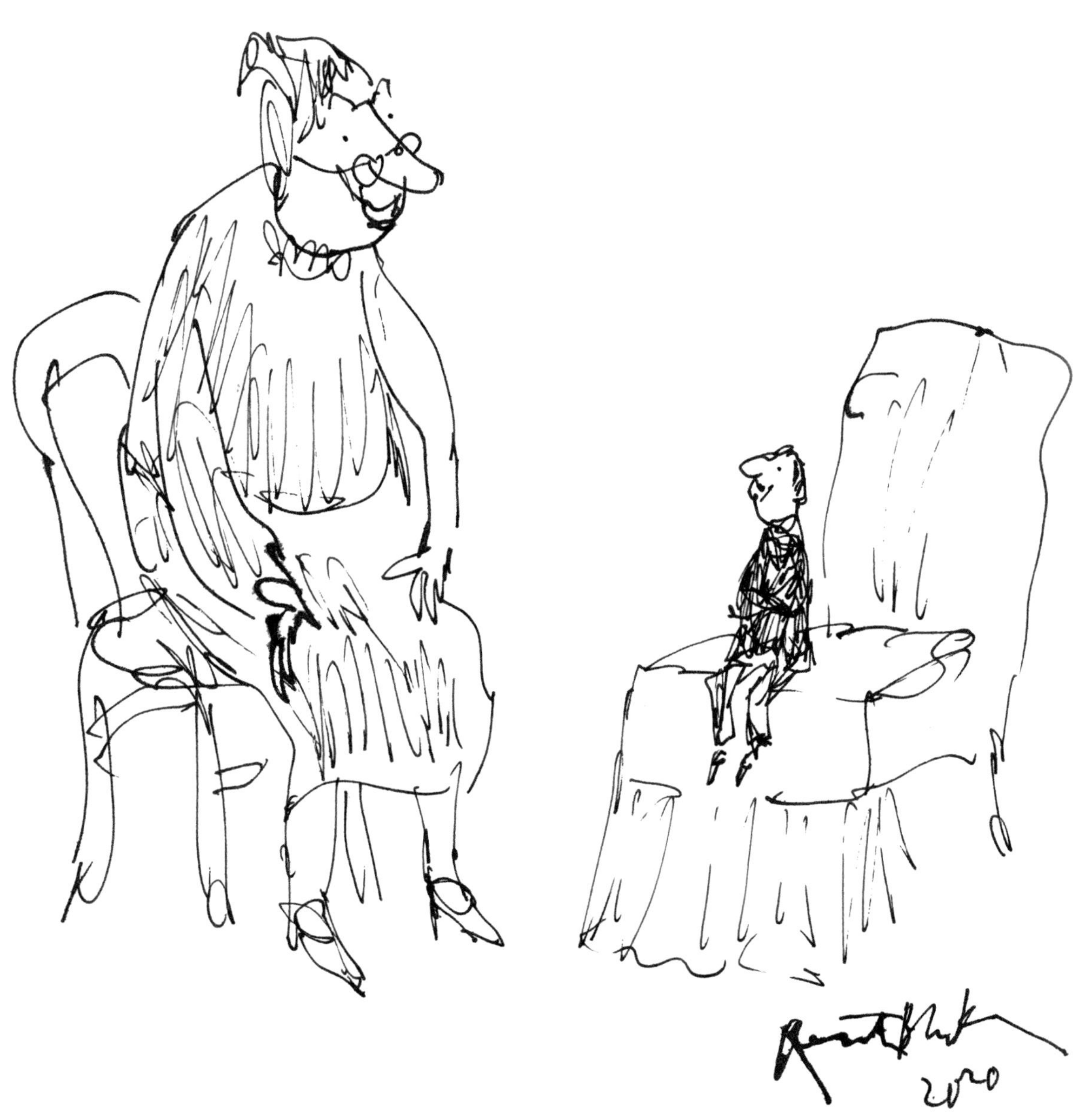

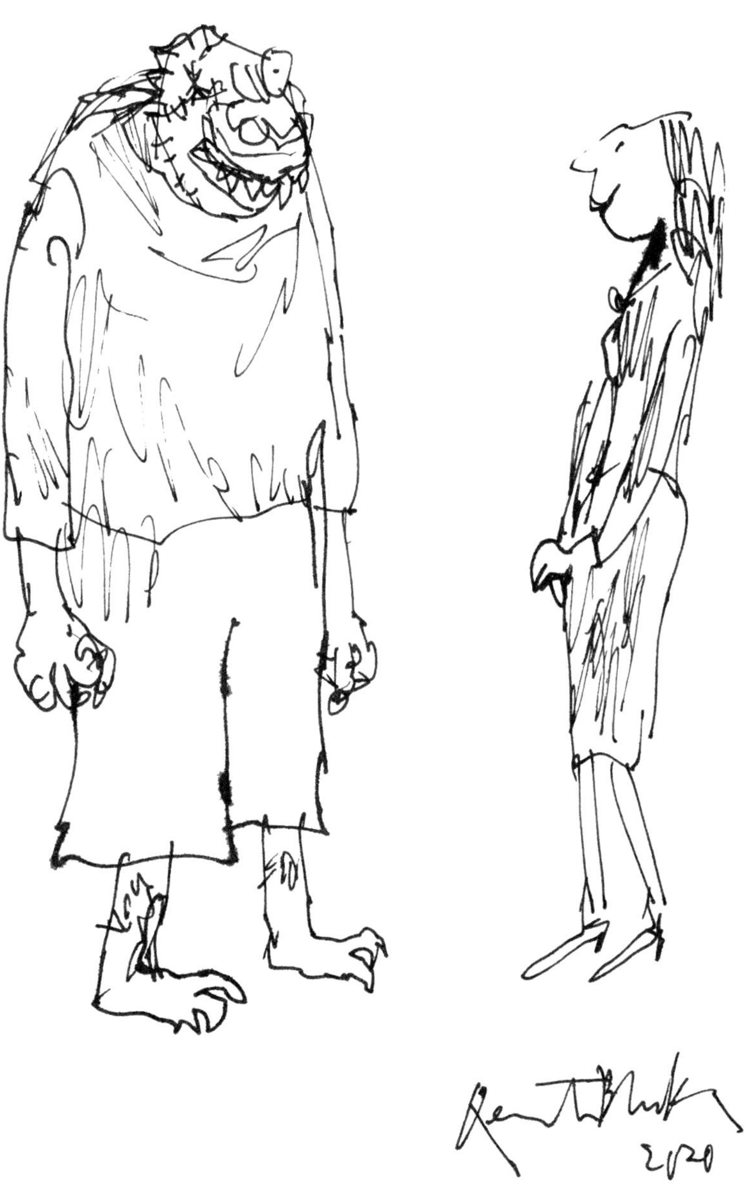

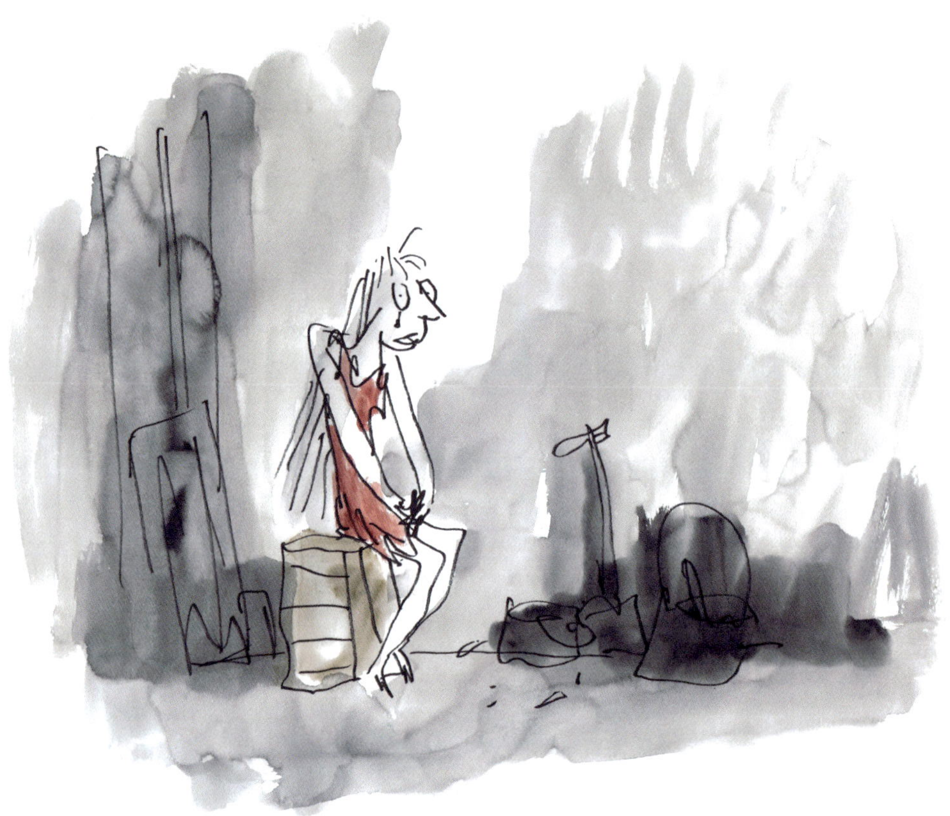

ABOVE & OPPOSITE – *Cinderella*, 2020

## *Comic Relief, Pantomimes*

For Christmas 2020 and 2021 actors and comedians took part in virtual pantomimes recorded online for the BBC. They asked Quentin if he would do drawings to set the scene for 'Cinderella' and 'Beauty and the Beast'. They were later auctioned in aid of the charity.

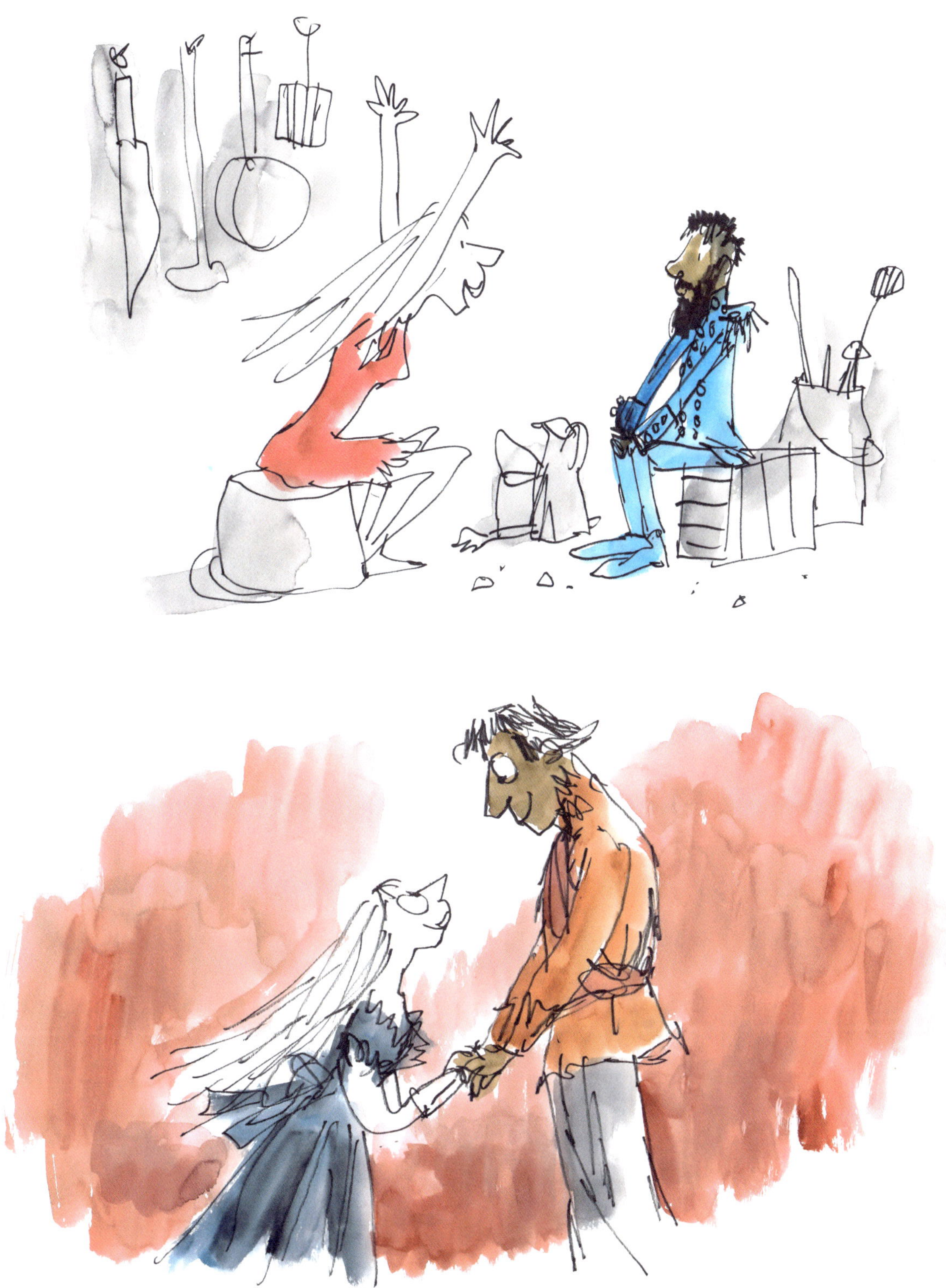

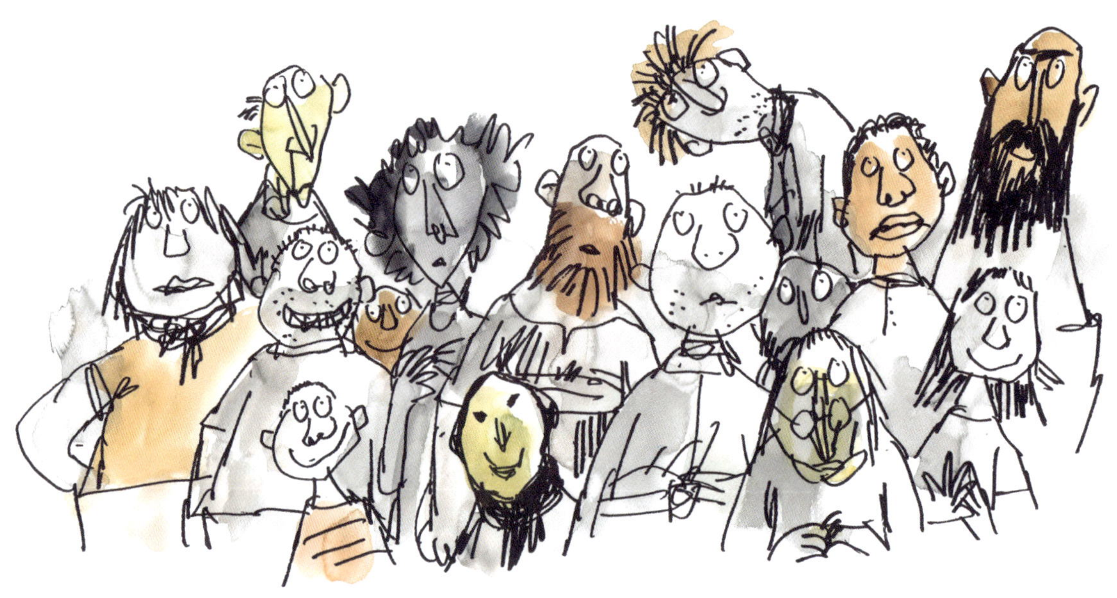

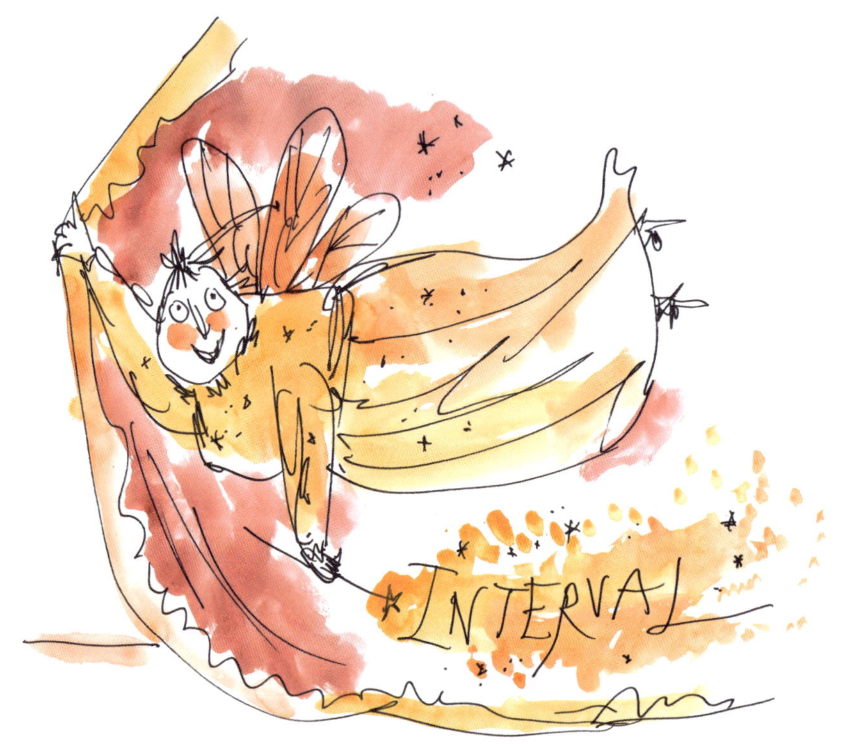


*Cinderella*, 2020

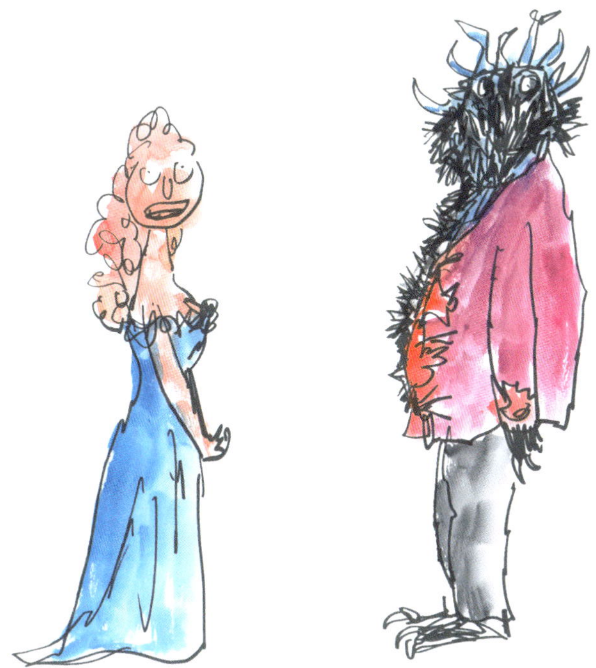

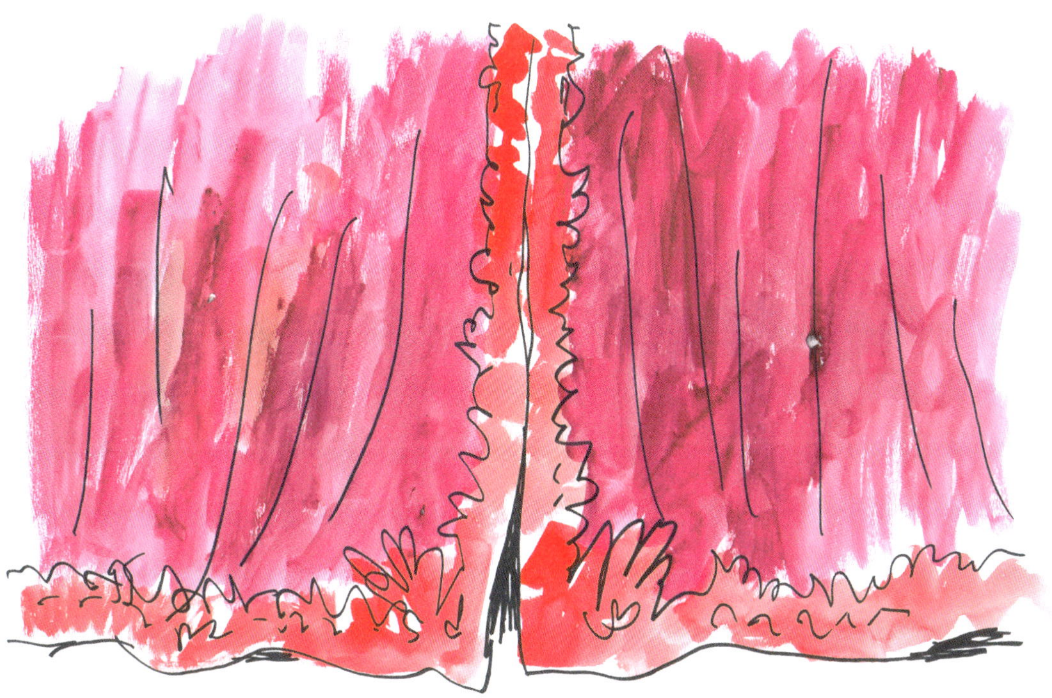

*Beauty and the Beast*, 2021

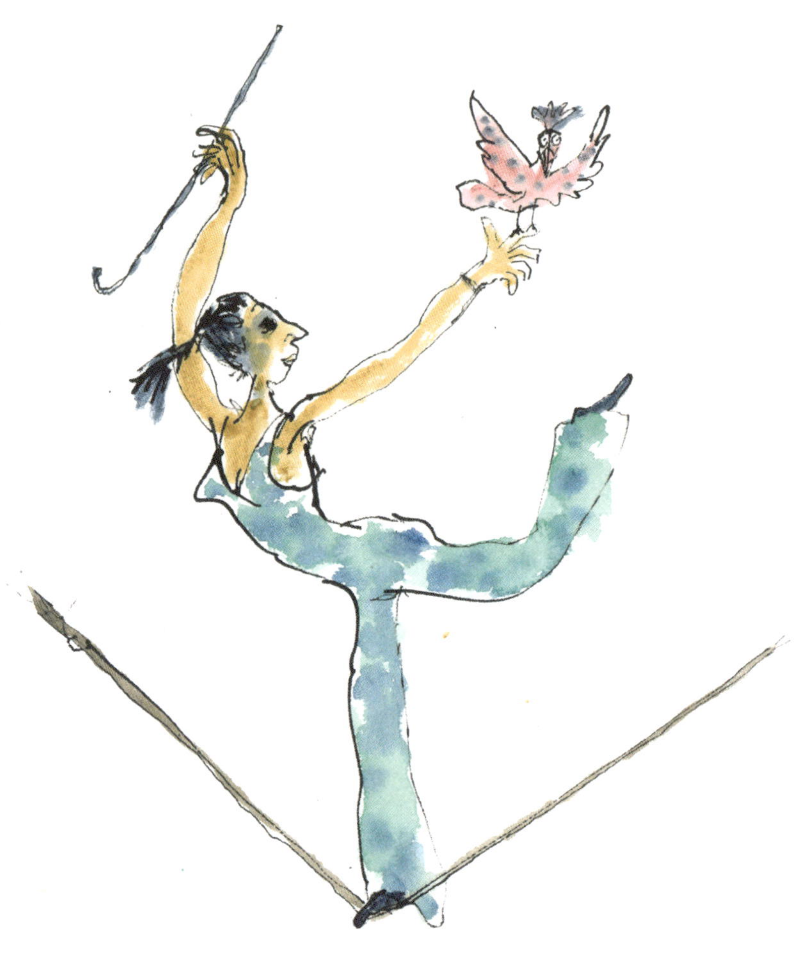

## Freedom from Torture

Founded in 1985, Freedom from Torture provide a wide range of support, including specialized therapy, for survivors of torture who have come to the UK to seek asylum. Quentin has supported them for many years with gifts of artwork for their auctions.

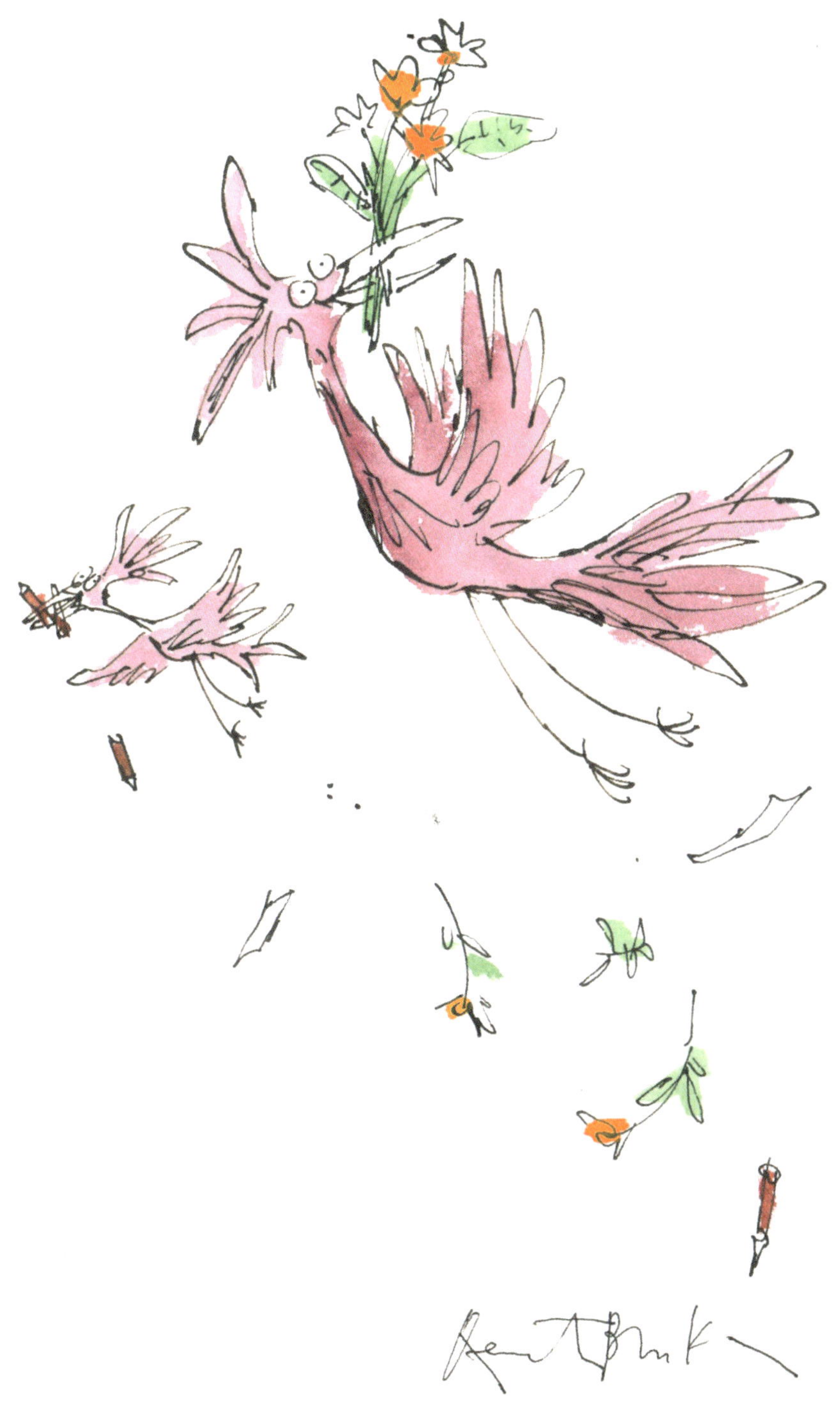

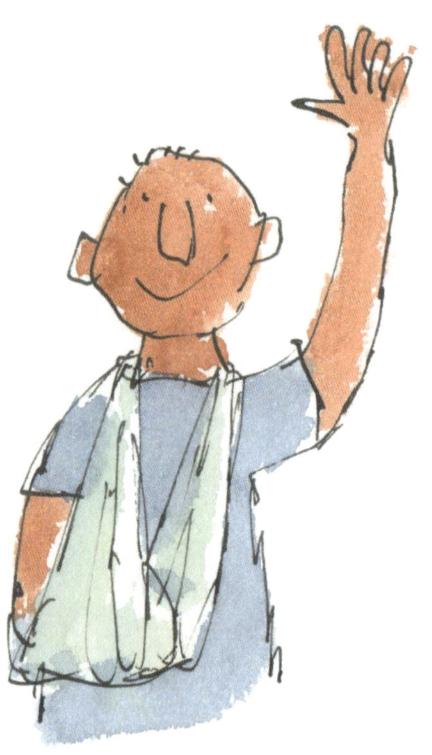

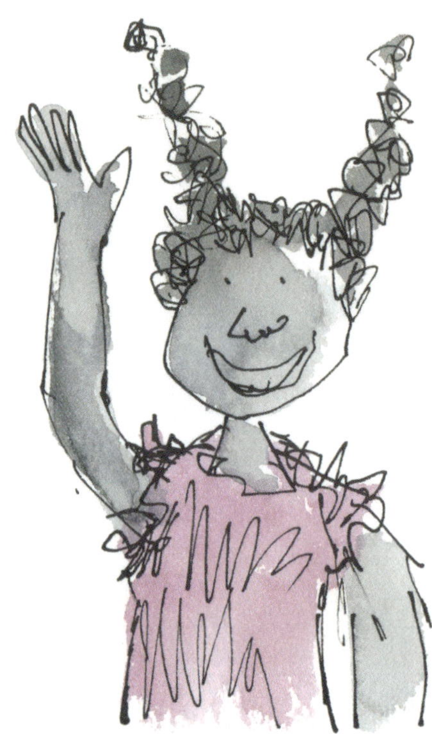

## Project Everyone

Project Everyone is a not-for-profit organisation who make campaign material to support the United Nations Global Goals, seventeen commitments which aim to address extreme poverty, climate change, and injustice and inequality.

When the UK hosted the G7 and the UN Climate Change Conference (COP26), Project Everyone joined seventy-five charities in a joint initiative to 'Crack the Crises' and spread a 'Wave of Hope' across the country. Quentin, and other illustrators, were asked to do drawings for people to decorate their windows with.

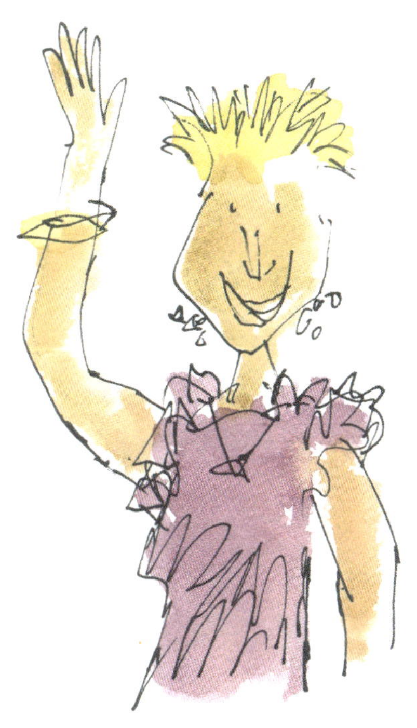

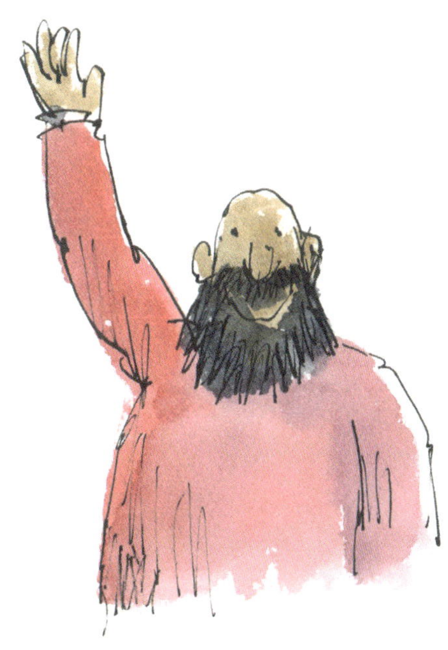

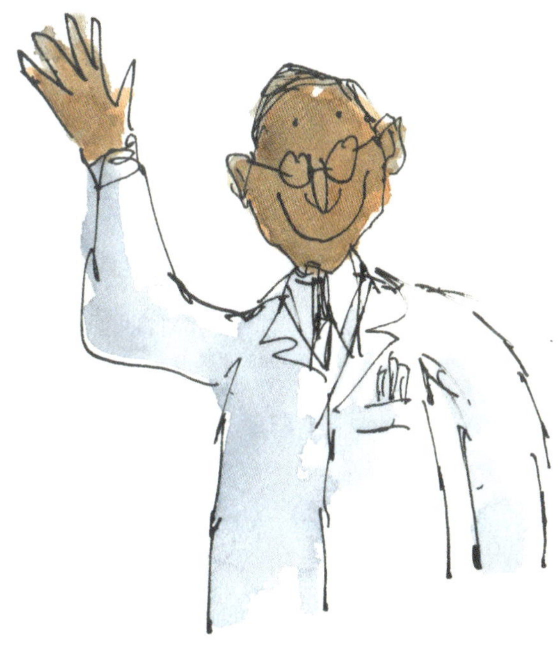

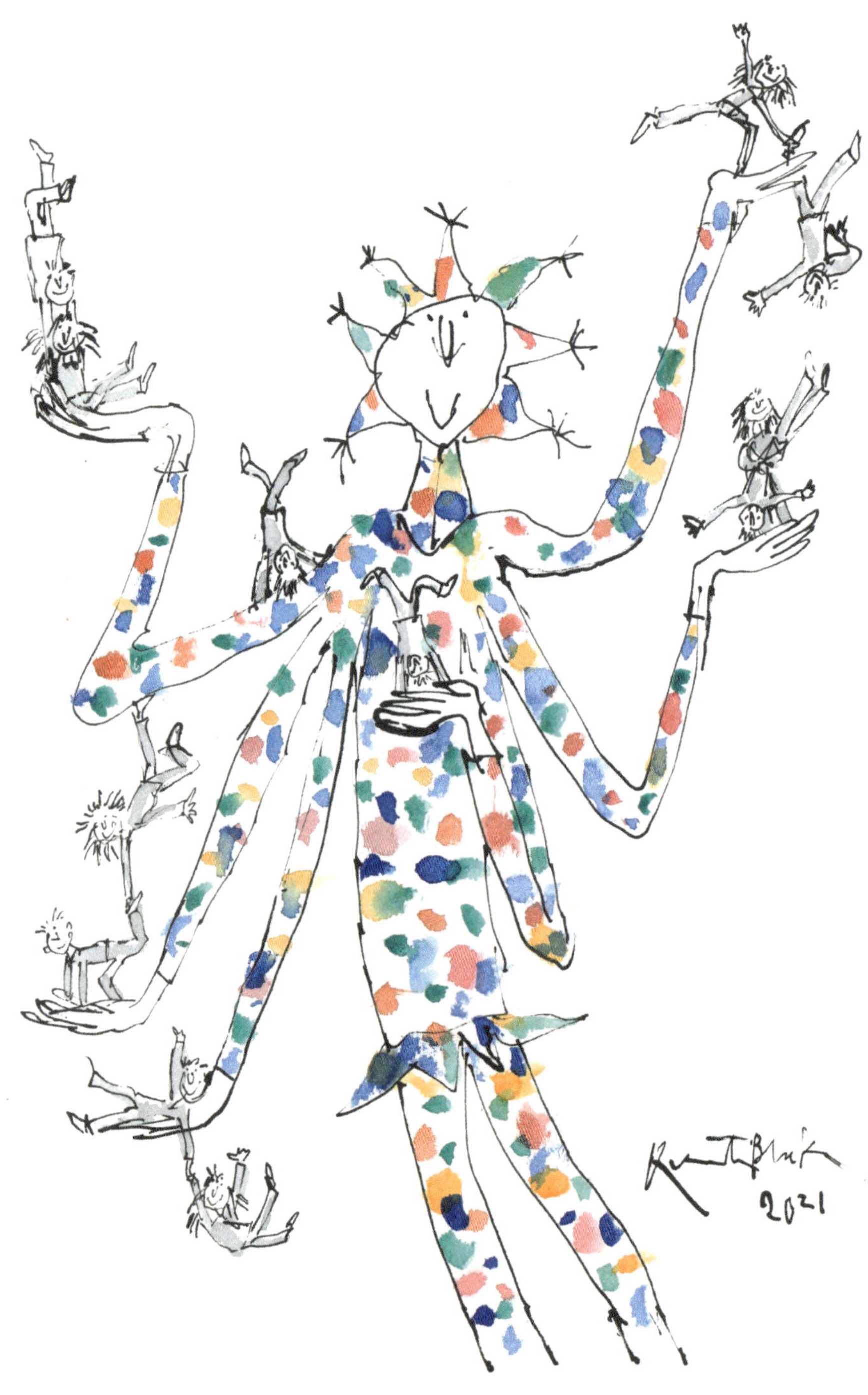

*Medical Aid for Palestinians*, Drawing for Limited Edition Print to Raise Funds, 2021

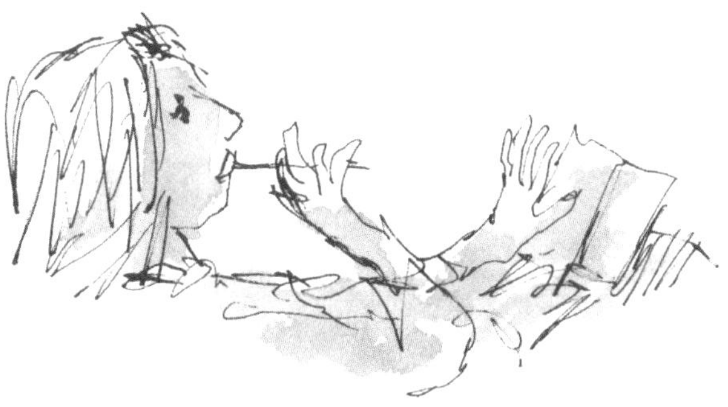

*Beyond Bea Stillbirth*, 2021

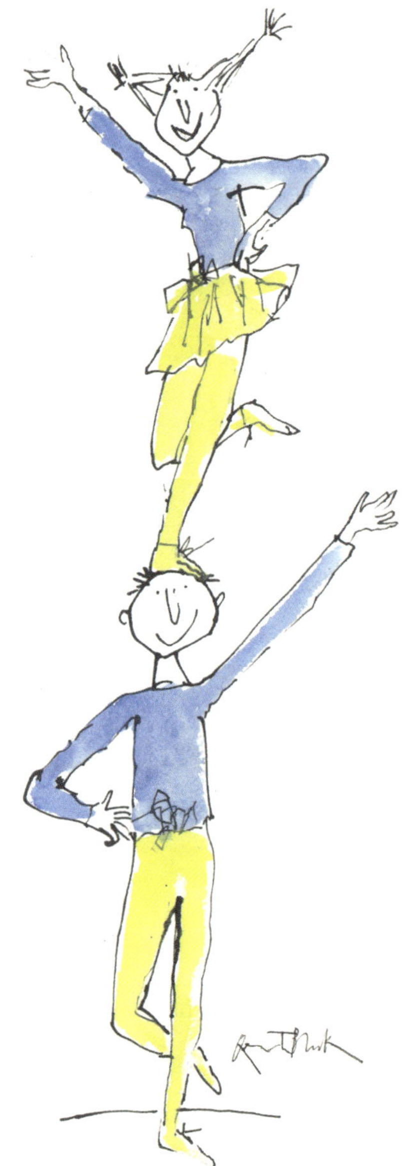

## Hope and Homes for Children

Hope and Homes for Children is an organisation that finds homes for orphaned children in loving families. Quentin did forty drawings for the charity's auction to raise funds for children in Ukraine in 2022.

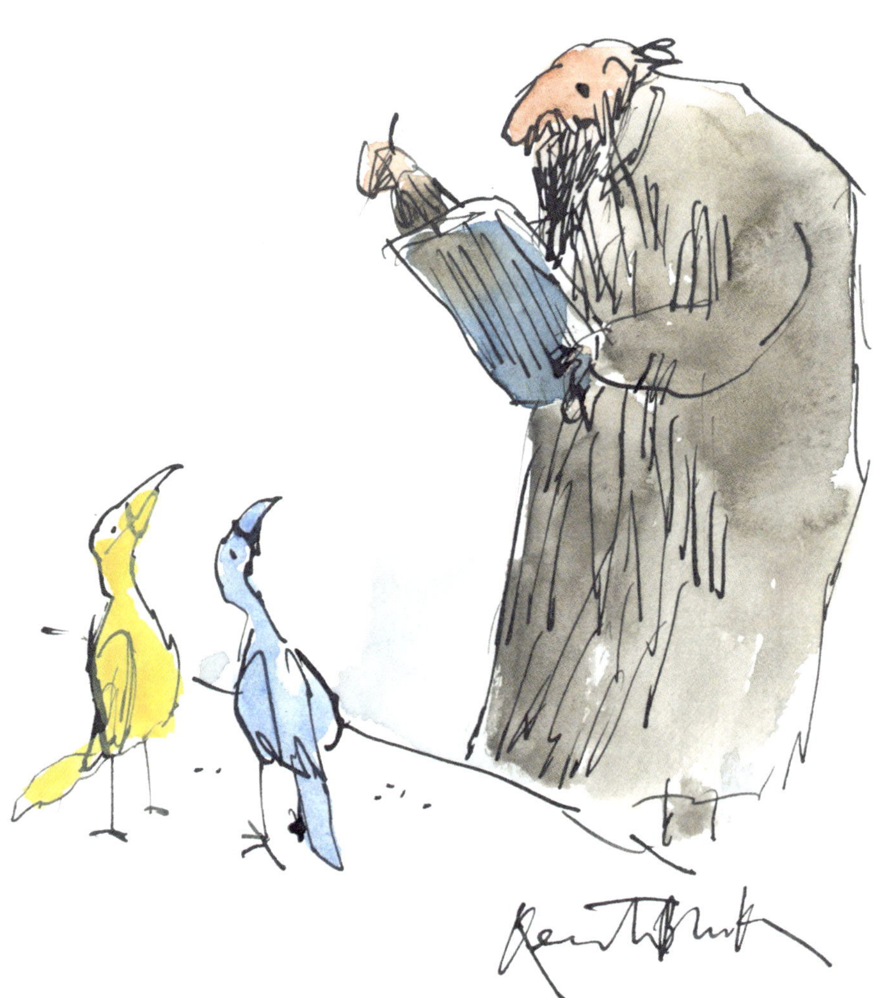

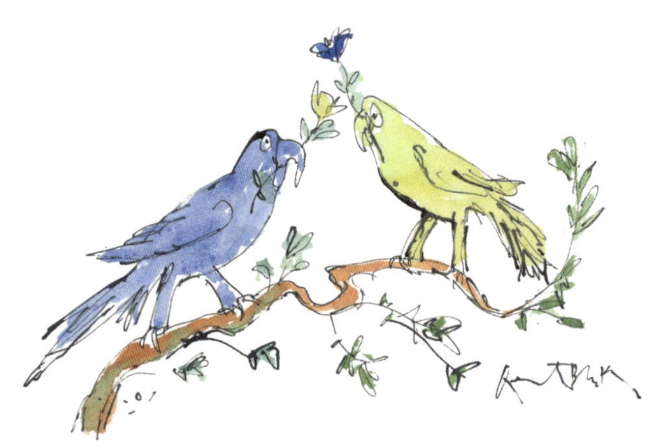

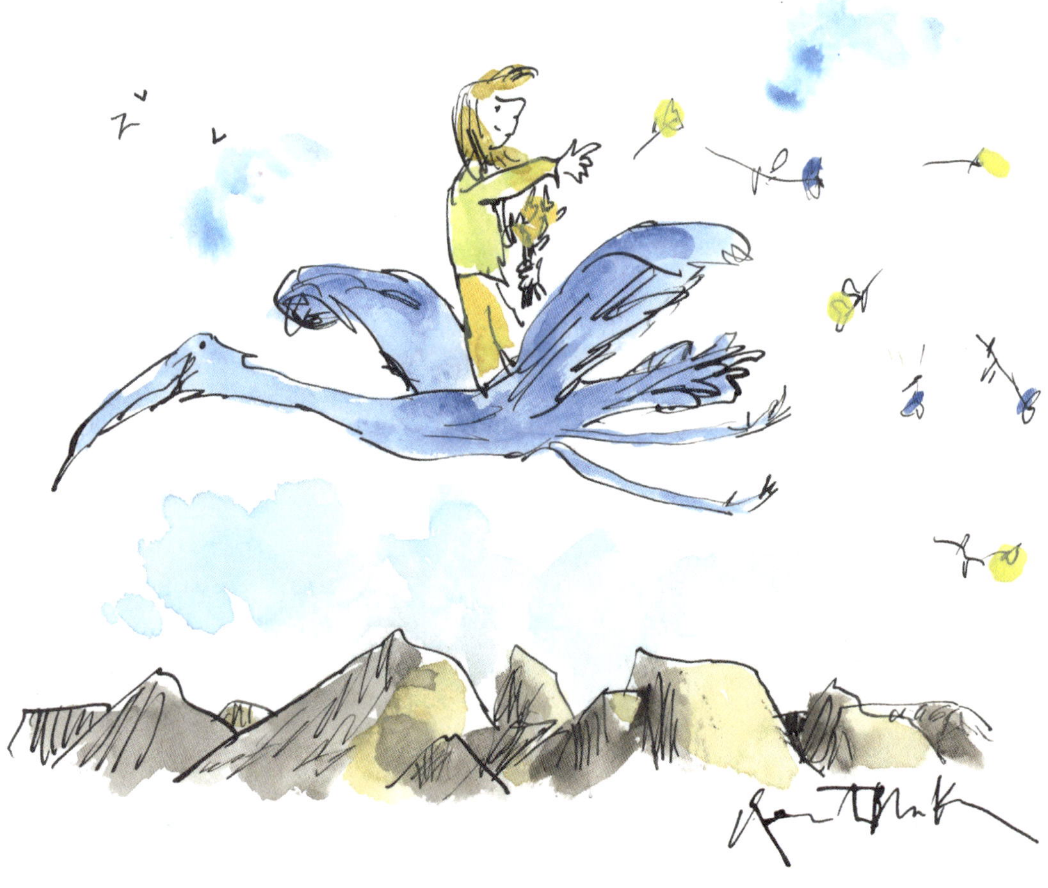

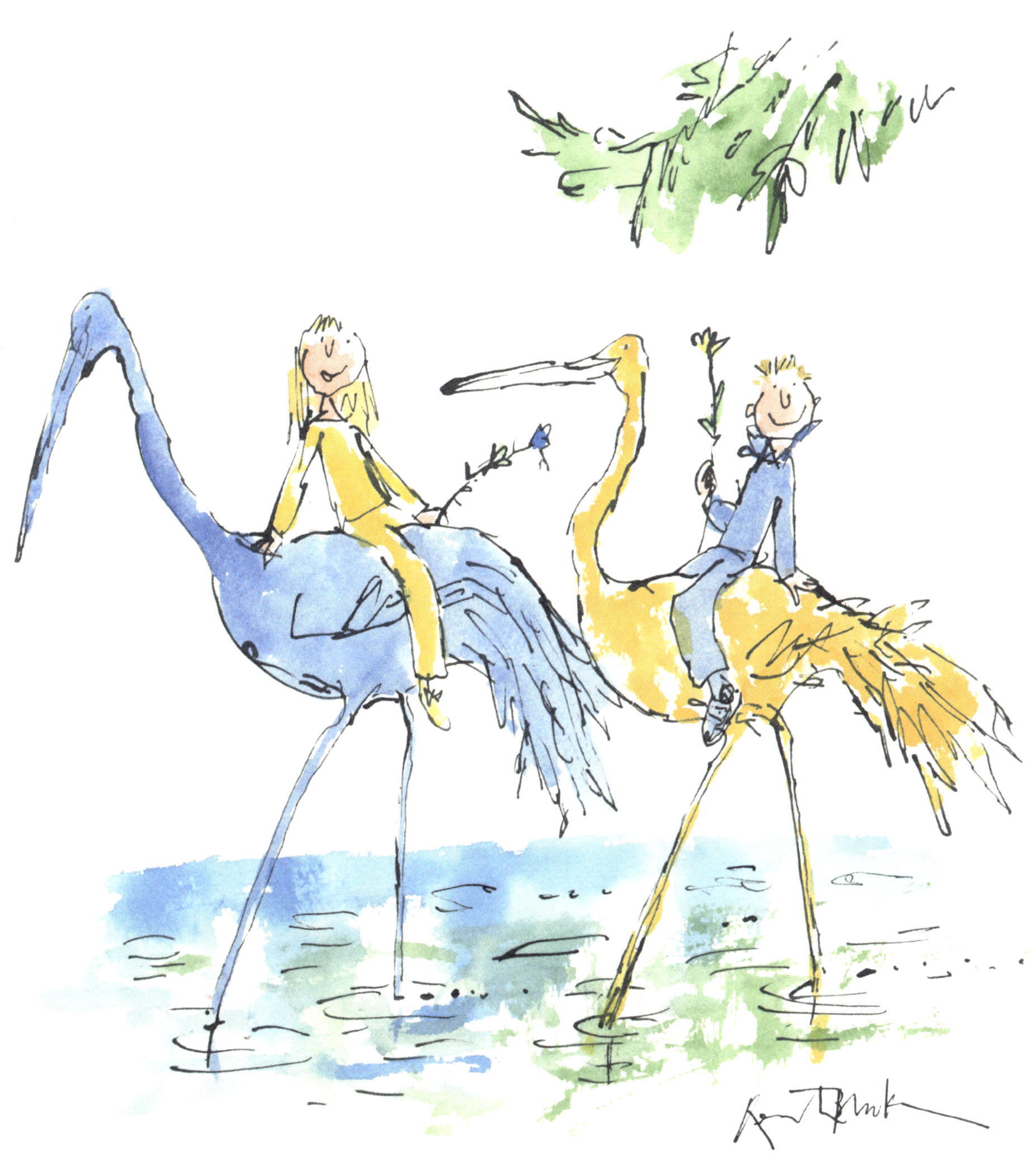



OPPOSITE & ABOVE – *Hope and Homes for Children*, 2022

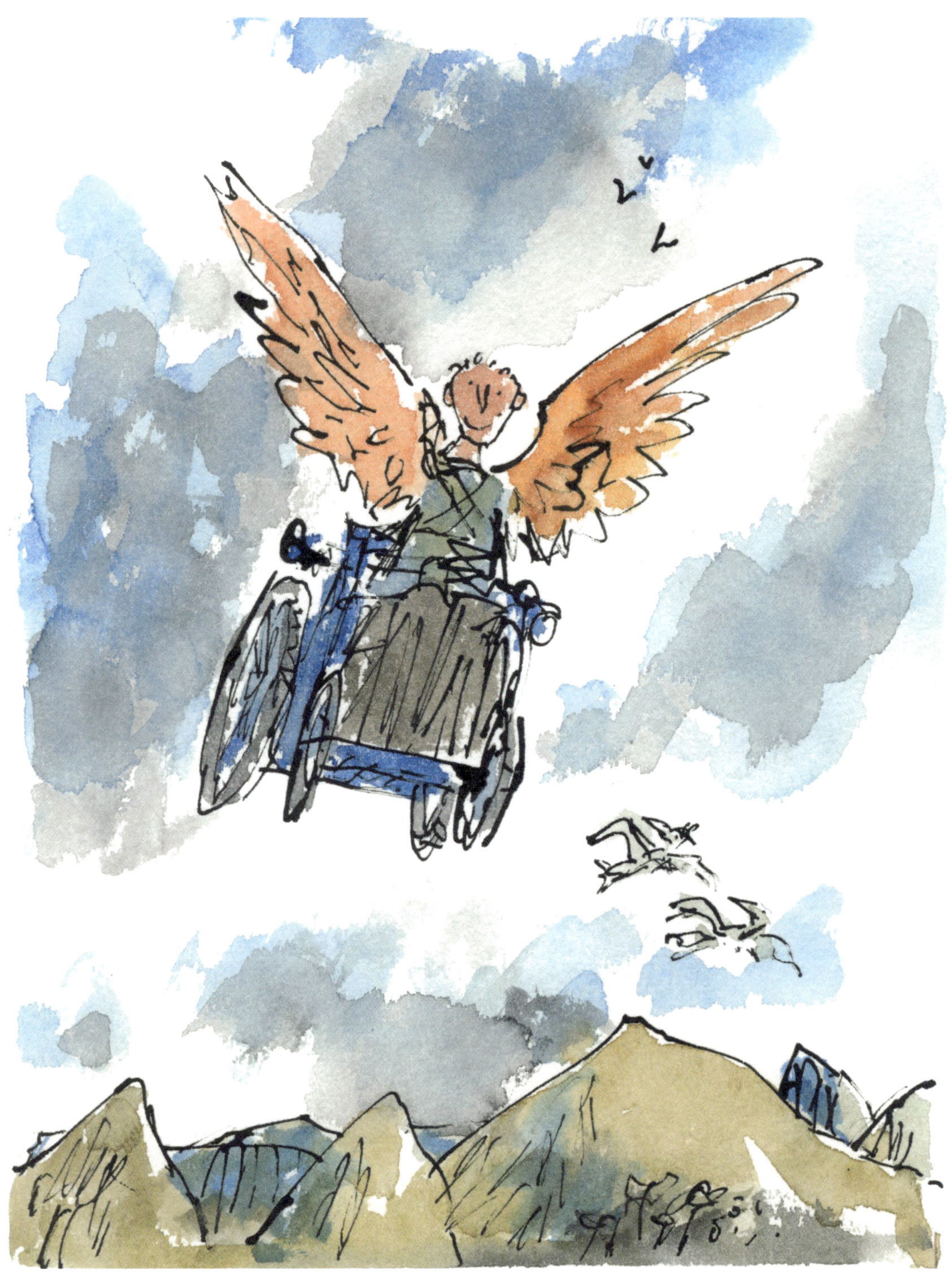

*Invictus Games,* produced as a limited edition run
of fifty prints to raise money for the games in 2022

*Blue Peter Badge to Encourage Reading,*
Original Illustration and Badge with Digitized Artwork, 2023

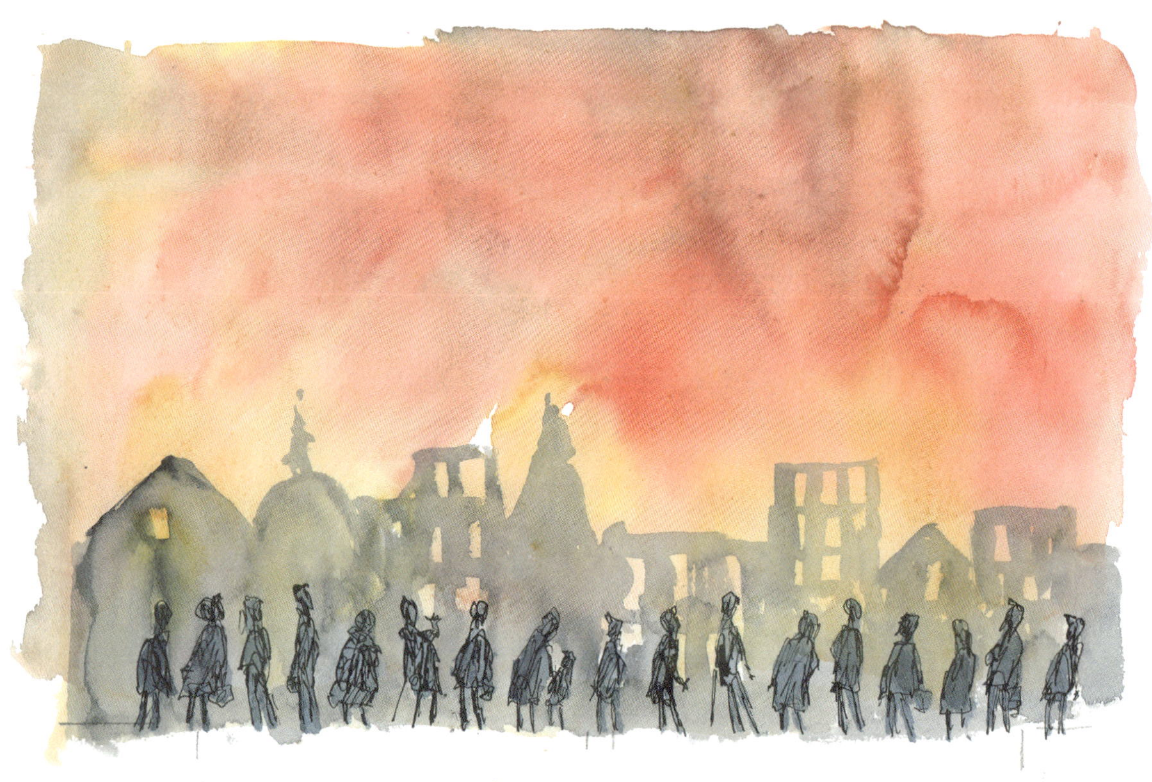

## ShelterBox

ShelterBox is a charity which supports people to rebuild their lives after a disaster or conflict. In their book, *Tamesis Street,* thirty authors tell one story of the effect of a flood on one community. Quentin did the cover artwork in 2021, pictured here.

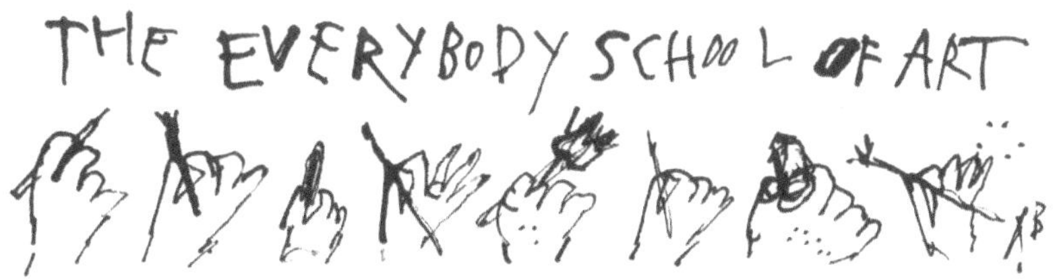

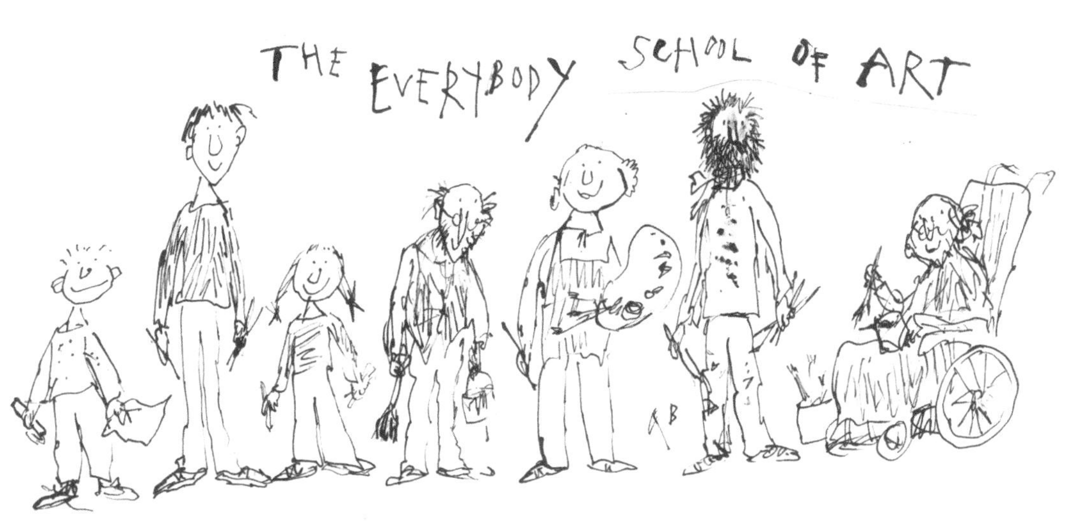

ABOVE – *Everybody School of Art,* 2022

## Everybody School of Art

Quentin created the logo and signage for the Everybody School of Art, a community art school in a converted mill in Halifax, 2022.

# Environmental Charities

Quentin's long-held belief in protecting the planet and its wildlife has involved him in several different charities.

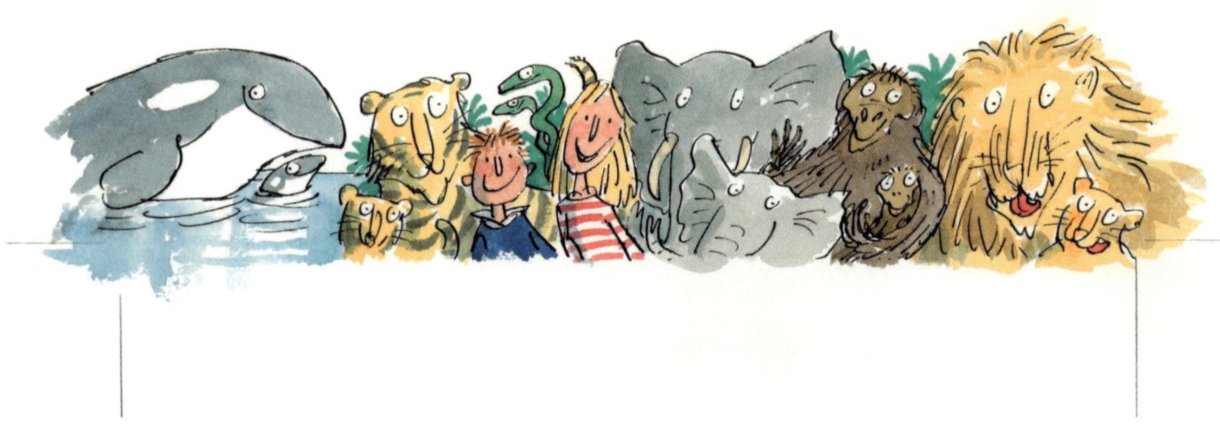

*Endangered Species Car Sticker,* 1996

## *Born Free Foundation*

This international wildlife charity protects wild animals in their natural habitat.

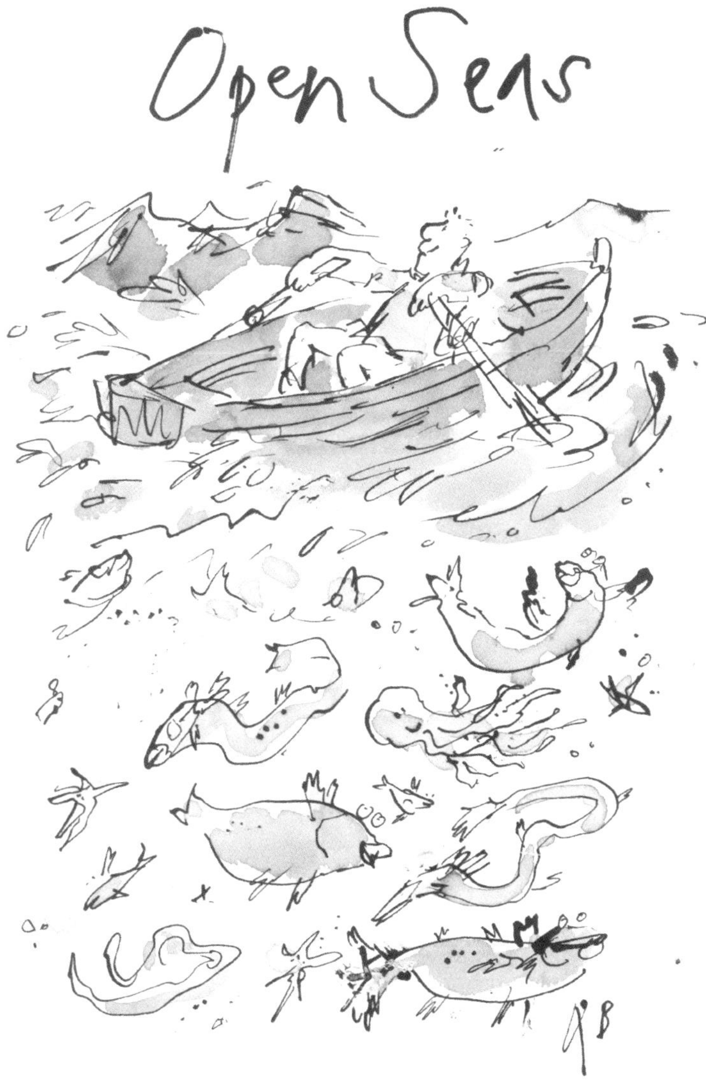

Open Seas, a charity committed to protecting the marine environment, 2024

## Open Seas

In 2023 Jamie Howard, a cousin of Linda Kitson's, Quentin's lifelong friend and fellow artist, rowed solo across the Atlantic on behalf of Open Seas, a charity committed to protecting the marine environment. Quentin drew the artwork for Jamie to use on social media and gave the original to him as a memento of his endeavours.

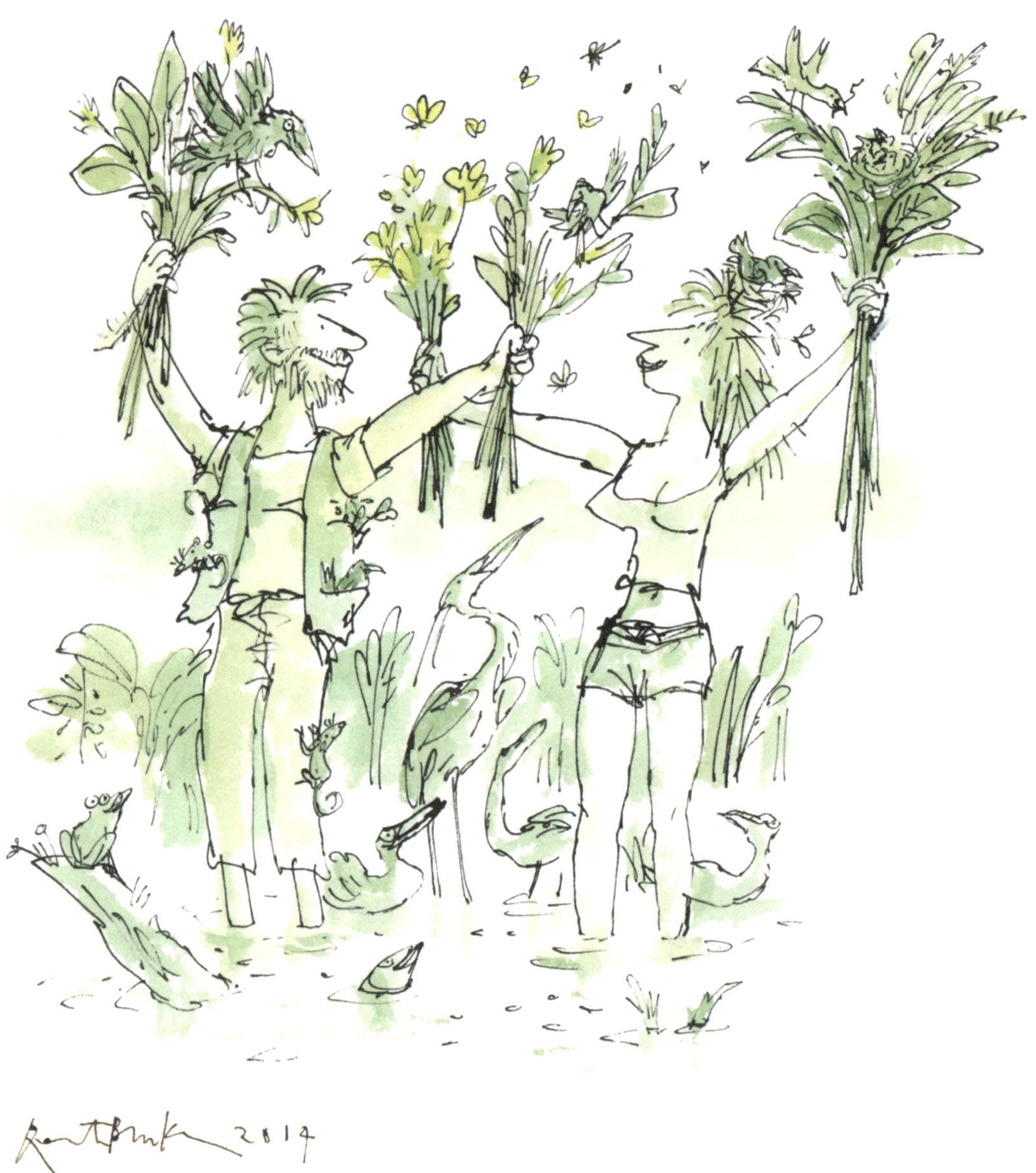

## *World Wildlife Fund*

Quentin created these prints in 2014 to support the World Wildlife Fund's Earth Hour, an annual event when people, businesses and communities turn off non-essential lights for an hour and do something positive for the planet.

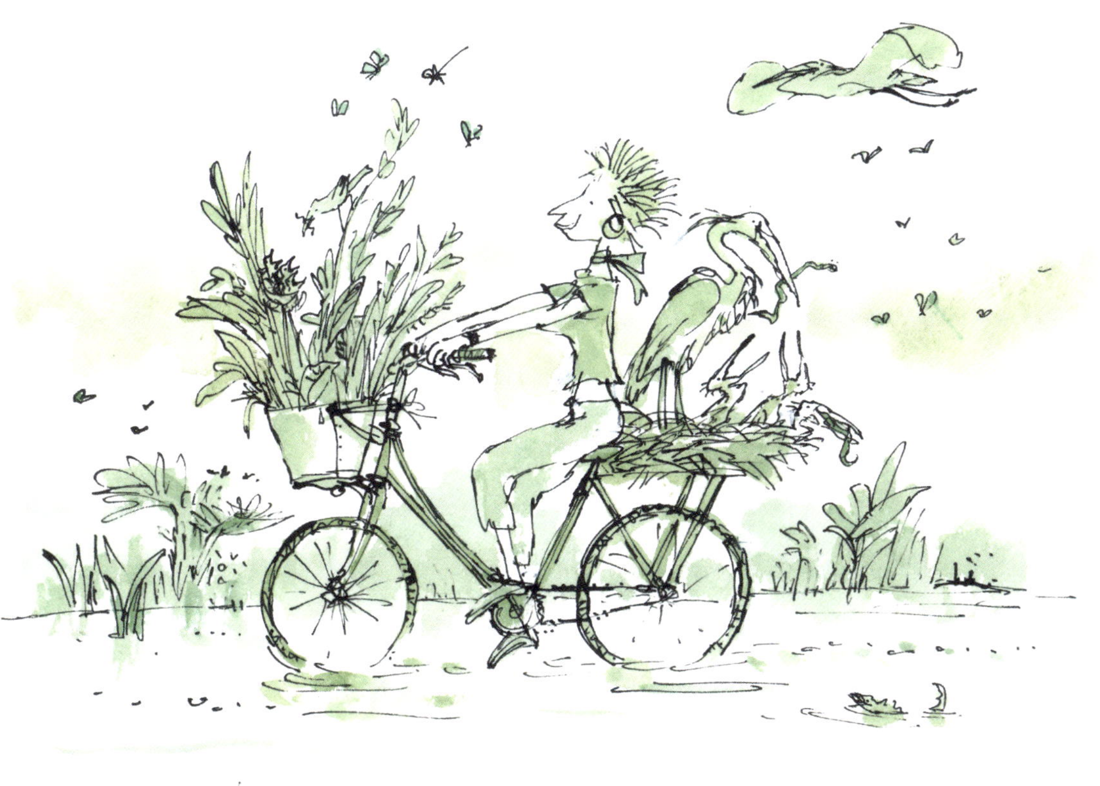

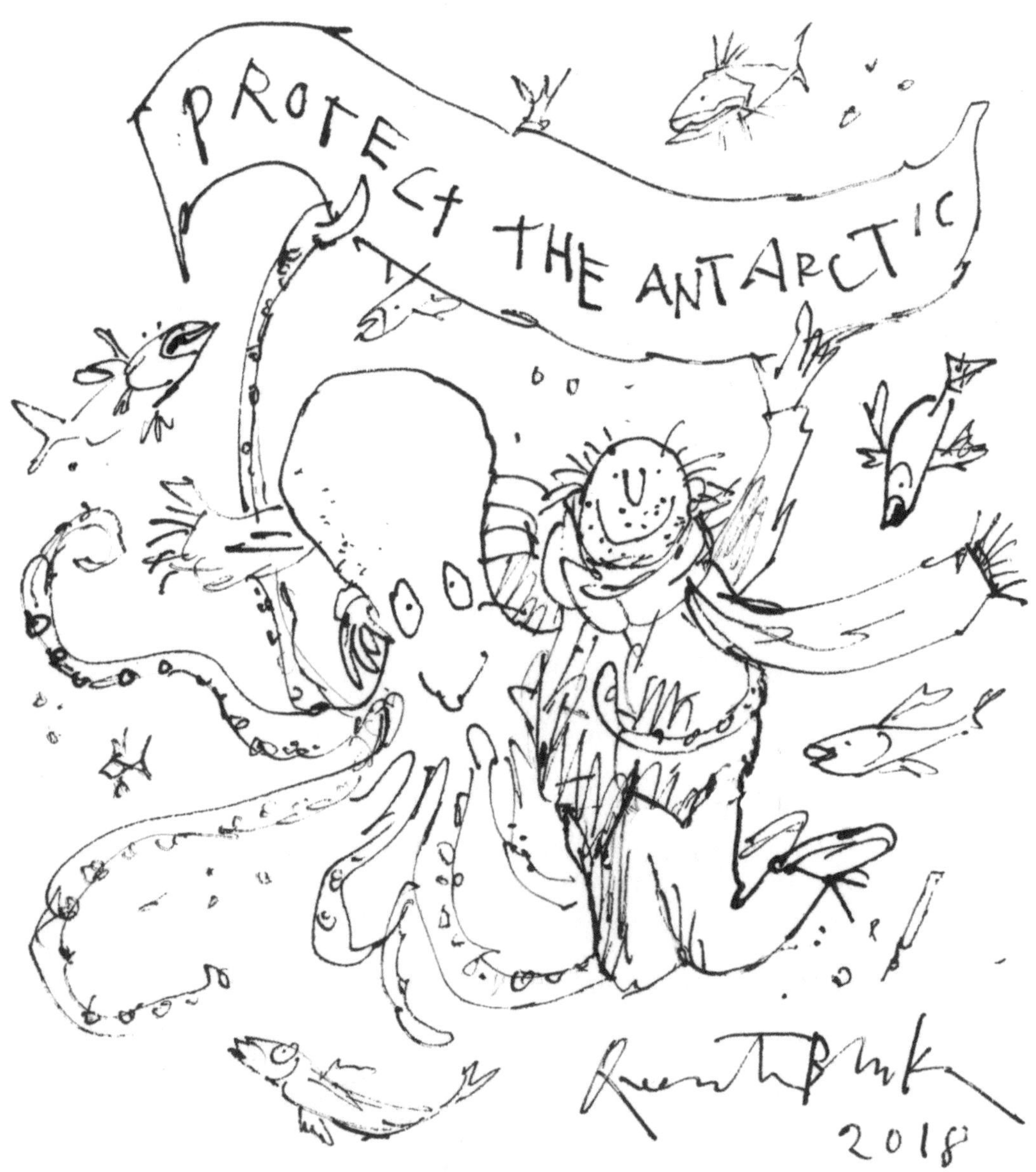


*Greenpeace*

Protect the Antarctic Campaign, 2018. The colour was added digitally by Greenpeace.

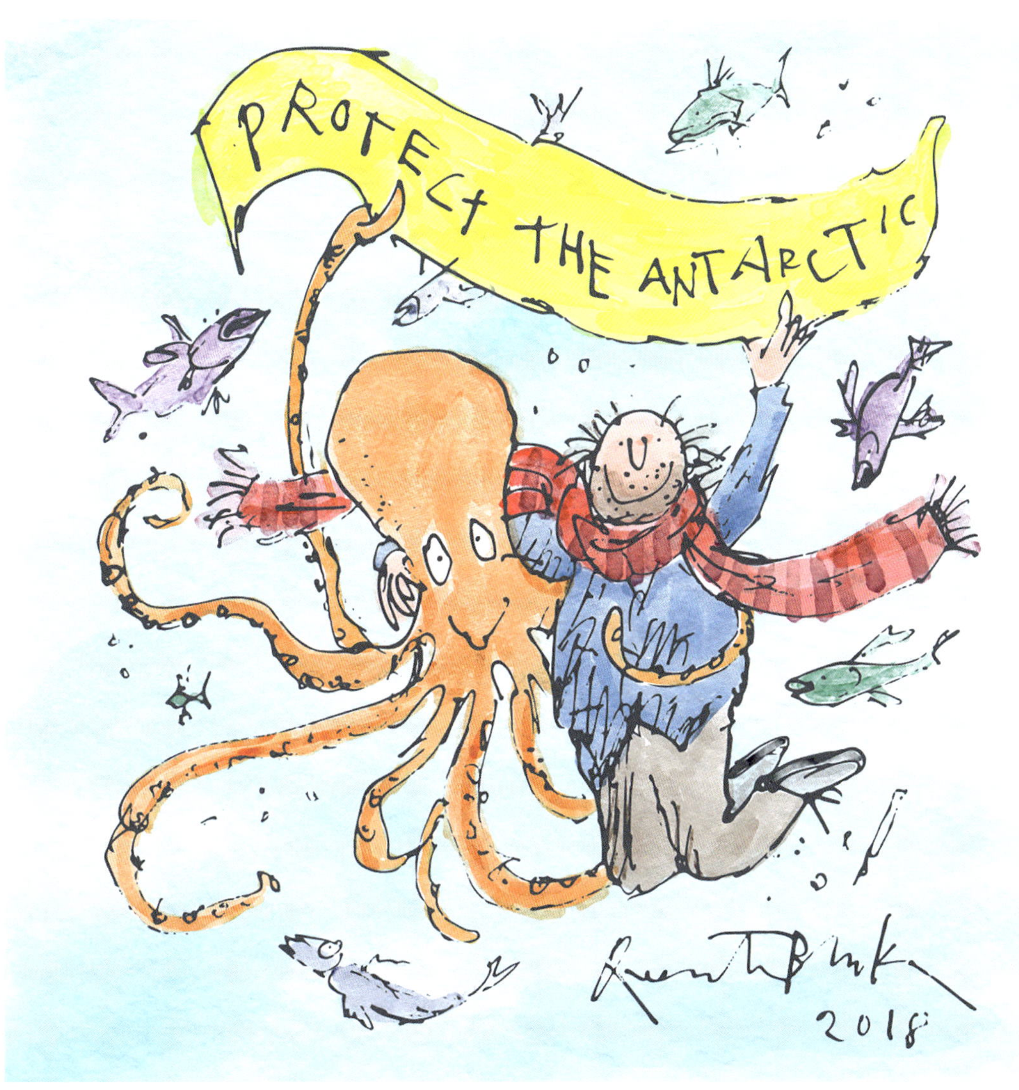
PROTECT THE ANTARCTIC
2018

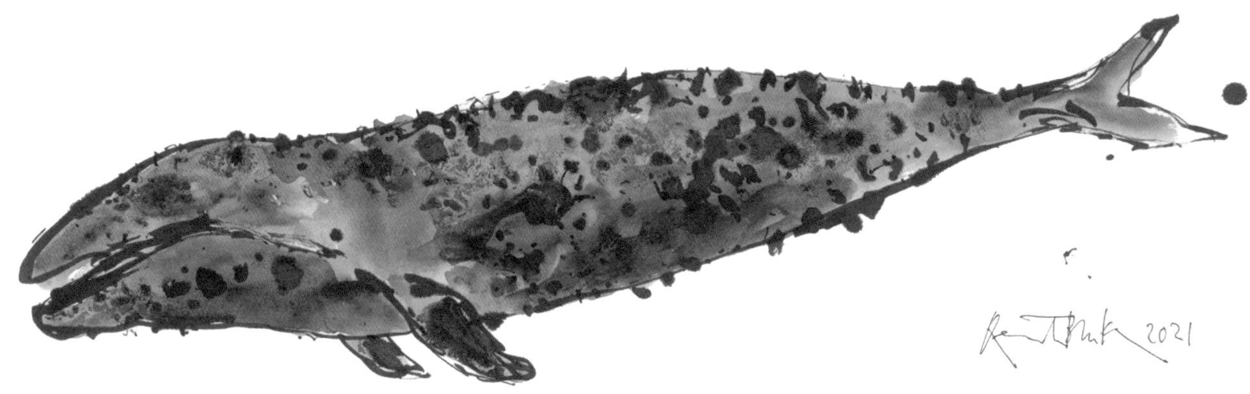

*Grey Whale,* for 'Draw the Oceans', an Online Drawing Challenge, 2021

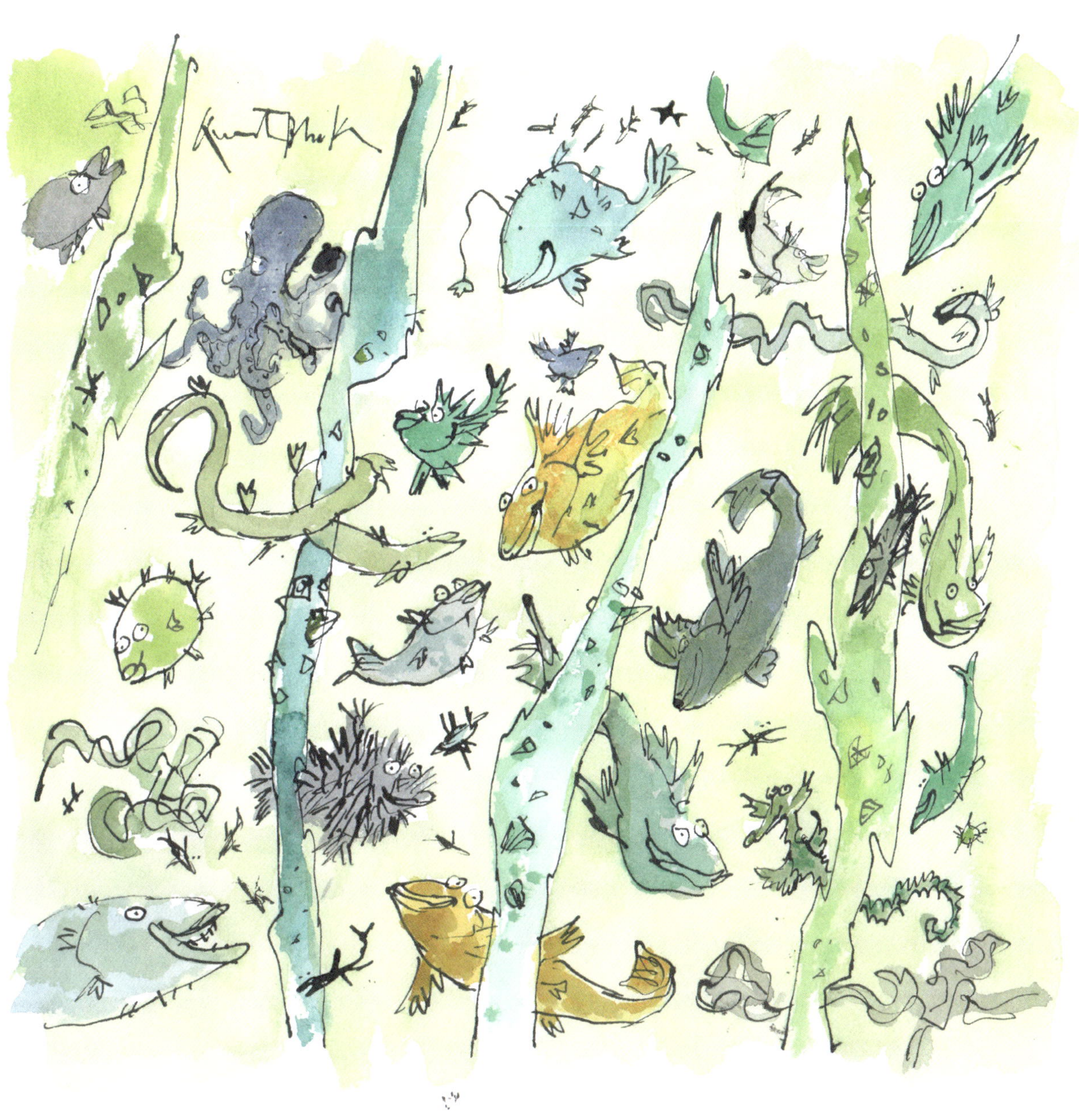

*Protect the Oceans Campaign,* 2019

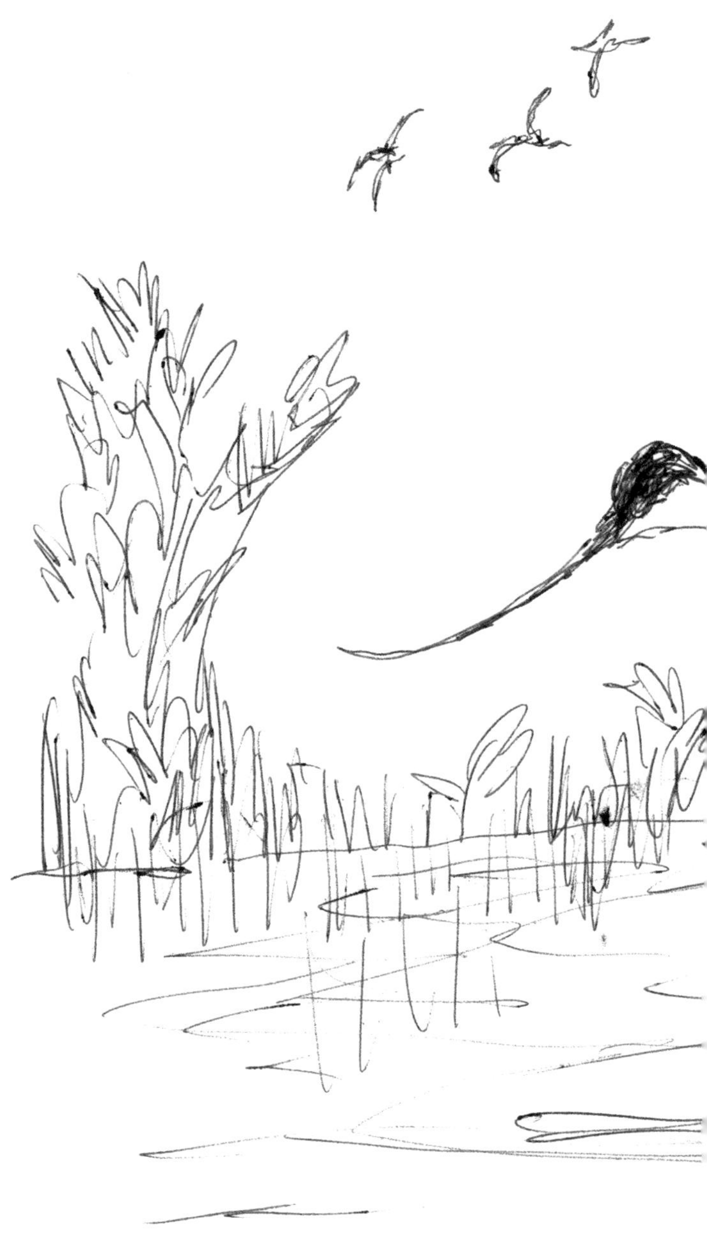

## *The Wildfowl and Wetlands Trust*

In July 2023 Quentin agreed to a year-long partnership with WWT in a project called Drawn to Water. They chose work from his archive of hundreds of illustrations of birds (and people) in, on and around water, and re-purposed them for their seasonal trails.

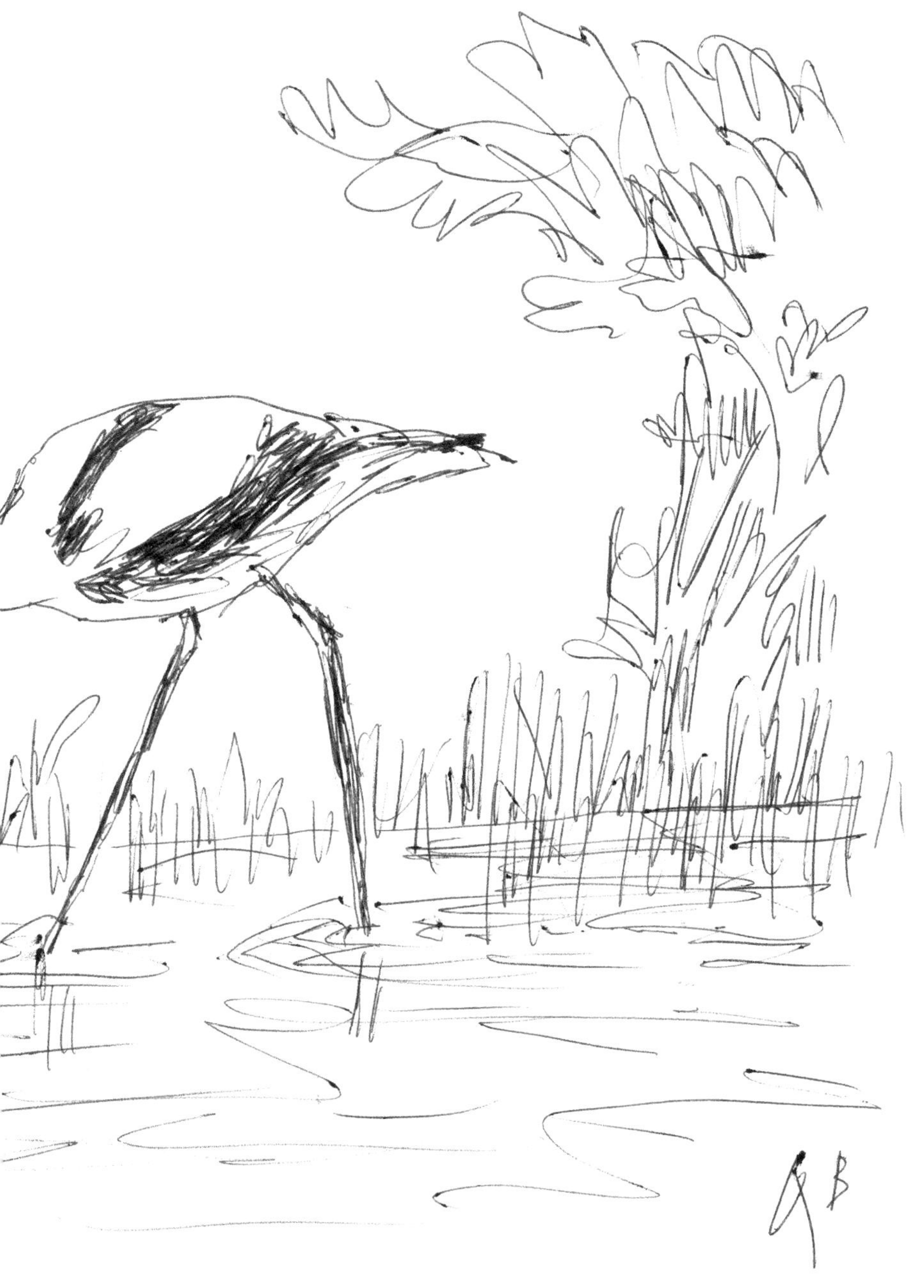

Quentin drew this avocet with a biro, which is currently one of his favourite drawing implements. He did it partly to demonstrate that you don't need complicated art materials to make a drawing and it was also used as a print for the charity as a legacy of the partnership. The print was framed and toured several of the WWT sites.

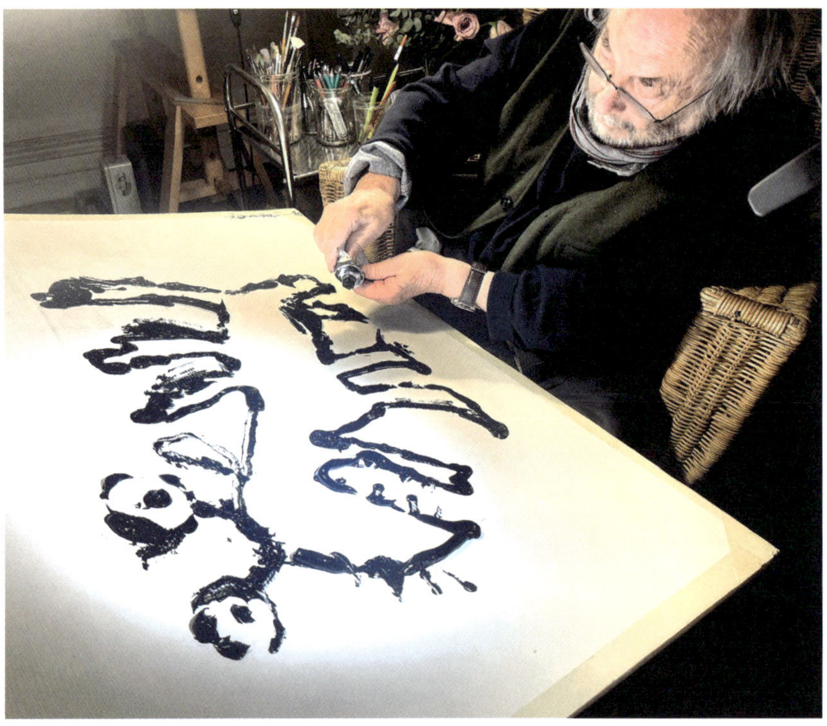

## Paintings for the Visually Impaired

Olivia Ahmad, the artistic director of the new Quentin Blake Centre of Illustration had written to Quentin about ideas for his gallery;

'…we are thinking about how people with different sensory needs can experience your work. Something that many galleries are doing is printing works in relief, which works very well. However, I wondered whether you might be interested in creating a set of drawings for people to touch and handle directly.'

This appealed to Quentin; he used acrylic paint squeezed straight out of the tube on to large pieces of paper so that the line could be felt as well as seen.

'I think the paintings should exist in different sizes as we need to take into account the first use of them. I'm not sure if you can get a mental picture from running your fingers over such a large painting.'

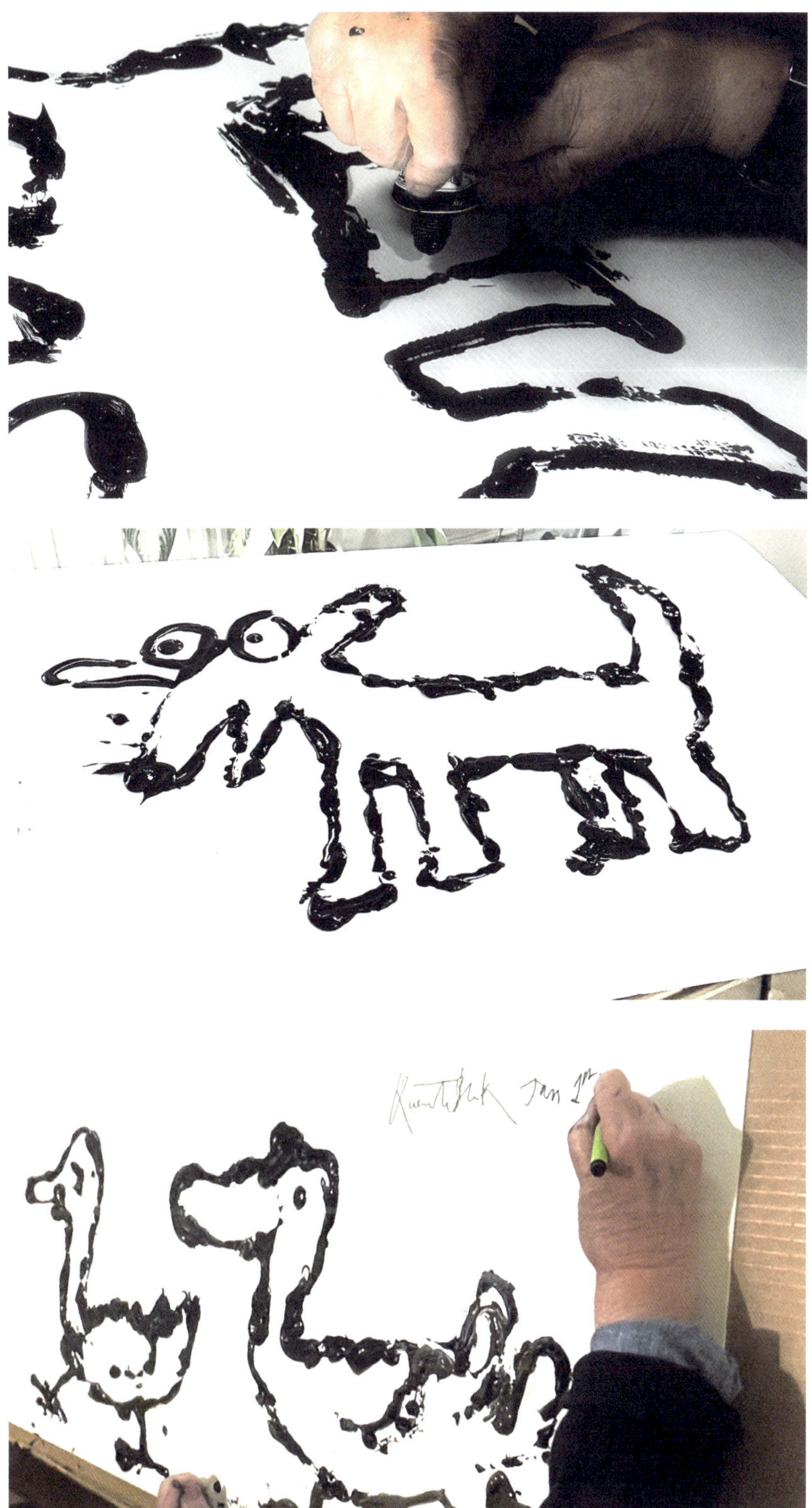

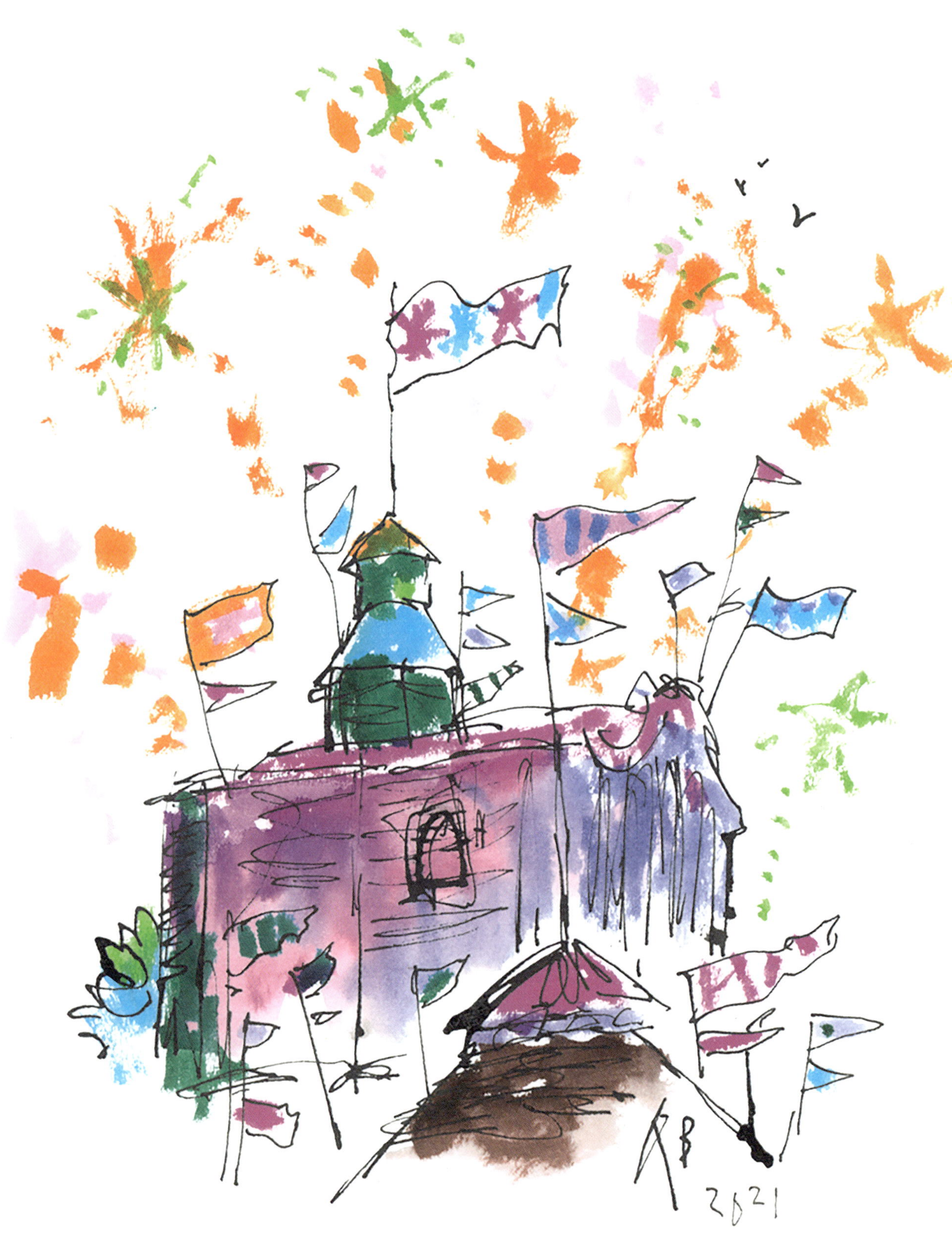

# The Quentin Blake Centre
# for Illustration

When Quentin was teaching illustration at the Royal College of Art, he felt the need for a museum where his students could see what their forebears and contemporaries were doing; a centre for 'the display and study and celebration of the art of illustration.' Somewhere with 'ILLUSTRATION above the door.'

As Jenny Uglow said in *The Quentin Blake Book,* 'Alert to the great tradition of illustration and its present wealth, and realizing there was no designated gallery, he led the drive to found the House of Illustration in 2014…. Another cause for celebration.'

The original House of Illustration closed its doors in King's Cross in 2020. Since renamed to honour its founder, a new site in Clerkenwell has been found to house the centre. This is what Quentin said at an event at the site in 2020:

'It will be the biggest space devoted to illustration probably in the world. So it will have the possibility of constant, and international, exhibitions. In fact illustration doesn't get so much notice because it isn't 'fine art' and it isn't in the Tate Gallery and so on, but it is, if you like, a vernacular; it's a language which everybody understands, they may look at it and not think that they're looking at art, but it's having the effect on them of art. It's a language which everybody can read, so to speak, and a lot of art happens in illustration and drawing which is not acknowledged. And so that will have a home here. Everybody can come together and they can look at drawing, they can do illustration projects, they can talk about the history of the thing.

This is my drawing of the building that we are in at the moment. If you go outside and look at it you will see that it's beautiful brickwork and it's a lovely shape. It's got history in it already, it was an industrial building and if we look round us where we are now you can see it's still a masterpiece of design and that's another reason why it's so good for it to be a home for illustration.'

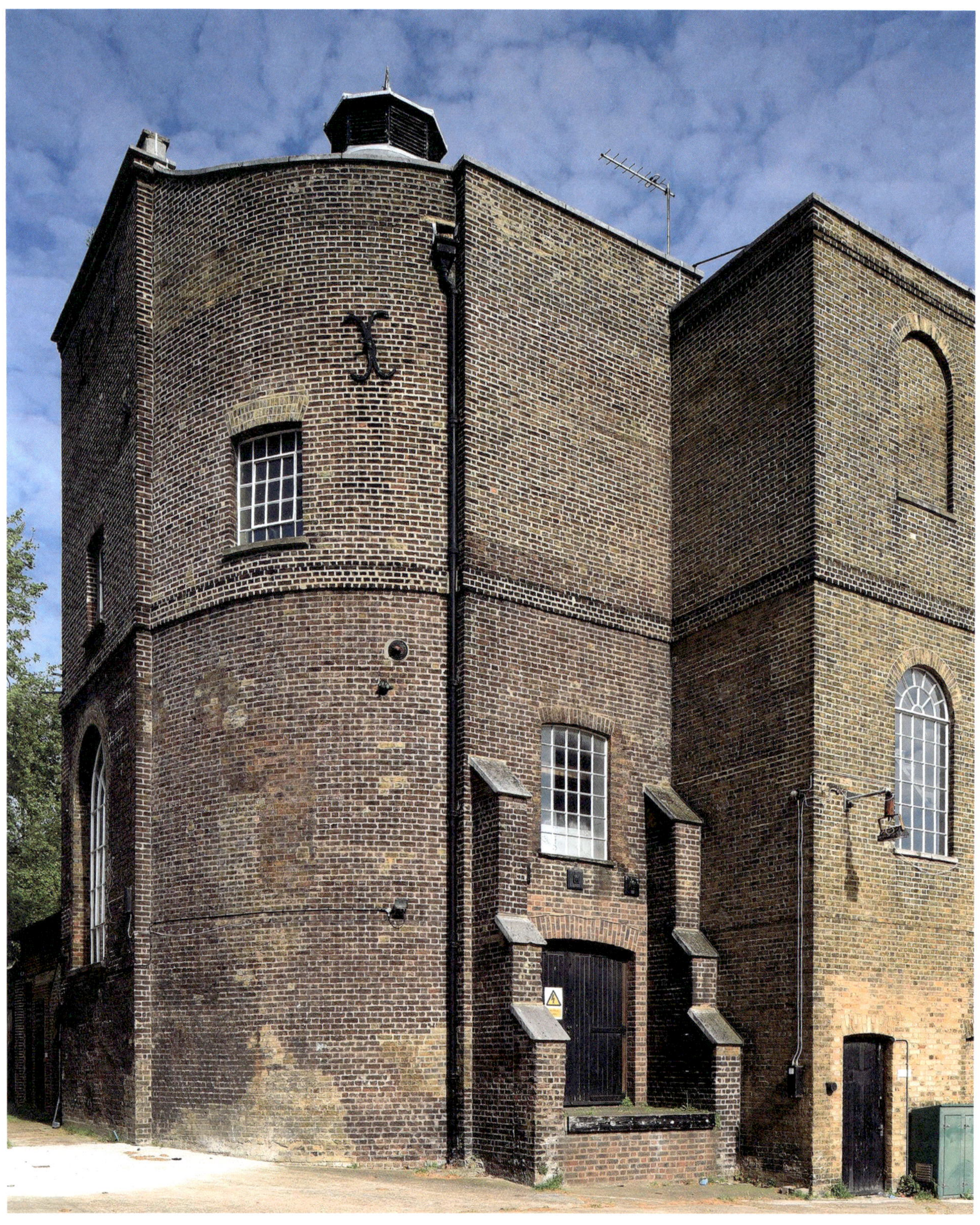

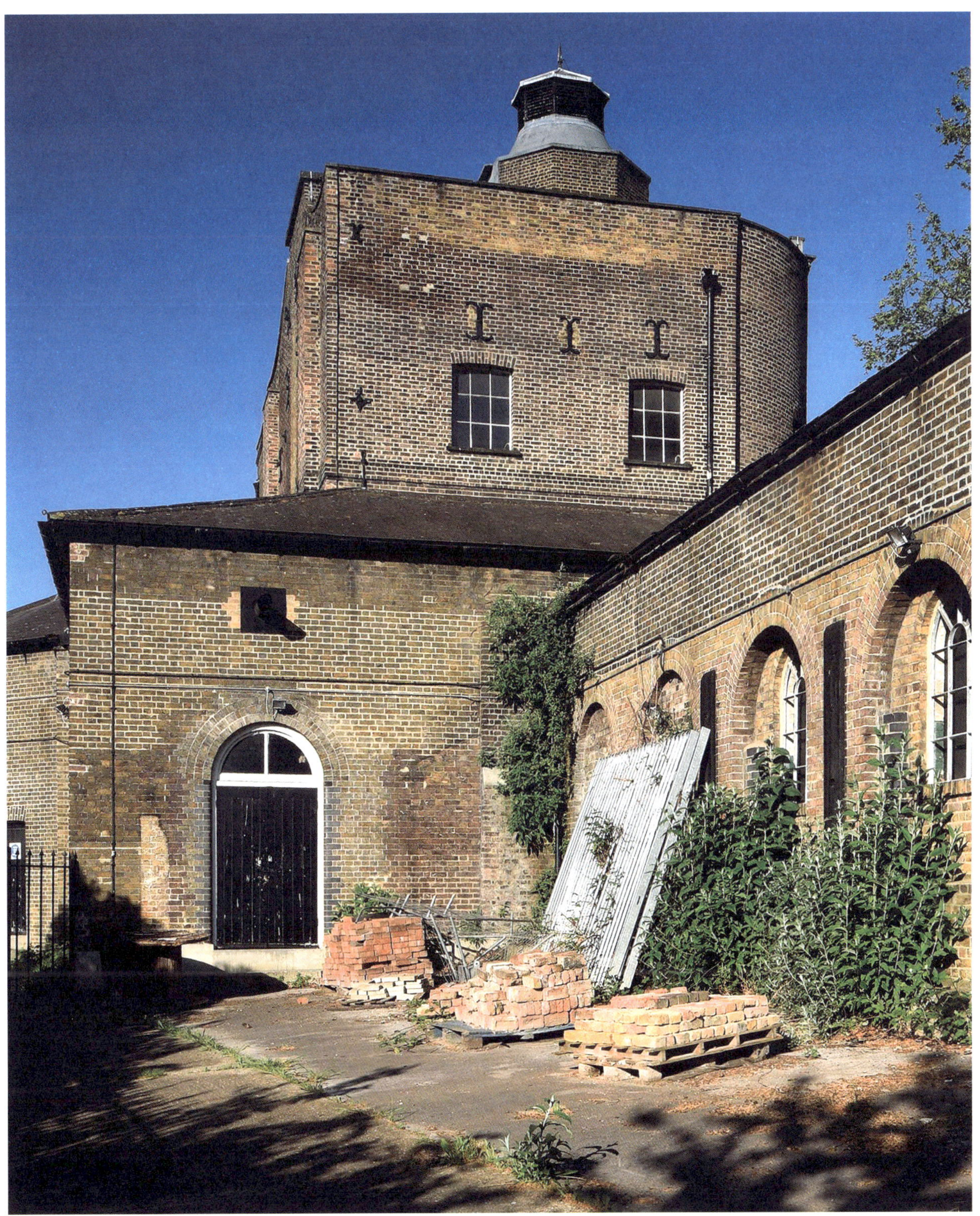

OPPOSITE & ABOVE – *The Quentin Blake Centre for Illustration*

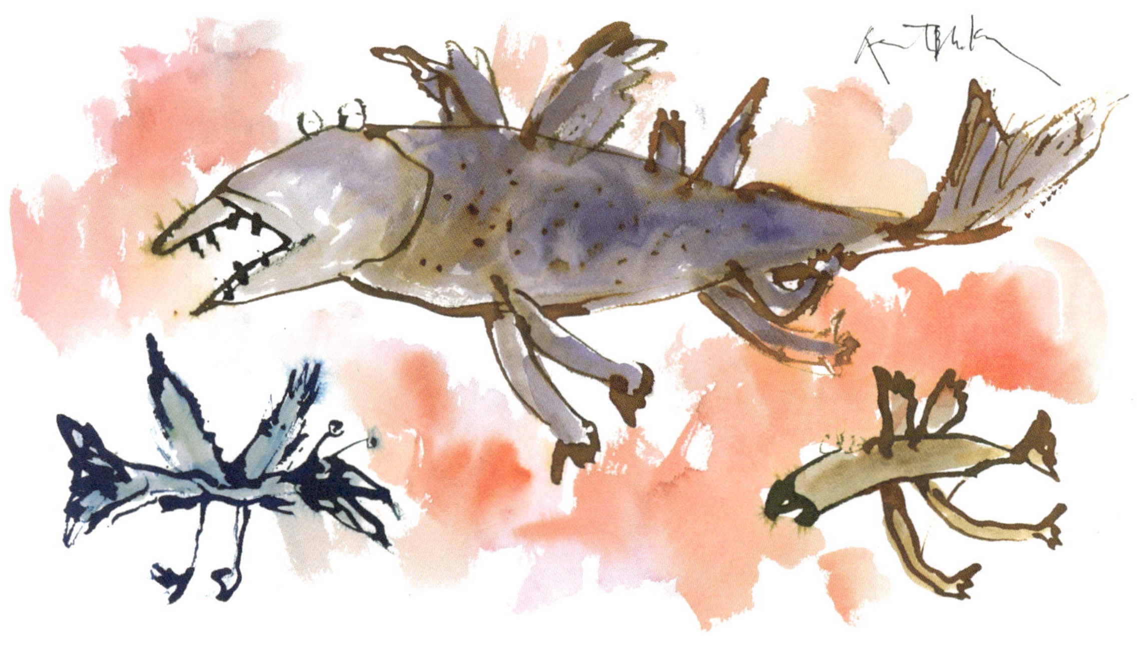

The site for the new Centre – New River Head, a group of historic, industrial buildings originally built to bring clean water into London – was generously purchased by Quentin, and the funds for the renovation have been raised by its dedicated executive team and board of trustees. As ever, Quentin has contributed his drawings for annual auctions in aid of the Centre. Some of the work is drawn specially for the auction and the rest is work he finds in the plan chests in his studio.

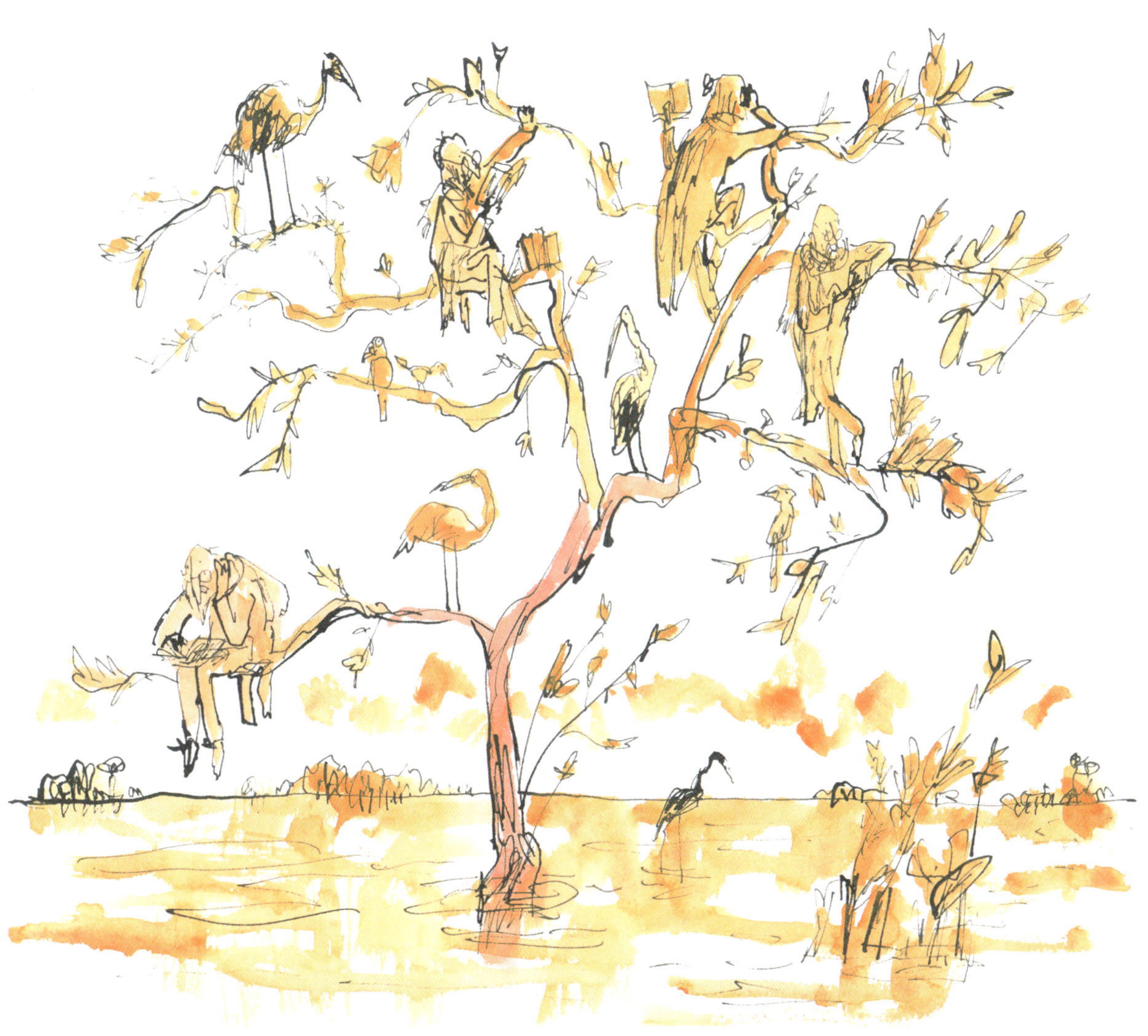

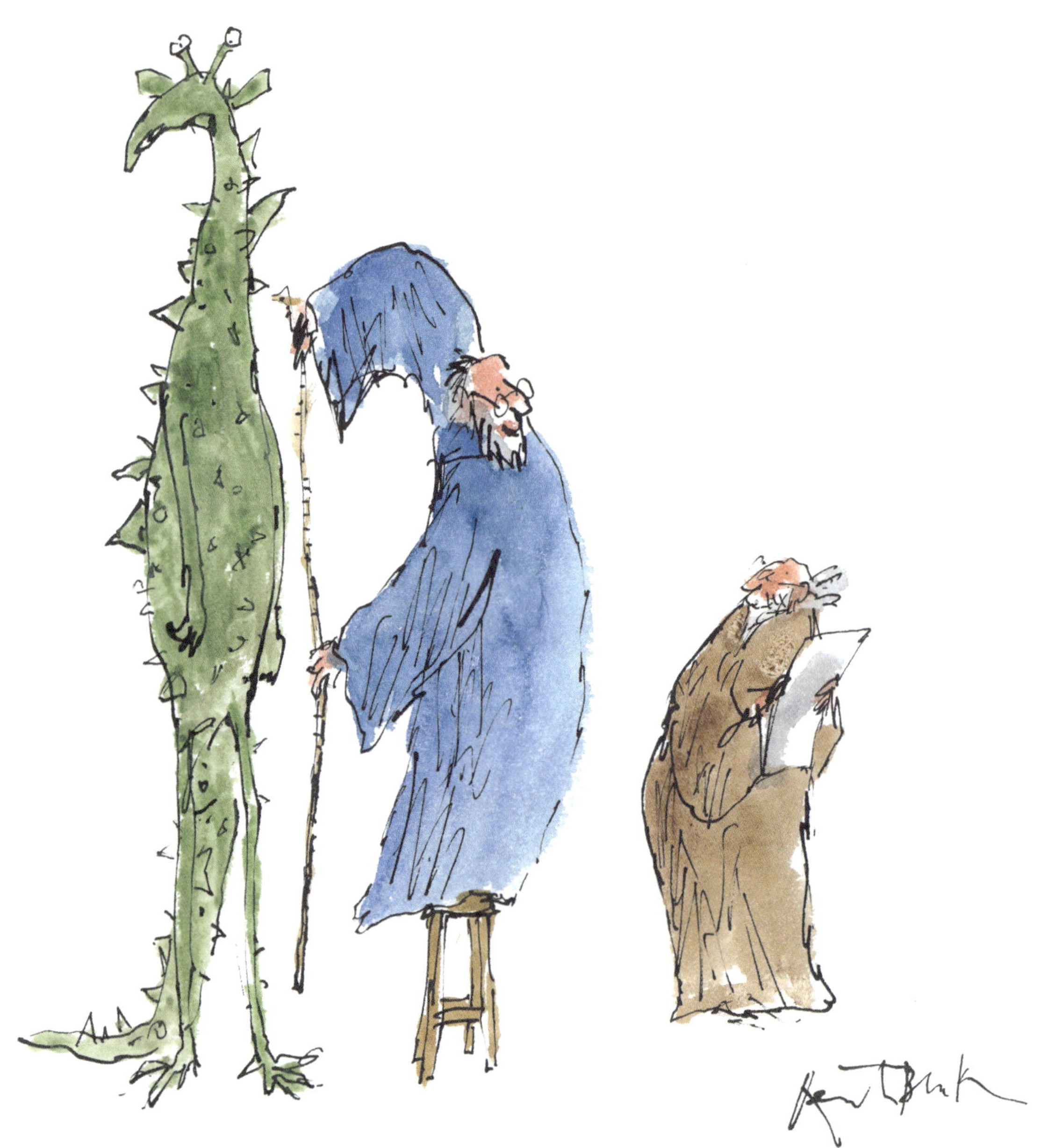

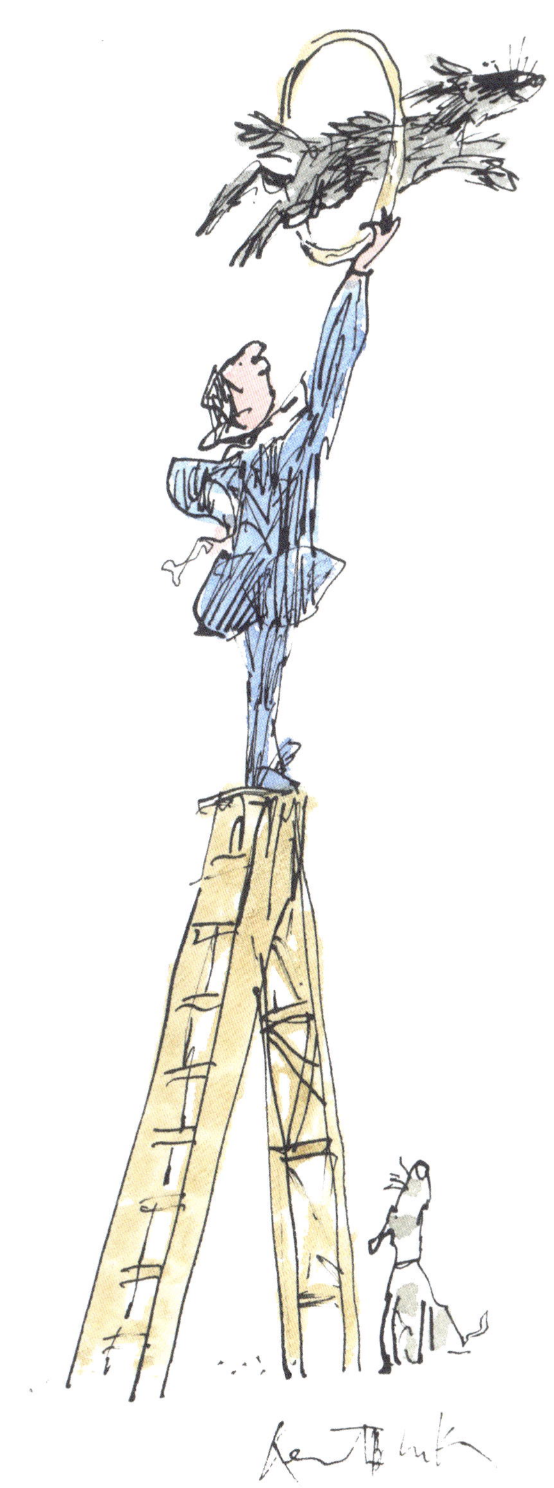

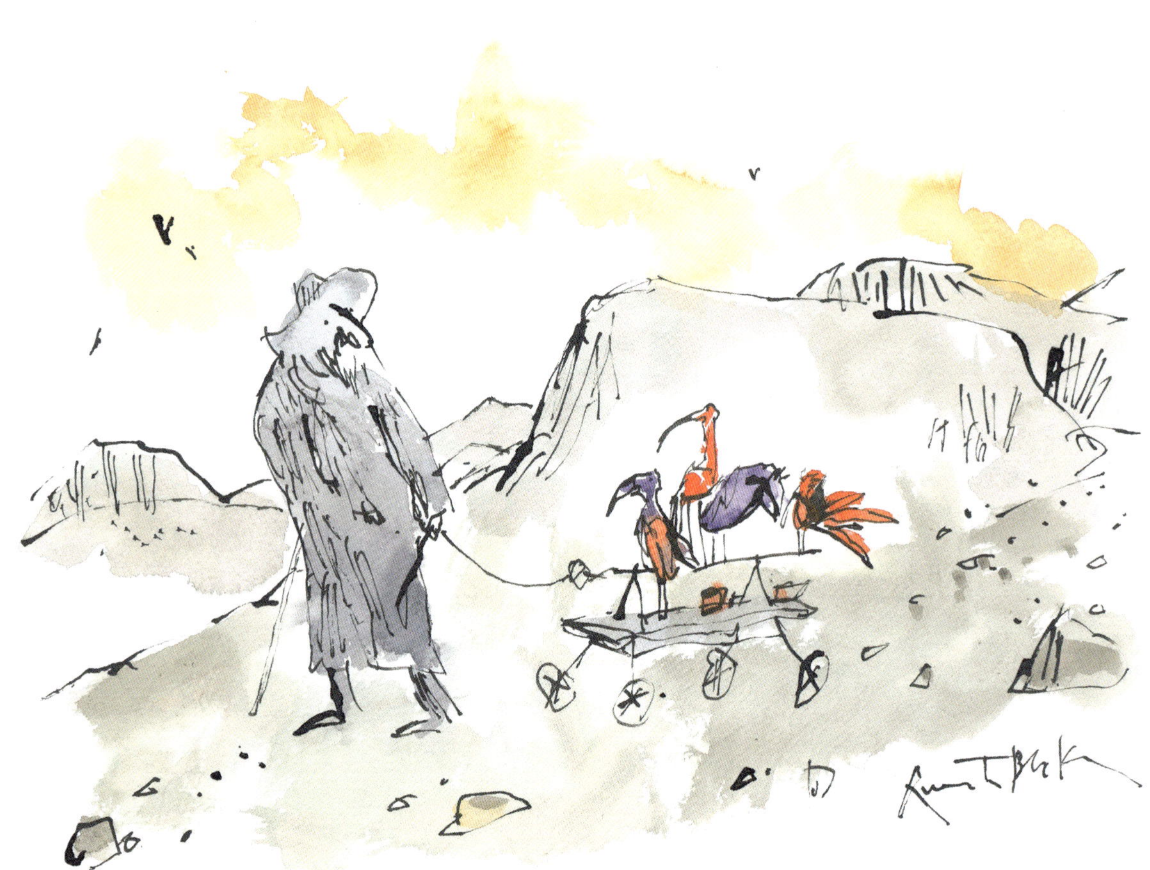

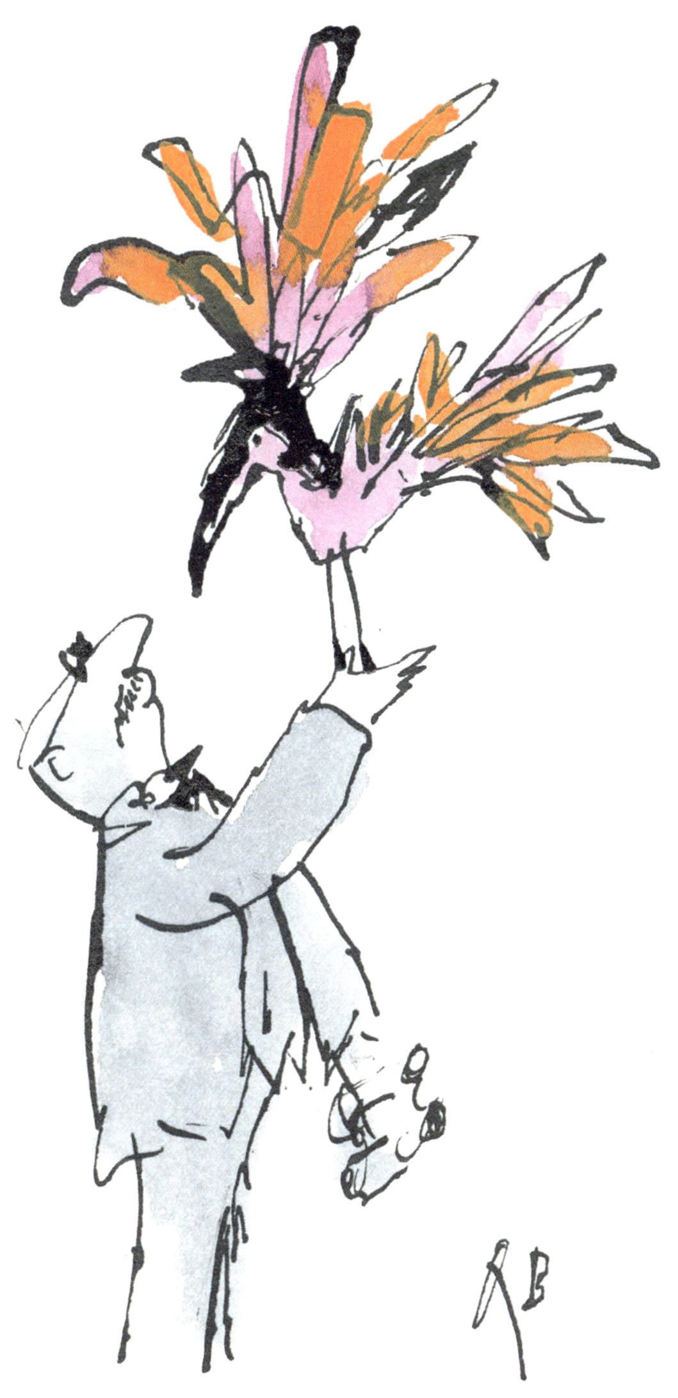

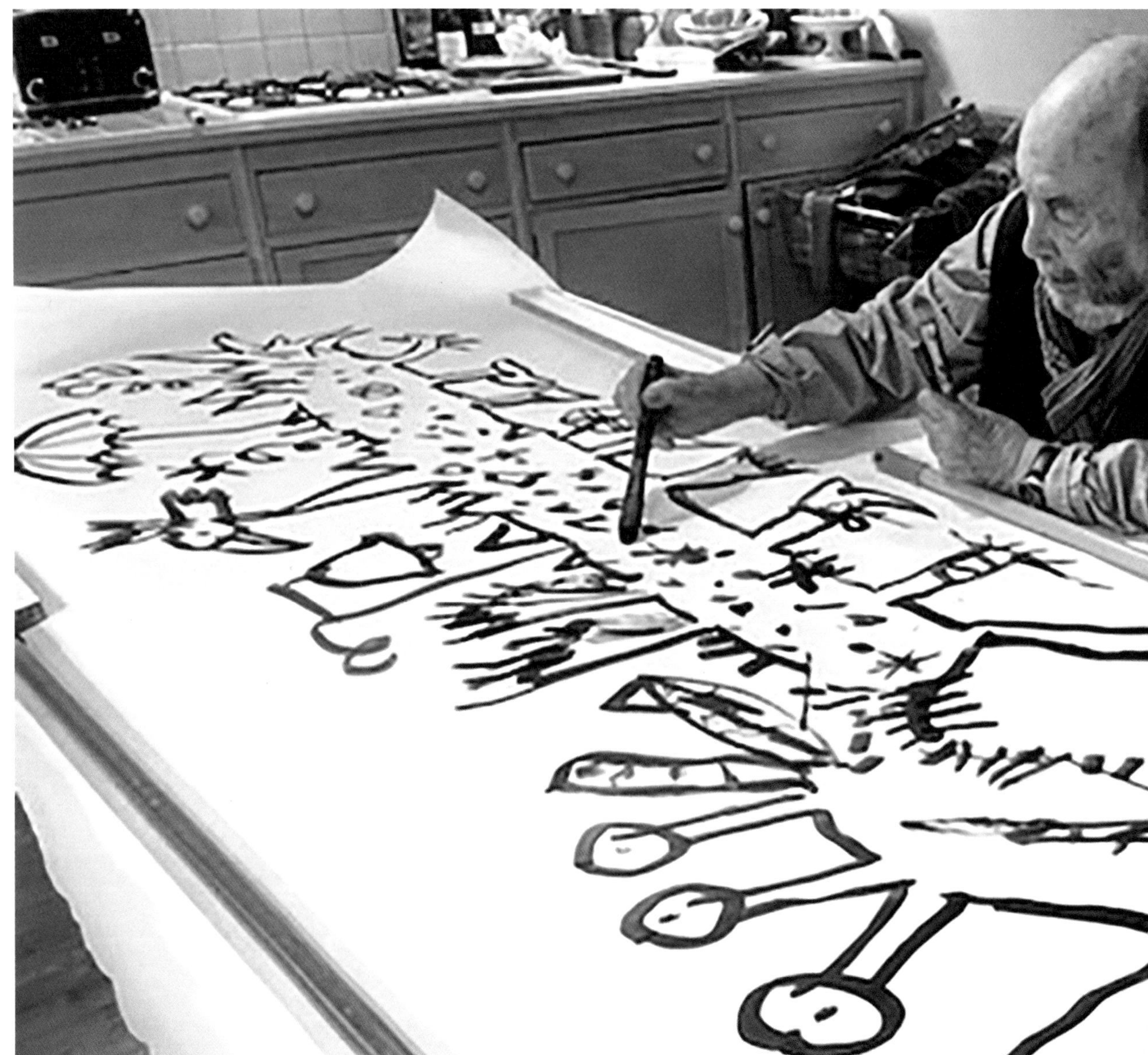

When, in September 2024, there was a breaking ground party to celebrate the start of the refurbishment of the site, Quentin couldn't come. In his place he sent a 3-metre-long creature, drawn on the afternoon of the party on his kitchen table using a long-armed shower cleaner, a broom handle and a ruler to keep it flat. With it was a note apologising for not being able to be at there and adding:

'I have only two pieces of advice. One is that you all enjoy yourselves this evening, and the other is that you should go home tonight and draw something.'

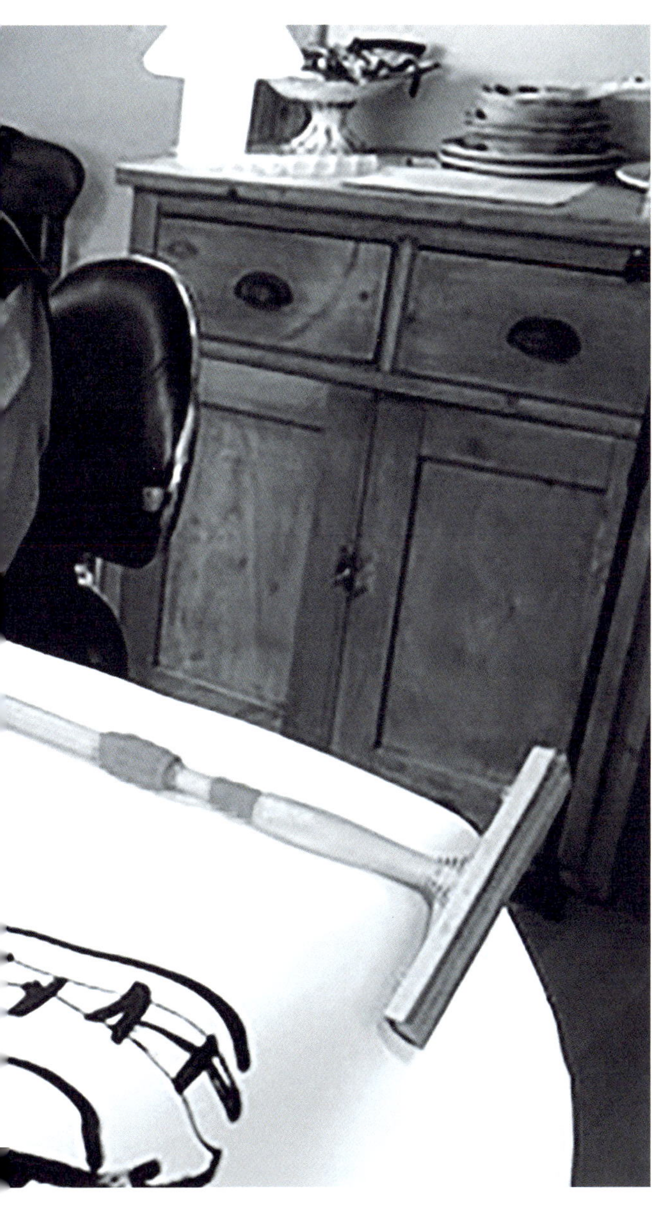

## Acknowledgments

My thanks to Linda Kitson, without whom this book would never have happened, and to Sophie Stericker and Liz Williams for their constant help and support. Also, to Lexi Burgess and Francis McCullagh for making this book so beautiful. And I'm grateful to Jenny Uglow for generously allowing me to quote from *The Quentin Blake Book* (Thames & Hudson, 2022).

But most of all my thanks to Quentin for entrusting me with editing this book.

FRONT COVER: Quentin Blake, Lettering, 2024

BACK COVER: Quentin Blake, Self-Portrait, for the Chislehurst and Sidcup Grammar School magazine, *The Chronicle,* 2017

TITLE PAGE: Illustration for Royal Boch Pottery Mug, 2003

CONTENTS PAGE: Illustration for the walls of the Kershaw Ward, 2005

First published in the United Kingdom in 2025
by Quentin Blake and Thames & Hudson Ltd
181A High Holborn, London WC1V 7QX

Artwork copyright © 2025 Quentin Blake,
except as follows:

Photo © Linda Kitson 6, 18, 19, 65, 80-81, 100, 105, 118, 140, 188, 193, 258- 259, 270-271;
Photo © Michael Walker/Troika 13, 14;
Photo © Burgess Studio 25, 26, 30, 33, 36, 37, 41, 48-49, 50, 116, 117, 122, 124, 125, 136, 137, 139, 141;
Illustration © Crown copyright 142;
Photo © Sunniver Molvaer 29;
Photo © Sam Mellish 41;
Photo © Tom Thistlethwaite 61, 62-63;
Photo © Graham Webb 84;
Photo © Phoebe Wingate 191;
Photo © Justin Piperger 262, 263

Text © Quentin Blake
All quotes are from conversations with Quentin or taken from *Laureate's Progress* (Jonathan Cape, 2002), *Words and Pictures* (Jonathan Cape, 2000), *Beyond the Page* (Tate Publishing, 2012) and *Pen, Ink and Places* (Tate Publishing, 2018).



www.quentinblake.com

British Library Cataloguing-in-Publication Data
A catalogue record for this book is available from the British Library.

ISBN 978-0-500-96638-9

Design by Burgess Studio

Credits
The Quentin Blake Archive

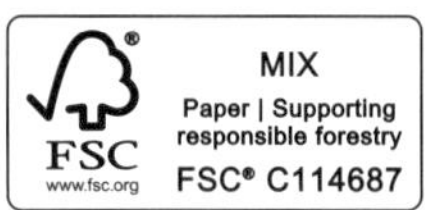


Be the first to know about our new releases, exclusive content and author events by visiting
thamesandhudson.com
thamesandhudsonusa.com
thamesandhudson.com.au